EXPLAINING THE IRAQ WAR

The almost universally accepted explanation for the Iraq war is very clear and consistent – the US decision to attack Saddam Hussein's regime on March 19, 2003 was a product of the ideological agenda, misguided priorities, intentional deceptions and grand strategies of President George W. Bush and prominent 'neoconservatives' and 'unilateralists' on his national security team. Despite the widespread appeal of this version of history, Frank P. Harvey argues that it remains an unsubstantiated assertion and an underdeveloped argument without a logical foundation. His book aims to provide a historically grounded account of the events and strategies which pushed the US–UK coalition towards war. The analysis is based on both factual and counterfactual evidence, combines causal mechanisms derived from multiple levels of analysis, and ultimately confirms the role of path dependence and momentum as a much stronger explanation for the sequence of decisions that led to war.

FRANK P. HARVEY was recently appointed University Research Professor of International Relations at Dalhousie University. He held the 2007 J. William Fulbright Visiting Research Chair in Canadian Studies (SUNY, Plattsburgh), is a Senior Research Fellow with the Canadian Defence and Foreign Affairs Institute, and was former Director of the Centre for Foreign Policy Studies at Dalhousie.

EXPLAINING THE IRAQ WAR

Counterfactual Theory, Logic and Evidence

FRANK P. HARVEY

CAMBRIDGE
UNIVERSITY PRESS

CAMBRIDGE UNIVERSITY PRESS
Cambridge, New York, Melbourne, Madrid, Cape Town,
Singapore, São Paulo, Delhi, Tokyo, Mexico City

Cambridge University Press
The Edinburgh Building, Cambridge CB2 8RU, UK

Published in the United States of America by Cambridge University Press, New York

www.cambridge.org
Information on this title: www.cambridge.org/9781107676589

First published 2012

Printed in the United Kingdom at the University Press, Cambridge

A catalogue record for this publication is available from the British Library

Library of Congress Cataloguing in Publication data
Harvey, Frank P.
Explaining the Iraq War : counterfactual theory, logic and evidence / Frank P. Harvey.
p.   cm.
Includes bibliographical references and index.
ISBN 978-1-107-01472-5 (hardback) – ISBN 978-1-107-67658-9 (pbk.)
1. Iraq War, 2003–Causes.   2. United States–Foreign relations–2001–2009.   I. Title.
DS79.757.H37 2011
956.7044'31–dc23
2011028336

ISBN 978-1-107-01472-5 Hardback
ISBN 978-1-107-67658-9 Paperback

To Anupa, my wife and BFF.
To Jay and Kalli G for being so perfect.
To Janet, Christine and Carolyn for their unconditional love.
To Sudershan and Ramesh for their endless support and limitless generosity.

CONTENTS

FIGURES

TABLES

ACKNOWLEDGMENTS

I am very grateful to the Social Sciences and Humanities Research Council of Canada and the Canada-US Fulbright program for generous financial support to complete the project. I would like to thank Jennifer Harris (Lucid Pulp) and Josephine Lane (Cambridge University Press) for their meticulous attention to detail as editorial assistants, and John Mitton for his outstanding research assistance. I would also like to thank Michael Brecher, Gary Goertz, Kim Richard Nossal, Richard Ned Lebow, Jack Levy, Denis Stairs, Philip Tetlock and two anonymous referees for very helpful comments, suggestions and insights on earlier drafts. Any errors are my own.

~

Introduction

The generally accepted historical account of the 2003 Iraq war is very clear – this was a war of choice, not one of necessity.[1] The decision to attack Saddam Hussein's regime on March 19, 2003 was a product of the political biases, misguided priorities, intentional deceptions and grand strategies of President George W. Bush and prominent 'neoconservatives', 'unilateralists' and 'Vulcans' on his national security team.[2] A few powerful ideologues exploited public fears (and international goodwill) in the aftermath of 9/11 to amplify Iraq's weapons of mass destruction (WMD) threat as a primary justification for an unnecessary, preventive invasion.[3] Disarming and democratizing Saddam's brutal regime were viewed as moral imperatives and considered essential to the long-term security interests of the United States. These imperatives, in turn, explain why the 2002 National Intelligence Estimate on Iraq was updated to exaggerate the scope of Baghdad's WMD–terrorism nexus. To fully appreciate the causal path leading to the onset of military hostilities in 2003, therefore, we need to understand George W. Bush the person, the powerful and determined neocons and unilateralists who advised him, and the package of prejudices, emotions, beliefs and values shared by those responsible for crafting the Bush Doctrine. In essence, neoconservatives, backed by other senior members of the Bush administration, abused their control of the White House to push the country into a war of choice that would otherwise never have happened – never!

The 'Bush-neocon-war' thesis, which I will label *neoconism*,[4] has emerged as *the* dominant narrative used to explain the US attack, essentially confirming Robert Kagan's (2008a) prediction that it would become the generally approved

---

[1] Haass 2009.
[2] For a discussion of the role played by 'Vulcans' and 'neoconservatives' on Bush's decision to invade, see Mann 2004. See also Halper and Clarke 2005.
[3] For an excellent treatment of the distinction between pre-emptive and preventive war in the context of democratic states, see Levy 2008a.
[4] There are risks when using the term *neoconism* to describe the 'theory' I critique in this book. Readers are therefore cautioned not to equate neoconservatism with 'neoconism'. The latter constitutes an explanation for the war that claims a Bush administration, guided by neocon advisers, constituted a necessary condition for invasion. This should not be confused with 'neoconservatives' or 'neocons' – the people neoconists blame for these mistakes.

1

story in history books.[5] It represents the prevailing consensus, theory or hypothesis running through dozens of the most popular books on the Bush administration, and hundreds of frequently cited (and widely circulated) scholarly articles, media reports and blog entries on the Iraq war.[6] There is of course some variation in the literature regarding the administration's underlying motivations, but the different 'goals' authors identify as central to the invasion (e.g., control over oil, democratization of the Middle East, eliminating Iraq's WMD threat and links to terrorism, fulfilling global obligations associated with American exceptionalism, feeding the security industrial complex, satiating the demands of the Israeli lobby, etc.) are typically filtered through a first-image (leadership) framework that assigns most causal weight to the prominent role of neoconservatives (and their allies in the administration) who crafted, implemented and directed US foreign policy toward invasion.

For the remainder of this study, therefore, neoconism refers to all first-image (leadership) explanations of the war that highlight any (or all) of the following ideologies as the main cause of the war – neoconservatism, unilateralism, hegemonic realism, democratic realism, democratic imperialism, democratic globalism, Wilsonian or Hamiltonian revivalism, or economic nationalism.[7] The common theme running through neoconist literature is the strong belief that something distinct about the Bush administration constituted a *necessary* condition for war. The specific descriptor one uses to define these policies, ideologies or principles is not particularly relevant to this exercise. Indeed, there are still ongoing debates over how to delineate the Bush Doctrine in relation to the expanding mosaic of ideological persuasions listed above. But these arguments are all firmly grounded in the same working assumption that some distinct (first-image) feature of the Bush administration accounted for the invasion.

Neoconism is defined further to include any other first-image theory of the war that blames Bush himself for being influenced by these powerful ideologues (e.g., because of the president's weak character, lack of intelligence or gullibility), or any related explanation that relies on Bush's idiosyncratic beliefs, religious values or decision-making style. Also included in neoconism are any accounts of the war that assign causal weight to Bush's psychological predispositions or pathologies – for example, his desire for revenge after Saddam Hussein's attempted

---

[5] Kagan 2008a.

[6] Prominent examples include Belsham Moki 2006; Bonn 2010; Buckley and Singh 2006; Burbach and Tarbell 2004; David 2010; Dodds 2008; Draper 2007; Duncan 2006, 2008; Eisendrath and Goodman 2004; Fukuyama 2006; Greenwald 2008; Heilbrunn 2008; Isikoff and Corn 2006; Kaplan 2008; Kaufmann 2004; Kellett Cramer 2007; Krebs and Lobasz 2007; Mazarr 2007; Oliphant 2007; Prados 2004; Record 2010; Ricks 2007; Risen 2006; Schmidt and Williams 2008; Smith 2006; Sniegoski 2008; Tunç 2005; Unger 2007 and 2008; Weisberg 2008; Western 2005.

[7] These ideological descriptors emerge from the neoconist literature included in endnote 6 above.

assassination of his father, or Bush's desire to prove his worth by finishing the job his father failed to complete in the 1991 Gulf war. The purpose of this book is to challenge the quality of each one of these first-image explanations, all of which encompass one or another dimension of the conventional wisdom – i.e., there was something specific to the Bush administration that, if absent, would have avoided war.

Notwithstanding its widespread appeal, however, neoconism remains an unsubstantiated assertion, a 'theory' without theoretical content, a position lacking perspective, and a seriously underdeveloped argument absent a clearly articulated logical foundation. Neoconism is, in essence, a popular historical account that overlooks a substantial collection of historical facts and relevant causal variables that, when combined, represent a serious challenge to the core premises of accepted wisdom. Yet, despite these serious deficiencies, the most popular first-image theory of the war has never been subjected to the kind of careful scrutiny it demands.[8] The theory has never been tested against competing models, explanations or levels of analysis.

For example, among the more obvious deficiencies with neoconism is the refusal on the part of its proponents to engage a significant portion of the intellectual legacy bequeathed by hundreds of scholars, practitioners and theorists working in the fields of political science, international relations, political psychology, intelligence studies, rational choice theory, conflict and war analysis, and US foreign and domestic policy studies.[9] In essence, the most popular explanation for the war has no significant grounding in the knowledge compiled over several decades on when, how and why powerful democracies such as the United States and Britain go to war. Almost every neoconist, for instance, assigns a remarkable measure of power and political influence to George W. Bush and a few key advisers. The only way to truly understand the onset of military hostilities in 2003, they argue, is to delve into George W. Bush's inner being, his idiosyncrasies, personality, and the unique perceptions, beliefs, values and weaknesses of key members of his team. "It should be no surprise," former

---

[8] The global popularity of neoconism was demonstrated most clearly by the success of Oliver Stone's *W* and Michael Moore's *Fahrenheit 9/11*. The fact that Moore's award-winning film broke attendance and global video sales records arguably illustrates the international appeal of the 'Bush-neocon-war' thesis.

[9] Oddly enough, neoconism has also been embraced by well respected international relations scholars who would otherwise downplay the role of idiosyncratic or domestic factors when explaining decisions to go to war. Perhaps the most notable example is Mearsheimer and Walt 2007. Apparently, despite their intellectual legacy extolling the explanatory relevance of structural factors (balance of power and state self-interests), these scholars are now prepared to discount system variables in favor of assigning significant causal weight to leadership and ideology – in this case, assigning significant influence to a few neocon leaders and a powerful domestic Israel lobby to explain the 2003 Iraq war. US self-interest, post-9/11 security threats associated with WMD proliferation and other realist, state-centric self-interests were irrelevant in this case.

Ambassador Michael Bell (2005) argues, "that the foreign policy of George W. Bush very much corresponds to the world as he sees it." Bell goes on to offer one of the clearest expositions of the conventional wisdom:[10]

> Bush's is a view driven by unshakeable moral conviction that literally pits the forces of good against the forces of evil. Evangelical Christianity, with its emphasis on struggle, is the essence of his fibre, something he puts on the public record at virtually every available opportunity. He has privately confided that the Divinity had spoken to him respecting his moral obligation to liberate Iraq and he has said nearly as much publicly ... This values-laden Bush vision was reinforced by the neo-conservative Washington cabal which had been amassing over several years. These individuals, led by Paul Wolfowitz (Deputy Secretary of Defense under Bush) had been speaking of war with Iraq considerably before George W. Bush became President. They see it as a necessary step in reforming the international order based on moral principles, which closely resemble those of the Christian right. They see liberal relativism as corrupt and believe that universalist templates can be imposed, that for instance the model of Eastern European democratization can be successfully implanted in the Middle East, if there is commitment and assertive American leadership. They believe a Hobbesian world dictates hard-nosed policy to achieve these ends. They contrast hard power – American instruments of pressure, the chief of which is the military – with the soft power favoured by Europeans and Canadians and detested by them ... They champion "coalitions of the willing," where the United States determines the course and others fall in, whether willing or coerced.

Like so many other neoconists, Bell's thesis fully embraces the view that leaders of large, powerful democracies have the capacity and authority to steer the ship of state in any direction they so choose, for any pathological, psychological, biological or, in this case, evangelical reason that compels them to do so. Now, consider the implications of this brilliantly conceived Machiavellian scheme – Bush's national security team managed, in a relatively short period of time in office, to create the necessary illusions to deceive the US public, con the national media, hoodwink Congress and trick senior officials from many other governments into wasting billions of dollars (and risking tens of thousands of lives, not to mention their careers and reputations) to accommodate the neocon team's irrational, religious and ideologically motivated package of prejudices.[11]

But those who continue to defend these 'leadership' theories of the war have ignored their obligation to engage decades of excellent research in the fields of international relations and comparative foreign policy, which caution against exclusive reliance on simplistic explanatory models that privilege the

[10] Bell 2005.
[11] Krauthammer sarcastically refers to "neocon sorcerers who magically foisted it upon what must have been a hypnotized President and vice president." See Krauthammer 2005.

psychological predispositions of particular leaders. Neoconism minimizes or excludes many other potentially useful independent variables that might otherwise inform our understanding of what actually transpired – e.g., intelligence failures, bureaucratic politics, groupthink, public fear and opinions after 9/11, the role of the media and its general coverage of the Iraq crisis, domestic politics and congressional support for war, US–UK cooperation, US–NATO–EU alliance politics and divisions, failed inspections regimes, institutional failures (the UN), threat perceptions and misperceptions by Saddam Hussein, and so on.

Of course, neoconist authors often claim to be offering more than simple leadership explanations by including references to other causal mechanisms or levels of analysis, but these 'theories' are often mentioned not to provide a comprehensive account of decisions leading to the US–UK invasion, but, once again, to defend a weak first-image theory of the war. The explanatory variables they cite are simply re-interpreted by neoconists as *effects* rather than *causes* in order to retain the privileged position of their first-image explanation of events. Bush and his advisers, in other words, fabricated the 'mistaken' intelligence, created the illusion of a security threat to manipulate public opinion, strategically managed the media spin to guide perceptions of Iraq's WMD, and carefully controlled the content and outcome of political debates in Congress, in European capitals and in the UN Security Council. Everything was controlled from above. In essence, neoconist theories about intelligence organizations, bureaucracies, domestic politics, interest groups, public opinion or Saddam's misperceptions are not studied as *independent* (causal) variables to help explain the war – instead, they are viewed as *dependent* variables (outcomes) explained with references to the overpowering influence of neoconservatives, unilateralists and evangelical realists bent on shaping and controlling US foreign policy toward the goal of invading Iraq. People, organizations, bureaucracies, public opinion and allies (Tony Blair) were all manipulated by these ideologues to facilitate their Grand Strategy.[12]

---

[12] Consider the 'interest group' thesis put forward by Halper and Clarke – they argue neoconservatives were essentially a powerful interest group that succeeded in pushing the country to war. But viewing neoconservatives as the most powerful interest group misinterprets the context within which many of the key domestic political debates played out from 2001 to 2003, and misses so much of what is intriguing about which interest groups actually determined the US–UK strategies that guided behavior and actions. As will be demonstrated in Chapters 2 and 3, neoconservatives in the administration actually lost many of these debates. Moreover, Halper and Clarke's take on the neoconservative interest group excludes from consideration so many other important groups whose competing interests were directly relevant to how events unfolded – e.g., British interests and related domestic political debates; French versus European interests; Russian interests; Saddam's interests. In fact, a more robust, historically informed application of interest group theory would not lead to the conclusion that neoconservatives, unilateralists or hegemonic realists prevailed as the dominant groups in this case.

Unfortunately, there has been no serious effort in the literature to explore the central question of whether George W. Bush and his neocon, unilateralist advisers actually deserve the credit assigned to them, or possessed anything approaching the magnitude of political power, influence or intelligence required to successfully transform American, British, EU, NATO and UN Security Council priorities and foreign policies. These important questions are never asked or answered. And the same fundamental error is repeated in many of the most popular neoconist texts that continue to generate very high Amazon.com sales rankings – a few examples are reviewed here to illustrate the point.

Jacob Weisberg (2008: 185) has argued, for example, that "George W. Bush did not arrive in the White House determined to invade Iraq." But Weisberg's explanation for the war inevitably returns to the same simplistic neoconist account:

> Bush's struggle to vindicate his family and outdo his father predisposed him toward completing a job his dad left unfinished ... *[I]t was his broader attempt to develop a foreign policy different from his father's that led him into his biggest mistake.* (Emphasis added)[13]

In his quest for 'answers,' Weisberg claims to have uncovered George W. Bush's deep psycho-pathological pedigree by rummaging through the psyches of the entire Bush family, like an archaeological dig, to reveal the biological origins of the compulsions that took the world's most powerful democracy to war. Conspicuously absent from Weisberg's analysis is any effort to engage the larger social, political or international context surrounding the specific strategies the United States and UK adopted throughout 2002–2003. Also missing in Weisberg's first-image neoconist account of the war is any reference to the policy-making process, or to the role played by so many other important participants who, presumably, were compelled to adopt positions because of their own distinct psycho-pathological pedigrees. Wouldn't we now need to carefully explore the family backgrounds of Colin Powell or Tony Blair to explain their preferences, decisions and actions? Wouldn't we have to perform the same sort of psycho-archaeological dig to understand the preferences expressed in speeches and editorials delivered at the time by Hillary Clinton, John Kerry or Al Gore? Each of these individuals strongly endorsed the policy recommendations on Iraq that were ultimately adopted by George W. Bush, Colin Powell and Tony Blair – i.e., authorization from Congress, deployment of troops and a new UN resolution (UNSCR 1441) to return inspectors with a robust inspections regime backed by a coercive military threat. These policy choices received widespread bipartisan support for very logical reasons that had very little (if anything) to do with Bush's psychology (a point to be explained in more detail in subsequent chapters).

[13] Weisberg 2008.

Also missing in Weisberg's account are many other important historical facts that turn his neoconist thesis on its head – George W. Bush's "biggest mistake," to use Weisberg's words, was based in large part on Bush's decision to *listen to* (and accept) the recommendations from his father and his father's former foreign and security policy advisers, James Baker and Brent Scowcroft (this is discussed in more detail in Chapters 2 and 3). In fact, most participants at the time uniformly *rejected* the alternative policies being pushed by Vice President Cheney and neoconservatives inside and out of the administration (e.g., Richard Perle, Paul Wolfowitz, Robert Kagan, William Kristol), who supported unilateral pre-emption and strongly favored bypassing Congress and the UN to avoid another round of endless inspections. Going back to the UN, they argued, was not in the best interests of the country. But they lost that battle when Bush, Powell, Blair and many other senior Republicans and Democrats in Congress rejected the neocons' and unilateralists' advice. In direct contrast to Weisberg's analysis, therefore, the strategy adopted by Bush to get inspectors back into Iraq (and every other decision associated with this widely supported foreign policy goal) had everything to do with a strong desire by Bush – shared by Powell, Blair, Gore and almost everyone – to re-invigorate a failing containment policy by reinforcing multilateral, UN inspections that demanded full and complete compliance.

Weisberg's version of history is essentially wrong – the crisis had nothing to do with an angry, vengeful president who, despite being afflicted by these dangerously misguided psycho-pathologies, managed to successfully convince dozens of presumably very bright, rational people (and allies) into coming along for the ride, all so he could 'outdo' his father. Leaving aside the factual errors throughout Weisberg's account, the author goes on to describe Bush's psychological profile as if these idiosyncrasies reveal all we need to know to understand why the invasion took place:

> Succeeding at foreign policy was the last most important way for George W. to prove himself in relation to his father. His struggle to come up with an *original doctrine* of his own frames not just his original mistake of launching an invasion of Iraq, but the more extensive international failure of his presidency ... Act one of the Bush Tragedy is the son's struggle to be like his dad until the age of forty. Act two is his growing success over the next fifteen years as he learned to be different. The botched search for a doctrine to clarify world affairs and the President's progressive descent into messianism constitute the conclusive act. (2008: 185, emphasis added)

There you have it – no need to engage decades of research by scholars in the subfields of international relations. The answer is pretty simple: George wanted to "prove himself" to his daddy by crafting an original, revolutionary approach to US foreign policy. Had Weisberg taken the time to study the contents of Bush's 2002 US National Security Strategy (USNSS) he would have noticed the striking resemblance to Clinton's 1999 USNSS and those of so many other presidents, replete with similar references to unilateralism, preventive diplomacy, American exceptionalism, the imperative to spread democratic institutions, the need to deal with rogue states (including Iraq) and the nexus between WMD proliferation and terrorism. These were staples of US foreign policy under Bush senior, Clinton and, now, remain central to Obama's foreign policy agenda (see Chapter 10). They will be staples of US foreign policy long after Obama leaves office. As will become clear in the Appendices of speeches and statements by senior Democrats included in Chapters 2 and 3, these principles were widely endorsed by almost everyone, including the other candidate for president in 2000, Al Gore.

As is common with most neoconist interpretations, Weisberg's account is derived from simplistic assumptions that leaders and their advisers design, construct and implement major foreign policy initiatives mirrored after their own images, personalities, beliefs and values – the country (and its allies) is somehow compelled by decree to follow these preferences regardless of the interests of the state. Societal pressures, political divisions, organizational and bureaucratic constraints, and international relations are consistently absent from these simplistic narratives of the war.

Lind's (2003) position, chastising neocons for taking advantage of "Bush's ignorance and inexperience," is another common variation on the neoconist theme, one that simultaneously slams Bush for being ignorant while assigning blame for the war on the cunning and brilliance of neocons who exploited the inexperienced president (and others) to satisfy their own agenda.[14] Unlike Weisberg's thesis, this version of the story discounts Bush's role (and presumably his personal goals and ambitions) and looks for answers from those surrounding the president. According to Lind, neocons "feared that the second Bush would be like the first ... and that his administration, again like his father's, would be dominated by moderate Republican realists such as Colin Powell, James Baker and Brent Scowcroft." But Lind, like Weisberg, overlooks the fact that neocons lost many of the key battles in the period leading to war. The evidence clearly shows that Democrats and non-neocon Republicans (Baker and Scowcroft) and left-of-center allies (Tony Blair) had a much greater impact on the plans and strategies Bush adopted from 2002 to 2003 – neocons failed at many key junctures to persuade Bush to adopt their preferred strategy of unilateral preemption without congressional or UN endorsement.

Another popular illustration of neoconism is Mann's (2004) *Rise of the Vulcans*[15] – a biographical sketch of the people advising Bush that claims to provide crucial insights into the personalities that shaped Iraq policy. Mann's intention is to present these biographical profiles as a way of explaining the war. But

---

[14] Lind 2003.   [15] Mann 2004.

another collection of personality sketches, while interesting, is never sufficient to provide a compelling, complete, theoretically informed account of the factors that led to war – it simply describes the individuals who were present at the time. The causal link between these personalities and the decision to invade is never fully explained.

Like Mann's work, the stated purpose of Isikoff and Corn's book (2006: vx)[16]

> is to examine the beliefs and the worldview of the Vulcans, Bush's foreign policy team, by tracing the histories of six of its leading members: Cheney, Rumsfeld, Powell, Armitage, Wolfowitz, and Rice. The aim is to try to understand *how and why* America came to deal with the rest of the world in the ways that it did during the George W. Bush administration. Where did the ideas of the Vulcans come from? Why did these six Vulcans, in particular, rise to the top of the Republican foreign policy apparatus? What was it in their background and experiences that *caused* them to make the choices they made after taking office in 2001 and after the terrorist attacks of September 11? (Emphasis added)

Bush is said to have played "only a supporting role" (2006: xix). The problem with these historical accounts is that the specific preferences defended by these Vulcans were *not* at all identical – there was no clear consensus in the administration on how to approach the Iraq impasse, or whether a renewed UN inspections regime was the right strategy. Again, as will become very clear in Chapters 2–8, both Colin Powell and Tony Blair (supported by CIA Director George Tenet) rejected key parts of the intelligence being pushed by Cheney, Rumsfeld and other central players within the Pentagon, especially distorted intelligence surrounding linkages between Saddam and Al-Qaeda (or 9/11), and aluminum tubes of uranium yellowcakes. They also successfully persuaded Bush to reject the alternative approach to Iraq recommended by Cheney and Wolfowitz – unilateral pre-emption.

What all of these neoconist texts consistently fail to reveal are the details of the case history, including the content, nature and relevance of important debates within the administration – and among senior officials from allied governments, who won and lost important political battles throughout this period. Also missing from neoconist accounts are the details of how these victories and defeats shaped the approach Bush ultimately adopted at crucial points in the crisis, and how the series of key decisions created the path-dependent momentum that led to war.

As Jonah Goldberg (2006) explains, there is a prevailing collective ignorance about history that often prevents us from finding the truth about past events: "as a culture, we have a tendency to look for our car keys where the light is good. Our usable past is the past that is illuminated to us."[17] Most treatments

---

[16] Isikoff and Corn 2006.   [17] Goldberg 2006.

of the Iraq war remain committed to collecting facts that are illuminated by simplistic theories analysts would like to validate, instead of trying to validate theories that are actually supported by an abundance of relevant facts. The focus therefore is typically (and exclusively) on Bush and the neocon leadership, which neoconists firmly believe deserve all of the blame for the catastrophic errors that led to this war. But almost no light is ever shed on the prominent role other non-neocons played in the decisions – senior Democrats in Congress, key allies such as Prime Ministers Tony Blair and John Howard (Australia), or the previous actions against Iraq throughout the eight years of the Clinton–Gore administration. Even less light is shed on the speeches delivered by senior Democrats passionately defending the authorization to use force based on what they considered to be factual evidence compiled from a decade of inspections. And virtually no light is shed on other psychological, domestic, political, organizational or international factors that constitute the complete history surrounding the decisions leading to the final choice to invade rather than extend inspections one more time. This project is designed to illuminate that history.

The following chapters will show, through a detailed assessment of all key decisions leading to the war, why the conventional story misses so much of what makes this case such a tragedy, a far greater tragedy than the one depicted by popular neoconist myths. Indeed, the facts are far more disturbing, because almost everyone involved in this crisis – from the left and right (Democrat and Republican), across three administrations, both inside and outside of American and British governments, within the United Nations and throughout key European capitals – helped set the stage for the final set of errors, decisions and actions that created the path-dependent and irreversible momentum to war. Neoconism misses the most relevant parts of the case history.

Logical implications of neoconism

The central tenet of neoconism is very clear and consistent – a Bush administration dominated by powerful neoconservatives was a *necessary* condition for the Iraq war. Advocates are not claiming a Bush victory was sufficient for the onset of hostilities three years later, but the conventional view is quite explicit about the crucial role played by neoconservatives pushing for the war; this is the foundational principle underpinning the prevailing consensus. If we extract the neocons from this popular story there would be nothing of substance left to distinguish the explanation from dozens of others.

Every necessary condition theory is logically connected to its sufficient condition counterpart – if X (neoconservatism) was a *necessary* condition for outcome Y (a US invasion of Iraq), then the absence of X would have been a *sufficient* condition for the absence of Y, by definition. As Goertz and Levy (2007) observe, "to assert a necessary condition is simultaneously to assert a (sufficient condition) counterfactual: they are bound together."[18] Now, consider the unmistakable counterfactual argument firmly rooted in neoconism – had a few more hanging chads remained intact in Florida in the 2000 election, the Iraq war would never have happened.[19] President Al Gore's preferences would have been guided by his team of non-neocon foreign policy advisers predisposed to providing advice based on their distinct experiences, values and ideological biases. A very different set of strategic priorities would have emerged to move the Gore administration, the country and international community down an alternative path away from war. In sum, if neoconservative preferences in a Bush administration were a necessary condition for war, then a Gore presidency would have been a sufficient condition for peace – the stronger one's commitment to the Bush-neocon-war thesis, the stronger the associated belief that a different president (especially a Democrat) would not have gone to war.

In fact, casual observers engaged in a cursory review of the literature will find some form of the same *Gore-peace* counterfactual repeated (and usually defended) by prominent scholars, filmmakers, comedians, journalists and Washington insiders on the left and right of the political spectrum. Consider the following illustrations. "I remain convinced," Madeleine Albright wrote in her 2003 *Foreign Affairs* article,

> had Al Gore been elected President, and had the attacks of September 11 still happened, the United States and NATO would have gone to war in Afghanistan together, then deployed forces all around the country and stayed to rebuild it … As for Saddam, I believe the Gore team would have read the intelligence information about his activities differently and concluded that a war against Iraq, although justifiable, was not essential in the short term to protect US security.[20]

Following news of another bombing at Bagram airfield in Afghanistan during the Bush administration, nationally syndicated talk-show host and comedian Bill Maher declared in one of his opening monologues: "I have zero doubt that if Dick Cheney was not in power, people wouldn't be dying needlessly tomorrow. I'm just saying if he did die … more people would live. That's a fact." Maher's counterfactual was followed by thunderous applause and laughter from the audience.[21] Banchoff (2004: 22) agrees with Albright and Maher: "President Gore would have approached the prospect of war with Iraq very differently," the author asserts, because he would have been motivated by "powerful forces in American domestic politics opposed to a purely national frame of reference

---

[18] Goertz and Levy 2007: 15.
[19] For some very convincing evidence supporting the strong likelihood of a Gore victory in the absence of a Nader campaign, please see Meyerson *et al.* 2004.
[20] Albright 2003.   [21] See Aaronovitch 2007.

and willing to embrace the strictures of multilateralism."[22] Prominent anti-war activist Tariq Ali (2004) makes the same point in his work:[23]

> Had Gore been elected, he would have gone to war in Afghanistan, but I doubt he would have gone to war in Iraq. This is very much a neocon agenda, dominated by the need to get the oil and appease the Israelis. This war in Iraq is very much something this administration went for. The defeat of this administration would be a defeat of the war party.

The identical *Gore-peace* counterfactual appears everywhere.[24] Its advocates encompass liberals, conservatives, Republicans, Democrats, realists, liberal internationalists, constructivists, socialists, globalists, feminists, Muslims, Christians and many others.[25] Of course, liberal and conservative neoconists

---

[22] Banchoff 2004. See also Ikenberry 2000.

[23] Tariq Ali (2004) quoted in Lance Selfa (2004: 4). WBAI-New York radio interview with British anti-war activist Tariq Ali can be found here: www.leftbusinessobserver.com/Radio. html.

[24] Dodds 2008; Schuler 2007; Weintraub 2003; www.nntpnews.net/f1012/if-gore-had-been-president-5938914/index4.html.

[25] A review of neoconist papers submitted to Annual Meetings of the International Studies Association from 2004 to 2008 included the following: **San Francisco 2008** – Chaudet, D., *The Neoconservative Movement at the End of the Bush Administration: Its Legacy, Its Vision, Its Political Future*; McDonald, M. and Jackson, R., *Selling War: The Coalition of the Willing and the "War on Terror"*; Monten, J. and Busby, J., *Winner Takes All: How did Unilateralism Triumph in the Republican Party?*; Van Apeldoorn, B. and De Graaff, J., *The Making of the "Long War": Neo-conservative Networks and Continuity and Change in US "War on Terror"*; Onea, T.A., *Jacksonian Idealism: Prestige, Iraq, and American Empire*; Macleod, A., *The Consequences of the "Day Nothing Much Changed" for Realist Theory*; Furmanski, L., *Eyes to Blind to See: Foreign Policy Making in the Bush Administration*; Martorana, G., *Evangelical Protestants: The Soteriological Impetus Behind Recent Foreign Policy Initiatives*; Saunders, E.N., *Wars of Choice: Leadership, Threat Perception, and Military Interventions*; Theurkauf, R.S., *Theological Identities in International Relations Theory*.

    Chicago 2007 – Boyle, M., *The War on Terror in American Grand Strategy*; Flibbert, A., *Who Lost Iraq? Policy Entrepreneurs and the War Decision*; Gadinger, F., *Practices of Security in the Light of 9–11: From a US-identity Crisis to a Crusade of Freedom*; Hanes, M., *Where You Stand, Where You Sit and How You Think; Bureaucratic Roles and Individual Personalities*; Hanes, M. and Schafer, M., *The Private-Psychological Sources of a Public War: Why George W. Bush went to War with Saddam*; Nabers, D. and Patman, R., *9/11 and the Rise of Political Fundamentalism in the US: Domestic Legitimatisation versus International Estrangement?*; Thrall, A. and Cramer, J., *Why Did the US Invade Iraq? Survey and Evidence*; Western, J., *Discounting the Costs of War in Iraq: Resurrecting the Ideology of the Offensive*.

    San Diego 2006 – Gourevitch, A., *National Insecurities: Narcissism, Neoconservatism, and the American National Interest*; Ish-Shalom, P., *The Civilization of Clashes: Neoconservative Reading of the Theory of the Democratic Peace*; Lobasz, J. and Krebs, R., *Fixing the Meaning of 9/11: Rhetorical Coercion and the Iraq War*; Morkevicius, V., *Faith-Based War? Religious Rhetoric and Foreign Policy in the Bush Administration*; O'Driscoll, C., *Anticipatory War and the Just War Tradition: Sufficient Threats, Just Fears, Unknown Unknowns, and the Invasion of Iraq*; O'Reilly, M. and Renfro, W., *Like Father, Like Son? A Comparison of the Foreign Policies of George H.W. Bush and George W. Bush*; Schonberg, K., *Wilsonian Unilateralism: Rhetoric and Power in American Foreign Policy since 9/11*.

embrace the *Gore-peace* counterfactual for different reasons. Conservatives, for example, are more inclined to believe President Gore would have lacked the intestinal fortitude to deal with Iraq's WMD, or, alternatively, would likely have ignored Iraq altogether.[26] Liberals, on the other hand, are more inclined to defend their version of the *Gore-peace* counterfactual with reference to some combination of Gore's superior intellect, his strong preference for multilateralism, his skills at managing Congress, or his even more impressive diplomatic skills when negotiating with allies. Neoconism is truly global in popularity, and, like many intellectual paradigms that share such widespread appeal, its proponents defend what they believe to be indisputable 'facts' – neoconists remain convinced that Al Gore's team would never have attacked Iraq – never!

Honolulu 2005 – Dunn, D., *The Transformation of American Foreign Policy and the Conflicting Strategies of the War on Terrorism*; Franke, V., *W's Manifest Destiny: Faith-Based US Foreign Policy for the 21st Century?*; George, J., *The Neo-Conservative Ascendancy and US Hegemony: History, Legacies and Implications*; Gill, S., *The New Imperialism and the War in Iraq*; Monten, J., *Neoconservatism and the Promotion of Democracy Abroad*; Payne, R. and Dombrowski, P., *Preemptive War: Crafting a New International Norm*; Sickles, M., *A Neoconservative Just War: Implications of the Iraq Campaign*; Stempel, J., *The Ideology and Reality of American Primacy: Hope, Error, and Incompetence*; **Honolulu Roundtables** – *The Sources of US Unilateralism: Using Perceptions of Foreign Policy Failures to Explain Neoconservatism*; *Presidential Character and the Decision-Making Process: Values, Political Strategy, and Loyalty as Independent Variables in the Foreign Policy of George W. Bush*.

Montreal 2004 – Attwood, T., *Hegemony and the Bush Administration's Foreign Policy: A Reconfiguration of American Grand Strategy*; Bozdaglioglu, Y., *Hegemonic (In)stability and the Limits of US Hegemony in the Middle East*; Buzan, B., *US Hegemony, American Exceptionalism and Unipolarity*; Bzostek, R. and McCall, K.W., *The Bush Doctrine: An Application of Crabb's Doctrinal Criteria and Illustration of Resulting Changes in American Foreign Policy*; Dietrich, J., *Candidate Bush to Incumbent Bush: The Development of an Internationalist, Unilateralist and Interventionist*; Dunn, D., *911, the Bush Doctrine and the Implications of the War on Iraq*; Entessar, N., *Permanent War, Elusive Peace: The Next US War in the Middle East*; Katzenstein, L., *Assessing US Intent in the Onset of the Iraq War*; Keller, J., *The Making of a Crusader: George W. Bush, September 11th, and the War Against Iraq*; Rodriguez, E., *George W. Bush And The End Of The New World Order*; Porpora, D., *Structure, Ideology, and the New American Hegemony*; Ryan, D., *Framing the Response: US Hegemony after September 11*; Wahlrab, A., *Realism, Security, and Democracy: A "Sophisticated" Realist Critique of the War on Terrorism*.

[26] See, for example, Frum 2004. Frum's analysis is not a particularly persuasive or well developed counterfactual of a Gore presidency – his piece spends no time establishing either a logical or empirical case to defend his central argument. The piece is essentially a political exercise in slamming Gore and the Democrats for being weak on security. In his defense, however, Frum never intended to produce a serious historical analysis of the war. Frum's *Gore-peace* counterfactual simply reconfirms many of the points Frum would make later in his 2005 book entitled *The Right Man: An Inside Account of the Bush White House*. This is not surprising: the best way to buttress a thesis extolling the virtues of Bush's leadership style after 9/11 is to argue that Al Gore would have been the wrong person for the job, including the wrong leader to address the Iraq impasse. However, for reasons outlined in Chapters 2 and 3, the notion that Gore would have been more inclined to downplay or ignore Iraq after 9/11 is simply not plausible, nor is it consistent with the facts from the case.

The 'what if Gore won' debate raised important enough questions about 9/11 and the Iraq war to be covered by *The Economist, Washington Post, Los Angeles Times* and *New York Times*.[27] The positions have merged into two camps: those who think things would have been very different – the dominant neoconist perspective – and a few holdouts who believe the outcomes would have been essentially the same.[28] Christopher Hitchens (2005a: n.p.), for example, offers his own take on the impact of a Democratic president after 9/11, arguing:

> You would have seen an exact switch. Richard Holbrooke's position (Holbrooke was Clinton's UN Ambassador and is a leading Democratic foreign policy thinker) would be Dick Cheney's position. The ones in the middle would have just done a switch, finding arguments to support or criticize the war. In fact, I remember that people in the Clinton administration spoke of an inevitable confrontation coming with Saddam. They dropped this idea only because it was a Republican president. That is simply disgraceful. It is likewise disgraceful how many Republicans ran as isolationists against [former Vice-President] Al Gore in the 2000 elections.[29]

Robert Kagan agrees:

> I think if Al Gore had been given the presidency after the 2000 election, it's entirely possible that he also might have gone to war in Iraq, because he was one of the leading hawks. I mean, people forget this now. He was one of the leading Iraq hawks in the Clinton administration. And after September 11th, I mean, I think it was possible.[30]

When asked by Tim Russert in 2004 whether he believed an Al Gore presidency would have been different, Nader responded, "Well, it wouldn't have been any different in terms of military and foreign policy." When asked whether Al Gore would have invaded Iraq, Nader replied, "He would have. I think he was a hawk. He may have done it in a different way. He and Clinton got through Congress a regime-change resolution as a pillar of our foreign policy."[31] Eyal Press' (2001) counterfactual thought experiment reads as follows:[32]

> While nobody can say for certain whether pressure from the right would have propelled Gore to deploy military force more aggressively and on a wider number of fronts than Bush has, there is broad agreement that such pressure would have been far greater with a Democrat in office – particularly with regard to Iraq. "With a Democratic president, I think the Republicans

---

[27] *The Economist* 2001a. The article hints that an experienced Holbrooke would have generated a stronger multinational coalition to deal with 9/11 and Afghanistan, and would have experienced soaring public approval. There is no real difference in the way history played out in this counterfactual. See also Kurlantzick 2004. For a rather large collection of counterfactual 'what if' studies, see Feltus and Ingraham 2000. See the following submissions to the *Washington Post* and *Los Angeles Times*: Martinez 2008 and McGough 2007.
[28] Santora 2007.   [29] Hitchens 2005a.   [30] Kagan 2008b.
[31] Nader 2004.   [32] Press 2001.

would have been calling for blood, saying it was the wimpish Clinton administration that left us with this Iraq problem," says former Carter administration official Gary Sick, a historian of US foreign policy and the Middle East
at Columbia University. "Of course, the irony is that it was Bush's father who
didn't finish the job during the Gulf War."

Albert R. Hunt (2001) makes a similar point:[33]

> In the same situation, the vocal right in Congress would have blamed Sept.
> 11 on the "weakness" of the Clinton-Gore policies. Jesse Helms would be
> ranting about the crippling of the CIA that began with Jimmy Carter and
> accelerated under Bill Clinton. (Somehow the Ronald Reagan, Bill Casey
> and George H.W. Bush years don't count.) The critics would go on to assert
> that capitulating to the Chinese with a semiapology when they downed a
> US plane only encouraged Osama bin Laden. If President Gore had waited
> almost four weeks to respond militarily – as President Bush prudently did –
> does anyone doubt the congressional mullahs would have embellished the
> "weakness" charge with protests about the pitiful state of the American mili-
> tary? … On homeland security there has been some criticism of President
> Bush, but it has been relatively mild. But suppose it had been Democrat Seth
> Waxman as attorney general and Robert Mueller as the new Gore-appointed
> FBI director when the same hijackers did exactly what they did.

As Joshua Kurlantzick (2004) reminds us:[34]

> Both wars enjoyed the support of Democratic heavy hitters in congress,
> including Senators Lieberman, Joseph Biden and John Kerry; Kerry himself
> made a big deal of backing the Iraq war resolution. Gore himself strongly
> backed Bush's invasion of Afghanistan and praised the idea of applying pres-
> sure on Iraq to force Saddam to come clean on WMD. Lieberman helped to
> shepherd the Iraq war resolution through congress. Fuerth, Gore's foreign
> policy adviser for decades, suggested that the US should "destroy the Iraqi
> regime, root and branch" if Saddam did not open his WMD programmes
> to the world … [T]he idea that a Democratic president would overhaul the
> substance of US foreign policy is a fantasy. The Bush administration's for-
> eign policies have not been hijacked by a cabal of extremists, as one might
> think from reading Al-Ahram or the Guardian. In fact, although a President
> Gore might have used 9/11 to reshape the world's institutions and so fight
> terror multilaterally, he would not have shied away from the aggressive use
> of US military power.

The Iraq war case also raises hundreds of other, secondary counterfactual questions: Woollacott (2004), for example, asks what would have happened had
Britain joined France and Germany in opposition to Bush's strategy, or refused
to endorse the final decision to go to war?[35] This would obviously have been
difficult for Blair in light of his statements, but it certainly would have made

[33] Hunt 2001.   [34] Kurlantzick 2004.   [35] Woollacott 2004.

Bush's decision to invade far more difficult and costly. But just as critics of the president's strategy are right to ask these sorts of counterfactual questions, it is just as legitimate (and helpful) to ask the other version of the same question: what would have happened had France and Germany joined the many other European states that supported the US–UK coalition? Would this level of endorsement have finally convinced Saddam that he no longer had allies in the UNSC and that an invasion (including moving onto Baghdad) was very likely? Would this more credible coercive threat have corrected Saddam's misperceptions, produced a higher measure of compliance and further undermined the case for war?

Or consider Christopher Hitchens' counterfactual argument (2005b):[36]

> Bad as Iraq may look now, it is nothing to what it would have become without the steadying influence of coalition forces. None of the many blunders in postwar planning make any essential difference to that conclusion. Indeed, by drawing attention to the ruined condition of the Iraqi society and its infrastructure, they serve to reinforce the point.

McGough (2007) looks at the same set of questions when he asks whether a post-9/11 Gore administration would have pursued the same anti-terrorism legislation or endorsed the same limitations to civil liberties central to the Patriot Act, including the Bush administration's wiretapping programs or the surveillance of domestic communications.[37] One could add extraordinary rendition or Guantanamo to the list of counterfactual studies.

John Heilemann (2006) asked an assortment of public figures to speculate about what might have happened in the absence of 9/11. Heilmann begins the *New York Times Magazine* counterfactual series with a warning:[38]

> We're well aware that the dangers of counterfactual speculation (If Bobby Kennedy had never been shot, then Nixon would never have been elected! So no Watergate! No Carter! No Reagan! Etc., etc., etc.) are almost as grave as those of unbridled futurism. But we also see the virtues of an approach that appeals both to left-brain analytics and right-brain imagination – and that, in the process, tends to uproot subterranean assumptions and challenge conventional wisdom.

Some of the series' entries read like Hollywood movie scripts, describing the political responses to chemical attacks throughout the United States (Sullivan's account). Others focus exclusively on a very specific alternate history dealing with US–China relations, or the New York real estate market. Al Sharpton's

---

[36] See Hitchens 2005b.   [37] McGough 2007.

[38] Heilmann 2006. The series included contributions from John Heilmann, Thomas L. Friedman, Andrew Sullivan, Fareed Zakaria, Jonathan Miller, Ron Suskind, Reverand Al Sharpton, among many others. An audio of the counterfactual discussion can be found here: www.npr.org/templates/story/story.php?storyId=5769540.

assertion that the Iraq war would not have happened without the 9/11 attacks is probably true, since there would have been no appetite whatsoever to re-invigorate the inspections process – at the time, France and Russia were trying to get sanctions on Iraq lifted. By contrast, Suskind's analysis is among the weakest. Consistent with his strong neoconist views, outlined in his books on the Iraq war, he insists that the Iraq war would have unfolded in much the same way even if the Bush administration did not experience 9/11.

Several things become immediately clear as one works through the various submissions to the *New York Times Magazine*. Many of the authors preferred to portray a world they would have liked to see rather than one that flows logically from the antecedent conditions they outline. Most of the counterfactuals dealing with Iraq were very brief, somewhat amusing and often politically motivated exercises that did not do justice to the details of the case history or take the time to explore the many psychological, political, domestic or international factors leading to the onset of hostilities in 2003. These weaknesses are common across most counterfactual analyses.[39]

All of the studies reviewed above illustrate the same basic problem – the *Gore-peace* and/or *Gore-war* counterfactuals embedded in existing literature on Iraq are based on superficial, incomplete and often ad hoc applications of counterfactual research and methodology. Although everyone appears to be engaged in this type of analysis, very few studies defend the arguments with anything approaching a careful analysis of the entire historical record. As Lebow (2000: 556) explains, "counterfactuals are frequently smuggled into so-called factual narratives."[40] *Gore-peace* counterfactuals, for example, are often inserted into

---

[39] Even major theoretical paradigms are grounded in counterfactual logic. Many realists believe international anarchy, self-interest and uncertainty produce security dilemmas that lead to conflict and war. In the absence of these enabling conditions, most realists would be inclined to concede the possibility of forms of sustained cooperation. Most institutionalists believe that lower transaction costs and higher transparency and trust lead to more cooperation, but in their absence conflict would be more likely and cooperation more difficult to sustain. Any theory or hypothesis can be reframed in counterfactual terms, revealing ways in which these 'necessary condition' versions of these theories can be legitimately tested. Gary Goertz and Harvey Starr provide one of the best discussions of an obvious point that is so often missed by scholars who claim to be testing theories they cannot test with the methods they use. Neoconism is another illustration of a generally accepted theory that is typically tested using a poorly designed theoretical framework of analysis. See Goertz and Starr 2003.

[40] Lebow 2000. Jack Levy (2008b: 636) also acknowledges the centrality of this type of reasoning: "One example of a minimal rewrite counterfactual is the proposition that if George W. Bush had not won the 2000 election, the United States would not have gone to war in Iraq. So the counterfactual's antecedent is quite plausible. The hypothesized consequent (President Al Gore not invading Iraq) is quite plausible but not certain, and the argument would have to include enabling counterfactuals such as how Gore would have reacted to 9/11." But very few studies actually include a discussion of these enabling counterfactuals and typically fall well short of the historical analysis required to defend these assertions.

stories about the Bush administration because this conclusion logically fits the Bush-neocon-war thesis regarding the overpowering influence of neoconservatives in 2003. Even serious scholars who are predisposed to carefully applying counterfactual methodology as a tool to enhance historical analysis have been seduced by the conventional story. In a widely circulated email exchange between the *Washington Post*'s Robert Kagan and historian Niall Ferguson (on the subject of the "legitimacy problem" of the United States), Kagan raised, in passing, the possibility that Al Gore would have faced similar post-9/11 pressures to enhance American security and would likely have endorsed a similar UN strategy to address the Iraq problem.[41]

> ROBERT KAGAN: So what would we have to do to rally Europeans to our side? The funny thing is, Bush actually tried. In moments of candour, honest Democrats such as Phil Gordon and Ivo Daalder (another Brookings scholar) admit that if Al Gore had been president in 2003, he would not have been able to win France's support for the invasion of Iraq, either. Nor can anyone who is not working for the Kerry campaign believe that the election of Kerry will magically transform our relations with the rest of the world. As Mead correctly insists, it is "wishful thinking" that "if we can just reverse and undo the changes of the Bush years we can get back to the calmer and more peaceful atmosphere of the 'post-historical' nineties."[42]
>
> NIALL FERGUSON: By the way, did you intend to imply that, if he had become president, Al Gore would have invaded Iraq too? I think not.

Ferguson is widely regarded as a leading expert on counterfactual analysis and, ironically, among its strongest advocates. Yet even he dismisses Kagan's counterfactual observation that Gore's team may have made many of the same decisions leading to war. Apparently, Kagan's hypothetical was so absurd, and the historical facts so clear-cut, that just the idea of engaging in a counterfactual study of a Gore presidency (the mother of all counterfactuals) was worthy of nothing more than a three-word reply – "I think not." The neoconist consensus is so powerful that even one of the strongest defenders of counterfactual analysis is prepared to summarily dismiss the thought of Al Gore going to war. Presumably, had Ferguson believed even a few of the key decisions would have been repeated by Gore (e.g., pushing for the return of inspectors after 9/11 and after a four-year absence of UN inspections; obtaining congressional authorization to use force; deployment of troops to establish a credible, compelling threat; demanding a strong, coercive UN inspections regime) then he would have qualified his reply to Kagan with these caveats. This exchange would have been far more interesting, but it did not take place.

---

[41] The full exchange can be found here: Kagan and Ferguson 2004.

[42] Kagan and Ferguson 2004.

Had Ferguson invested a little more time contemplating the exercise, he would have discovered that a carefully constructed counterfactual analysis of the major domestic and foreign policy decisions between 2002 and 2003 strongly supports the view that President Gore would have been compelled to follow the same general path to war – not because he would have preferred war to peace, but because he would have concluded that the same, UN-based multilateral strategy offered the best hope of compelling Saddam to comply with disarmament objectives without having to go to war. The path-dependent decisions that created the momentum toward invasion would almost certainly have been repeated under a Gore presidency. In fact, the recommendations explicitly endorsed by Gore in two major speeches in 2002 were identical to those ultimately adopted by Bush, Powell and Blair in 2002–2003. In direct contrast to standard accounts of the war, Democrats played a major role in the crisis while neoconservatives were largely irrelevant to how events unfolded.

And yet it is virtually impossible today to find a single Democrat who was in Congress in October 2002 (during the vote to authorize the use of military force) or anyone from the former Clinton–Gore administration who is prepared to accept the view that Gore would have made many of the same decisions after 9/11, especially the big decisions leading to invasion. These conclusions prevail despite the fact that many of these same Democrats explicitly *supported* and defended each of the key decisions made by George W. Bush to get inspectors back into Iraq, to obtain congressional support, to deploy troops to the region, and to craft a strongly worded unanimous UN resolution on inspections. Indeed, Al Gore and Richard Holbrooke praised the Bush administration when they adopted this multilateral strategy (see Chapter 2).

Despite the fact that everyone seems to be engaged in counterfactual analysis, or endorses one or another of the counterfactual conclusions described above, no one has produced a carefully constructed counterfactual history using a rigorous application of the approach. To date, despite its apparent popularity, few scholars have actually applied the techniques for testing causal claims, competing social scientific hypotheses on the war, or assessing the validity of different historical accounts. In sum, notwithstanding its widespread use and surface appeal, no one has used the technique well enough to inform our analysis of this crucial case.

If there are compelling, historically informed reasons why Gore would have been pressured after 9/11 to make many (I will argue *all*) of the same major decisions on Iraq, this evidence would logically run counter to the standard narrative embedded in neoconism and provide powerful disconfirmation of accepted wisdom.[43] For example, the stronger the case that Al Gore shared the same

---

[43] In contrast to the conventional wisdom being challenged in this book, readers should consider other important (but largely marginalized) research emphasizing the continuity of the 'Bush Doctrine' with historical traditions in US foreign policy. See, for example, Gaddis

conclusions about Iraq's WMD, the weaker the claim that neoconservatism was required to form that perception. Similarly, if Al Gore had faced the same domestic pressure to approach the UN for a strong, multilaterally endorsed resolution to force Saddam to comply with robust inspections, then neoconservatism is irrelevant to that small part of the story. And if Gore is on record explicitly recommending the multilateral strategy and tactics adopted by Bush and Blair – and then praising them when these policies were adopted – then, once again, neoconservatism is irrelevant to explaining these preferences.

The book's main objective is to challenge conventional wisdom by demonstrating that all major decisions from 2002 to 2003 were endorsed by Al Gore, his team and most other senior Democrats in power at the time. The book's main thesis is *not* that Gore's behavior would have been identical to Bush's – there is no need to meet that standard in order to take Gore down a similar path to war. To push the 'path' analogy a little further, Gore's pace, stride and movements would have been different, but not his general direction or destination. The differences would have been largely inconsequential in competition with the pressures to make the same big decisions that produced the path-dependent outcome.

The following chapters will focus on an eighteen-month period from September 2001 to March 2003, starting from a relatively straightforward and perfectly realistic antecedent condition – a Gore victory in 2000. The primary objective of the project is to challenge neoconism, a widely accepted interpretation of decisions leading to the US invasion of Iraq in 2003, by explaining why Gore would have followed a very similar path leading to the same outcome (with a few important differences to be discussed in later chapters). Comparative counterfactual analysis and theory-based process tracing are used to produce a stronger explanation of all key decisions, choices and tactics adopted by George W. Bush and Tony Blair during this period.

It is important for readers to understand the central goal of this exercise – it is not simply to defend an interesting counterfactual theory of a Gore presidency; the primary objective is to use the Gore counterfactual as a methodological tool to provide a more compelling (and complete), logically informed, theoretically grounded account of the Bush presidency as well as the strong support Bush received from both Democrats and Republicans for the decisions he and Blair made. Consistent with standard social scientific techniques and conventional statistical analysis, I am simply changing a single variable (the presidency) to carefully probe the impact this change would have had on behavior and

---

2004; Leffler 2005; Lynch and Singh 2008. This point parallels the main thesis developed in this book – that is, that structural factors (domestic and international) external to the Bush administration would have pushed Gore down a very similar path. See also Hurst 2005. Ironically, prominent neoconservatives have also rejected the claim that their views were really that influential – see Kagan 2002, 2006 and 2008b.

outcomes. The counterfactual approach forces us to examine the relative impact of other important societal, political and international factors affecting US–UK policy decisions. Combining these factors produces a richer, more plausible and far more persuasive explanation for the war that is significantly stronger than the first-image thesis offered by neoconists.

The findings outlined in this book are significant, for two reasons – one theoretical, the other relevant to policy. First, if weak arguments are assigned such a high degree of credibility throughout the academic and policy communities in the *absence* of supporting evidence, or if alternative explanations are summarily rejected despite the *presence* of strong confirming evidence, then we are destined to produce incomplete or, worse, dangerously erroneous lessons from one of the most important wars in decades. The value of any contribution to knowledge should be directly proportional to the scope of the consensus being challenged – the more sweeping the accepted wisdom on the crucial role of neoconservatism, the more pressing the obligation to challenge that view, and the more valuable the conclusions if neoconism is largely disconfirmed or refuted as an explanation of the war. The primary task of this book is to carefully unpack the conventional narrative by challenging each and every aspect of its logical, empirical and theoretical foundations.

Second, if neoconism remains the most widely accepted explanation for the 2003 Iraq war despite the serious deficiencies outlined in this book, then we are destined to disregard the right correctives (and institutional reforms) that are likely to prevent these mistakes from reoccurring in the future – if we continue to believe the war was a neoconservative plan, then we are not likely to focus our attention on the institutional reforms required to improve, for example, the faulty intelligence-gathering routines that produced the consensus on Saddam's WMD. If we believe that only a few cherry-picked intelligence errors (aluminum tubes, uranium from Africa, Saddam's ties to Al-Qaeda or 9/11, etc.) were responsible for shifting public and political opinions on the war, then we are likely to ignore the hundreds of pages of intelligence reports that were wrong in favor of focusing exclusively on mistakes that played no role in the support Bush received for war. And, finally, if we remain convinced the president selected a strategy pushed by neoconservatives, or that Democrats had nothing to do with this crisis or the WMD consensus, then our understanding of that part of American history will remain incomplete and dangerously inaccurate. A clear understanding of how we got from Afghanistan to Iraq is essential for theory and policy, and this imperative is more pressing precisely when the overwhelming consensus regarding this history is so very wrong.

In sum, a carefully constructed counterfactual analysis of the major domestic and foreign policy decisions leading to the 2003 Iraq war strongly supports the view that President Gore (along with most Democrats) would have been compelled to follow the same path. Again, the argument is *not* that Gore's behavior would have been identical. But differences are not always path changing and often represent descriptive details that do not have a substantive (theoretically relevant) effect on the foreign policies in question.

Chapters 1 and 2 will focus on the values, (mis)perceptions and beliefs held (and clearly articulated) by senior Democrats throughout this period, including Al Gore and every member of his national security team. The political context of key policy debates preceding the war will be discussed in Chapter 3, followed by a review of American societal pressures and public opinions on Iraq after 9/11 (Chapter 4), political consensus in Congress regarding Iraq's WMD threats (Chapter 5), pervasive intelligence failures and related bureaucratic constraints (Chapter 6), international politics and diplomacy in the United Nations (Chapter 7), and the serious miscalculations and misperceptions by Saddam Hussein regarding Washington's resolve and strategic intentions (Chapter 8). These factors, derived from multiple levels of analysis and firmly rooted in international relations and foreign policy theory, will be combined to provide a more plausible explanation for Bush and Blair's decision to invade in March 2003 based on path dependence and momentum (Chapter 9). Chapter 10 provides a final collection of observations, conclusions and final thoughts.

Comparative counterfactual analysis
and the 2003 Iraq war

The value of counterfactual historical analysis

Counterfactual historical analysis is regarded across multiple disciplines as a powerful tool for evaluating popular accounts of major events in history, or for testing different theories scholars offer to resolve questions about causation – but it only works if it is done well.[1] Lebow (2006: 4) describes counterfactuals as

> past conditionals or, more colloquially, "what if" statements about the past. They alter some aspect of the past (e.g., doing away with a person or event, changing a critical decision or outcome, inserting an event or development that never happened, or making it take place sooner or later than it did), to set the stage for a "what might have been" argument ... They entail small, plausible changes in reality that do not violate our understanding of what was technologically, culturally, temporally or otherwise possible.[2]

The method has been used by prominent scholars to weigh competing explanations for world wars, the end of the Cold War, the escalation of contemporary international crises and many other transformative events in world history.[3] "Good counterfactual thought experiments," Lebow (2000: 555) reminds us, "differ little from 'factual' modes of historical reconstruction [and] are an essential ingredient of scholarship. They help determine the research questions we deem important and the answers we find to them. They are necessary to evaluate the political, economic, and moral benefits of real-world outcomes. These evaluations in turn help drive future research."[4] Contrary to popular assumptions, there is no significant (or theoretically relevant) distinction between factual and counterfactual reasoning; both dimensions of any explanation must

---

[1] Tetlock and Belkin 1996. [2] Lebow 2006.
[3] See Ferguson 2000; Lebow 2000; Levy 2008a; Tetlock and Belkin 1996; Tetlock and Lebow 2001. For case study applications, see Collier and Mahoney 1996; Fearon 1991; King and Zeng 2002, 2005 and 2006; Levin 2004; Lewis 1973a; Murphy 1969; Ragin and Becker 1992; Tetlock 1999; Thorson and Sylvan 1982.
[4] Lebow 2000: 555.

be processed for a credible theory to emerge.[5] Whenever we isolate what we believe to be an important cause of some act or event, the validity of that claim demands simultaneous exposure to some counterfactual proof that, in the absence of these conditions, the event would not have occurred. As Lebow (2000: 556) explains:

> Any sharp distinction between factuals and counterfactuals rests on questionable ontological claims. Many of the scholars who dismiss counterfactual arguments do so because they do not believe they are based on facts ... Even when evidence is meager or absent, the difference between counterfactual and "factual" history may still be marginal. Documents are rarely "smoking guns" that allow researchers to establish motives or causes beyond a reasonable doubt. Actors only occasionally leave evidence about their motives, and historians rarely accept such testimony at face value. More often historians infer motives from what they know about actors' personalities and goals, their past behavior and the constraints under which they operated.[6]

Testing counterfactuals is essentially what we do as social scientists – we change a variable and track its relative impact on outcomes in our search for necessary and/or sufficient causes. Consequently, each contribution to the literature on the Iraq war is based on both 'factual' and 'counterfactual' claims. For example, every book supporting the Bush-neocon-war theory (almost all of them) requires that we accept as 'fact' the *Gore-peace* counterfactual – both parts of the argument (as with any causal claim) are inseparable, because you can't accept the validity of one (neoconism) without simultaneously requiring the validity of the other (*Gore-peace*).

Counterfactual analysis is not just another option for comparing different interpretations of history – the approach is fundamental to any serious historical inquiry focused on testing competing social scientific theories.[7] In fact, working through the logical and historical consequences of changing the value of hypothesized causal variables or shifting the presence of enabling conditions is standard social science; there is no meaningful distinction, therefore, between

---

[5] Lebow (2000: 551, 556): "The difference between so-called factual and counterfactual arguments is greatly exaggerated; it is one of degree, not of kind ... Counterfactuals are frequently smuggled into factual narratives."

[6] Lebow 2000.

[7] "If we hypothesize that x caused y," Lebow (2000: 561) explains, "we assume that y would not have happened in the absence of x – *centris paribus*." For excellent overviews of counterfactual analysis and necessary condition reasoning, see Levy (2008a) and Goertz and Starr (2003: 54–5). According to the latter authors, "The correlation universe is occupied by those who focus on hypotheses about classes of events (wars), while those who have proposed necessary condition versions of causation tend to examine cause in the context of a single event ... As one moves from qualitative to quantitative analysis, the focus moves from the causes of effects to the effects of causes."

factual and counterfactual analysis. "History can be rendered counterfactual free," Tetlock *et al.* (2000: 18) explain, "only if those who study it are prepared to eschew all causal inferences and limit themselves to strictly descriptive narratives of what happened."[8]

Some skeptics will immediately reject the use of counterfactual analysis to refute the dominant 'Bush-neocon-war' thesis, or, for that matter, any theory. But there is no significant (or relevant) theoretical distinction between factual and counterfactual reasoning; both dimensions of any explanation must be processed for a credible theory to emerge. Whenever we isolate what we believe to be an important cause of some act or event, the validity of that claim demands simultaneous exposure to some counterfactual proof that, in the absence of these conditions, the event would not have occurred.

Plausibility is one of the more central prerequisites for producing relevant, logically consistent and historically accurate counterfactual claims. The more specific, limited (minimal re-write condition) and plausible the historical alteration, the more realistic the counterfactual argument, and the more helpful it will be for revealing important causes associated with past events. With these requirements in mind, counterfactual analysis demands a meticulous attention to the details of the case and an appreciation of the compound (ripple) effects these small, realistic changes are likely to have on subsequent actions. The very plausible, minor change related to the counterfactual in this study includes, among other conceivable events: a few more hanging chads during the recounting of precinct votes in Florida following the 2000 US presidential election; or an alternative US Supreme Court ruling on the methods used in Florida to recount electoral ballots; or Al Gore's successful bid to retain the electoral college votes by winning his own state of Tennessee; or a decision by Ralph Nader to pass on running in the 2000 election.[9] Any of these minor changes represents an independently sufficient initial condition that would have given Al Gore a victory in the 2000 election, so the plausibility of this particular historical alteration is very high. The objective from this point on is to explore the effects of this minimal re-write of history on key decisions related to the Iraq crisis. The facts from the case, outlined in considerable detail in the following chapters, are used

---

[8] Tetlock *et al.* 2000.

[9] The proximity of a Gore victory did not rest exclusively on a few hanging chads in Florida. In the absence Ralph Nader's candidacy, most informed observers strongly believe Gore would have easily won the 2000 election. Consider some of the numbers in a report by Meyerson *et al.* (2004): "Nader got 97,488 votes in Florida. Al Gore would have been President had he gotten even 1 percent of those. In New Hampshire, too, Nader's 22,198 votes dwarfed the 7,211 vote margin by which Bush won the state. In other states, Gore barely dodged Nader's bullet. Nader got 21,251 in New Mexico, which Gore squeaked out by 366 votes. Nader got 94,070 votes in Wisconsin, which Gore won by only 5,708 votes. Nader got 29,374 votes in Iowa, which Gore won by 4,144. And Nader won 5 percent of the vote in Oregon, which Gore won by one-half of 1 percent."

to assess the relative strengths of two competing counterfactuals: *Gore-war* and *Gore-peace*.

Lieberfeld's (2005: 12) analysis of a Gore presidency illustrates the typically weak counterfactual assertions rooted in neoconism – his arguments capture the mistaken assumptions underpinning conventional wisdom and reveal the absence of any serious application of counterfactual methodology when using history to defend *Gore-peace*:

> A starting point for assessing the causal influence of a leader's psychology might be to ask whether in similar circumstances a different leader would have behaved similarly: Would Democrat Al Gore … have decided to invade Iraq had [he] been elected in 2000? … *If we doubt this … then the causes of the decision appear to be located primarily in Bush's personal psychology, or in his ideological influences and those of his key advisors.* (Emphasis added)[10]

But every scholar, including neoconists such as Lieberfeld, shares an important obligation to go well beyond relying exclusively on "doubt" about whether Gore would have followed the same path. The obvious error with Lieberfeld's analysis is that 'doubts' are not 'facts' and do not prove anything. All relevant historical facts from the case must be examined and should take precedence over doubts when drawing important conclusions about the relevance of leadership or psychology – in fact, superficial subservience to a few doubts should never constitute sufficient evidence to support any theory. Yet, because the accepted wisdom is so sweeping, neoconists are rarely challenged to defend assertions like Lieberfeld's. A decidedly weak 'if-then' (counterfactual) hypothesis can be put forward as a 'fact' requiring no proof or further elaboration. But neoconists should embrace the burden of proving their *Gore-peace* counterfactual beyond simply expressing a few doubts about the *Gore-war* alternative.

Proponents of both sides of this debate should confront the entire historical record to construct the strongest possible case to confirm their respective

---

[10] Lieberfeld 2005: 12. According to the author's account of underlying ideological reasons for the war, "Neoconservatism's ideological roots lie in the crusading liberalism and anticommunism of the Cold war. Neoconservatives – many with ties to lobbying groups such as the Committee on the Present Danger (which warned that the Soviet Union would win the arms race), the Project for a New American Century, and the American Enterprise Institute – are convinced that US security depends on a policy of forward leaning, anti-isolationist confrontation, rather than containment or accommodation of adversaries, or on multilateral approaches to security. Along with hawkish liberals, they see the War on Terror in the same light as US-led wars against fascism and totalitarianism, and envision the US as a benevolent global hegemon that uses its power to promote democracy. Bush administration neoconservatives and Straussians – students and followers of Leo Strauss, a political philosopher who escaped to the US from Nazi Germany – became conditioned during the Cold war to seeing the world in terms of continual, potentially existential threats."

counterfactuals while presenting the strongest possible evidence to disconfirm its mirror-image counterpart.[11] And in the process of constructing these cases, counterfactual analysis can produce more compelling, historically informed, theoretically grounded accounts of key choices made by Bush and Blair from 2002 to 2003 that set their countries on a path to war. The next section explains how such a research program should be designed, and why it will contribute to constructing a better theory of the Iraq war.

Comparative counterfactual analysis (CCA)

Every causal theory makes both historical and counterfactual claims, and, with respect to the latter, at least two mutually exclusive counterfactual arguments emerge from every thesis. According to neoconism, for example, the conventional view maintains that a Gore administration would not have gone to war, while its mirror-image counterpart asserts that Gore would have followed the same path as Bush. The question at the heart of this analysis is which counterfactual receives the strongest support from the facts and evidence derived from a careful (and complete) review of the relevant historical record? The evidence for and against both counterfactuals must be discussed together, because the strengths of one are directly relevant to uncovering the weaknesses of the other and vice versa. They should not be studied in isolation, yet neoconists never engage these important counterfactual questions.

As Pelz (2001: 92) explains, historians typically apply one of two positivist methods when trying to uncover the 'truth' about any explanation or proposition surrounding an important historical event – they gather all relevant evidence in support of the proposition being tested, or they clearly specify what facts would disprove, disconfirm or falsify the proposition and fail to uncover any evidence.[12] Fearon (1991: 171) raises the same point: for any hypothesis of the form X (neoconservatism) being a cause of Y (war),[13]

> analysts have available a choice between two and only two strategies for "empirically" assessing this hypothesis. Either they can imagine that (X) had been absent and ask whether (Y) could have (or might have) occurred in that counterfactual case; or they can search for other actual cases that resemble the case in question in significant respects, except that in some of these cases (X) is absent (or had a different value).

---

[11] The approach, Lebow (2001: 27) explains, is very useful for refuting competing explanations. "Because every argument has its related counterfactual, critics have two strategies open to them: they can try to offer a different and more compelling account, or they can try to show that the outcome in question would still have occurred in the absence of the claimed causes."

[12] Pelz 2001: 92.   [13] Fearon 1991.

The comparative counterfactual analysis (CCA) introduced here simultan-eously applies both methods to both counterfactual claims.[14] Lewis' (1973a) and Fearon's (1991) seminal work on the subject do not explicitly recommend sim-ultaneous comparison of competing counterfactual scenarios, but I would argue that this is exactly what needs to be done to evaluate their relative strengths.

If the Gore-war counterfactual (*Gore-war*) is more plausible, historically con-sistent, theoretically grounded and logically compelling than the Gore-peace counterfactual (*Gore-peace*), then these findings would constitute powerful grounds for rejecting neoconism, because many of the same pressures that would have pushed Gore to make similar decisions *also* explain the calculations Bush and his team made at the time. The stronger the evidence supporting the *Gore-war* path, the weaker the evidence that neoconservatism was relevant.

With the previous points in mind, consider the two competing counterfac-tuals associated with neoconism in relation to the relevant evidence we should expect (and *not* expect) to find (see Figure 1.1).

Proponents of neoconism have relied exclusively on evidence corresponding to category D – that is, they tend to profile Bush and key members of his national security team, or refer to other authors who do the same thing. Amazon.com, for example, lists dozens of memoirs by former Bush administration officials crammed with facts, details and personal anecdotes about their experiences during this period. Although all of these contributions help us paint a much clearer picture of what went on from 2002 to 2003, each entry produces dimin-ishing returns over time – they do not provide better explanations for the onset of hostilities. In essence, the literature on Iraq remains grounded in category D, and tends to ignore any and all falsifying evidence from category C. The reason, of course, is that neoconists would never expect to find much if any evidence corresponding to category C (*Gore-war*). Surprisingly, a review of the case his-tory confirms the exact opposite to be true – there is considerably more (and stronger) counterfactual evidence corresponding to C and almost no evidence to support A.[15]

---

[14] Using Lewis' (1973a) work on counterfactual reasoning as a guide, the following will help to clarify the logical underpinnings of CCA. According to neoconism, if Gore was president (X), then war with Iraq would not have happened (Y). But this is true, Lewis points out, "[I]f and only if there is a possible world in which (X) and (Y) are true [*Gore-peace*] *that is closer to the actual world than any possible world* in which (X) is true and (Y) is false [i.e., *Gore-war*]: that is, a world in which (X) and (Y) are both true [*Gore-peace*] is less of a deviation than a world in which (X) is true and (Y) is false [*Gore-war*]" (emphasis added).

[15] Figure 1.1 is a standard conceptual template used by those engaged in evaluating *necessary* and/or *sufficient* condition theories and logic (Harvey 1998, 1999; Most *et al.* 1989; Goertz and Starr 2003). There is no question that neoconism is a *necessary* condition theory that should be subjected to *both* confirming (Category A and D) and disconfirming (Category B and C) evidence. With respect to Category B evidence, despite the same administration in the White House, run by the same powerful preventive war mongering neocons, they *did not* come close to dealing with Iran and North Korea the same way. And, notwithstanding

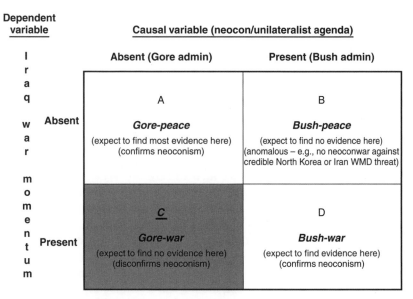

Dependent variable	Causal variable (neocon/unilateralist agenda)	
Iraq war momentum	**Absent (Gore admin)**	**Present (Bush admin)**
Absent	A *Gore-peace* (expect to find most evidence here) (confirms neoconism)	B *Bush-peace* (expect to find no evidence here) (anomalous – e.g., no neoconwar against credible North Korea or Iran WMD threat)
Present	*C* *Gore-war* (expect to find no evidence here) (disconfirms neoconism)	D *Bush-war* (expect to find evidence here) (confirms neoconism)

Figure 1.1 Neoconism (*Iraq war momentum* is a far more accurate conceptualization of the dependent variable than *Iraq war*, because it avoids the common mistake of assuming that only one decision (i.e., the final decision to go to war) is the only relevant outcome to explain – it isn't. The only way to truly understand the onset of the Iraq war is to explain each of the many key decisions that constituted the path dependent momentum pushing the US–UK coalition over the line. War was a product of that momentum and must be understood in this context).

To illustrate the relationship between historical evidence and the categories in Figure 1.1, consider Bush's endorsement, early in 2002, of the policies recommended by Colin Powell, Tony Blair, Al Gore and Richard Holbrooke (widely regarded as Gore's likely pick for Secretary of State). All of these important political leaders strongly encouraged the President to reject the neoconservative preference to deal with Iraq through unilateral pre-emption (without congressional authorization or UN approval). The United States did not require such

the fact that Iran and North Korea constituted more obvious nuclear threats than Iraq, a multilateral strategy was adopted. Now, if the preferences of a powerful neoconservative cabal explain the Iraq war, then why were these same ideologically motivated policy preferences absent when dealing with the other two-thirds of the axis of evil? It should be noted that category B evidence partially disconfirms the sufficient condition version of neoconism and is not directly relevant to questions surrounding *necessity*. Evidence from Categories A and C, on the other hand, are directly relevant to testing the more widely accepted *necessary* condition version of neoconism.

endorsement, many prominent neocons argued, because of the many pre-existing UN resolutions compiled over the previous decade. Going back to the UN at this stage, only to get bogged down in another round of endless inspections, was not consistent with US national interests. But Powell, Blair, Holbrooke, Gore, many other distinguished Democratic senators and several senior former Republican advisors to President George H.W. Bush (for example, James Baker and Brent Scowcroft) encouraged the President to take a more moderate approach. In several high level meetings, speeches and op-eds, they all strongly recommended congressional endorsement and a new UN resolution. Despite equally passionate recommendations by Dick Cheney, Donald Rumsfeld, Paul Wolfowitz, Richard Perle, Robert Kagan and William Kristol (of the Project for a New American Century) to bypass the UN and another round of inspections, the President rejected the neocons' and unilateralists' arguments.

In sum, contrary to conventional neoconist wisdom, the historical evidence on this important decision corresponds to category C. One of the clearest indications that Al Gore fully endorsed President Bush's decision to go to Congress and return to the UN for a strong multilateral resolution can be found in an interview he gave on November 19, 2002:[16]

> I think the president deserves credit for getting a unanimous vote in the Security Council. I think he and Secretary Powell did an excellent job of wrestling to the ground and negotiating a unanimous resolution. Now they changed their policy in the process of doing that and they traded off a lot of things and the new policy is much closer to what I was talking about in San Francisco than what they were embarked on sometime before. It doesn't surprise me because I think the international political realities push in that direction.
>
> … I think there's been progress in the last two months. I think that the President clearly changed course and decided to invest heavily in the United Nations to the point where, you know, those on the right wing in his party are beginning to criticize what he's done.
>
> *Question from Charlie Rose* – You seem to be saying, whether the President was listening to Colin Powell, Brent Scowcroft, you or others … in terms of the arguments being made, he seems to have moved to a more moderate position with respect to Iraq in your judgement.
>
> It certainly seems that way to me. And rather than more moderate, I would say more realistic. You can't just thumb your nose at the entire world and say we're going to go and do whatever we want to do regardless of the consequences. That may feel good to say that but you're going to stir up a lot of opposition to the US around the world and buy us some trouble on down the road … I think that investing as heavily as he did in the United Nations process, I think was wise.

---

[16] See Gore 2002e.

The quote from Gore's interview with Charlie Rose (and Holbrooke's interview with Rose included in Appendix 3.1), taped shortly after Bush decided to go back to the UN to negotiate a strong UN resolution to return inspectors, represents so much more than another Gore statement endorsing multilateralism – it is a direct quote from Al Gore praising President Bush for *rejecting* the neoconservative (unilateralist) approach to the crisis in favor of the alternative (i.e., assertive multilateralism) that Gore explicitly outlined and recommended in his Commonwealth Club of California (CC) and Council on Foreign Relations (CFR) speeches in 2002. The quote is directly relevant to partially confirming the interpretation of the case history defended in this book, an interpretation that is inexorably connected to defending the counterfactual claim that Gore and Holbrooke would have followed a very similar path.

The real debate at the time was between those in favor of unilateral pre-emption and those pushing the UN-backed multilateral disarmament strategy. The latter approach received widespread bipartisan support, which explains why Bush ultimately adopted the policy and why Gore would have as well. In fact, Gore's strong preference for this approach was outlined in CC and CFR speeches.[17] At the time, Gore was also issuing statements strongly endorsing regime change in Iraq:[18]

> I've made it clear, I'm in favor of a regime change there, of him being removed from power. Now that's been taken off the table as a goal by the present administration at least formally … I'm sure [Bush and Blair] would still like to see him removed from power, but they've removed that as a formal goal. Now I've said repeatedly, you know, I think that he needs to be removed. I've said that if you're going after Jesse James you ought to organize the posse first, well I think they've made good steps in organizing a posse.

In essence, Gore was endorsing an even stronger, more forceful multilateral policy (consistent with his push for 'assertive multilateralism' and 'forward engagement') to ensure the regime was toppled. With this in mind, the claim by some leaders, including Canadian Prime Minister Jean Chretien, that regime change would not have been the policy of a Democratic government, is patently false.

These are crucially important facts often missed by neoconists, who constantly implore us to acknowledge the role Bush officials played in creating the necessary political context to sell the war. These common assertions and themes run through many (perhaps all) standard accounts, including Kaufmann (2004) and Kellett Cramer (2007) – their specific thesis regarding the "failure of the marketplace of ideas" is addressed below.

To begin, neoconism is based on the mistaken assumption that only one dominant 'context' prevailed when in fact there were really two, and the context

---

[17] See also Gore 2002a and 2002b.   [18] Gore 2002e.

pushed by neoconservatives, nationalists, unilateralists and hegemonic realists – that is, the imminent threat from Saddam; distorted intelligence; yellow-cakes; aluminium tubes; the need for a pre-emptive unilateral strike against Iraq; rejecting any need to go back to Congress for authorization or to the United Nations for legitimacy; sufficiency of previous UN resolutions to justify intervention; dismissing the case for returning UN inspectors, or relying on coalition partners for support and so on – was *not* the context that ultimately prevailed or the one that determined perceptions and strategies. Nor was it the context (or set of assumptions about WMD) that guided decisions at crucial points from 2002 to 2003. The perspective (and myths) pushed by neoconservatives and unilateralists, in other words, was *not* the context that led to a multilaterally endorsed, UN-run inspections regime supported and defended by Bush, Powell and Blair, and widely supported by so many other senior Democrats and Republicans in Congress and elsewhere. The imminent threat and distorted intelligence perspective endorsed by Cheney, Rumsfeld, Wolfowitz, Perle, Feith, Kagan, Kristol, the PNAC and others was *rejected* by most participants. If the ideas and policies that prevailed at the time were widely supported, then, by logical extension, the marketplace of ideas succeeded. These facts are absent from conventional accounts.

To be clear on this point: the argument here is not that Gore would have become a neoconservative, pre-emptive unilateralist or hegemonic realist, but he would certainly have remained committed to the liberal international principles outlined throughout the 2000 campaign and in the 2002 speeches to the CC and CFR (see Appendix 3.1).[19] These principles, not the ones pushed by ideologues and unilateralists in the administration, were essentially the principles adopted by Bush.

Each of these important historical facts (and many others covered throughout the remainder of this book) contributes to establishing the relevant context(s) and domestic political debates that prevailed at the time. It is critically important when interpreting context, therefore, to understand who shaped what context(s) for what reasons, based on what arguments and evidence. And then, in light of the prevailing context, what impact these debates had on the decisions and policies selected. Claiming that context mattered does nothing to explore the details of the case history to understand the causal effects of context on the policy path selected. The neocon-unilateralist perspective was obviously *not* necessary to defend the decisions, strategies and policies Bush and Blair adopted (and Al Gore and Richard Holbrooke praised). Once again, these details are missed (and often intentionally ignored) in standard narratives that continue to buttress the conventional wisdom.

These facts also represent a serious challenge to the arguments put forward by Kaufmann (2004), Kellett Cramer (2007), Krebs and Lobasz (2007) and many

---

[19] Gore 2002a and 2002b.

other proponents of neoconism who maintain that the Iraq war was the quint-essential illustration of the 'failure of the marketplace of ideas.' This standard view is firmly rooted in a fundamental misreading of relevant context(s) and an incomplete account of the historical facts surrounding the case. The market-place of ideas (MoI) 'succeeded' – the policy preferences and decisions taken at the time emerged from a widespread consensus on the nature of the threat (it was not imminent so did not require unilateral pre-emption) and appropriate responses (congressional authorization and multilateral inspections). The pol-icy Kaufmann (2004) and others claim was so central to the outcome (unilateral pre-emption and distorted intelligence) was largely marginalized by those who successfully pushed the alternative approach Bush ultimately endorsed. No dis-cussion of the MoI can logically ignore the consensus that drove the decisions in the sequence unfolding throughout 2002–2003. It is not enough to conclude that the marketplace of ideas failed simply because the end product, invasion, is viewed as such a serious mistake. Occasionally, as in this case, consensus around the need for a multilateral solution to a lingering foreign policy problem can result in decisions that take the country to war. Most neoconist critics (many of them staunch multilateralists) refuse to believe this can happen.

If Kaufmann (2004), Krebs and Lobasz (2007), Kellett Cramer (2007), or any other proponent of "threat inflation" have all *mistakenly* concluded that the MoI failed, and the historical record actually shows that the marketplace succeeded, then any explanation for why the MoI failed makes no logical sense. The key to this debate, therefore, is to establish whether or not the MoI succeeded or failed, rather than simply assume failure because that interpretation is more consistent with the popular neoconist account of history. Contrary to popular accounts, the evidence shows that the path adopted by Bush and Blair was widely endorsed by the American public (see the opinion polls described in Chapter 6), Congress, almost every other senior political adviser on the left and right of the political spectrum (see Appendices), and many other world leaders. The marketplace of ideas succeeded in marginalizing the neoconservatives' unilateralist policy pref-erences in favor of a widely accepted and rational multilateral path produced by an open political debate in the United States between unilateralists and mul-tilateralists. The latter policy path made more sense to more people, precisely *because* officials accepted the generally held, non-distorted interpretation of the threat. If a widely accepted, non-distorted version of the threat was sufficiently worrisome to explain the policy adopted, then threat inflation is *not* a necessary condition explaining the war. In sum, Kaufmann and others are wrong about the relationship between the "constructed threats" they repeatedly highlight and the outcome (war) they criticize, because they miss too much of the relevant history.

The choices made in 2002–2003 were based on a strong conviction that effective inspections must be backed by coercive threats. But, for reasons out-lined later, this preferred strategy was destined to fail – paradoxically, because forceful, coercive diplomacy to create rigid inspections stood the best chance of dealing with the crisis peacefully. Nevertheless, that same strategy produced a sequence of events and perceptions that led to invasion. The collection of theories described in the book to explain this failure include: the cyclical nature of intelligence failures and correctives (as distinct from intelligence distortions); escalatory logic of coercive diplomacy; misperceptions by Saddam Hussein; domestic politics; public opinion; path dependence/momentum). All of these important details, historical facts and relevant theories are excluded from accounts pushed by proponents of the conventional wisdom.

The evidence compiled in the following chapters is consistently missing from neoconist texts, because most of this information directly challenges the validity of standard narratives. As discussed earlier (and in more detail in Chapter 2), Bush and Blair 'rejected' the preferences of neoconservatives in favor of an alternative strategy endorsed by almost everyone else. Similarly, the facts revealed in Chapter 5 clearly establish that distorted intelligence and imminent threat myths pushed by neoconservatives were not relevant to the overwhelming support Bush received from both Democrats and Republicans authorizing the use of military force. These facts are absent in neoconist accounts despite their relevance to disconfirming the most popular account of the war, and their revelation is helped by the demands of comparative counterfactual analysis (CCA).

Everyone is engaged, in one form or another, in counterfactual reasoning; the difference is that this project is considerably more systematic and rigorous in its effort to link theory to the factual evidence and counterfactual reasoning. The only truly hypothetical condition is tied to a minimum re-write of history that assumes a few more hanging chads remained intact in the 2000 presidential election – that is really the only variable explicitly changed. The following chapters, however, focus almost exclusively on the established historical facts to produce a better explanation for the 2003 Iraq war, supported by an impressive collection of international relations and foreign policy theories that go well beyond neoconists' first-image 'leadership' story.

Benefits of comparing competing counterfactual histories

There are several important features of CCA that facilitate the resolution of debates over the causes of the Iraq war. First, the approach requires that we engage both counterfactuals simultaneously to uncover all category A (confirmation of neoconism) and category C (disconfirmation) evidence. If neoconists are perfectly willing to accept the *Gore-peace* counterfactual embedded in their preferred theory of the war, they cannot then logically dismiss (or shy away from) the wealth of disconfirming evidence supporting *Gore-war*. In other words, the quality of a counterfactual claim cannot be evaluated in isolation – its strengths and weaknesses must be assessed in relation to its mirror-image counterpart, because the strengths of one version of history automatically reveal weaknesses of the other.

Second, CCA forces neoconists to confront the logical implications of their own theory. Viewed in comparative counterfactual terms (see Figure 1.1), for example, proponents of *Gore-peace* cannot simply accept their preferred counterfactual merely because it is logically consistent with neoconism – the real strengths of *Gore-peace* (and neoconism) can only be determined by comparing this version of history against its *Gore-war* counterpart. The fact that Gore was not a neoconservative is not evidence confirming the Bush-neocon-war theory – it is simply a restatement of the same weak interpretation of history. In order to test the theory, one would have to establish (rather than simply assert through additional category D evidence) whether neoconservatism was really that relevant to the strategy adopted by Bush and Blair. As will be shown in the next chapters, the ideology was virtually irrelevant to those choices.

Third, CCA is a natural corrective to standard approaches in which a researcher begins with entrenched (often politically motivated) assumptions about George W. Bush and his team, a preferred theory he/she wishes to reconfirm, and a collection of cherry-picked observations selected exclusively to fit some predetermined theoretical template or caricature – e.g., the 2003 Iraq war confirms *realism* because it was a unilateral decision to rationally protect US security interests without any consideration of domestic opposition or multilateral consensus. The support for realism rests entirely on whether the above description of US actions is consistent with the historical record. In this case, the description does not fit the facts surrounding the crisis, yet these superficial conclusions are common in the literature. The CCA approach introduced in this study unpacks the details of the case history first – e.g., leadership, society and public opinion, domestic politics, intelligence organizations, Saddam Hussein's leadership and the legacy of relations with the Iraqi regime, and international politics – not to 'verify' a specific theory, but to evaluate the relative strengths of two competing counterfactuals. The counterfactuals are then evaluated with reference to common criteria for assessing the logical, empirical and theoretical strengths of these claims. All relevant theories (from any levels of analysis) are identified throughout the exercise to provide the most comprehensive explanation for behavior, choices and decisions during the relevant period. The objective of CCA, in other words, is to avoid privileging or precluding any specific theory, level of analysis or paradigm.

Fourth, when combined with theory-guided process tracing, CCA facilitates both idiographic and nomothetic methods of analysis. As Bennett and George (2001: 144–5) point out,

> Process tracing is the attempt to trace empirically the temporal and causal sequence of events within a case that intervene between independent variables and observed outcomes … Process tracing can help identify a specific

causal process that may explain an instance of a particular phenomenon. It
can also inductively identify general causal mechanisms that may be at work
in other cases, and it can test whether a given causal mechanism is at work
in a particular case ... While process tracing shares some of the basic features of historical explanation, historians and political scientists differ in the
types and uses of process tracing that they emphasize because historians are
most interested in explaining particular cases and political scientists seek
to develop and test generalizable theories that explain categories of cases or
phenomenon.[20]

The authors go on to note, "political scientists employ process tracing not only
to explain specific cases but also to test and refine theories, to develop new theories, and to produce generic knowledge of a given phenomenon. Such process
tracing, which converts a historical narrative in an analytical causal explanation
couched in explicit theoretical forms, is substantially different from historical
explanation."[21] But the distinction between explanation/theory and description/
history is often overplayed.[22] CCA goes a long way toward synthesizing historical
detail and theoretical relevance – it is as close as one could get to what Tetlock
and Belkin (1996: 6) describe as "joint idiographic-nomothetic counterfactual,"
combining "the historian's interest in what was possible in particular cases with
the theorist's interest in identifying lawful regularities across cases, thereby
producing theory-informed history."[23] CCA accomplishes both by providing
a detailed case history of an important event, but it does so through process
tracing to uncover the multiple pressures (causal mechanisms) across different
levels of analysis that reveal common patterns associated with prominent theories of war – e.g., intelligence failures, groupthink, misperception theory, political psychology, coercive diplomacy, path dependence, momentum and crisis
decision-making. The objective is to combine history and social science, facts
and covering laws.

More specifically, using both CCA and process tracing together combines
what historians claim is essential for strong idiographic analysis – historical
detail – with a clear commitment to systematic empirical and theoretical analysis to produce a better theory/explanation for the 2003 war. The approach
requires the analyst to be very precise about the claims embedded in their
respective accounts of history, the assumptions that guide their analysis, the evidence they offer to support those claims, the variables they choose to highlight
and the conclusions they draw from their analysis. CCA compels scholars to be

---

[20] Bennett and George 2001.   [21] Bennett and George 2001: 148.

[22] Pelz (2001: 95) believes that "[p]olitical scientists are primarily interested in the necessary
conditions that explain a majority of similar cases, while historians are more interested in
explaining the entire history of a single case in all its detail." For another discussion of these
differences, and an excellent review of reasons why they are often exaggerated, see Levy
(2001) and Jervis (2001).

[23] Tetlock and Belkin 1996: 6.

very clear when interpreting the relationship between the facts of the case and the decisions that led to war. Neoconists have shied away from approaches like CCA that demand this kind of careful attention to historical detail. Each of the next seven chapters represents an important piece of the larger case against conventional wisdom.

Replying to critics of counterfactual reasoning

Before moving on to the substance of the argument it might help to address common criticisms of counterfactual analysis, many of which are put forward by skeptics who do not understand the approach, refuse to appreciate the contributions it can make to resolving debates about causation, or overlook the fact that their own approach is firmly rooted in counterfactual reasoning.

The most common error critics make when challenging counterfactual analysis is the insinuation that these methods are "superfluous to serious scholarship."[24] Edward Hallett Carr is credited with a critique that continues to carry weight given his reputation as a widely respected historian: "one can always play a parlor-game with the might-have-beens of history. But they have nothing ... to do with history."[25] Carr refers to counterfactual analysis as "'Geschichtswissenschlopff', or unhistorical shit." But as Tetlock *et al.* (2000: 18) explain, there are serious problems with this common argument: "whenever we make the apparently factual claim that factor x made a critical causal contribution to outcome y we simultaneously make a critical counterfactual claim that, in a logical shadow universe with factor x deleted, outcome y would not have occurred."[26] This point is missed by neoconists who simultaneously reject the utility of counterfactual methods for testing their popular Bush-neocon-war thesis while remaining absolutely convinced of the *Gore-peace* counterfactual embedded in their own neoconist theory. Their entire argument is based on a predetermined conclusion that Gore would have made none of the same decisions that created the path-dependent momentum to war. Skeptics who repeat Carr's criticism often misunderstand the relationship between factual and counterfactual reasoning – you cannot defend conclusions derived from one approach without at least some reference to the conclusions derived from the other.

Second, what Carr and others fail to acknowledge in their critique is that historians who shun counterfactual analysis are just as susceptible to producing crap in the name of traditional historical research. In fact, a counterfactual analysis of the 2003 Iraq war clearly reveals a very common failure on the part of contemporary 'historians' to compile all relevant facts and historical evidence from the case. The conventional story re-interprets or ignores a great deal of information that is absolutely crucial to producing informed opinions about

---

[24] Tetlock *et al.* 2000: 18.   [25] Carr 1961: 127.   [26] Tetlock *et al.* 2000.

what actually happened from 2002 to 2003, who pushed what policies, why they succeeded and failed, and how these battles over policies and strategies affected the outcome. Many of the books and articles claiming to provide a detailed history of the case, or a strong explanation for the war, have excluded a good part of the historical record revealed by counterfactual reasoning, and it is neoconism in particular that has produced a dangerously incomplete account of actions throughout this period. The problem is not with counterfactual analysis, the problem is with poor factual and historical analysis – CCA simply forces scholars to apply both factual and counterfactual methods to produce the best historical account possible. Without counterfactual reasoning, the standard histories of the war will remain seriously flawed and incomplete. The solution is to adhere to strict rules for doing factual history, counterfactual history and process tracing, and this is guided by a strong commitment to the highest standards of empirical research and theoretical analysis to improve our understanding of one of the most important wars in decades.

Third, contrary to what many critics will argue, the objective here is not simply to provide an interesting counterfactual story of a Gore presidency or engage in a "parlor game." The objective is to challenge neoconism by revealing serious theoretical, logical and empirical flaws – and, in the process of disconfirming the standard account, provide a much better explanation for the Bush–Blair decision to go to war in 2003. Counterfactual analysis is used to test factually based theories of the Iraq war, because these facts are often overlooked in traditional accounts. Indeed, as is clear from a brief review of standard narratives on the war, there is no requirement to engage the facts that disprove neoconism unless forced to do so through CCA.

Conclusions and objectives moving forward

With the preceding analysis in mind, several questions emerge as central to the investigation. What collection of specific historical facts would we need to see to support one or the other counterfactual? What behavior, actions, beliefs, perceptions, speeches or stated policy preferences would we need to identify, and how should we interpret or classify this evidence in light of the logic stipulated in Figure 1.1? In an effort to provide a more substantive treatment of the evidence supporting the *Gore-war* counterfactual, the remainder of the book will focus on the following seven factors:

Chapter 2 – Al Gore's values, policy preferences and misperceptions;
Chapter 3 – Gore's advisers' values, policy preferences and misperceptions;
Chapter 4 – domestic and congressional politics and political support;
Chapter 5 – organizational routines, American intelligence failures and miscalculations;
Chapter 6 – society, the media and public opinion;

Chapter 7 – international politics, global WMD consensus and UN power balancing;

Chapter 8 – Saddam's intelligence failures and miscalculations.

These factors, derived from multiple levels of analysis and firmly rooted in international relations literature, combine to provide a better theory of the 2003 invasion. The theory, based on path dependence and momentum, is summarized in Chapter 9.

A form of *theory guided process tracing* will be used to cover important details from the case history that are often excluded from popular accounts (Falleti 2009; George and Bennett 2005; George and McKeown 1985).[27] The approach helps to connect historical evidence surrounding each decision with relevant theories described in the book. Process tracing facilitates "theoretically explicit narratives that carefully trace and compare the sequences of events constituting the process (and) capture the unfolding of social action over time in a manner sensitive to the order in which events occur" (Aminzade 1993: 18).[28] Getting this order correct is essential to the quality of a historical account and, by extension, the empirical evidence required to support (or refute) the counterfactual claims being made in the book. George and McKeown (1985: 35) add that process tracing "uncovers what stimuli the actors attend to; the decision process that makes use of these stimuli to arrive at decisions; the actual behavior that then occurs; the effect of various institutional arrangements on attention, processing, and behavior; and the effect of other variables of interest on attention, processing, and behavior." In sum, process tracing exposes, for each decision-maker or participant at each point in time, all relevant information they relied on to form perceptions, priorities, expectations, preferences and, ultimately, *context* and choices. My objective is to carefully work through the entire process by embracing complexity, nuance and detail, and by appreciating the full context and chronology of events and choices as they unfolded at crucial points in time.

[27] Falleti 2009; George and Bennett 2005; George and McKeown 1985.
[28] Aminzade 1993.

2

Leadership, political context(s) and the Iraq war

The Bush-neocon-war thesis requires, in part, some clear proof that the Bush administration succeeded in pushing a set of policies that were different from those recommended by prominent Democrats or non-neoconservative Republicans at the time – evidence that would correspond to categories A or D from Figure 1.1. However, if the policies strongly recommended by prominent Democrats (including Al Gore) were identical to those adopted by Bush, Powell and Blair (category C), this would pose a serious challenge to neoconism. The evidence indicates that prominent Democrats and Republicans at the time, including Al Gore, Joseph Lieberman, Richard Holbrooke, Brent Scowcroft and James Baker strongly endorsed the policies and strategies that were ultimately selected by Bush, Powell and Blair. More damaging to neoconism is the fact that these policies were recommended by a majority of political leaders at the time, and adopted by the president, precisely because they provided a more appealing alternative to the pre-emptive, unilateralist strategy recommended by prominent neoconservatives. The fact that neoconservatives lost key debates at crucial stages of the policy process disconfirms a central part of standard historical accounts, but the point is never raised by neoconists.

Two common errors committed by proponents of neoconism

When forced to contemplate the likelihood of a Democratic administration making many of the same decisions from 2002 to 2003, the typical reaction from neoconists is to dismiss the *Gore-war* counterfactual by raising the *political context* argument. *Gore-war*, they argue, completely ignores the extent to which ideologues in the Bush administration constructed the political context for war – they (not the Democrats) were responsible for assembling, manipulating and disseminating the 'evidence' surrounding Iraq's WMD to increase support for an invasion that was all but inevitable given their preferences. The belief that a few officials on Bush's team constructed the dominant threat narrative to defend their 'war of choice' runs through many (perhaps all) standard accounts – the thesis, discussed in Chapter 1, is commonly framed in terms of the "failure of the marketplace of ideas" (Kellett Cramer 2007; Kaufmann 2004; Krebs and Lobasz 2007) and re-emerges in other forms through neoconist accounts of 'threat inflation,' 'distorted intelligence,' 'rhetorical coercion' and 'the absence of imminent threat' (see Chapter 5 for a more detailed assessment of these pressures).

According to these popular accounts, the political context largely constructed by the Bush administration would not have prevailed in the absence of the administration responsible for creating it. Yet scholars who defend this position typically commit two serious errors when constructing their historical accounts of the war. First, they assume only one dominant perspective was sold to the American public (and Congress), and the myths about 'imminent threats' at the center of this perspective were responsible for shaping perceptions and policy preferences. Second, the conventional account typically assumes that only one major decision is relevant to understanding what happened – the final decision to invade Iraq. These two guiding assumptions consistently overlook (or ignore) important facts surrounding the case.

One versus two dominant perspectives on the Iraqi threat and appropriate responses

In order to correct the first error, readers should have a very clear, undistorted understanding of the *two* dominant perspectives that emerged at the time, which of the two versions of the facts represented the most widely shared and influential opinions guiding solutions to the Iraq problem, and how the outcomes of these policy battles affected specific decisions taken at each stage of the crisis. As was briefly covered in Chapter 1, the views being pushed by neoconservatives and unilateralists in the administration were not the ones that ultimately shaped specific choices throughout this period. The imminent threat context exploited by Cheney, Rumsfeld, Wolfowitz, Perle, Kagan, Kristol, the PNAC, etc. was *rejected* by leading Democratic and Republican officials at the time. Instead, a more reasonable interpretation of the Iraq threat led to the multilaterally endorsed, UN-sponsored inspections regime that was ultimately adopted by Bush. In fact, when the administration's UN-based disarmament strategy was revealed to Rumsfeld during a Pentagon press conference, it was clear from his response that he was not only surprised by the revelations about Bush's decision to support Blair but more than a little concerned that his administration would even consider going down this path:

> I wasn't aware that the United States was pressing for a [UN] resolution for inspections. And I don't believe it's correct. I think the president's speech is the United States government's position. There are various other countries that are floating resolutions of various types, including a number that involve inspections. There's no question about that, and certainly they are being discussed with the United States representatives. But I – to my knowledge, the United States has not proposed any resolution that suggests inspections … [I]nspections do have a place in the world if the country

is cooperative. And the goal is disarmament. The goal is not inspections. And inspections can work if a country is cooperative and they want to prove to the world that they have, in fact, disarmed. That is when inspections work because you can go in and inspect and then validate what that country has done by way of disarming. In this instance, one would – to favor inspections, one would have to make a conscious judgment that Iraq was cooperative. And that means they'd have to review the past decade and come to that conclusion. And that's a difficult thing for a reasonable person to do, it seems to me.[1]

Vice President Dick Cheney, among the more prominent ideologues in the administration neoconists blame for the war, was actually quite upset when he *lost* the debate over strategy. According to Tenet (2007: 318–19):

> The meeting on Saturday morning, September 7 (2002), sparked considerable debate about the wisdom of trying to revive a UN inspection regime. Colin Powell was firmly on the side of going the extra mile with the UN, while the vice president argued just as forcefully that doing so would only get us mired in a bureaucratic tangle with nothing to show for it other than time lost off a ticking clock. The president let Powell and Cheney pretty much duke it out. To me, the president still appeared less inclined to go to war than many of his senior aides.[2]

Confirmation of Cheney's reaction was provided by Alastair Campbell (Tony Blair's director of communications and strategy).[3] As Campbell notes in entries for the September 2002 Camp David meetings (with senior members of the US and UK national security teams), Blair saw himself as the point person to get Bush to accept the UN approach and "felt that his job was to sell the case for the UN route to Cheney" (Campbell and Stott 2007: 634–5). Campbell describes Cheney as "pissed off" when it became clear that Bush was going back to the UN for a new resolution and a return of inspectors. He goes on to describe Cheney as looking "very sour throughout, and after dinner, when Tony Blair and Bush walked alone to the chopper. Bush was open with [Blair] that Cheney was in a different position," obviously because of his strong preference for the pre-emptive unilateral route. Blair and Campbell (and Powell) regarded Bush's adoption of their policy as a major victory. Both understood that Powell had a great deal to do with the success but there was no question that the Powell–Blair team succeeded in thwarting the considerably more unilateralist approach recommended by Cheney and others. At dinner that night after the final decision had been made, Bush joked with Campbell: "I suppose you can tell the story of how Tony flew in and pulled the crazed unilateralists back from the brink."

These important historical details rarely if ever appear in standard neoconist accounts despite their relevance for understanding the debates that prevailed at

---

[1] US Department of Defense 2002.   [2] Quoted in Tenet 2007: 331.
[3] Campbell and Stott 2007.

the time. Al Gore (and almost everyone else) rejected neoconservative recommendations in favor of mounting a passionate plea to push the country down a very different, multilateral path. In the process, the neocon-unilateralist perspective was marginalized, along with its distorted interpretation of the intelligence (see Chapter 5). None of these distortions were necessary to defend the decisions, tactics and policies Bush and Blair adopted.

Clearly, Gore's preferences for assertive multilateralism and forward engagement would not have automatically led to a decision to attack Iraq. Nevertheless, assertive multilateralism would have cautioned against pushing Iraq to the back burner after 9/11, and would rationally have led to a series of choices (starting with a decision to return inspectors) that would take Gore's team down a very similar path closer to war. It was the combination of these key decisions (along with all other factors tied to coercive diplomacy, Saddam's misperceptions, and un-distorted intelligence errors covered in the remaining chapters) that resulted in the final decision.

Al Gore's interview with Charlie Rose (described at length in Chapter 1) serves to confirm this version of history – Gore explicitly endorses the strategy adopted by Bush and Blair, precisely because that approach rejected the recommendations being endorsed by neoconservatives. These facts are inexorably connected to supporting the *Gore-war* interpretation of the case history, and are directly relevant to disconfirming neoconism (category A) because, during this very important stage in the sequence of events leading to war, Gore and Bush were in sync. The fact that Rose and Gore joked about the possibility that Bush actually listened to Gore's speeches speaks directly to the counterfactual point. Praise for the decision was nicely captured by O'Hanlon's piece on "how the hardliners lost":[4]

> Colin Powell has carried the day on what may be the most important national security debate of the Bush presidency ... There is now a real possibility that the President[,] together with the Secretary of State, will achieve a peaceful outcome in Iraq that rewrites the books on coercive diplomacy – as well as the early histories about who really calls the shots in this administration.

O'Hanlon's *Washington Post* article is one of many illustrations of the widespread sentiment following the decision to negotiate the passage of a unanimously endorsed UN resolution to return inspectors. Many others praised the decision at the time for obvious reasons: because it hit the right balance between hardliners who pushed for unilateral pre-emption without congressional or UN endorsement, and their critics who believed another UN resolution was essential to establishing legitimacy. Of course, no one at the time fully understood what this diplomatic 'success' meant, or how subsequent

---

[4] O'Hanlon 2002.

decisions ostensibly designed to reinforce the requisite coercive threats would set the stage for war.

No single piece of evidence presented in this book (including relevant quotes from Gore defending Bush's approach) constitutes sufficient evidence to confirm the *Gore-war* counterfactual – the Rose interview obviously does not take us right to war. Every statement and speech included in Appendices 2.1 and 2.2, along with all other pieces of evidence discussed in this chapter and throughout the book, must be viewed in their entirety when assessing competing counterfactuals and when challenging the dominant narrative. But the Rose exchange does go a long way toward challenging the view that neocons dominated the entire agenda, or that a Democratic administration, led by Gore, would have done things much differently.

Decision-making context(s): one versus
multiple decisions leading to war

A second major error plaguing conventional accounts of the war is the assumption that only one decision is relevant to understanding what happened – the decision to invade Iraq. This simplistic account of history leaves out almost everything that is essential to appreciating what actually happened, how decisions unfolded over time, who supported these decisions, how these decisions were mutually reinforcing and interdependent, how the choices at each stage had a direct effect on perceptions of risks and costs of available options moving forward, and how, when combined, these choices led to the invasion. In reality, context evolves over time and changes whenever a specific decision is taken and publically defended. It was this collection of specific choices that created the path to war.

The path to war unfolded through several stages, arguably beginning with the expulsion of inspectors in 1998. The final decision to invade was a consequence of a series of choices made from 2002 to 2003 by multiple actors in the United States and UK, each decision receiving widespread bipartisan support from Congress and the British parliament. Consider the following examples of key decision points: (T1) address the absence of inspectors by working through the UN for a post-9/11, multilaterally endorsed response to the failing containment and sanctions regimes (neocons and unilateralists strongly recommended against this option, preferring instead to bypass the UN by relying exclusively on existing UN resolutions); (T2) obtain congressional authorization (neocons and unilateralists argued against going to Congress); (T3) deploy troops to the region, which are backed by congressional authorization to enhance the credibility of the coercive threat needed for a strong UN resolution; (T4) with troops deployed to the region, approach the United Nations to obtain a unanimously endorsed resolution to re-start coercive inspections; (T5) negotiate a strong resolution with a very clear mandate and rigid requirements demanding full, complete and unfettered compliance; (T6) reject Iraq's report as inadequate proof of disarmament (Blix was equally critical of this report); (T7) interpret subsequent reports by Blix as inadequate evidence of full and complete compliance; (T8) go back to the UN to negotiate a second resolution (against the strong recommendations of unilateralists and neocons), one with a clear timeline and explicit threat of military action (consistent with both the UK and Canadian proposals); (T9) reject France's demands to exclude reference to a timeline and explicit military threat, which would have virtually eliminated the coercive power associated with the deployment of hundreds of thousands of troops in theatre; (T10) back off from regime change commitment by demanding the departure of Saddam, his sons and senior leadership (against the recommendations of unilateralists and neoconservatives, who favored a much stronger commitment to regime change); (T11) respond to the rejection of the final offer to Saddam by mounting an invasion with the full support of the UK, most other European powers, several other coalition partners, and a number of regional allies, including critics of the war (Harvey 2004). In light of these key decision points, it is clear that this is not a story of a single decision to invade Iraq, and neoconservatives lost most of the crucial decisions along the way – each of the decisions altered the context moving forward, raising the value and appeal of some options and, once they were selected, affecting the value and appeal of other choices. Decisions have consequences and each decision in the sequence had consequences that, as the remainder of the book will establish, created the momentum toward the final stage, war.

These multiple decisions also reveal important anomalies that directly challenge core tenets of conventional wisdom, because both the overall multilateralist strategy and many of the specific choices along the way were *opposed* by neocons and unilateralists – the latter two groups were not running the show. The extent of bipartisan support for the overall strategy and related decisions was considerably more widespread than standard narratives ever acknowledge.

Looking at the case history from the perspective of a sequence of decisions is beneficial for several reasons. First, it helps to clarify how the overall strategy unfolded. Previous decisions have an effect on the willingness to accept (or discount) subsequent choices and reveal the difficulties that come with revisiting the wisdom of discarded alternatives. A sequence approach also helps to clarify how the coercive diplomatic strategy was applied and the consecutive (and increasingly more costly) threats and signals that were issued over time. The approach also forces the researcher to uncover relevant debates and outcomes in their proper context, and determines how these outcomes were ultimately responsible for the decisions that pushed the United States and UK along the path to war.

Of course, the reason why neoconists overlook these sequential details and multiple decision points is simple – avoiding this complexity and nuance helps to sustain the conventional wisdom. The larger the number of actors and the

more complex (interdependent) the decisions in the sequence, the more difficult it is for neoconists to sustain the view that a single person (or a small group
of ideologues) were capable of controlling the entire process toward a single
objective. It is also much easier for neoconists to criticize the final decision to go
to war rather than assessing the quality of a much larger collection of rational,
interim decisions that received widespread bipartisan support at the time. Yet
all of the key decision points from 2002 to 2003 reveal important anomalies
that directly challenge core tenets of conventional wisdom, because the overall multilateralist strategy adopted by Bush and Blair, along with specific tactical choices at each stage, were *opposed* by neocons and unilateralists. Many
of those in Congress who voted against authorization (e.g., Carl Levin) did so
not because they rejected the general WMD case against Saddam, but because
they wanted the president to approach the UN first to obtain international support – which Bush, Powell and Blair ultimately accomplished anyway through
UNSCR 1441.

Some neoconists might offer a slightly watered down version of their *Gore-
peace* counterfactual in which the Gore administration makes all of the same
choices except for the very last decision to go to war. But there are two problems with this line of reasoning. First, even if this was the case, this counterfactual would still constitute a major challenge to the 'failure of the marketplace of
ideas' thesis defended by Kaufmann. This alternative version of neoconism suggests that the marketplace was working perfectly well up to the very last stage,
but scholars who defend the 'failure of the marketplace' thesis never qualify
their arguments in these weak neoconist terms. Second, for reasons discussed
in this and subsequent chapters, the notion that Gore's team would have made
all of the same decisions and still prefer the status quo at the eleventh hour is not
at all persuasive. The risks and political costs would have been too high in the
context of the first post-9/11 presidential election campaign. Why would Gore's
team act so logically and consistently with respect to all previous decisions but
behave so differently at the very end? What evidence do we have from Gore's
or Holbrooke's statements or speeches that would support that counterfactual
claim? And, most important, how does that counterfactual case compare, in its
entirety, with the one developed in this book?

The final choices at each stage of the crisis, including the end point, were
guided by a strong conviction, shared by many, that effective inspections must
be backed by a coercive military threat and deployment of troops to the region.
But this preferred strategy was destined to fail, paradoxically, because coercive
diplomacy through rigid inspections stood the best chance of dealing with the
crisis peacefully. Nevertheless, that path produced a sequence of events and
perceptions that escalated to a point where invasion was considered less risky
than the status quo in March 2003. The next section of this chapter will further
explore the leadership qualities of Gore and other senior Democrats that support *Gore-war* and disconfirm *Gore-peace*.

Gore's right-of-center leadership and hawkish foreign policy legacy

By any measure, including conservative Republican standards, Gore was a for-eign policy hawk. He consistently opposed efforts to cut defense spending, sup-ported Reagan's decisions to bomb Libya, invade Grenada, aid the Contras in the 1980s, and fund the B-1 and B-2 bomber and MX missile programs. Gore, along with Senator Joe Lieberman (his 2000 running mate), strongly endorsed the 1991 Gulf War by opposing a significant majority of other Democrats in the Senate at the time. As vice president, Al Gore supported national missile defense and military actions in Bosnia (lift-and-strike policy, 1993–1995) and Kosovo (1998). In the 2000 election campaign, Gore recommended increas-ing the defense budget by as much as $100 billion over ten years, compared to Bush's $45 billion proposal. Perhaps most relevant to the counterfactuals in question, Gore consistently adopted the hardest line in the Clinton administra-tion when dealing with Saddam Hussein. President Clinton's decision to end the bombing campaign against Iraq in 1998 (Operation Desert Fox) did not rely on unanimous consent among his advisers – Secretary of State Albright, Defense Secretary Cohen and Vice President Gore all opposed halting the strikes at that time, despite the absence of UN Security Council endorsement.[5] Gore also strongly endorsed American retaliatory strikes against Sudan and Afghanistan, in response to the terrorist strike on the USS *Cole*, without first obtaining multi-lateral support from the UN Security Council.

The consensus with respect to Gore's influence on foreign policy in the Clinton administration is very clear – Gore was Clinton's most important foreign policy adviser (Cockburn and St. Clair 2000; Kengor 1997; Turque 2000).[6] In fact, Gore was selected as vice president in 1992, in large measure, to address Clinton's weaknesses in this regard and to balance the ticket with a right-of-center foreign policy platform. According to Cockburn and St. Clair (2000: 218), "Gore had virtually unprecedented influence in the formation of foreign policy, and not only with respect to Iraq." Gore's former chief of staff, Roy Neel, explains why Clinton deferred to Gore on Iraq policy – "He knows it. He had credibility on it because of his background and expertise and because he voted with Bush on the Gulf war. Clinton is perfectly comfortable to let Gore exploit this issue on his own."[7] These are significant points that are directly related to the counterfactual exercise – they suggest that major foreign policy initiatives during the Clinton administration, especially on Iraq, are likely to be close approximations of what we would expect to see from Gore. Former UN Ambassador Bill Richardson

---

[5] See *New Republic* 1998.
[6] Cockburn and St. Clair 2000; Kengor 1997; Turque 2000. See Kengor (1997: 16–18) for Gore's evolving views on Iraq and Saddam Hussein.
[7] Cockburn and St. Clair 2000: 211.

described Gore's influence this way: "Gore comes in at the end, summarizes, moves the President his way."[8]

Hartung (2000) provides some additional evidence regarding Gore's (and Lieberman's) consistently right-of-center foreign policy preferences, many of which were outlined during their 2000 campaign:[9]

> As Vice President, Al Gore has carefully distanced himself from the Clinton Administration's modest steps toward relaxing economic and travel restrictions between the United States and Cuba. On October 4, The New York Times asked Gore, "Would you press for the lifting of sanctions?" Gore answered: "No, no, I'm a hardliner on Castro."
>
> Peace Action, the nation's largest grassroots peace group, highlighted six issues in its latest Presidential voter guide. On five of these, Gore and Bush agreed: "Increase Pentagon spending" (Yes), "Spend $60 billion or more on 'Star Wars' anti-missile system" (Yes), "Give aid to Colombian army guilty of human rights violations" (Yes), "End sanctions on food and medicine to civilians in Iraq" (No), and "Require labor rights and environmental protections in all trade agreements" (No).
>
> Gore was an early and consistent supporter of using force in the Persian Gulf. In 1991, he and Lieberman were two of only ten Democrats in the Senate to vote for the resolution authorizing the air war against Iraq. Lieberman also called for the use of US ground troops to drive Saddam Hussein from power, despite the fact that such a move would have violated the UN resolution that had authorized US intervention in the conflict.
>
> Lest we think his views have mellowed with age and experience, Gore has a section on his campaign web site entitled "Gore Backed Use of Military Force When Necessary to Protect US Interests and Values," in which he proudly proclaims that he "argued strongly for punitive air strikes against the Serbs," "supported air strikes and continuous patrolling of the no-fly zone to contain Saddam Hussein," and "supported military retaliation against Osama Bin Laden for terrorist attacks against US embassies in East Africa." [This retaliation included the bombing of a building in the Sudan that was later determined to be a pharmaceutical factory with no documented connection to bin Laden.]

Turque goes on to point out that it was Gore who pushed Clinton to launch cruise missile strikes against Iraqi targets following news of the plot to kill President George Bush during his visit to Kuwait in 1993. Gore was among the strongest supporters of continuing air strikes in 1998 to force Radovan Karadzic and Slobodan Milosevic back to the bargaining table to sign the Vance–Owen peace plan. Presidential historian Richard Neustadt is quoted in Turque's book as having "a clear impression that [Gore] would have been more forthcoming with force much earlier" (2000: 274). In the 1990s, Gore and several Republicans were consistently strong supporters of the controversial policy to lift the arms

---

[8] Quoted in Cockburn and St. Clair 2000: 221.   [9] Hartung 2000.

embargo imposed on Bosnian Muslims (which Bosnia Serbs managed to bypass with support of Serbian leader Milosevic) and strike Serb targets in Bosnia-Herzegovina. Gore's comments in the Oval Office during a national security meeting in July 1995 convey the passion underlying his position (shared by National Security Adviser Anthony Lake and UN Ambassador Madeleine Albright) to push for a stronger stance by the United States. Bob Woodward's recollection of Gore's statement reads as follows:

> My 21 year old daughter asked about that picture. What am I supposed to tell her? Why is this happening and we're not doing anything? My daughter is surprised the world is allowing this to happen. I am too ... the cost of this is going to cascade over several decades. It goes to what kind of people we are. Acquiescence is the worst alternative ... We have to come up with something practical to make military sense. Acquiescence is not an option.[10]

The reference was to a *Washington Post* picture of young Muslim women hanging from a tree reportedly after committing suicide. Gore supported Anthony Lake's proposal to apply coercive diplomacy reinforced by a massive NATO bombing campaign that ultimately led to the signing of the Dayton Peace Accords. As Turque infers (2000: 342) – "*Where Clinton's instincts were to accommodate and placate, Gore drew sharper lines on moral questions and tended to view the world as more starkly divided between good and evil*" (emphasis added). This, once again, was a policy position considerably more in line with the Republicans, who were emphasizing the unique obligation of the United States to stabilize dangerous regions through democratization and reform.

Gore strongly defended President Clinton in 1998 against claims that Operation Desert Fox (the major bombing campaign punishing Iraq for non-compliance with UN resolutions and inspections) was nothing more than a wag-the-dog initiative designed to distract the American public from the impending House vote on four articles of impeachment in the Monica Lewinsky trial:

> Anybody who thinks for one minute that Bill Cohen, a former member of the Senate Republican caucus, or Hugh Shelton, a four-star general of the Green Beret Special Forces branch of the Army, would sit in these meetings and be a part of some politically motivated plan is just crazy. No serious person can look at the facts and come to that conclusion.[11]

As it turned out, the "facts" about Saddam's WMD that Gore was referring to were less than accurate, as would be the case in 2003. Nevertheless, the same logical argument Gore offered to defend Clinton in 1998 could just as easily be applied in defense of Bush and Blair in 2003; they were also supported by four-star

---

[10] Woodward quoted in Cockburn and St. Clair 2000: 221.
[11] Quoted in Turque 2000: 354–5.

generals and several very bright non-neocon Republican and Democratic leaders who authorized the use of force against Iraq.

In a 1998 CNN interview with Larry King, arranged by the vice president to defend the administration's decision to launch Operation Desert Fox, Gore explained:

> We tried to make this inspection regime work, and Saddam would not cooperate. In fact, he obstructed the inspectors. And so we are going to take the other alternative available to us, to use our military to degrade his ability to get weapons of mass destruction and threaten his neighbors. We'll make an assessment whenever this military action is completed. If at some point in the future he decides to try to continue to threaten his neighbors and get weapons of mass destruction, we may have to do it again ... We have strong support from around the world. The British are participating. We have strong support in the region. We're very pleased with the level of support for this. I think people all over the world are really fed up with Saddam Hussein.[12]

Of course, Gore strongly supported the Iraq (and Kosovo) air strikes in 1998 despite the fact that none of these operations were endorsed by a United Nations Security Council resolution coming anywhere close to what Bush and Blair managed to negotiate in 2002 (UNSCR 1441). Nor did Clinton and Gore obtain congressional authorization to use force – in fact, the 1998 Iraq Liberation Act (ILA) explicitly *excluded* the application of US military force in order to get the resolution passed in Congress. Nevertheless, Clinton and Gore continued to refer to the ILA whenever they defended the bombing campaign. Their arguments appear to be virtually identical to those offered by Bush, Powell and Blair in 2002–2003:

> If you allow someone like Saddam Hussein to get nuclear weapons, ballistic missiles, chemical weapons, biological weapons, how many people is he going to kill with such weapons? He's already demonstrated a willingness to use these weapons. He poison gassed his own people. He used poison gas and other weapons of mass destruction against his neighbors. This man has no compunction about killing lots and lots of people. So this is a way to save lives and to save the stability and peace of a region of the world that is important to the peace and security of the entire world.[13]

Neoconists are fond of extracting similar sentiments from speeches delivered by Bush administration officials as definitive proof of a predilection toward invasion, but they never acknowledge the fact that almost everyone else in Washington, on both sides of the aisle, shared these exact same views, including Al Gore.

[12] Gore 1998b.   [13] Gore 1998b.

As Sanger (2000) concludes, there was no question during the 2000 election that Gore's team was working hard to define the vice president as a staunch liberal internationalist and assertive multilateralist, in direct contrast to Bush's more isolationist and realist positions.[14] This was certainly the typical storyline covered by all major media outlets at the time, and it is clear that both the Gore and Bush teams exploited these differences at every opportunity – indeed, Gore wore this image as a badge of honor, milking his Bosnia, Kosovo and Iraq legacies. This is *not* the profile of a leader who would be concerned about the application of coercive military force. In Al Gore's own words:[15]

> Despite our swift victory and our efforts since, *there is no doubt in my mind that Saddam Hussein still seeks to amass weapons of mass destruction.* You know as well as I do that as long as Saddam Hussein stays in power there can be no comprehensive peace for the people of Israel or the people of the Middle East. We have made it clear that it is our policy to see Saddam Hussein gone. (Emphasis added)
>
> We have used force when necessary, and that has been frequently. And we will not let up in our efforts to free Iraq from Saddam's rule. Should he think of challenging us, I would strongly advise against it. *As a senator, I voted for the use of force, as Vice President I supported the use of force. If entrusted with the Presidency, my resolve will never waiver. Never waiver.* (Emphasis added)

It is very hard to parse statements like this, and even harder to imagine, after the trauma of 9/11, that Gore would be less inclined to follow the policy he outlined. Why would anyone with these beliefs oppose the option of getting inspectors back into Iraq to disarm Saddam after 9/11 – options he explicitly endorsed in 2002?

Turque's (2000: 293) biography of Gore describes efforts by Dick Morris (the policy brain behind the Clinton administration and self-described inventor of 'triangulation')[16] to use Gore as the conduit through which Morris could persuade Clinton and other advisers to move to the center or center-right of the policy spectrum. Popular rather than ideologically informed/motivated positions on key debates were regarded as the key to political success, which Clinton not only accepted but used effectively (according to Morris' memoirs) to win re-election. Turque's assessment is consistent with general impressions of Gore's foreign policy legacy. It is highly unlikely that Gore would have been inclined when in power to accept a radical departure from right-of-center preferences on foreign policy, especially if these positions received widespread public and bipartisan political support. Rejecting the neoconservative preferences for unilateral pre-emption in 2003 in favor of going back to the UN for coercive

---

[14] Sanger 2000.   [15] Gore 2000b.

[16] Essentially co-opting Republican policies and exploiting centrist positions of key initiatives.

inspections was the perfect mix of policies that would have matched Gore's foreign policy legacy – these preferences also match those Al Gore outlined in his 2000 campaign and the Council on Foreign Relations and Commonwealth Club speeches on Iraq he delivered in 2002.

Gore's support for unilateralism ('if necessary') and endorsement of 'axis of evil'

A portion of chapter eight in Bob Woodward's (2004) book, *Plan of Attack: The Definitive Account of the Decision to Invade Iraq*, was dedicated to tracking the origins of the "axis of evil" reference in Bush's January 2002 State of the Union address.[17] Woodward provides some fascinating details about why changes were made to the version included in speech writer David Frum's original draft, which used "axis of hatred." Woodward believed this part of the story was important enough to devote several pages to the subject, perhaps because he, like many others (including neoconists) believed the "axis of evil" reference was a clear articulation of the Bush Doctrine and Washington's Iraq policy. At the time, however, they were not regarded as anything approaching a novel thought or the cornerstone of a revolutionary US foreign policy initiative or grand strategy. For many critics, however, these three words constituted Bush's declaration of war.

These issues are directly relevant to the counterfactual evidence supporting category A versus category C evidence (from Figure 1.1) – Gore endorsed the "axis of evil" statement in a speech he delivered in 2002 to the Council on Foreign Relations, and also expressed support for occasionally applying unilateralist strategies when multilateral efforts fail:

> The Administration in which I served looked at the challenges we faced in the world and said we wished to tackle these *with others, if possible; alone, if we must*.[18]

> Since the State of the Union, there has been much discussion of whether Iraq, Iran and North Korea truly constitute an *"Axis of Evil."* As far as I'm concerned, there really is something to be said for occasionally putting diplomacy aside and laying one's cards on the table. There is value in calling evil by its name. One should never underestimate the power of bold words coming from a President of the United States.[19]

These sentiments are not exclusive to Al Gore; they were shared by many other senior Democratic leaders, including the 2004 Democratic presidential candidate, John Kerry – "With John Kerry as commander-in-chief, we will never wait for a green light from abroad when our safety is at stake."[20] Now consider the profile of Gore's running mate in the 2000 campaign, Joe Lieberman, who was

---

[17] Woodward 2004.   [18] Gore 2002a.   [19] Gore 2002a.
[20] Kerry (2004) quoted in www.isreview.org/issues/37/one_agenda.shtml.

put on the ticket in part because he was a foreign policy and defense hawk as well, especially on Iraq. "Since September 11," Eyal Press (2001) observes, "no member of the Senate has voiced more hawkish views about the scope of the war than Joseph Lieberman, the man who would have been Gore's vice president."[21] Press continues:

> In numerous speeches and newspaper articles, Lieberman has argued that Saddam Hussein's "special hatred for America" calls for aggressive action to topple the Iraqi dictator – a perspective in line with that of Paul Wolfowitz, Bush's deputy secretary of defense. Such statements prompted the conservative strategist William Kristol, a well-known (neoconservative) hawk, to tell the Los Angeles Times that Lieberman's views are "closer to us than parts of the Bush administration."

Kagan (2006) reminds us that Lieberman

> was the leading sponsor of a Senate [Iraq Liberation Act] resolution, which eventually passed with 98 votes, to provide money to Iraqis for the express purpose of overthrowing Hussein. This was what made him attractive to Democrats in 2000. It made him a fitting companion to that other hawk on the ticket, Al Gore. For remember, Gore, too, had gained the nomination as a relative hard-liner on foreign policy, including policy on Iraq.[22]

Any reasonably balanced assessment of the ideological divide separating Gore–Lieberman from Bush–Cheney in the 2000 campaign would conclude that the Democratic ticket was considerably more passionate about the need for assertive multilateralism, and more willing to apply military force for national security and humanitarian reasons. Bush's foreign policy platform, on the other hand, was informed by an alternative vision most succinctly captured by Condoleezza Rice's 2000 *Foreign Affairs* article entitled "Promoting the National Interest." It was the first and clearest explication of the doctrine Bush went on to defend in the campaign.[23] Rice and Bush were very critical of the Clinton–Gore policy that replaced "national interest" with "humanitarian interests or the interests of the international community." This was a common critique repeatedly issued by Bush to challenge what he regarded as Clinton's seriously mistaken policies in Bosnia and Kosovo, followed by a recommendation to withdraw US forces from Bosnia – a strategy quickly denounced at the time by Al Gore and Madeleine Albright as misguided.[24] A senior Bush spokesperson defended the governor's policy preferences during the campaign:

> The role of the US military is not to be all things to all people. Bush does not support an open-ended commitment to keep our troops as peacekeepers in the Balkans ... Gore seems to have a vision of an indefinite US military deployment in the Balkans. He proved today that if he is elected, America's

[21] Press 2001.   [22] Kagan 2006.   [23] See Rice 2000.   [24] Holmes 2000.

military will continue to be overdeployed, harming morale & re-enlistment rates, weakening our military's core mission.[25]

If Bush and Cheney were compelled after the trauma of 9/11 to dismiss these isolationist sentiments in favor of a more assertive foreign policy agenda, what logical argument could neoconists offer to explain why Al Gore, Richard Holbrooke and Joe Lieberman would follow a different path? If one traces the content or underlying themes running through Gore's unwavering defense of American foreign policy, particularly when he was vice president (see Appendix 2.1), he was consistently defending the central principles of what later became his 2000 foreign policy platform: 'assertive multilateralism,' 'liberal internationalism,' 'cooperative security' and 'forward engagement.' By logical implication, wouldn't they be *more* inclined in the aftermath of 9/11 to select the path consistent with the policies they forcefully defended throughout the previous eight years, or the policies recommended in Gore's 2002 speeches on Iraq?

Similarly, there would have been no reason for Gore to change his mind about the Iraq threat *after* a four-year absence of inspectors. Previously entrenched concerns about Saddam's WMD were reinforced when inspectors left in 1998 and were subsequently amplified after 9/11; the generally accepted (non-distorted) estimates were never seriously challenged by anyone. Some of the best work on the role of cognitions in foreign policy decision-making (Janis 1972; Janis and Mann 1977; Jervis 1976; Lebow 1984) has consistently argued that beliefs and perceptions change very slowly (if at all) and only after a significant amount of new information comes in.[26] Without inspectors on the ground, however, there was no new information on Iraq's WMD on which to rely – inspectors who left in 1998 believed Saddam retained proscribed weapons.[27] In light of the 9/11 commission report confirming Washington's 'failure to imagine' serious security threats, the notion that Gore would have downplayed Iraq's WMD threat in this environment is simply not plausible. Gore "repeatedly portrayed himself as a man who has come to believe in vigorous American intervention abroad," David Sanger observed, "a reversal of Democratic philosophy for most of the time since the end of the war in Vietnam."[28]

Finally, with respect to the standard neoconist refrain that Gore preferred multilateralism, these common assertions are far from factual and are rarely if ever exposed to the kind of historical (contextual) analysis one would need to defend these claims. The evidence clearly demonstrates Gore's strong

---

[25] Holmes 2000.

[26] Janis 1972; Janis and Mann 1977; Jervis 1976; Lebow 1984.

[27] See Ritter 1999. Despite being one of the strongest critics of the war, Ritter includes very detailed appendices describing the WMD weapons (biological and chemical) he believed Saddam retained, notwithstanding years of inspections.

[28] Sanger 2000. Sanger was a senior *New York Times* correspondent covering Gore's debate performances, interviews and foreign policy speeches during the 2000 campaign.

preference for *instrumental* multilateralism rather than the more *principled* approach preferred by Europeans – a partiality motivated by their relative military weakness. Gore and members of what would have been his national security team certainly endorsed multilateralism when allies are on side, but were always perfectly willing to bypass these strictures when the values and interests of major powers diverged (see Chapter 7). President Clinton and Vice President Gore bypassed the UN Security Council when they launched Operation Desert Fox in 1998, ignored the call for a UN resolution when they launched attacks on Serbian positions in Bosnia in 1995, and rejected calls for UN endorsement prior to the Kosovo bombing campaign in 1998. With respect to whether Gore would have been more inclined to wait for additional countries to join the coalition against Iraq, recall that France, Germany and Belgium were the 'exceptions' in Europe. A majority of major players in *old* and *new* Europe supported the Bush–Blair strategy. Any post-9/11 American leader facing the 2004 presidential election campaign would have understood the enormous political risks of defending the status quo – ongoing inspections with no clear resolution – while covering the mounting costs of sustaining 200,000 or more US troops in theater. Giving France a veto over US (or UK) security policy would not have been a very appealing option for any astute political leader.

Additional category 'C' evidence supporting *Gore-war*

With respect to uncovering additional counterfactual evidence from Gore's past, consider the large collection of statements by Al Gore cited in Appendix 2.1. The evidence collected here represents only a small fraction of hundreds of similar statements by Gore (and senior Democratic advisers he would almost certainly have consulted as members of his national security team: see Chapter 3 and Appendix 3.1), all available in the public domain and all partially responsible for reinforcing the exact same consensus on Iraq's WMD that Bush, Powell and Blair defended.[29] In fact, none of the statements issued by Al Gore throughout his entire political career came close to presenting an image of a leader inclined to follow a completely different (*Gore-peace*) path away from the one he himself recommended in 2002.[30]

---

[29] For a considerably larger collection of relevant quotes, please see www.davidstuff.com/political/wmdquotes.htm (accessed October 2010).

[30] See, for example, the explanation Gore offered in support of the Iraq war resolution in 1991, his speeches on Iraq and US foreign and security policy as vice president, his strong endorsement of the 1998 Iraq Liberation Act calling for regime change, his subsequent defense of Operation Desert Fox, statements made throughout the 2000 election campaign and related presidential debates on foreign affairs, interviews, press conferences and two major speeches in 2002. All support or explicitly endorse the policies adopted by Bush, Blair and Powell, in line with the *Gore-war* counterfactual.

Five months after the end of the Iraq war, and well after the Iraq Survey Group failed to find stockpiles of WMD, Al Gore offered the following admission:

> I'm convinced that one of the reasons that we didn't have a better public debate before the Iraq War started is because so many of the impressions that the majority of the country had back then turn[ed] out to have been completely wrong. Leaving aside for the moment the question of how these false impressions got into the public's mind, it might be healthy to take a hard look at the ones we now know were wrong and clear the air so that we can better see exactly where we are now and what changes might need to be made.[31]

Like many of his fellow Democrats in the years after the Iraq war, Gore would obviously prefer to 'leave aside' any question of how so many of these false WMD impressions made their way into the public's mind, perhaps because he played such a large role in reinforcing that consensus when he was in power. In light of the large collections of statements included in Appendix 2.1, there is very little evidence from Gore's past that would provide even a hint that he had serious reservations about using military force to address a threat from Saddam Hussein. Nor does Gore appear to be the type of leader who, if bolstered by strong support from Prime Minister Tony Blair, would capitulate to a French refusal to endorse military action against Iraq if Saddam failed to comply with UNSCR 1441. This is not the profile of a leader with a foreign policy legacy that would be inclined to take the country down a completely different path on Iraq.

Iraq versus other foreign policy priorities

The evidence clearly shows that Al Gore was not in favor of unilateral pre-emption and would not have pushed this policy as a serious option in the absence of an imminent threat. But these preferences are entirely consistent with the counterfactual case I am developing in this and subsequent chapters. Without Bush, the views of neoconservatives and unilateralists would not have been relevant to establishing the context surrounding Iraq in a Gore administration.

We know that Gore rejected the more extreme items in the distorted intelligence case being put forward by Cheney and the Pentagon, rejected the imminent threat argument and related case for unilateral pre-emption, and pushed (along with many others) for a policy recommending a return to Congress and the UN for a strong resolution and coercive inspections. An 'imminent' threat from Iraq, in other words, was not necessary to push the policy Gore endorsed, and the one Bush and Blair adopted to deal with the Iraq impasse. In fact, it was the absence of an imminent threat that was so central to the justification Gore offered in 2002 to defend his alternative – retain a focus on Al-Qaeda (once

---

[31] Gore 2003.

major combat operations in Afghanistan were completed) and deal with Iraq '*simultaneously*' through UN inspections.

Neoconist critics have argued that Iraq would have been relegated by a Gore administration to the back burner, to be contained and managed through other multilateral efforts while the United States focused on defeating Al-Qaeda, or nuclear proliferation in Iran, North Korea or the former Soviet Union. But there are several problems with this position. First, those were not the policies Gore articulated in the 2002 CFR and CC speeches, or during his 2000 campaign. None of the statements included in Appendix 2.1 elevates Iran or North Korea (or global warming, for that matter) to more prominent positions in the list of US foreign and security policy priorities. Anyone making the counterfactual claim that a Gore, Holbrooke and Lieberman team would have seriously considered such a significant shift in priorities after 9/11 would need to provide very clear evidence to the point, or at least offer compelling re-interpretations of all the statements included in Appendices 2.1 and 2.2 (and Appendix 3.1).

Second, even if we accept the view that Gore would have focused significantly more attention on the multilaterally endorsed Afghanistan intervention by deploying, say, an additional 50,000 to 80,000 troops to the region, the overall impact on Washington's Iraq policy would have been negligible. A larger, even more successful Afghanistan operation that, for instance, succeeded in killing more Taliban fighters or capturing Osama bin Laden would have increased rather than decreased the likelihood of shifting to the next foreign policy challenge – getting inspectors back into Iraq to address heightened fears of WMD after 9/11. One of the reasons the Afghanistan operation was so successful was the political endorsement and military support from a large coalition of NATO allies. Gore would have received the same support. If, on the other hand, the Afghanistan operation looked similar to what unfolded under the Bush administration (a relatively quick military victory), then, once again, there would have been mounting pressure from Republicans and many senior Democrats to deal with the 'other' lingering foreign policy threat that played such a large role in the Clinton–Gore administrations – Saddam's WMD and the absence of inspectors. The more relevant question, therefore, is whether Gore's team would have made the same big decisions after a relatively quick victory in Afghanistan. The point is that Iraq would have remained important enough to begin the process of returning inspectors, and the only way to get inspectors back into Iraq with a robust mandate is to follow the same basic strategy.

Third, Iraq as a foreign policy priority was appealing precisely because of the legacy of seventeen previous UN resolutions, the absence of inspectors since 1998, and a failing containment and sanctions regime. In essence, Iraq was the ideal candidate for the application of assertive multilateralism; the same strategy would have been considerably more difficult to apply against Iran, North Korea or global warming. Moreover, Holbrooke (Gore's likely choice for secretary of state) is on record (in a major speech delivered before leaving his position as UN ambassador) predicting that the next president would have to focus on Iraq:

> Saddam Hussein's activities continue to be unacceptable and, in my view, dangerous to the region and, indeed, to the world, not only because he possesses the potential for weapons of mass destruction but because of the very nature of his regime. His willingness to be cruel internally is not unique in the world, but the combination of that and his willingness to export his problems makes him a clear and present danger at all times.[32]

The next administration, Holbrooke concluded, "will have to deal with this problem, which we inherited from our predecessors and they now inherit from us" (Aita 2001). Tony Blair also admitted, "Look, if Bush hadn't been exercised after 9/11 about these issues I would have been worrying about them, and I raised them with him before 9/11."[33] Gore, Lieberman and Holbrooke would have been compelled after 9/11 to favor an approach in line with the one Gore outlined in the 2000 campaign and recommended in 2002. If ignoring Iraq was not an option, then a return of inspections would have been seen as the most appealing liberal internationalist approach to a lingering foreign policy challenge that had been exacerbated by the absence of inspections and which they were now facing in a post-9/11 environment. The counterfactual claim that Iraq would have been ignored or downplayed in a Gore administration is not consistent with the historical record.

Fourth, we know that Iraq was a central foreign policy preoccupation throughout the two Clinton–Gore administrations – it was important enough to start a major strategic bombing campaign in 1998. The issue would have remained an important foreign policy concern in 2002, especially after 9/11, because inspectors were essential for re-invigorating containment and for monitoring the arms control piece of the sanctions and oil-for-food programs. Gore provided no indication in his campaign speeches (or those he delivered in 2002) that he was inclined to shift focus away from Iraq, and his team would not have been inclined to do so in the face of serious criticism from the media, Congress and the American public slamming the Clinton–Gore policies that led to the departure of UN inspectors in 1998. This is not to imply that the blame Gore would almost certainly have received for the absence of inspectors would have been sufficient to lead to war. But these pressures (along with many other factors introduced throughout the book) would have placed Gore in a very difficult position, especially in light of a legacy of powerful statements on Iraq and the WMD threat. Even if Gore had been inclined to avoid or downplay the Iraq threat (note: the evidence outlined above does not support this counterfactual assertion), Gore's team would have been criticized for shifting the focus away from their responsibility for the absence of UN inspectors – a very difficult position to be in after 9/11.

[32] Aita 2001.   [33] Woodward 2004.

Fifth, it is useful for readers to recall one of the more significant lessons emerging from the 9/11 Commission hearings at the time – that 9/11 was the product of a systemic *failure of imagination*. When the most powerful nation on earth is tasked with a policy directive to routinize, bureaucratize and institutionalize the exercise of 'imagination,' and when this authoritative recommendation is assigned to multiple federal, state and municipal governments and organizations by one of the most important bipartisan committees in American history (a committee widely supported by an American public scarred by the trauma of 9/11), it's not unreasonable to expect Gore's team would have seen this as the worst possible time to downplay the WMD threat from Iraq, a threat he was largely responsible for identifying in every one of his speeches on the subject (see Appendix 2.1). Downplaying the Iraq threat by describing it as less important than other foreign policy issues would have convinced most people that Gore just didn't get it. That is not the message Gore, Holbrooke, Lieberman, Fuerth or any one of Gore's hawkish advisers would have wanted to spread as they approached the first post-9/11 presidential election. All of these factors would have made congressional authorization, a unanimous UN resolution and the return of UN inspectors backed by a coercive inspections regime look *very* attractive as a foreign policy agenda. Gore, like Bush, would likely have benefited from rally-around-the-flag effects after 9/11, helping Gore's team push this agenda forward.

The most common mistake in the literature on Iraq is the general assumption that the only way to move closer to war is with neoconservatives, hegemonic realists and/or unilateralists in power. But there is no need for Gore to place Iraq on the top of his priority list to appreciate the wisdom of returning inspectors or obtaining congressional authorization to bolster his bargaining leverage for negotiating a new, unanimously endorsed UN resolution. Nor is it necessary for Gore to believe Iraq poses an imminent threat for him to see the appeal of these same basic strategies (see Chapter 5).

Evaluating alternative approaches to the Iraq impasse

Whenever neoconists defend their *Gore-peace* counterfactual, it is essential that they consult the facts from the relevant historical record, especially evidence that disconfirms their thesis. Good counterfactual analysis must always rely on factual history. Analysts should also include a balanced assessment of alternative policies available to decision-makers at the time. In this case, most of the policy alternatives for dealing with Iraq were widely regarded as failing. To begin, containment required inspections, now absent since 1998.

Focusing exclusively on the same 1998 air strike strategy was not a realistic option for Bush (or Gore), because bombing suspected WMD sites would provide no useful information in the absence of inspectors (or any other intelligence assets on the ground) capable of providing reliable after-action reports on damage. Secretary of defense, William Cohen, and chairman of the Joint Chiefs of Staff, Hugh Shelton, repeatedly declared at the time that the purpose of Operation Desert Fox was to degrade the regime's ability to develop and deliver chemical, biological and nuclear weapons. The 1998 bombing operation was a pretty clear admission by the administration that containment was failing and required a more forceful military response. The after-action reports in December 1998 were anything but encouraging – again, because there was really no way to confirm successful depletion of Saddam's WMD without inspectors. A similar operation in 2003 would have failed for the same reasons – Saddam could simply take reporters to document the effects of bombed-out sites, none of which would reveal stockpiles of WMD. This would have confirmed, once again, the futility of US–UK attacks and the excessive pain and suffering inflicted on civilian populations. Public opinion in the region would turn against US officials for producing far worse conditions for Iraqis without any signs of progress on disarmament.

The sanctions regime was also failing, as the Duelfer Report (2004) confirmed:

> The introduction of the Oil-For-Food program (OFF) in late 1996 was a key turning point for the Regime. OFF rescued Baghdad's economy from a terminal decline created by sanctions. The Regime quickly came to see that OFF could be corrupted to acquire foreign exchange both to further undermine sanctions and to provide the means to enhance dual-use infrastructure and potential WMD-related development. By 2000–2001, Saddam had managed to mitigate many of the effects of sanctions and undermine their international support. Iraq was within striking distance of a de facto end to the sanctions regime, both in terms of oil exports and the trade embargo, by the end of 1999.[34]

The oil-for-food program and sanctions regime were being abused by senior members of the UN (see Paul A. Volcker's report to the Independent Inquiry Committee), and by Saddam's selective distribution of oil contracts to France, Russia and China.[35] Even those indicted for corruption acknowledged the widespread nature of the problem – Benon V. Sevan (2005), a senior UN representative responsible for UN oil contracts, believed that almost everyone was at least partially complicit in the abuse and corruption:[36]

> On no occasion did OIP or I personally withhold material information from the Security Council members, the secretary general and his deputy. OIP informed the 661 Committee not only on surcharges but also on

---

[34] Duelfer 2004.

[35] See the Independent Inquiry Committee into the United Nations Oil-for-Food program, Chaired by Paul Volcker (former Chairman of the United States Federal Reserve): www.iic-offp.org.

[36] Sevan 2005.

at least 70 occasions of contracts reflecting suspicious pricing (and hence possible kickbacks), yet the committee declined in every instance to act. Similarly, I informed the US government, effectively the policeman for sanctions violations in the Gulf, of maritime smuggling on a massive scale that was occurring, to no avail.

The extent of the problems with the OFF program was detailed in several editorials throughout this period.[37] A wealth of circumstantial evidence against Sevan was revealed, including bank statements verifying large sums of money being deposited into a New York account between 1998 and 2003, and other evidence of corruption, wire fraud, kickbacks and money laundering. Getting agreement on stronger sanctions was certainly an option, but agreement on sanctions was never the problem – it was getting UNSC members to enforce existing sanctions.

The United States and UK were also losing the PR campaign surrounding the sanctions regime, all while Saddam Hussein generated billions in profits – almost everyone at the time believed the regime was investing a good portion of these funds into reconstituting (and hiding) his WMD programs, a reasonable presumption of guilt in light of his behavior over the previous decade. Readers will also recall Osama bin Laden's declaration in one of his videotaped messages that "a million innocent children (are) dying at this time ... in Iraq."[38] At the time, the most widely circulated (and hugely exaggerated) assessment of the effects of sanctions was disseminated by the United Nations Children's Emergency Fund (UNICEF). According to UNICEF, 200 children were dying every day from the effects of a draconian sanctions regime – 5,000 Iraqi children under the age of five were reportedly dying each month. These figures were constantly repeated by virtually every US newspaper. As James B. Steinberg (Clinton's deputy national security adviser from 1996 to 2000) admitted in his assessment of the serious problems with their sanctions and containment policies:[39]

> The media has made it so that you cannot succeed in your foreign policy practice now, unless you have good communications strategy ... On Iraq, we were having a huge problem because we had been totally unable to convince the international community about why we were pursuing the policy that we were pursuing. The allies would say: "We can't support it because it's opposed by the people in the wider Arab world." Even though we convinced them we had the right policy, we failed because we were ineffective in convincing people that it was Saddam who was causing the suffering of his own people. We didn't have an effective communication strategy and we hadn't developed strong enough support on the Hill.

[37] Editorial, 2005. UNcorruptible? WashingtonPost.com, August 10: A16; see also Editorial, 2005. Oil-for-bribes program. *Washington Times*, August 10.
[38] Quoted in Leigh and Wilson 2001.
[39] Quoted in Daalder and Destler (moderators) 2000.

The other linchpin of containment was the no-fly zone, which was also failing. It was costly to deploy, the flights were continuously shot at, it presented a potentially risky situation to be in for a president after 9/11 contemplating a response to this kind of aggression, and the UK issued notice that it would no longer participate – the no-fly zone was becoming an increasingly unilateral initiative that would be viewed by Gore as less appealing than the multilateral return of inspections. The cost of two no-fly zones amounted to about $1 billion every year, and after the Afghanistan operation and mounting costs of 9/11 security, the no-fly zones became a lot harder to sustain. As Ricks (2007: 43) explained, the no-fly zones kept "Air lift, AWAC command-and-control aircraft, and re-fuellers – extremely busy. By late 2001, parts of the US military felt badly stretched by enforcing the policy of containment."[40] By 2003, the total number of sorties for the no-fly zone was around 34,000 – the equivalent of the 1991 Gulf war every three years. The most obvious indication that the entire containment policy wasn't working was the decision to push for the Iraq Liberation Act, passed in 1998 – the policy that changed exclusive reliance on containment by making regime change the official policy.

Kenneth Pollack (2002) provides one of the most sweeping and clearly articulated critiques of containment:[41]

> Serious inspections of Saddam's WMD programs stopped long ago. Fewer and fewer nations respect the UN-mandated constraints, and more and more are tired of constantly battling with Saddam to force him to comply. Ludicrous Iraqi propaganda about how the economic sanctions are responsible for the deaths of more than a million people since 1991 is now accepted at face value the world over. A dozen or more nations have flown commercial airliners into Iraq to flout the ban on air travel to and from the country – a ban they now claim never existed, but one that was a well-respected fact just a few years ago. Smuggled Iraqi oil flows via Jordan, Syria, Turkey, and the Persian Gulf states at a rate more than double what it was in 1998. Iraq is increasingly able to get its hands on prohibited items such as spare parts for its tanks and planes and equipment for its crippled logistical system. Most stunning of all, the Chinese were recently caught building a nationwide fiber-optic communications network for Saddam's regime; the key nodes of this system were destroyed by US airstrikes in January 2001. If respect for the sanctions has already eroded to the point where the Chinese are willing to sell Iraq such critical technology, how long will it be before someone proves willing to sell tanks? Or missiles? Or fissile material?
>
> The current administration's unhappy experience in trying to sell "smart sanctions" to the international community shows just how bad the situation

---

[40] Ricks 2007.
[41] Pollack 2002. Pollack was one of many who identified the most serious problems with the containment policy before the Iraq war. These are sentiments shared by senior foreign policy advisers in the Clinton administration.

is ... France, Russia, China, and others have opposed the plan because Baghdad fears, correctly, that if it were accepted some form of international military and financial controls might be prolonged.

The Gulf Cooperation Council (Bahrain, Kuwait, Oman, Qatar, Saudi Arabia, and the United Arab Emirates) ... profit from the smuggling, all have populations opposed to enforcing the sanctions, and all except the GCC and Iran are now highly vulnerable to Iraqi economic pressure. So no matter what they may say publicly, none of them is likely to help much in blocking the flow of oil, money, and contraband.

Restoring a serious and sustainable containment regime would require an entirely new set of arrangements ... Such a deal is unimaginable in the UN Security Council today, where many of the members compete to see who can appease Iraq most. And although in theory similar reforms could be imposed by the United States unilaterally, any attempt to do so would soon run into passionate international opposition, crippling US diplomacy long before it had much effect on Saddam. Reforming containment enough to make it viable, therefore, is simply not in the offing.

With respect to additional confirmation that containment was widely regarded as failing, consider statements by Secretary of State Madeleine Albright on November 10, 1999, as she addressed the public and reporters at the Chicago Hilton and Towers.[42] She was responding to questions about the devastating effects of sanctions on Iraq civilians and children:[43]

> Saddam Hussein had been acquiring weapons of mass destruction. We carried out, with the help of an alliance, a war in which we put Saddam Hussein back into his box. The United Nations voted on a set of resolutions which demanded Saddam Hussein live up to his obligations and get rid of weapons of mass destruction ... There has never been an embargo against food and medicine. *It's just that Hussein has just not chosen to spend his money on that. Instead, he has chosen to spend his money on building weapons of mass destruction, and palaces for his cronies.* (Emphasis added)

Albright clearly believed the Clinton administration had failed to contain Saddam – sanctions did not prevent him from obtaining WMD.

Given the legacy of failed policies of containment, air strikes, no-fly zones and sanctions, defending the status quo in 2002 evolved into an increasingly costly proposition after 9/11. With these serious problems in mind, Gore, his advisers and the larger Democratic leadership in Congress would have found

---

[42] Quoted in Proulx 1999.

[43] Albright openly declared her view that the reported deaths of hundreds of thousands of Iraqis (including mostly children, according to a well circulated UNICEF report) was acceptable to deal with Saddam's defiance of UN resolutions and related WMD threats. When asked by Leslie Stahl in May 1996 whether the policy was justifiable, Albright replied, "Yes, I think the price is worth it." In addition to losing the PR battle, the status quo of containment was failing, as she declared in 1999.

it very appealing to negotiate a unanimous resolution to return inspectors – something the Clinton team could not accomplish. The opportunity to reinstate UN inspectors with a much stronger mandate would have been a popular option for Gore given his preference for assertive multilateralism, now a more realistic proposition in light of the international goodwill following the 9/11 attacks. Returning inspectors, in other words, was the best all-round solution to re-invigorating a crucial piece of the Clinton–Gore containment policy. The problem, of course, is that all of the other rational decisions associated with making this policy work pushed the country closer to war.

In sum, there is more than one way an administration can arrive at the conclusion that the best approach to Iraq is by returning UN inspectors:

(1) they can get to this conclusion by rejecting unilateral pre-emption or distorted intelligence (which is what Bush, Powell and Blair did); or
(2) they can arrive at the same conclusion by rejecting the status quo (failed policies of containment and sanctions) in favor of doing more after 9/11 by going back to the UN to get inspectors back in.

The latter is consistent with the counterfactual path Gore would have selected, especially if neoconservatives and unilateralists weren't around to push the other option. And these preferences are entirely consistent with Gore's belief that the United States should continue to focus on Al-Qaeda (as the priority) and Iraq 'simultaneously.'

Clearly, critics of *Gore-war* are correct to speculate that other options would have been made available to a different administration, but these options are not infinite. Some options tend to emerge because they make more sense in the context of the general consensus at the time and the legacy of Gore's position (and previous actions) on Iraq. Once specific decisions are taken, however, others logically follow. And, for reasons explained in the remainder of the book, the cumulative weight and impact of these choices combined to push the country closer and closer to war.

Other critics will reject as insufficient any of the evidence from Gore's speeches as confirmation of the *Gore-war* counterfactual, but, again, nothing here is meant to suggest that any of these items is sufficient. The evidence from Gore's past, including the very large collection of speeches on Iraq, must be viewed along with all other evidence when judging the relative strengths of competing *Gore-war* versus *Gore-peace* counterfactuals. If neoconists remain committed to the view that speeches can't confirm anything, they would then have to explain why they continue to rely on speeches from a few members of the Bush administration when bolstering their interpretation of events. Even if we agree to exclude speeches, neoconists would still need to explain how other variables (domestic, political, bureaucratic, institutional, organizational, international) would be any more likely to lead Gore down a different path. As the remaining chapters demonstrate, these other factors provide even stronger support for *Gore-war*.

Gore's position on Iraq's WMD

As the evidence from Appendix 2.1 indicates, Gore agreed with the general (as distinct from the distorted, neocon) consensus on Iraq's WMD programs. Neoconists are inclined to describe Gore's views on WMD as considerably more measured, but this watered-down version of Gore's position is not at all consistent with the facts. A brief review of Gore's speeches and statements on Iraq, or those delivered in Congress in support of the Iraq Liberation Act (1998), or the many speeches on Iraq by Clinton, Cohen, Berger, Kerry or Albright throughout the previous administration (see Appendices 3.1 and 3.2), or any of the speeches delivered by senior Democrats in Congress in support of the October 2002 resolution authorizing the use of force all clearly establish the fact that most Democrats, including Gore, were convinced that Saddam's WMD posed a serious threat to the United States and its allies.

Assessing the causal impact of 'relevant' differences

When conducting counterfactual analysis, researchers should never be satisfied with their strong suspicions that things would have been different. They should always push the point by asking important questions about what these differences would have been, providing logical reasons why they would have emerged, and explaining how these differences would have influenced decisions, policies and outcomes. For example, it is certainly conceivable (indeed likely) that Gore and Holbrooke would have been much better negotiators and would not have stoked the same ideological divisions with other European and UN members that were so easily exploited by Rumsfeld and Cheney. In the absence of neocons and unilateralists in the administration, perhaps Gore's team could have generated more support for a stronger initial or even second resolution. But this counterfactual argument still takes us down the path to war, now with a second resolution, a timeline for inspections (that would continue to reveal evidence of material breach) and a threat of force directed at a leader who, it turns out, could not provide the evidence of disarmament everyone was demanding (see Chapter 8).

Counterfactual historians could also speculate that a *risk-averse* personality (assuming Gore and his team could be shown to be predisposed to these tendencies) would have preferred to avoid war because of the risks associated with civilian casualties, the absence of support in the region, or the probability of a civil war. On the other hand, risk aversion could just as easily predict a preference for war, because doing nothing or conceding to French intransigence could have been regarded by Gore (as it was by Bush) to be a risky proposition in light of post-9/11 concerns about WMD proliferation and terrorism. A risk-averse politician could also be persuaded to act on the basis of the high political costs associated with conveying weakness as they approach the first post-9/11 presidential election in 2004. Risk aversion could also logically be tied to a decision by Gore to prepare a much larger invading force to increase the probability of winning both the conventional war and post-conflict peace and stability during the reconstruction phase. Of course, a much larger pre-deployment force also increases the costs of sustaining a larger force in theater if inspections are extended indefinitely. Risk aversion, in other words, predisposes Gore to reject France's request that a timeline and military option be taken off the table at the eleventh hour. In sum, risk aversion, like any other personality trait, does not privilege or preclude any outcome, nor does it automatically define the choices leaders will make. The final judgements about the role of personality must be subjected to the kind of careful analysis that links options to a clear assessment of costs, benefits and utility.

Counterfactually relevant speeches and statements

The material included in Appendix 2.1 (and 3.1) constitutes an important part of the counterfactual case in favor of *Gore-war*. Among other contributions, the quotes clearly support the view that Gore and Holbrooke would have pushed a liberal internationalist agenda, favored a multilateral approach to addressing the Iraq impasse after 9/11, but would not have succumbed to the pressure by other Security Council members to rely on a second unanimous resolution before punishing Iraq for non-compliance with UNSCR 1441.

The quotes included in the Appendices are not meant as sufficient evidence to encapsulate the totality of the argument I am making in defense of *Gore-war*. Therefore, critics cannot challenge the counterfactual by simply isolating and then rejecting as insufficient a few select quotes from the Appendices. I am not claiming these quotes constitute evidence that takes the Gore team directly to war – that is a caricature of my counterfactual case and anything but a fair portrayal of the comparative methodology used in the book. My arguments are considerably more layered and encompass several causal mechanisms across multiple levels of analysis. Evidence from speeches is only one aspect of the larger story.

Moreover, these quotes not only constitute strong (but partial) evidence in favor of *Gore-war*, they also serve as powerful disconfirmation of the alternative neoconist view that Gore's policy preferences, as expressed in these speeches, were completely distinct from those adopted by Bush and Blair (*Gore-peace*). They were not. Comparative counterfactual analysis forces proponents of both counterfactuals to confront the implications of historical evidence. In other words, neoconists cannot simply challenge the evidence in terms of whether it supports *Gore-war*, but must also deal with the question of how far the evidence takes us from the *Gore-peace* alternative they are defending. The speeches included in Appendix 2.1 certainly raise questions about *Gore-peace* assumptions that the former vice president was a peacenik, averse to the application of military force, suspicious of the general consensus on intelligence regarding Iraq's WMD program or more inclined to have US security policy dictated by multilateral consensus in the UN.

Political speeches have always been accepted by historians and social scientists as a crucial body of evidence to reveal leaders' personality traits, values, beliefs, priorities and policy preferences. Gore's speeches are important in this case because they tell us a great deal about his views on Iraq. However, it would be a mistake to assign equal explanatory weight to any quote selected from one of Gore's speeches – informed judgements about which of Gore's statements are more or less relevant is an important consideration for good counterfactual analysis. Where and when was the speech delivered? How many speeches were delivered expressing the same or similar sentiments? How does the content of the selected speech relate to confirming or disconfirming the counterfactual claims? How does the historical sequence (timing) and political context of the speech relate to each of the two counterfactual claims?

With respect to political context, some statements by Gore (or his advisers and leading Democrats) are more likely than others to provide relevant information about policy preferences, because they were delivered at a time and place that closely approximates the antecedent condition at the center of the counterfactual. For example, arguably the most relevant speeches, statements or comments by Gore are those he delivered in December 1998 when he was vice president and a senior member of President Clinton's national security team, dealing with an almost identical military crisis and contemplating the use of military force to compel Hussein to comply with UN inspections. These situations reveal clear evidence about Gore's foreign policy, his beliefs about the utility of coercive military force, his perceptions of Saddam Hussein and concerns about weapons of mass destruction, etc, and this information is directly relevant to how a counterfactual Gore presidency would have handled the Iraq crisis from 2002 to 2003.

Similarly, the sequence and timing of specific statements is important, so those delivered, for example, during the 2000 presidential campaign are helpful in as much as they provide insights into Gore's foreign policy preferences at a time when political costs and benefits are at their maximum. Speeches delivered by Gore when he was out of power but still considering the possibility of becoming a leading Democratic candidate for the 2004 election are also relevant. For example, two major speeches and an important interview on Iraq in 2002–2003 (to the Council on Foreign Relations, the Commonwealth Club of San Francisco and in conversations with PBS' Charlie Rose) are directly relevant, because Gore used these opportunities to outline specific recommendations on Iraq in the context of establishing an alternative to the neoconservative path being championed by Cheney, Rumsfeld and Wolfowitz. These two major speeches were delivered a year before the war, when the Bush administration had begun to consider different approaches for dealing with the lingering Iraq problem. Gore articulated the main elements of a UN-based multilateral alternative to unilateral pre-emption.

Perhaps the least relevant speeches are those delivered when Gore was out of office, long after the war (and after no WMD were found), with no plans to return. These statements carry virtually no political risks whatsoever and are freed from the social, political, military or international pressures leaders face when in power. In a GQ interview in 2006, Gore all but acknowledged the difference inside and outside of government – when answering a question about being out of political office, Gore admitted, "Well, you know the old Kris Kristofferson song that Janis Joplin made famous, 'Me and Bobby McGee'? It has a great line: *Freedom's just another word for nothing left to lose. There's some aspects of that involved here*" (emphasis added).[44] Gore went on in the same interview to claim that he would have heeded the warnings about terrorism had he been president in 2000. Gore admitted that "it's almost too easy to say, 'I would have heeded the warnings,'" but left little doubt that he thought the president hadn't done as much as he should have when warned by the CIA in the summer of 2001 that bin Laden was determined to attack the United States.

> In fact, I think I would have, I know I would have … We had several instances when the CIA's alarm bells went off, and what we did when that happened was, we had emergency meetings and called everybody together and made sure that all systems were go and every agency was hitting on all cylinders, and we made them bring more information, and go into the second and third and fourth level of detail.[45]

But Gore's record when in power throughout the previous decade – in fact, the record of the Clinton administration – does not support that position. National Security Adviser Sandy Berger rejected, on four separate occasions, warnings from Richard Clarke about Al-Qaeda and possible targets for bin Laden's location. Even with detailed intelligence on Al-Qaeda training in Afghanistan, there was not much that could be done in the absence of a 9/11 attack, and when action was taken – for example, in Sudan – the administration was severely criticized for failing to resolve the problem. After the Sudan bombing error, Berger was very reluctant to do anything that would risk civilian casualties. To claim in 2006 they would have had more "emergency meetings" than Bush's team says nothing about the kind of operational planning they would have been required to put in place to resolve the Al-Qaeda problem.

Other relevant speeches include those by senior Democratic leaders in Congress whose opinions Gore would have sought for support or guidance.

---

[44] www.gq.com/news-politics/newsmakers/200611/al-gore-interview-truth-inconvenient.
[45] www.gq.com/news-politics/newsmakers/200611/al-gore-interview-truth-inconvenient.

Arguably the most relevant of all would be statements by senior Democrats on the floor of the House or Senate justifying their decision to authorize the president to use all necessary means to force Saddam's compliance. Consistent with category C evidence, there are dozens of major speeches by senior Democrats regarding their impressions of intelligence on Iraq's WMD that turned out to be completely wrong – neocons were not the only ones making these arguments. The WMD consensus was firmly rooted well before the Bush administration took office.

The sheer volume of statements that share a particular perspective on a key issue is also relevant when assessing a leader's perceptions, assumptions and foreign policy preferences. Obviously, Gore spent a good part of his entire political career making speeches on Iraq, repeating the same concerns about Saddam's WMD threat, the regime's use of chemical weapons against Saddam's own people, the value of regime change and democratization, and the importance of maintaining a credible coercive threat to manage the crisis.

As Eyal Press (2001) argues:[46]

> While nobody can say for certain whether pressure from the right would have propelled Gore to deploy military force more aggressively and on a wider number of fronts than Bush has, there is broad agreement that such pressure would have been far greater with a Democrat in office – particularly with regard to Iraq. "With a Democratic president, I think the Republicans would have been calling for blood, saying it was the wimpish Clinton administration that left us with this Iraq problem," says former Carter administration official Gary Sick, a historian of US foreign policy and the Middle East at Columbia University. "Of course, the irony is that it was Bush's father who didn't finish the job during the Gulf War."

In sum, counterfactually relevant speeches convey a great deal of information. They tell us more about the priorities of these individuals (all else being equal) when they're faced with similar challenges and forced to suffer political consequences. Statements that confer costly signals are not easily reversible and therefore more risky – they should carry more counterfactual weight, because they are closer to the real preferences we would expect to see under the relevant counterfactual circumstance.

Admittedly, the collection of speeches or policy statements from Appendix 2.1 is not sufficient in and of itself to provide definitive proof of the priorities Gore and his team would have followed in 2002–2003. But equally relevant to the case supporting *Gore-war* is the almost complete absence of speeches we would expect from a leader more inclined to pursue a different, *Gore-peace* path. Proponents of neoconism share the obligation to identify speeches that are consistent with category A evidence (from Figure 1.1). The problem is that there is no record of a speech by Gore worthy of being classified as category

---

[46] Press 2001.

A evidence – no speeches rejecting the general WMD consensus, or recommending we ignore Iraq, or endorsing a strategy that was different from the UN-based, multilateral approach Bush and Blair adopted, or questioning the need to return inspectors with a strong mandate, or challenging the wisdom of deploying troops to the region to enforce compliance with UN resolutions. Even among those who rejected Cheney's imminent threat argument, the return of inspectors with a strong coercive mandate (backed by a military threat) was still considered by them to be among the most reasonable solutions to the disarmament impasse. Neoconism fails by comparison.

Gore's speeches to the Commonwealth Club and Council on Foreign Relations (2002)

Two speeches in particular are arguably more relevant than most when defending competing counterfactual claims about Gore's approach to Iraq, because they were delivered during the crucial 2002–2003 period – one to the Council on Foreign Relations (CFR) in February 2002, the other to the Commonwealth Club (CC) of San Francisco in September of the same year. Both are useful for gaining insights into Gore's position on Iraq, WMD and the application of coercive military diplomacy. But the CC speech is particularly useful *because it is the one most often cited by neoconists and proponents of Gore-peace when defending their counterfactual claims.* For this reason the CC speech deserves special attention precisely because it is used to support both sides of this debate.

Commonwealth Club (CC), San Francisco, September 2002

The first speech, to the CFR, was delivered six months after the 9/11 attacks and a full year before the Iraq war. The second speech, to the CC, was delivered six months before the March 2003 invasion and around the first anniversary of the 9/11 attacks. Throughout this period, senior administration officials, decision-makers and opinion leaders were establishing their respective positions on how the United States should address the impasse over Iraq, the absence of inspectors since 1998 and the failing containment strategy. One side of the debate included prominent neoconservatives, nationalists and unilateralists who were forcefully pushing for a policy of unilateral pre-emption based on Iraq's material breach of existing UN resolutions, ongoing WMD programs and ties to terrorism. Those supporting this view included Vice President Cheney, Secretary of Defense Donald Rumsfeld and other senior officials in the Pentagon and National Security Council, and leading neoconservative intellectuals such as Richard Pearle, William Kristol and Robert Kagan. The other side in the debate was recommending a multilateral approach backed by congressional authorization, a new UN resolution and another round of rigid inspections backed by a military threat. Those embracing the multilateral strategy included key administration officials (Colin Powell and George Tenet), former senior Republican advisers to George H.W. Bush (James Baker, Brent Scowcroft, Lawrence Eagleburger), almost every Democratic member of Congress (and many Republicans), several former advisers to President Bill Clinton, key allies (Tony Blair, John Howard and Silvio Berlusconi), and, of course, Al Gore and Richard Holbrooke. This is the relevant political context for interpreting the content of Gore's 2002 CC speech – it was delivered *before* Bush, Powell and Blair selected the UN-based strategy to deal with Iraq, before the deployment of troops to the region and before the unanimous passage of UNSCR 1441, which declared Iraq in material breach and demanded full, complete and unfettered compliance with the disarmament demands.

In addition to overlooking the context of Gore's CC speech, scholars on both sides of the Iraq war debate have intentionally selected specific parts of the speech to defend one of two mutually exclusive interpretations of Gore's position. For example, Carl Rove interprets a selection of quotes from the CC speech to illustrate Gore's support for the war, essentially to defend Rove's claim that Democrats shared the same views about Saddam's WMD and therefore would have done the same thing (*Gore-war*).[47] In his review of Rove's book, *Time* magazine's Joe Klein accuses the former chief of staff of completely misinterpreting Gore's anti-war sentiments in the same CC speech:[48]

> Rove offers a damning list of Democratic politicians acting like politicians – making bellicose statements prior to the war, then criticizing Bush for rushing in when no WMD turned up. Touché. But then he goes a step too far. "Perhaps the most pathetic display of hypocrisy came from one of America's most embittered politicians: former Vice President Al Gore," Rove writes. He proceeds to quote a 2002 Gore speech: "We know that [Saddam] has stored away supplies of biological weapons and chemical weapons throughout his country." Rove's busy-beaver oppo researchers should get credit for digging up that one … except that it was delivered in the midst of a *vehement antiwar speech*. Gore, in fact, was making a wise argument: war was not justified even if Saddam had WMD. But taking those sorts of lines out of context is how you hammer your opponents in political campaigns. (Emphasis added)

The fact is that Joe Klein is guilty of the exact same crime – defending the *Gore-peace* counterfactual by focusing on his preferred selection of quotes from the same CC speech and taking them out of context to suggest it was an anti-war speech. This was not an anti-war speech delivered on the eve of battle – it was delivered six months *before* the war essentially to articulate Al Gore's contribution to a crucially important domestic political debate between neoconservative unilateralists and assertive multilateralists (or

[47] Rove 2010.   [48] Klein 2010.

liberal internationalists). The CC speech was Gore's effort to make the strong-est case possible for going back to the UN to get inspectors back into Iraq – the other side believed this would be a huge waste of time. Gore's views were shared by Colin Powell and Tony Blair, and it was their position in the debate that persuaded Bush. Gore's position won, but the many decisions that fol-lowed this key victory (decisions designed to ensure the success of inspec-tions) were largely responsible for the path-dependent momentum that led the United States and UK closer to war.

The problem with selective quotations is that almost every major political speech is designed to include arguments that concede points to both sides. Some parts of Gore's CC speech read like a strong endorsement of a hard-line position to force the Iraq regime to comply with existing UN resolutions, even acknowledging at one point the possibility (and legitimacy) of unilateral action based on pre-existing resolutions. But other parts of the same speech read like a clear indictment of the Bush administration's policy of unilateral pre-emption, in which Gore criticizes the government for refusing to engage allies and undermining Washington's capacity to successfully deal with the larger war on terror.

To illustrate the point about mutually exclusive inferences, consider the fol-lowing two excerpts from Gore's CC speech:

(A) I believe that we are perfectly capable of staying the course in our war against Osama Bin Laden and his terrorist network, while simultan-eously taking those steps necessary to build an international coali-tion to join us in taking on Saddam Hussein in a timely fashion. All Americans should acknowledge that Iraq does indeed pose a serious threat to the stability of the Persian Gulf region, and we should be about the business of organizing an international coalition to eliminate his access to weapons of mass destruction. Iraq's search for weapons of mass destruction has proven impossible to completely deter, and we should assume that it will continue for as long as Saddam is in power. Now, let's be clear, there's no international law that can prevent the United States from taking action to protect our vital interests when it is manifestly clear that there is a choice to be made between law and our survival. Indeed, international law itself recognizes that such choices stay within the purview of all nations. I believe, however, that such a choice is not presented in the case of Iraq. Indeed, should we decide to proceed, our action can be justified within the framework of international law rather than requiring us to go outside the frame-work of international law. In fact, even though a new United Nations resolution might be helpful in the effort to forge an international con-sensus, I think it's abundantly clear that the existing UN resolutions passed 11 years ago are completely sufficient from a legal standpoint so long as it is clear that Saddam Hussein is in breach of the agree-ments made at the conclusion of the Persian Gulf War … we know that he has stored away secret supplies of biological weapons and chemical weapons throughout his country … *The president should be authorized to take action to deal with Saddam Hussein as being in material breach of the terms of the truce and, therefore, a continuing threat to the security of the region. To this should be added that his continued pursuit of weapons of mass destruction is potentially a threat to the vital interests of the United States. But Congress should also urge the president to make every effort to obtain a fresh demand from the Security Council for prompt, unconditional compliance by Iraq within a definite period of time.* If the Council will not provide such language, then other choices remain open. In any event, the president should be urged to take the time to assemble the broadest possible international support for his course of action. Anticipating that the president will probably still move toward unilateral action, the Congress should establish now what the administration's thinking is regarding the aftermath of a US attack for the purpose of regime change. I believe that the congressional resolution should also make explicitly clear that authorities for taking these actions are to be presented as derivatives from existing Security Council resolutions and from international law, not requiring any formal new doctrine of preemption, which remains to be discussed subsequently in view of its great gravity … There is a case to be made that further delay only works to Saddam Hussein's advantage, and the clock should be seen to have been running on the issue of compliance for a decade, therefore not needing to be reset again to the starting point. (Emphasis added)

(B) I am deeply concerned that the course of action that we are presently embarking upon with respect to Iraq has the potential to seriously damage our ability to win the war against terrorism and to weaken our ability to lead the world in this new century … To begin with – to put first things first – I believe we should focus our efforts first and foremost against those who attacked us on September 11th and who have thus far gotten away with it. The vast majority of those who sponsored, planned and implemented the cold-blooded murder of more than 3,000 Americans are still at large, still neither located nor apprehended, much less punished and neutralized. I do not believe that we should allow ourselves to be distracted from this urgent task simply because it is proving to be more difficult and lengthy than was predicted. Great nations persevere and then prevail. They do not jump from one unfinished task to another … And the president is proclaiming a new, uniquely American right to preemptively attack whomsoever he may deem represents a potential future threat … If you're going after Jesse James, you ought to organize the posse first. Especially if you're in the middle of a gunfight with somebody who's out after you … Now one of the central points I want to make here today is that we have an obligation to look at the relationship between our war against terrorism and this proposed war against Iraq. We have a goal of regime change in Iraq, we have had for a number of years. We also have a clear goal of victory in the war against terror. In the case of Iraq, it would be difficult to go it alone, but it's theoretically possible to achieve our goals in Iraq unilaterally. Nevertheless, by contrast, the war against terrorism manifestly requires a multilateral approach. It is impossible to succeed against terrorism unless we have secured the continuing, sustained cooperation of many nations. And here's one of my central points; our ability to secure that kind of multilateral cooperation in the war against terrorism can be severely damaged in the way we go about undertaking unilateral action against Iraq … Now we have seen the assertion of a brand new doctrine called "preemption," based on the idea that in the era of proliferating weapons of mass destruction, and against the background of a sophisticated terrorist threat, the United States cannot wait for proof of a fully established mortal threat, but should rather act at any point to cut that short. The problem with pre-emption is that in the first instance it is not needed in order to give the United States the means to act in our own defense, either against terrorism in general or against Iraq in particular … But to the extent that we have any concern about international support, whether for its political or material value or for its necessity in winning the war against terrorism, hurrying the process could be costly. Even those who now agree that Saddam Hussein must go may divide deeply over the wisdom of presenting the United States as impatient for war.

Selective quoting can produce two almost mutually exclusive positions – one supporting a unilateral, coercive military strategy to deal with a clear WMD threat from Saddam backed by the legitimacy of existing UN resolutions; the other clearly rejecting unilateral pre-emption (and the case for an imminent threat) in favor of focusing on the war on terror and dealing with Iraq through multilateral diplomacy and a new UN inspections regime. But what appears through selective quotations to be two mutually exclusive positions can be easily reconciled if the speech is read in its entirety and understood in the context of the heated political battle playing out at the time. As Gore explains, "I'm speaking today in an effort to recommend a specific course of action for our country, which I sincerely believe would be better for our country than the [unilateral pre-emption] policy that is now being pursued by President Bush." Gore went on to argue that it doesn't really matter whether US officials could make a legal case for unilateralism in light of Saddam's failure to comply with existing resolutions – it is still wise for the United States to work with allies to negotiate a new, coercive resolution to enforce compliance with disarmament demands. Both quotes are entirely consistent with the position Gore was endorsing at the time – Saddam is a serious (but not imminent) threat that should be dealt with in the right way, through coercive diplomacy, rigid inspections backed by a credible threat from allies, authorization from Congress and a new UN resolution.[49] As Gore explains:

[49] And this is how the speech was interpreted by major media outlets – as a warning against unilateral pre-emption and a call to multilateral diplomacy to get inspectors back in (see

Congress should also urge the president to make every effort to obtain a fresh demand from the Security Council for prompt, unconditional compliance by Iraq within a definite period of time. If the Council will not provide such language, then other choices remain open. In any event, the president should be urged to take the time to assemble the broadest possible international support for his course of action ... I believe that we are perfectly capable of staying the course in our war against Osama Bin Laden and his terrorist network, while *simultaneously* taking those steps necessary to build an international coalition to join us in taking on Saddam Hussein in a timely fashion. (Emphasis added)

In sum, contrary to Klein's interpretation, this was not an anti-war speech – it was Gore's best effort to articulate the case against an immediate unilateral, preemptive war in September 2002 without congressional authorization and in the absence of another UN resolution. This was a speech laying out the same recommendations that were being pushed by Tony Blair, Colin Powell, James Baker, Brent Scowcroft and Bush's own father. As Scowcroft explains, the best way to deal with Saddam is "to get the UN to insist on an inspection regime that is no notice, any time, anywhere, and so on. The administration says Saddam would never agree to it. But if he doesn't agree to it that gives you the casus belli that we don't really have right now."[50] As with all of the arguments offered by critics of the Bush administration's early policy on Iraq, Gore's CC speech was not a speech criticizing the government for the decisions taken *after* September 2002 (in line with Gore's and Scowcroft's recommendations) that were ultimately responsible for the path-dependent momentum that led to invasion in March 2003 (*Gore-war*). The evidence supports the view that the same series of rational decisions would have led to identical pressures to make the next decision in the sequence of moves leading to the brink of war (see Chapter 9 for a more detailed discussion of path dependence and war).

Conclusions

One of the reasons the conventional wisdom has become so entrenched, and why the many historical details included in this and subsequent chapters rarely appear in neoconist accounts, is that so few people involved at the time (Democrats or Republicans) are willing to take credit for the decisions that ultimately led to war. Why would they? It's so much more convenient (and politically astute) to blame the entire thing on a few powerful neoconservatives and unilateralists. The truth, however, is considerably more complex and interesting. Contrary to neoconists' assertions, then, the *Gore-war* counterfactual does

---

Mercurio 2002). The speech also reveals that Gore accepted the legal basis for intervening in Iraq based on previous resolutions, but nevertheless warns against the option in favor of multilateral diplomacy backed by the threat of force.

[50] Quoted in Cosgrove-Maher 2002.

not suffer from logical errors or factual omissions, although the conventional wisdom certainly does.

If Gore believed in the utility of coercive diplomacy and threats of military force, the importance of democratization and spread of liberal values to enhance American security, American exceptionalism, 'assertive multilateralism', 'forward engagement' and preventive action to deal with threats before they emerge, etc., then all of this evidence should lead to important counterfactual conclusions about what Gore would have done to handle the Iraq impasse after 9/11. War would certainly not have been an immediate impulse, but it wasn't for Bush or Blair either, despite the efforts by neoconservatives to handle the Iraq problem earlier and alone. An immediate, unilateral pre-emptive strike against Iraq would not have been considered a winning political or military option by Gore, but, in the end, Bush and Blair rejected that option as well. The pressure Bush experienced from Cheney was less relevant to the outcome in this case than the pressure he received from Blair and Powell.

The next chapter examines the preferences of those who would most likely have been advising a Democratic president.

Appendix 2.1

Key speeches, campaign statements and foreign policies on Iraq

Al Gore – 1991 to 2003

Senator Al Gore

1991 Desert Storm

• (April 18, 1991) On the issue of removing Saddam's ruling clique: "Unless we do that, we run the risk that the Kurds will still not go back to their homes, and that they will stay in these camps for a long time ... That is now a risk that we're running unless we find a way to get Saddam Hussein and his ruling clique there out of power."[51]

• (April 18, 1991) "In my opinion, Madam President, and I want to state this clearly, President Bush should not be blamed for Saddam Hussein's survival to this point. There was throughout the war a clear consensus that the United States should not include the conquest of Iraq among its objectives. On the contrary, it was universally accepted that our objective was to push Iraq out of Kuwait, and it was further understood that when this was accomplished, combat should stop. That is also why, after it became apparent that Iraqi forces were being routed, pressure mounted rapidly here and abroad to proclaim a cease-fire. If it was a mistake to believe that Saddam Hussein would be a prompt political casualty of the war, as the debacle it turned out to be for Iraq, that his rule would end shortly

---

[51] Gore 1991b.

after the defeat of his armies, then that was a mistake widely shared throughout our country."[52]

Vice President Al Gore

1998 Desert Fox bombing campaign against Iraq

• (December 16, 1998) *Larry King*: "The President pointed out that everyone agreed with this decision: the Security Council, the Joint Chiefs, yourself. Since he did mention you, was that tough for you to say yes to an OK to bomb people?" *Gore*: "No, it was not, because if you allow someone like Saddam Hussein to get nuclear weapons, ballistic missiles, chemical weapons, biological weapons, how many people is he going to kill with such weapons? He's already demonstrated a willingness to use these weapons; he poison gassed his own people. He used poison gas and other weapons of mass destruction against his neighbors. This man has no compunctions about killing lots and lots of people. So this is a way to save lives and to save the stability and peace of a region of the world that is important to the peace and security of the entire world."[53]

• (December 16, 1998) Describing Saddam as a mass murderer: "You know, back in November (1998), when we were on the brink of military action then, Saddam Hussein suddenly waved the white flag and said, 'I give in, I'll do whatever you want.' And we left our forces in the region. We can't leave them there indefinitely. We left our forces in the region and told him, 'OK, look, we'll give you one more chance. If you show a sign that you're not going to cooperate, then we're going to take military action, and there won't be any intervening diplomacy either' ... Remember, Peter, this is a man who has used poison gas on his own people and on his neighbors repeatedly. He's trying to get ballistic missiles, nuclear weapons, chemical and biological weapons. He could be a mass murderer of the first order of magnitude. We are not going to allow that to happen. We are going to win this confrontation."[54]

2000 election campaign

• (January 5, 2000) "I was one of only a handful of Senators in the Democratic Caucus in the Senate when Saddam Hussein was in Kuwait. And the argument was made that sanctions would suffice to push him out of Kuwait and get rid of that threat that he was posing virulently to all of the Middle East region. And I voted to authorize the use of force. And it felt like a lonely vote at the time. And it was tough. But I was glad that I did it. And I think, in retrospect, it definitely turned out to be the right thing."[55]

• (April 30, 2000) Saddam Hussein "has been in power for much longer than we would like," but "some of what is now under way, with respect to Iraq, in

[52] Gore 1991a.   [53] Gore 1998b.[54]   Gore 1998a.   [55] Gore 2000a.

[the Clinton] administration, is not something we can talk about in the public arena."[56]

• (April 30, 2000) Gore campaigned in 2000 on a platform of building a "New Security Agenda," arguing that "threats that were once local can have consequences that are regional and global." The United States should play an active role in "reinvigorated international and regional institutions" toward "confronting threats before they spiral out of control." Gore also favoured efforts to resist "new isolationism."[57]

• (April 30, 2000) "We need to pursue a policy of *'Forward Engagement'* – *addressing problems early* in their development before they become crises; addressing them as close to the source of the problem as possible; and having the forces and resources to deal with those threats as soon after their emergence as possible" (emphasis added).[58]

• (May 23, 2000) Gore makes reference to a plan to meet in June with Iraqi opposition forces to "see Saddam Hussein gone. I will encourage them to further unite in their efforts against Saddam. We have made it clear that it is our policy to see Saddam Hussein gone … And if entrusted with the presidency, my resolve will never waver."[59]

• (August 1, 2000) Gore announces "A New Agenda for the New Decade," his plan to "build a public consensus supporting US global leadership." He argues "our leaders should articulate a *progressive internationalism* based on the new realities of the Information Age: globalization, democracy, American pre-eminence, and the rise of a new array of threats ranging from regional and ethnic conflicts to the spread of missiles and biological, chemical, and nuclear weapons. This approach recognizes the need to revamp, while continuing to rely on, *multilateral alliances that advance US values and interests.* A strong, technologically superior defense is the foundation for US global leadership … The US must speed up the 'revolution in military affairs' that uses our technological advantage to project force in many different contingencies involving uncertain and rapidly changing security threats – including terrorism and information warfare" (emphasis added).[60]

---

[56] Gore 2000c.   [57] Gore 2000b.   [58] Gore 2000b.

[59] See Gore 2000d. See also Sobieraj 2000.

[60] Gore 2000f. What is so surprising is the absence of any difference between these policy prescriptions and those statements pegged with the 'neoconservative' title when delivered by Rumsfeld, Wolfowitz or Cheney. They were consistent with the proposals expressed in Quadrennial Defense Reviews and other strategic documents produced during the Bush administration. The goals of "promoting the spread of political and economic freedom," and plans regarding "where and how we are willing to use force" are virtually indistinguishable from Bush policies.

- (October 3, 2000) "I want to make it clear: Our military is the strongest, best-trained, best-equipped, best-led fighting force in the world and in the history of the world. Nobody should have any doubt about that, least of all our adversaries or potential adversaries. I will do whatever is necessary in order to make sure our offices stay the strongest in the world. In fact, in my 10-year budget proposal, I have set aside more than twice as much for this purpose as Gov. Bush has in his proposal."[61]

- (October 4, 2000) *Statement from reporter*: "Bush made nation-building a point of difference with you [in the October 3, 2000 debate]." *Gore's response*: "I think that phrase taps into a legitimate concern about how far we should go and how long we should be involved. But it's not a new mission. The Marshall Plan was about nation-building. And the generation that won World War II, having seen the catastrophe of the interwar period in the 20s and 30s, wisely decided that nation-building was a preferable alternative to World War III. And it was a stunning success."[62]

- (October 11, 2000) "Our greatest national strength comes from what we stand for in the world. It is a great tribute to our founders that 224 years later this nation is now looked to by the peoples on every other continent and the peoples from every part of this earth as a kind of model for what their future could be. Even the ones that sometimes shake their fists at us. As soon as they have a change that allows the people to speak freely, they're wanting to develop some kind of blueprint that will help them be like us more: freedom, free markets, political freedom ... The power of example is America's greatest power in the world. And that means, for example, standing up for human rights. It means addressing the problems of injustice and inequity along lines of race and ethnicity here at home because in all these other places around the world where they're having these terrible problems when they feel hope it is often because they see in us a reflection of their potential."[63]

- (October 11, 2000) On the subject of nation building: "Like it or not, the US is now the natural leader of the world. All these other countries are looking to us. Now, just because we cannot be involved everywhere and shouldn't be doesn't mean that we should shy away from going in anywhere. But there is a difference [with Bush] here. *This idea of nation building is kind of a pejorative phrase, but think about the great conflict of the past century, World War II. And acting upon the lesson of WWI, in the aftermath of WWII, we laid down the Marshall Plan*; we got intimately involved in building NATO and other structures there. We still have lots of troops in Europe. And what did we do in the late 40s and 50s and 60s? We were nation building" (emphasis added).[64]

---

[61] Gore 2000g.   [62] Gore 2000h.   [63] Gore 2000i.   [64] Gore 2000i.

• (October 11, 2000) "We have to keep a weather eye toward Saddam Hussein because he's taking advantage of this situation [in Israel] to once again make threats and he needs to understand that he's not only dealing with Israel, he is dealing with us … We have maintained the sanctions. I want to go further. I want to give robust support to the groups that are trying to overthrow Saddam Hussein. Some say they're too weak to do it. But that's what they said about those opposing Milosevic in Serbia."[65]

Former Vice President Al Gore

February 12, 2002

• (Council on Foreign Relations speech) Defending Bush's 'Axis of Evil' description: "I also support the President's stated goals in the next phases of the war against terrorism as he laid them out in the State of the Union. What I want to talk about tonight are the fundamental, strategic questions before us as a nation. What are the next steps in the war against terrorism? And beyond immediate next steps, what is the longer-range plan of action? And finally, what should be done to deal with root causes of this threat? Since the State of the Union, there has been much discussion of whether Iraq, Iran and North Korea truly constitute an 'Axis of Evil.' As far as I'm concerned, there really is something to be said for occasionally putting diplomacy aside and laying one's cards on the table. There is value in calling evil by its name. One should never underestimate the power of bold words coming from a President of the United States. Jimmy Carter's espousal of human rights as an integral part of American foreign policy was in truth the crucial first step towards the democratic transformation of Latin America. And Ronald Reagan's blast against 'the evil empire' was a pivotal moment reminding everyone that there was more at issue in the struggle between east and west than a contest for power." [66]

• (2002 Council on Foreign Relations speech) "Even if we give first priority to the destruction of terrorist networks, and even if we succeed, there are still governments that could bring us great harm. And there is a clear case that one of these governments in particular represents a virulent threat in a class by itself: Iraq. As far as I am concerned, a final reckoning with that government should be on the table. To my way of thinking, the real question is not the principle of the thing, but of making sure that this time we will finish the matter on our terms. But finishing it on our terms means more than a change of regime in Iraq. It means thinking through the consequences of action there on our other vital interests, including the survival in office of Pakistan's leader; avoiding a huge escalation of violence in the Middle East; provision for the security and interests

---

[65] Gore 2000i.   [66] Gore 2002a.

of Saudi Arabia, Turkey and the Gulf States; having a workable plan for preventing the disintegration of Iraq into chaos; and sustaining critically important support within the present coalition."[67]

• (2002 Council on Foreign Relations speech) The Bush administration must be "prepared to go [to] the limit" against Saddam in Iraq. "In 1991, I crossed party lines and supported the use of force against Saddam Hussein, but he was allowed to survive his defeat as the result of a calculation we all had reason to deeply regret for the ensuing decade. And we still do. So this time, if we resort to force, we must absolutely get it right. It must be an action set up carefully and on the basis of the most realistic concepts. Failure cannot be an option, which means that we must be prepared to go [to] the limit. And wishful thinking based on best-case scenarios or excessively literal transfers of recent experience to different conditions would be a recipe for disaster."[68]

• (2002 Council on Foreign Relations speech) "When all is said and done, I hope that when the people of our country next return the White House for a time to the Democratic Party, our leadership then will be big enough to salute the present administration for what it will have done that is wise and good. And to build upon it forthrightly. Towards that end, we must now expand our concept of what is needed to reach the goals upon which we all agree. The United States needs to create a world made more just and more hopeful, not just a world made more profitable for ourselves. I hope that this President's record makes it damn hard for the competition to complain about his record in foreign policy. That may be bad for the loyal opposition. But it's good for the people, who deserve it. And I promise my support for whatever he may do in support of that prayer."[69]

February 13, 2002

• *New York Times* headline on Gore's Council on Foreign Relations speech: "*Gore, Championing Bush, Calls For a 'Final Reckoning' With Iraq.*"[70]

(November 19, 2002) – interview with Charlie Rose
(see detailed discussion in Chapter 2)

• (November 19, 2002) The timing and context of the interview is important. This exchange with PBS's Charlie Rose followed the September Commonwealth speech, the October authorization and Bush's UN speech, and occurred after seven weeks of negotiations to get a unanimous UN vote in favour of UNSCR 1441 to return inspections.[71]

---

[67] Gore 2002a. [68] Gore 2002a. [69] Gore 2002a. [70] Nagourney 2002.
[71] Gore 2002e.

Appendix 2.2

Key speeches, statements and foreign policies on Iraq

Given Gore's prominent role in the Clinton administration's foreign policy, it is not unreasonable to assume that Gore either provided his views on the content or generally agreed with the administration's impressions of the facts and evidence regarding Iraq's WMD stockpiles described in Clinton's 1998 speeches. There is no evidence on record, either before or after Gore left office, to indicate that he questioned any of this evidence. All of his speeches and statements on Iraq since 1998 endorsed and supported these impressions, which were the last official statements from the administration in power prior to the departure of UNSCOM inspectors and leaving the status of Iraq's WMD unanswered for four years.

President Clinton 1998

• (February 17, 1998) Excerpts from Clinton's address to Joint Chiefs of Staff and Pentagon:[72]

> We have to defend our future from these predators of the 21st century. They feed on the free flow of information and technology. They actually take advantage of the freer movement of people, information and ideas.
>
> And they will be all the more lethal if we allow them to build arsenals of nuclear, chemical and biological weapons and the missiles to deliver them. We simply cannot allow that to happen.
>
> There is no more clear example of this threat than Saddam Hussein's Iraq. His regime threatens the safety of his people, the stability of his region and the security of all the rest of us.
>
> … Iraq repeatedly made false declarations about the weapons that it had left in its possession after the Gulf War. When UNSCOM would then uncover evidence that gave lie to those declarations, Iraq would simply amend the reports.
>
> For example, Iraq revised its nuclear declarations four times within just 14 months and it has submitted six different biological warfare declarations, each of which has been rejected by UNSCOM.
>
> In 1995, Hussein Kamal, Saddam's son-in-law, and the chief organizer of Iraq's weapons of mass destruction program, defected to Jordan. He revealed that Iraq was continuing to conceal weapons and missiles and the capacity to build many more.
>
> Then and only then did Iraq admit to developing numbers of weapons in significant quantities and weapon stocks. Previously, it had vehemently denied the very thing it just simply admitted once Saddam Hussein's

---

[72] www.articles.cnn.com/1998–02–17/politics/transcripts_clinton.iraq_1_national-security-american-people-freedom?_s=PM:ALLPOLITICS.

son-in-law defected to Jordan and told the truth. Now listen to this, what did it admit?

It admitted, among other things, an offensive biological warfare capability[,] notably 5,000 gallons of botulinum, which causes botulism; 2,000 gallons of anthrax; 25 biological-filled Scud warheads; and 157 aerial bombs.

... Despite Iraq's deceptions, UNSCOM has nevertheless done a remarkable job. Its inspectors[,] the eyes and ears of the civilized world[,] have uncovered and destroyed more weapons of mass destruction capacity than was destroyed during the Gulf War.

This includes nearly 40,000 chemical weapons, more than 100,000 gallons of chemical weapons agents, 48 operational missiles, 30 warheads specifically fitted for chemical and biological weapons, and a massive biological weapons facility at Al Hakam equipped to produce anthrax and other deadly agents.

Over the past few months, as they have come closer and closer to rooting out Iraq's remaining nuclear capacity, Saddam has undertaken yet another gambit to thwart their ambitions. (Emphasis added – Clinton references nuclear capacity as late as 1998)

By imposing debilitating conditions on the inspectors and declaring key sites which have still not been inspected off limits, including, I might add, one palace in Baghdad more than 2,600 acres large by comparison, when you hear all this business about presidential sites reflect our sovereignty, why do you want to come into a residence, the White House complex is 18 acres. So you'll have some feel for this.

One of these presidential sites is about the size of Washington, DC. That's about[,] how many acres did you tell me it was? 40,000 acres. We're not talking about a few rooms here with delicate personal matters involved.

It is obvious that there is an attempt here, based on the whole history of this operation since 1991, to protect whatever remains of his capacity to produce weapons of mass destruction, the missiles to deliver them, and the feed stocks necessary to produce them.

The UNSCOM inspectors believe that Iraq still has stockpiles of chemical and biological munitions, a small force of Scud-type missiles, and the capacity to restart quickly its production program and build many, many more weapons.

... Iraq must agree[,] and soon, to free, full, unfettered access to these sites anywhere in the country. *There can be no dilution or diminishment of the integrity of the inspection system that UNSCOM has put in place.* (Emphasis added)

Now those terms are nothing more or less than the essence of what he agreed to at the end of the Gulf War. The Security Council, many times since, has reiterated this standard. If he accepts them, force will not be necessary. If he refuses or continues to evade his obligations through more tactics of delay and deception, he and he alone will be to blame for the consequences.

I ask all of you to remember the record here[,] what he promised to do within 15 days of the end of the Gulf War, what he repeatedly refused to do, what we found out in 1995, what the inspectors have done against all odds.

We have no business agreeing to any resolution of this that does not include free, unfettered access to the remaining sites by people who have integrity and proven confidence in the inspection business. That should be our standard. That's what UNSCOM has done, and that's why I have been fighting for it so hard. And that's why the United States should insist upon it.

Now, let's imagine the future. What if he fails to comply, and we fail to act, or we take some ambiguous third route which gives him yet more opportunities to develop this program of weapons of mass destruction and continue to press for the release of the sanctions and continue to ignore the solemn commitments that he made?

Well, he will conclude that the international community has lost its will. He will then conclude that he can go right on and do more to rebuild an arsenal of devastating destruction.

And some day, some way, I guarantee you, he'll use the arsenal. And I think every one of you who [has] really worked on this for any length of time believes that, too.

Now we have spent several weeks building up our forces in the Gulf, and building a coalition of like-minded nations. Our force posture would not be possible without the support of Saudi Arabia, Kuwait, Bahrain, the GCC states and Turkey. Other friends and allies have agreed to provide forces, bases or logistical support, including the United Kingdom, Germany, Spain and Portugal, Denmark and the Netherlands, Hungary and Poland and the Czech Republic, Argentina, Iceland, Australia and New Zealand and our friends and neighbors in Canada.

That list is growing, not because anyone wants military action, but because there are people in this world who believe the United Nations resolutions should mean something, because they understand what UNSCOM has achieved, because they remember the past, and because they can imagine what the future will be depending on what we do now. (Emphasis added)

… Now, let me say to all of you here[,] as all of you know the weightiest decision any president ever has to make is to send our troops into harm's way. And force can never be the first answer. But sometimes, it's the only answer.

… But Saddam Hussein could end this crisis tomorrow simply by letting the weapons inspectors complete their mission. He made a solemn commitment to the international community to do that and to give up his weapons of mass destruction a long time ago now. One way or the other, we are determined to see that he makes good on his own promise.

Saddam Hussein's Iraq reminds us of what we learned in the 20th century and warns us of what we must know about the 21st. In this century, we learned through harsh experience that the only answer to aggression and illegal behavior is firmness, determination, and when necessary action.

In the next century, the community of nations may see more and more the very kind of threat Iraq poses[,] now a rogue state with weapons of mass destruction ready to use them or provide them to terrorists, drug traffickers or organized criminals who travel the world among us unnoticed.

If we fail to respond today, Saddam and all those who would follow in his footsteps will be emboldened tomorrow by the knowledge that they can act with impunity, even in the face of a clear message from the United Nations Security Council and clear evidence of a weapons of mass destruction program.

But if we act as one, we can safeguard our interests and send a clear message to every would-be tyrant and terrorist that the international community does have the wisdom and the will and the way to protect peace and security in a new era. That is the future I ask you all to imagine. That is the future I ask our allies to imagine.

• (March 3, 1999) President Clinton's 1999 Report to Congress after Desert Fox: "On October 31, Iraq announced that it was ceasing all cooperation with UNSCOM. In response to this decision, the Security Council on November 5 unanimously adopted Resolution 1205, which condemned Iraq's decision as a 'flagrant violation' of the Gulf War cease-fire Resolution 687 and other relevant resolutions. Resolution 1205 also demanded that Iraq immediately rescind both its October 31 decision and its decision of August 5. This came after the passage on March 3, 1998, of Resolution 1154, warning Iraq that the 'severest consequences' would result from Iraq's failure to cooperate with the implementation of Resolution 687."[73]

• (March 3, 1999) "Iraq's actions were a material breach of the Gulf War cease-fire resolution (UNSC Resolution 687), the February 23, 1998, Annan-Aziz Memorandum of Understanding, and Iraq's November 14 commitment to the Security Council. The threat to the region posed by Iraq's refusal to cooperate unconditionally with UNSCOM, and the consequent inability of UNSCOM to carry out the responsibilities the Security Council entrusted to it, could not be tolerated. These circumstances led the United States and the United Kingdom to use military force to degrade Iraq's capacity to threaten its neighbors through the development of WMD and long-range delivery systems. During Desert Fox, key WMD sites and the facilities of the organizations that conceal them, as well as important missile repair facilities and surface-to-air missile sites, were attacked. Operation Desert Fox degraded Saddam's ability to threaten his neighbours militarily."[74] The following excerpts from the report go on to list additional WMD evidence:

Chemical Weapons
After Iraq's November 15, 1998, pledge of unconditional cooperation with weapons inspectors, UNSCOM began to test the Iraqi promise. In a November 25 letter, Iraq continued to deny that it ever weaponized VX nerve agent or produced stabilized VX, despite UNSCOM's publicly stated

---

[73] Clinton 1999a.   [74] Clinton 1999a.

confidence in the Edgewood Arsenal Laboratory finding of stabilized VX components in fragments of Iraqi SCUD missile warheads. Iraq alleges that the presence of VX was a deliberate act of tampering with the samples examined in the United States.

… On November 30, the Iraqis failed to meet a deadline to provide various documents Chairman Butler requested pertaining to Iraq's chemical weapons program. Included in this request was the Iraqi Air Force file of documents found previously by UNSCOM inspectors that details chemical weapons expended during the Iran-Iraq war. We understand that UNSCOM believes the file indicates that Iraq's official declarations to UNSCOM have greatly overstated the quantities of chemical weapons expended, which means that at least 6,000 chemical weapons are unaccounted.

In a January 25, 1999, report to the UN Security Council President, UNSCOM identified as a priority chemical weapons disarmament issues: VX, the 155 mm mustard shells; the Iraqi Air Force file of chemical weapons documents; R-400 bombs filled with CBW (field inspections needed); and chemical weapons production equipment (field verification is needed for 18 of 20 shipping containers UNSCOM knows were moved together). On monitoring, the report identified as priorities the ability to verify Iraqi compliance at listed facilities and to detect construction of new dual-use facilities.

Biological Weapons

Iraq has failed to provide a credible explanation for UNSCOM tests that found anthrax in fragments of seven SCUD missile warheads. Iraq has been claiming since 1995 that it put anthrax in only five such warheads, and had previously denied weaponizing anthrax at all. Iraq's explanations to date are far from satisfactory, although it now acknowledges putting both anthrax and botulinum toxin into some number of warheads.

Iraq's biological weapons (BW) program – including SCUD missile BW warheads, R-400 BW bombs, drop-tanks to be filled with BW, spray devices for BW, production of BW agents (anthrax, botulinum toxin, aflatoxin, and wheat cover smut), and BW agent growth media – remains the "black hole" described by Chairman Butler. Iraq has consistently failed to provide a credible account of its efforts to produce and weaponize its BW agents.

During the period November 17 to December 2, 1998, an undeclared Class II Biosafety Cabinet and some filter presses were discovered; these items are subject to declarations by Iraq and biological monitoring.

On November 18 and 20, Chairman Butler again asked Iraq's Deputy Prime Minister for information concerning Iraq's biological weapons programs. Iraq has supplied none of the information requested.

In the January 25, 1999 report to the UN Security Council President, UNSCOM identified as a priority biological weapons disarmament issue Iraq's incomplete declarations on "the whole scope of the BW program." The declarations are important because "Iraq possesses an industrial capability and knowledge base, through which biological warfare agents could be produced quickly and in volume." The report also identified the importance of monitoring dual-use biological items, equipment, facilities, research, and acquisition at 250 listed sites. The effectiveness of monitoring is "proportional to Iraq's cooperation and transparency, to the number of monitored sites, and to the number of inspectors."

Nuclear Weapons

After Iraq unconditionally rescinded its declarations of non-cooperation on November 15, the IAEA began to test the Iraqi pledge of full cooperation. The IAEA Director General Mohammed El-Baradei's December 14 report on Iraqi cooperation stated: "The Iraqi counterpart has provided the necessary level of cooperation to enable the above-enumerated activities [ongoing monitoring] to be completed efficiently and effectively." In its 6-month report to the Security Council on October 7, the IAEA stated that it had a "technically coherent" view of the Iraqi nuclear program. At that time, the IAEA also stated its remaining questions about Iraq's nuclear program can be dealt with within IAEA's ongoing monitoring and verification (OMV) effort. In the IAEA's February 8 report to the UN Security Council it reiterated this position.

Nonetheless, Iraq has not yet supplied information in response to the Security Council's May 14 Presidential Statement. This statement noted that the IAEA continues to have questions and concerns regarding foreign assistance, abandonment of the program, and the extent of Iraqi progress in weapons design. Iraq has also not passed penal legislation prohibiting nuclear-related activities contrary to Resolution 687.

In a February 8, 1999, report to the UN Secretary Council President, IAEA Director General Mohammed El-Baradei summarized previous IAEA assessments of Iraq's compliance with its nuclear disarmament and monitoring obligations. The report restates that "Iraq has not fulfilled its obligation to adopt measures and enact penal laws, to implement and enforce compliance with Iraq's obligations under Resolutions 687 and 707, other relevant Security Council resolutions and the IAEA OMV plan, as required under paragraph 34 of that plan." The IAEA states that the three areas where questions on Iraq's nuclear disarmament remain (lack of technical documentation, lack of information on external assistance to Iraq's clandestine nuclear weapons program, and lack of information on Iraq's abandonment of its nuclear weapons program) would not prevent the full implementation of its OMV plan.

… Conclusion: Iraq remains a serious threat to international peace and security. I remain determined to see Iraq comply fully with all of its obligations under Security Council resolutions. The United States looks forward to the day when Iraq rejoins the family of nations as a responsible and law-abiding member. I appreciate the support of the Congress for our efforts and shall continue to keep the Congress informed about this important issue.

• (October 2, 2002) Addressing the ruling UK Labour Party conference in Blackpool: "I believe we have to stay at this business until we get all those biological and chemical weapons out of there … If the inspections go forward, perhaps we can avoid a conflict … Until they fail, we don't have to cross bridges we would prefer not to … Saddam Hussein, as usual, is bobbing and weaving. We should call his bluff … Of course, we have to stand against weapons of mass destruction – but, if we can, we have to do it in the context of building the international institutions that in the end we will have to depend upon to guarantee the peace and security of the world and the human rights of all people."

Statement by President Bill Clinton following the signing of the Iraq Liberation Act

October 31, 1998

Today I am signing into law H.R. 4655, the "Iraq Liberation Act of 1998." This Act makes clear that it is the sense of the Congress that the United States should support those elements of the Iraqi opposition that advocate a very different future for Iraq than the bitter reality of internal repression and external aggression that the current regime in Baghdad now offers.

Let me be clear on what the US objectives are:

The United States wants Iraq to rejoin the family of nations as a freedom-loving and law-abiding member. This is in our interest and that of our allies within the region.

The United States favors an Iraq that offers its people freedom at home. I categorically reject arguments that this is unattainable due to Iraq's history or its ethnic or sectarian make-up. Iraqis deserve and desire freedom like everyone else.

The United States looks forward to a democratically supported regime that would permit us to enter into a dialogue leading to the reintegration of Iraq into normal international life.

My Administration has pursued, and will continue to pursue, these objectives through active application of all relevant United Nations Security Council resolutions. The evidence is overwhelming that such changes will not happen under the current Iraq leadership.

In the meantime, while the United States continues to look to the Security Council's efforts to keep the current regime's behavior in check, we look forward to new leadership in Iraq that has the support of the Iraqi people. The United States is providing support to opposition groups from all sectors of the Iraqi community that could lead to a popularly supported government.

On October 21, 1998, I signed into law the Omnibus Consolidated and Emergency Supplemental Appropriations Act, 1999, which made $8 million available for assistance to the Iraqi democratic opposition. This assistance is intended to help the democratic opposition unify, work together more effectively, and articulate the aspirations of the Iraqi people for a pluralistic, participatory political system that will include all of Iraq's diverse ethnic and religious groups. As required by the Emergency Supplemental Appropriations Act for FY 1998 (Public Law 105–174), the Department of State submitted a report to the Congress on plans to establish a program to support the democratic opposition. My Administration, as required by that statute, has also begun to implement a program to compile information regarding allegations of genocide, crimes against humanity, and war crimes by Iraq's current leaders as a step towards bringing to justice those directly responsible for such acts.

The Iraq Liberation Act of 1998 provides additional, discretionary authorities under which my Administration can act to further the objectives I outlined above. There are, of course, other important elements of US policy. These include the maintenance of UN Security Council support [for] efforts to eliminate Iraq's prohibited weapons and missile programs and economic sanctions that continue to deny the regime the means to reconstitute those threats to international peace and security. United States support for the Iraqi opposition will be carried out consistent with those policy objectives as well. Similarly, US support must be attuned to what the opposition can effectively make use of as it develops over time. With those observations, I sign H.R. 4655 into law.

3

Democratic national security advisers

Clearly, presidential advisers have a direct impact on the selection and ranking of important foreign policy issues, how these issues are framed, and the information presidents are provided when choosing from among competing options for dealing with crises.[1] The influence of advisers will vary, but, in the interest of comparing the quality of counterfactual claims, it's important to ask who Gore would have selected for his national security team, and what their views, opinion, beliefs and recommendations would likely have been based on relevant statements and speeches on either Iraq or Bush's foreign policy.

The quotations included in Appendices 3.1 and 3.2 clearly convey the views held by Gore's senior advisers and confirm their support for the same liberal internationalist, assertive multilateral policies the former vice president defended throughout his political career. There is no reasonable explanation why, for example, Senators Hillary Clinton and John Kerry would authorize the use of force in October 2002 to buttress the UN-based multilateral approach to inspections but reject the same policy if it was put forward by a Democratic president.

Among the more crucial pieces of evidence supporting *Gore-war* are statements by Richard Holbrooke, Gore's likely choice for secretary of state. These sentiments clearly express a very strong rejection of European-style multilateral consensus (or unanimity) in the UNSC when crafting US national security policy, especially when confronted with an opponent who was failing to comply with demands tied to a coercive military threat. The fact that Holbrooke doesn't believe the US requires UN approval is *not* an insignificant point in relation

---

[1] See McDermott 1992. President Jimmy Carter's interpretation of risks and costs and his choice of the rescue mission option were affected by competing frames (losses vs. gains) presented to him by key advisers. Similarly, George W. Bush assessed risks and costs through two competing frames – one focusing on unilateral pre-emption presented by neocons, the other, recommended by Powell, Blair and many other Democratic and Republican advisers. In the end Bush selected what he perceived at the time to be the less risky option of multilateral disarmament and a return of inspection with another UN resolution and rejected the unilateral pre-emption doctrine being pushed by neocons. The risks and costs of each decision associated with this strategy were perceived at each stage to be lower than alternatives. See also Redd 2002.

to a counterfactual argument about the advice Gore would be getting from his secretary of state on the application of coercive diplomacy. The logical linkage between these quotes and the counterfactual case defended here should be clear, if not self-evident.

The list of entries in Appendices 3.1 and 3.2 also includes quotes from those who would almost certainly have played leading roles on Gore's national security team. If senior Democrats at the time were making consistent arguments about Saddam's WMD and the importance of a credible inspections regime, then this evidence is relevant to challenging the underlying neoconist assumptions that things would have been very different under a Democratic administration. Again, these quotes are *not* included here to defend a simplistic counterfactual claim that they constitute *sufficient* evidence to confirm Gore would have invaded Iraq. The quotations, like those from Gore, must be viewed along with all other evidence compiled in every chapter.

In light of the many statements collected in these Appendices related to this chapter, the question is: which of the two competing counterfactuals is supported by views articulated by this group of advisers? To the extent that these views are indistinguishable from the policies George W. Bush adopted, the evidence would help to disconfirm the claim that neoconservatism was relevant to this story.

According to most assessments of Gore's likely cabinet picks in 2000, the list of individuals who at the time were expected to be approached for key positions on Gore's national security team included, among others: Richard Holbrooke (secretary of state), Leon Fuerth, Sandy Berger, George Mitchell and Wesley Clark.[2] Urbina (2000) describes a 25-person advisory group that included many people the vice president often turned to for advice on foreign policy. In one particularly ironic speculation about Gore's team, Eyal Press (2001) suggested:[3]

> Gore would likely have named his longtime aide Leon Fuerth as national security adviser, former ambassador to the United Nations Richard Holbrooke as secretary of state, and a centrist figure such as former Georgia Senator Sam Nunn as secretary of defense. Other possibilities for the latter post include former CIA Director James Woolsey and Paul Wolfowitz, who is admired by Martin Peretz, one of Gore's closest friends.

The latter two (Woolsey and Wolfowitz) were among the more prominent neoconservatives responsible for pressuring George W. Bush to adopt a pre-emptive unilateral approach to Iraq. In fact, James Woolsey was Gore's pick for Clinton's CIA director. Similar predictions about Gore's foreign policy team were offered by Albert Hunt (2001):[4]

---

[2] Urbina 2000. See also Broder 2000; *The Economist* 2001a.
[3] Press 2001.   [4] Hunt 2001.

Dick Holbrooke at State, Sam Nunn at Defense, Leon Fuerth as national
security adviser and George Mitchell as a roving troubleshooter – would be
equal in experience, expertise and resolve. They also would be bolder.

The overwhelming consensus was that Gore's national security team would
include many of the following advisers – Leon Fuerth (senior Gore adviser and
top choice for national security adviser);[5] Joseph Lieberman (vice presidential
candidate); Madeleine Albright, Richard Holbrooke (the latter a leading candidate for secretary of state); Sandy Berger, Carl Levin, John Kerry, Joe Biden
(all senior Democratic foreign policy advisers); Bill Richardson (UN ambassador under Clinton); Sam Nunn, Wesley Clark (both candidates for secretary
of defense); Richard N. Gardner[6] and Robert E. Hunter (often consulted on US
foreign policy during the 2000 campaign);[7] Anthony Lake; Ashton B. Carter;[8]
William Cohen; and academics Bruce Jentelson,[9] Graham Allison, Joseph Nye
Jr. and Joan Edelman Spero.

Other likely additions to Gore's national security team included: Marc C.
Ginsburg, Meldon Edises Levine, James R. Sasser, Laura D'Andrea Tyson, Carter
Eskew and Tony Coehlo, but the size of the list is less relevant than the fact that
none of these candidates had views on Iraq that were markedly different from
those expressed by advisers whose comments are included in Appendix 3.1.
The consensus on Iraq was pretty clear – they all repeatedly expressed strong

---

[5] Leon S. Fuerth was national security adviser to Vice President Al Gore, co-chair of Gore's
foreign policy advisory committee, and Gore's primary foreign policy adviser and consultant
for more than twenty years, often helping craft Gore's speeches. Fuerth also sat on Clinton's
foreign policy 'Principals Committee' with Madeleine Albright, William S. Cohen and
Sandy Berger. Biographical information obtained from the Council on Foreign Relations:
www.cfr.org/thinktank/experts.html.

[6] CFR – Richard N. Gardner was a foreign policy adviser to then-Senator Al Gore in his first
attempt at the Democratic presidential nomination and was a key member of Clinton's foreign policy advisory team during the 1992 presidential campaign. Biographical information
obtained from the Council on Foreign Relations: www.cfr.org/thinktank/experts.html.

[7] CFR – Robert E. Hunter was a member of Jimmy Carter's National Security Council as director of west European affairs (1977–1979) and then director of Middle East affairs (1979–
1981). From 1993 to 1998, he was ambassador to NATO and a founder of the National
Endowment for Democracy. He was also a senior foreign policy adviser during Bill Clinton's
1992 presidential campaign. Biographical information obtained from the Council on
Foreign Relations: www.cfr.org/thinktank/experts.html.

[8] CFR – Ashton B. Carter is professor of International Affairs at Harvard's Kennedy School
who served in the Clinton administration as assistant secretary of defense for international
security policy. Biographical information obtained from the Council on Foreign Relations:
www.cfr.org/thinktank/experts.html.

[9] CFR – Bruce W. Jentleson was Gore's senior foreign policy adviser for the Gore–Lieberman
2000 campaign and co-chair of Gore's foreign policy team; he also served as foreign policy adviser to Senator Al Gore in 1987–1988. He too was on the Clinton–Gore transition
team in 1992. Biographical information obtained from the Council on Foreign Relations:
www.cfr.org/thinktank/experts.html.

support for the decisions by Bush, Powell and Blair to pursue the UN-based multilateral approach to disarming Iraq. Both Les Aspin and William Perry, each of them former secretaries of defence (whose selections to the post were strongly endorsed by Gore when he was vice president) *supported* the 2003 decision to invade.

The strength of the *Gore-war* (category C) counterfactual is derived from the fact that each of these prospective advisers (and many of those who would have surrounded the team) shared a collection of values, beliefs and perceptions about Iraq that mirrored those held by most Democrats and Republicans at the time. It would not have mattered who was in the National Security Agency, CIA, state department, defence or Joint Chiefs of Staff, because their views on Iraq's WMD were virtually identical – aside from Wolfowitz and Woolsey, they all rejected the approach recommended by unilateralists and neoconservatives in the Bush administration in favor of a strategy outlined by Gore in the 2000 campaign and in his 2002 CFR and CC speeches (reviewed at the end of Chapter 2). In fact, both Leon Fuerth and Richard Holbrooke were likely directly responsible for the content of these two speeches.

Leon Fuerth – leading candidate for national security adviser

Biographies on Gore highlight his close working relationship with Leon Fuerth (Cockburn and St. Clair 2000; Kengor 1997; Turque 2000).[10] Fuerth held the senior adviser position throughout Gore's tenure as vice president, a status confirmed by almost every media report on Gore's senior advisers, speech writers or campaign team during the 2000 presidential race. Sciolinoi (2000) describes the relationship in a way that encapsulates a common theme in media coverage of Gore and the origins of his foreign policy positions:

> It is Leon Sigmund Fuerth, Mr. Gore's longest-serving aide, who has acted as his elder adviser on national security matters for two decades. The two men know each other so well that, like an old married couple, they can communicate through a grimace or a glance.[11]

According to Turque (2000: 239), Leon Fuerth strongly encouraged Senator Gore to support the controversial 1991 Gulf War resolution granting George H.W. Bush the authorization to use "all necessary means" to get Saddam out of Kuwait. At the time, Gore was one of only a few Democrats to support the resolution, along with his 2000 vice presidential running mate, Joe Lieberman. According to Anthony Lake (national security adviser during Clinton's first term and nominated for CIA director in Clinton's second term), Fuerth would

---

[10] Cockburn and St. Clair 2000; Kengor 1997; Turque 2000. See Kengor 1997: 16–18 for Gore's evolving views on Iraq and Saddam Hussein.

[11] Sciolinoi 2000.

typically offer what Lake characterized as the "contrarian point of view" to produce "spasmodic displeasure of the other principles."[12] That view would typically be the most hawkish on the Principals Committee – it was unprecedented to have a vice presidential adviser acquire this kind of access, but it was equally unprecedented to have a vice president with this kind of control over foreign policy.

One of the standard Democratic lines both Fuerth and Gore often used in their speeches on Iraq was to blame Bush senior for not following through with regime change in 1991 and essentially creating the threat Washington was now forced to deal with in 2002–2003. During the 2000 campaign, Fuerth (then national security adviser to Gore) and Robert Zoellick (foreign policy adviser to Texas Governor George W. Bush) addressed the Washington Institute's annual Soref Symposium. Fuerth noted:[13]

> With respect to Saddam Hussein, I think we have come to the same understanding, which is, so long as he is in power he is a menace. He is, however, to be fair, a legacy bequeathed to us by the last Bush administration, which had a sword at his throat at the end of the Gulf War but elected not to use it.

Even before the trauma of 9/11 or the failure of Saddam to demonstrate full and complete compliance with a strongly worded UNSCR 1441 threatening 'serious consequences,' Fuerth maintained:

> Ultimately, Saddam Hussein is going to make a mistake. He is going to make a mistake that plays into our hands. The art of it will be to be poised to respond to that mistake when it occurs, because that mistake will confer upon us the legitimate right to deal with him.

Among Saddam's many 'mistakes' was his inability (or unwillingness) to satisfy the strict demands stipulated in UNSCR 1441 (see Chapter 8). Fuerth's views on Iraq remained consistent throughout the 2002–2003 crisis; it was a position that was fully in sync with Gore's and one he repeatedly articulated in debates with prominent neoconservatives:

> America's choices are not limited to attack or neglect. There can be an interim program for Iraq. We should reheat the demand for international inspectors and return to the Security Council for "smart" sanctions. We should take the position that if Mr. Hussein blocks inspection of facilities suspected of being used for manufacturing weapons of mass destruction, the United States will destroy those sites. Further, we should develop the capabilities of the Iraqi National Congress, help the Kurds while making clear that we are not supporting a Kurdish state, and use covert action across its full potential ... Our hand could be forced by convincing evidence that Saddam Hussein was a

---

[12] Cockburn and St. Clair 2000: 218.   [13] Fuerth and Zoellick 2000.

central actor in the use of anthrax as a weapon against us or by some new
move on his part that threatens his neighbors. Absent such developments,
the United States should focus on destroying what threatens us most: the
ability of terrorist organizations to organize and to attack through a dispersed network; literally, the globalization of terror.[14]

His priority was a return of inspections, because without them there would be
no way to verify whether other elements of the strategy were working, no way
to reinvigorate containment, and no way to confirm the effectiveness of "smart"
sanctions. In several other speeches throughout 2002–2003 (quoted below),
Fuerth makes an even stronger case in favor of inspections and a clear resolution
with very rigid standards for compliance.

In May 2002, five months before Gore delivered his Commonwealth Club
of Californian (CC) speech, Fuerth defended the same policies in a roundtable
discussion with neoconservative James Woolsey at the Democratic Leadership
Council.[15] The exchange provides some very relevant insights into Fuerth's
views, the advice he was giving Gore at the time, and the importance he placed
on constructing and articulating an alternative 'Democratic' position to distinguish it from the doctrine of unilateral pre-emption being touted by certain elements within the Bush administration. The exchange (and another with
neoconservative Richard Perle, cited below) reveal virtually identical themes
to those outlined in Gore's 2002 CFR and CC speeches, further reinforcing
the counterfactual claim that liberal internationalism, assertive multilateralism and forward engagement were among the central principles guiding senior
members of Gore's national security team. Fuerth endorsed the generally
accepted views on Iraq's WMD threat, supported the initiatives to prioritize
the disarmament of Iraq, acknowledged the need to approach Congress, and
embraced the benefits of at least approaching the UN for another resolution
and, hopefully, a much stronger inspections regime. Although both Fuerth and
Holbrooke were skeptical about the chances of actually obtaining another UN
resolution, they believed the effort alone was essential to acquire a measure of
legitimacy (above and beyond pre-existing UN resolutions) to support a decision to invade if necessary. Fuerth, like Gore, believed the UN strategy would
accomplish three things: establish the seriousness and credibility of US intentions to address the disarmament impasse one way or another, demonstrate the
resolve to compel Saddam to accept a new round of rigid inspections, and either
confirm non-compliance (thereby justifying a military option) or achieve full
and complete compliance and disarmament. Either outcome would serve US
interests.

"We need to get rid of Saddam Hussein," Fuerth argued, "at a time that we
have prepared under conditions that we have set in motion."[16] He went on to
recommend a return to the UN and "draconian weapons-inspection rules." This

---

[14] Fuerth 2002a.   [15] Fuerth 2002b.   [16] Quoted in Noonan 2002.

was in direct contrast to the views expressed by Perle, Woolsey and Zoellick – all prominent neoconservatives associated with the Project for a New American Century – who rejected the call for a return to the UN for perpetual negotiations over what they considered another useless resolution to restart yet another round of endless and ineffective inspections. As Noonan (2002) explains in her summary of the exchange:

> One does get a sense of what a Gore administration foreign policy might have been from Mr. Fuerth, who himself might have become an NSC advisor for President Gore. One senses that policy would be marked by talking, hoping, waiting and worrying. There's a lot to worry about so that's not all bad, but it's not all good either. From Mr. Perle, on the other hand, we get a sense of impatience: move, and now!

Fuerth was making these recommendations to be patient a full year *before* the war, and before Bush, Powell and Blair adopted the same approach. In another widely publicized debate with Richard Perle (2002), Fuerth argued:[17]

> Well, my first impulse is to begin by simply saying that a lunge is not the same thing as a policy or a strategy (and) (t)hat is not something that can be done by simply pivoting out of Afghanistan and moving on to the attack in Iraq.

The need to focus on Al-Qaeda and Afghanistan was a point Gore would subsequently highlight in his CC speech. But Fuerth goes on to clarify his point (as did Gore):

> This does not mean that we should simply hope that Saddam Hussein keeps out of trouble. In the meantime, there are plenty of things that we can do to make sure that he is occupied with defending himself from those things that we need [to] set in motion. In time, maybe the Iraqi National Congress [INC] could become an effective force. For anybody who has dealt with it at this time, I don't think that is now ... *We would need to work at it. In time, the United States can, by hammering away at the need for a return to very draconian inspection rules[,] begin to prepare people's thinking for a move that we might ultimately make when the moment is ripe to demand those rules or to demand the right to take action in our own self defense under the existing UN security resolutions.* (Emphasis added)[18]

Perle's reaction provides some of the clearest insights into the nature of the domestic political battle playing out between neoconservatives, on the one hand, and, on the other, Powell, Blair, Gore, Holbrooke, Fuerth, the Democratic leadership and most Republicans:

[17] Fuerth and Perle 2002.   [18] Fuerth and Perle 2002.

It's all very well for Leon to say that the Iraqi National Congress, an umbrella group of opponents to Saddam, is not ready. For eight years nothing was done to make them ready in his administration. And for the first year of the Bush administration nothing has been done to make them ready. And I have the feeling that nothing will be done to make them ready until we face the decision that the removal of Saddam Hussein is imperative. At that point, we will set in motion what it takes to make them ready. [19]

The option of helping the INC may look good on paper, Perle argued, but it was a pipe dream – nothing had been done during the previous administration to push this policy along. Fuerth essentially agreed:

I had the Iraqi National Congress in a meeting with the vice president of the United States for two days. I no sooner got back to London than they sent me a dispatch saying they had split. Now, the INC consists of gentlemen who have taken their lives in their hands by publicly opposing Saddam Hussein, *but it does not consist of people who have yet demonstrated the slightest ability to operate as the sharp spear point of an operation on the ground. Maybe they could be trained. But not in a couple of weeks. And not in a couple of months. You wouldn't want to bet the foreign policy of the United States and its regional policy and standing on the INC and their ability to operate miraculously in concert with American air power.* (Emphasis added)[20]

Like Perle, Fuerth was not persuaded that support for the INC was the best option, which is why he recommended the UN-based multilateral inspections route.[21] But consider Richard Perle's case against inspections, a position shared by almost every neoconservative inside and outside of Washington:

I hope no one would consider it unfair or ad hominem if I make the observation that the inspectors were shown the door during Leon's administration. Indeed, I think one of the reasons for Saddam's growing strength in the region is the fact that he defied the United States and the western coalition and got away with it. *I don't believe inspections will add to our security. I don't believe we will find anything because the database that had once been established has been destroyed. And it is the proverbial needle in a haystack, and Saddam controls the haystack. He controls the rules of engagement. What*

---

[19] Fuerth and Perle 2002.   [20] Fuerth and Perle 2002.

[21] Fuerth offered similar negative assessments of the plan to support the INC in hopes that they would overthrow Saddam. See Fuerth 2002b. Regarding the Democratic Leadership Council, Fuerth said: "Notwithstanding the uniformly negative assessments of the State Department, the Department of Defense, and the CIA, I believed that the opposition might be developed into a useful external voice for liberation – but over a period of time and with some intensive work. The idea that it could organize inside Iraq to create the means to overthrow the regime never seemed credible to me – and does not seem credible now. Saddam runs a ruthlessly effective intelligence system, and there were good reasons to be pessimistic about the INC's chances of creating an internal resistance that would survive."

has been negotiated for a possible resumption of inspections is a much less robust inspection machine than we had before. And Hans Blix is no Richard Butler. So I think the prospects of meeting our security requirements by sending inspectors in are nugatory and it would be a great mistake to insist on the return of the inspectors. Because if Saddam were shrew enough to take us up on it, it might make it more difficult for us to act in other respects. (Emphasis added)[22]

Vice President Dick Cheney, like Perle, Woolsey, Zoellick and those responsible for crafting the infamous 1997 letter on behalf of the Project for a New American Century (Robert Kagan and William Kristol), did not support another round of Iraq debates in Congress or going back to the UN, or a return of inspectors.[23] Fuerth goes on in the exchange to clarify the distinction between the multilateral (coalition building) approach he and many others were recommending and the unilateral alternative Cheney and Perle were trying hard to persuade Bush to adopt:

> There are ways of accepting from other countries what they can do and blending that into what we can do, even if the mix is pretty heavily in our favor. The alternative is to emphasize that they're good for nothing and we don't really give a damn what they offer us, and we'll go it alone, and we're probably better off without them because they're impediments. That's only a slight overstatement of your attitude, and what it guarantees us is that the other governments of the world will say that if that is your attitude, go your way, because we're not following you. And then the question is, do you really think that we can[,] through military power alone[,] prevail over the longer term against [the] rest of the world which is either hostile or indifferent?[24]

Fuerth's preference for the multilateral route was further confirmed in his response to the following question from a reporter: "I'm David Greenway from the Boston Globe. Do you think, either one or both, do you think that we should follow President Bush's suggestion that we get inspectors back into the country? And if you agree, how do we do it?" Fuerth's reply was clear and unequivocal:

> I certainly believe that President Bush was right to demand the return of inspection to Iraq. I also believe that that is a drumbeat that we should pick

---

[22] Fuerth and Perle 2002.

[23] The 1997 PNAC letter is the one neoconists claim represents the smoking gun, proving neoconservative influence on plans to invade Iraq. James Woolsey, CIA director during the Clinton administration, was a co-signatory to the 1997 and 1998 PNAC letter to Clinton pushing regime change in Iraq. It was also co-signed by Elliott Abrams, Richard L. Armitage, John Bolton, Francis Fukuyama, Robert Kagan, William Kristol, Richard Perle, Donald Rumsfeld, Paul Wolfowitz and Robert B. Zoellick. This letter represents the main principles of the neocon strategy, *but* it is a far more forceful set of recommendations that did not support approaching Congress or the UN – in fact, it strongly recommended against this policy because it was not consistent with US interests, and offered no reference to relying on allies.

[24] Fuerth and Perle 2002.

up, because the rest of the world understands without inspections there, Saddam Hussein is free to do God knows what at whatever pace he can muster. I also believe that it's in this area where the United States should insert a twist. That is to make it clear that we are on an extremely short leash, a hair trigger, when it comes to any interference with the operation of these teams. But if they are denied access to a location, a location can cease to exist. At our pleasure. I do not know whether Saddam Hussein will ever consent to the readmission of inspectors with a mandate to operate on very draconian terms. *His refusal to do so should be part of a continuous campaign to be used against him to prepare the world for the action that we should take.* (Emphasis added)[25]

Fuerth was recommending the application of very clear coercive military threats to compel Saddam's compliance, and he argued that the US would have the right to move forward if Saddam refused or failed in this regard. This strategy was endorsed by almost everyone at the time, except for neoconservatives, but it was a rational strategy that produced a serious (almost irresolvable) dilemma – the new UNSC resolution 1441 demanded a draconian inspections regime with a very short leash; in Fuerth's words, a "hair trigger when it comes to any interference with the operation of these teams." But the same resolute and clearly articulated threat strategy, which stood the best chance of succeeding by disarming Saddam peacefully, is also the strategy that moves the country ever closer to war. Paradoxically, it was the absence of WMD that prevented Saddam from demonstrating compliance with the draconian disarmament requirements stipulated in UNSCR 1441. For reasons covered in more detail in Chapter 8, Saddam was either unable or unwilling to satisfy these demands, and members of the US–UK coalition were not prepared to damage their credibility by accepting Saddam's non-compliance. In fact, even if Bush accepted the neocons' preference for immediate, unilateral action based on existing UN resolutions, Fuerth believed Bush would still have received support from most Democrats.

> Should this president decide to act on [Perle's] course, I'm inclined to believe that he would have the support of most democrats. When the last president chose to make a fairly heavy response against Iraq, he was accused in the midst of that action of letting the tail wag the dog to conceal other problems. I wish retroactively that we could have called upon the same spirit of support that I think you can rely upon in the future should circumstances be reversed.[26]

In response to a question about the "relative priority" of Iraq versus going after Al-Qaeda, Fuerth's response was identical to the one Gore outlined in his Commonwealth Club speech – we can do both 'simultaneously.' As Fuerth explains:

---

[25] Fuerth and Perle 2002.   [26] Fuerth and Perle 2002.

I think that is walking and chewing gum at the same time, actually. That's the ability to modulate the intensity of what you are doing and to design a rate of progress for it and to try to carry that out. As opposed to a binary approach in which you conclude that you've got to do one thing immediately regardless of its consequences for the other.[27]

Fuerth goes on in the exchange to explain why focusing exclusively on Al-Qaeda would not likely resolve that problem, either – he (like Gore) *did not* think it was wise to wait for a final resolution to Al-Qaeda before moving on to Iraq, because no one at the time honestly believed the terrorist threat was resolvable in that sense. Again, both he and Gore were convinced both problems could be addressed if handled in the right way, and the right way was through UN inspections and assertive multilateralism:

We should deal with the set of terrorists who are at present the most menacing while getting ready to deal with Saddam Hussein in good time, and under terms that we have prepared. I do believe that in the end it begins to boil down to a list of things that need to be put into position and credible periods of time in which to get them done … [T]his is not an argument for remaining immobilized, it is an argument for arming carefully and preparing carefully, and in the meantime for acting rapidly and decisively to deal with the manifestation of the terrorist threat that has damaged us so badly at this point, and which is still in a position to damage us again.[28]

The policy recommended by Fuerth (and Gore), and adopted by Bush and Blair, unfolded over the next twelve months – a considerably longer period of diplomacy and preparation than Perle and other neocons were recommending at the time. Weisberg's (2002) coverage of the Fuerth–Perle debate nicely highlights what turned out to be the central division between neocons and almost everyone else in the multilateralist camp.[29] Referring to the debate, Weisberg interprets the key distinction this way:

Even many prominent Iraq skeptics such as Leon Fuerth, the man who would have been Al Gore's Condi Rice, sound more like fledgling hawks than outright doves these days. In a recent debate with *echt* hawk Richard Perle, Fuerth argued not that we shouldn't go to war with Iraq at all, but that we shouldn't attack Iraq just yet … But if the justification for war is going to be Iraq's so-called "WMD" capability, it will be politically necessary to begin by demanding a resumption of the UN inspection program that Saddam unilaterally terminated in 1998. The opinion of many Iraq watchers is that Saddam, crazy like a fox, would agree to renewed inspections, both because he doesn't want to die and also because he knows he can hide some of his collection of poisons, as he has in the past. Under tougher rules of engagement, of the kind Robert Wright proposes, playing cat-and-mouse with inspectors could lead to a US attack.

---

[27] Fuerth and Perle 2002.   [28] Fuerth and Perle 2002.   [29] Weisberg 2002.

Fuerth also endorsed the view that President Bush did not need another resolution such as UNSCR 1441 to formally approve the resumption of hostilities –
previous congressional or UN votes were sufficient to establish the 'legal' case.
However, Fuerth, Gore and many others recommended going back to the UN
to establish the 'political' case for war *anyway*. The distinction between the
'legal' and 'political' case nicely captures the central dividing line between neocons and multilateralists – the latter was found to be more appealing to a larger coalition of states and leaders.[30] One final exchange, a point–counterpoint
between Leon Fuerth and James Woolsey, reinforced the unilateralist–multilateralist divide.[31] Fuerth begins the exchange by "stipulating a few points that
are not at issue:"

> Saddam Hussein is a continuing menace to the United States, and a final
> reckoning with him is in order. Replacing him, though necessary, is not suf-
> ficient. The entire political system he created must also be rooted out. Our
> objective should be the restoration of democratic governance in Iraq, and
> we should indeed reject the view that the Iraqi people are capable of living
> under no other rule but despotism. Finally, it is vital to the future security
> and stability of the region that Iraq remain intact.

Ironically, Fuerth was outlining important conditions for regime change that are
usually ascribed to neocons by their critics – a set of ideologically motivated plans
to uproot the entire political system of Iraq with the intention to restore democratic governance to enhance American security. Fuerth goes on to list several
key recommendations that served as the centerpiece of the policy endorsed at
the time by Gore, most other Democrats and non-neocon Republicans:

1. Ease the rhetoric about an early resort to force, but don't take that option off
   the table.
2. Try to corner Saddam on weapons of mass destruction and international
   inspections.
3. Use covert action to undermine Saddam's image of full control within Iraq.
4. Keep looking for any likely Iraqi allies, and give them our help, but without
   betting the farm on them.

Powell managed to obtain support from Saudi Arabia, Jordan and Egypt, and,
several months later, acquired support from France, China and Russia to
endorse UNSCR 1441 declaring Iraq in material breach and threatening military force. The scope of support Washington received from allies in the Middle
East and Europe (including from those who claimed to be against the war) was
quite significant.[32]

5. Be prepared – on any credible provocation – to destroy as much military-
   industrial infrastructure as we can in a powerful, if limited, raid.

[30] Tully 2002.   [31] Fuerth 2002b.   [32] See Harvey 2004.

Keep in mind, this was a recommendation Fuerth was making *before* a new UN resolution (1441) was signed threatening serious consequences. In essence, Gore's closest adviser was recommending the application of military force without UN endorsement, because no one at the time believed the Security Council would endorse a new resolution threatening 'serious consequences.'

6. Push for an international indictment of Saddam Hussein as a war criminal ... A legal indictment would be especially persuasive with our European allies.

Indicting Saddam as a war criminal is perhaps the clearest indication possible that Fuerth fully endorsed the principle of regime change.

7. Figure out now what we would be prepared to do inside Iraq after Saddam goes, because we cannot accept the kind of dithering that the administration is passing off as policy in post-Taliban Afghanistan. A post-Saddam Iraq would require a major commitment from the United States. If the administration isn't prepared for that, it should back off.

These are the same themes running through Al Gore's CC speech – Washington must commit sufficient resources to the operation to ensure a successful post-conflict reconstruction effort once the regime falls. Fuerth concludes his thoughts with a warning to Democrats who might consider rejecting these tactics or the overall strategy:

> Finally, a word for Democrats. *The moment of truth over Iraq – whether it comes sooner or later – requires broad-based support. For whatever reason, that kind of support was not available from the Democratic Party (with some notable exceptions) when the United States was deliberating whether, and in what way, to deal with Saddam's occupation of Kuwait 12 years ago. Thus Democrats now need to be clear about three things: Saddam Hussein cannot coexist with the vital security interests of the United States; his departure cannot be brought about except under conditions of grave crisis; and that event and its accomplishment require true bipartisan leadership.* (Emphasis added)

It is important to note that Fuerth's recommendations were made in May 2002 – a little under a year before the March 2003 invasion. Nowhere in the speech does Fuerth raise concerns about the application of this kind of coercive diplomacy – he believed, as did Gore, that the approach carried risks but was the best alternative available. President Bush and Secretary of State Colin Powell proceeded over the next eight months to carefully mobilize domestic support for authorization, and then another seven weeks to use that authorization to successfully negotiate a unanimous UN resolution few people expected was possible. This was a textbook application of Fuerth's (and Gore's) recommendations for dealing with Iraq, which managed to achieve results not even he expected.

The position Fuerth and Gore developed at the time must be viewed in the context of the evolving political debates in which Washington officials were engaged. Fuerth repeatedly juxtaposed his solution against the pre-emptive unilateral option – it was a rejection of what he and many others viewed as a dangerous policy, and an even more dangerous precedent. These arguments were being made very early in the process, before congressional authorization and well before Powell's seven-week diplomatic coup in which he managed to convince France and Russia to sign onto a very strong UN resolution giving Saddam one last chance to comply. The sequence and content of these contributions to the debate are crucial to establishing the *Gore-war* counterfactual.[33] Fuerth was not arguing in favor of exclusive reliance on principled (European style) multilateral consensus or unanimity – it was an argument for instrumental multilateralism, or "multilateralism American style" (Kagan 2002).[34]

Richard Holbrooke – leading candidate for secretary of state

Richard Holbrooke was considered by most observers in 2000 to be Gore's obvious choice for secretary of state. In his departing speech at the end of his tenure as UN ambassador under Clinton, Holbrooke predicted the Iraq issue will emerge as a *major* problem "we inherited from our predecessors and they now inherit from us."[35] Holbrooke was referring to the need to address the WMD threat and the challenge the next administration would have moving the policy of regime change forward, a policy Holbrooke fully supported:

> [T]his [Bush] administration has (rightly) called for regime change. Unfortunately, few other nations in the world, and especially in the region, will openly subscribe to such a goal. Other nations will probably seek to

[33] Fuerth (2005) takes credit for the concept of "forward engagement": "I began to think about a forward-looking system which I eventually called 'forward engagement' to try to get at what might be in the longer range, and what might be done immediately that could have a positive impact on what was coming." Fuerth says in the interview that he is looking forward to the day Saddam is gone, but argues in favor of using military force responsibly. Since he would no doubt include the 1998 Iraq and 1998 Kosovo bombing campaigns as 'responsible' (he and Gore supported these attacks), it is clear that Fuerth, like Gore, does not define 'responsible' in terms of exclusive commitment to UNSC endorsement or consensus. Clearly, both Fuerth and Gore defended the application of US military force in a coercive way to establish the credibility of a threat and to enforce compliance with US interests or compliance with UN resolutions. Gore introduces "forward engagement" in major speeches throughout the presidential campaign, which became an important component of his liberal internationalist foreign policy platform, along with assertive multilateralism and cooperative security (see Appendix 3.1). Similar linkages can be drawn out between Fuerth's statements about Iraq in the relevant time period and the CFR and CC speeches delivered by Gore in 2002.

[34] Kagan 2002.

[35] As previously noted, Holbrooke believed Iraq would be a major issue.

limit any [new Security Council] resolution to the issue of weapons of mass destruction. This is, however, less of a problem than it initially may appear. If military action against Baghdad begins, it will soon become evident that it is impossible to eliminate weapons of mass destruction without a change in regime ... Whatever happens, once launched, the effort against Saddam Hussein cannot be stopped until its goal is achieved and the overwhelming power of the United States has prevailed. The President will have American support for the difficult decisions he will soon have to make, but it would strengthen his position greatly if he remembered the importance of using every non-military tool at his disposal to build international support – starting with the UN Security Council.[36]

When Bush finally decided to heed the warnings from Powell and Blair (and, now, Holbrooke) to reject unilateral pre-emption by approaching Congress for authorization, and then the UN for another coercive resolution to return inspectors, Holbrooke praised Bush for doing the right thing.[37] To avoid concerns about using selective quotations from an important interview with Charlie Rose, a good part of Holbrooke's recorded statements are included here:

Disorganized and full of disarray the President straightened all that out with a beautifully crafted, beautifully delivered speech a week ago at the UN where he didn't change his positions an inch. Within a week Saddam Hussein blinked, he backed off to the extent of this letter ... that's in a week. The United States is now on the right track, whatever your goal, because Saddam has made this gesture. But I certainly agree with Secretary Powell that it's not enough and there needs to be an embodying Security Council resolution as we move forward. I think Saddam Hussein is far away the most dangerous person in leadership in the world today and removing him, which is not related to September 11th, is a legitimate goal just as removing Milosevic was a legitimate goal and you and I spent a lot more time in Milosevic than Iraq ... The undertaking of a vast military operation on the premise it will be a success is always a gamble. Now let me be clear, I believe we will succeed militarily, I think with Saddam's forces at 1/3 of the size they were 12 years ago, our force is stronger, and with much stronger, better precision guided munitions and missiles and high incidence of defection among the Iraqis, every day now American and British forces are taking down anti aircraft systems in the no fly zone ... I don't want to use a word like cake walk, that's too contemptuous to the men and women who risk their lives, but I think the odds heavily favor us in a military conflict. But we can't do it alone, we need the Turks, we need the British, we need

---

[36] Holbrooke 2002a.

[37] Holbrooke 2002b. In fact, Holbrook admitted shortly after the war started that he believed Congress gave the president all the authority he needed to go ahead with intervention, and, in his view, previous UN resolutions on Iraq would have provided sufficient international legal authority to justify the attacks. See Schiff 2003.

the support of at least one or two Arab states in the region and there is the post period.[38]

... I don't think if it's one resolution or two is the governing issue. What is the governing issue is that the US keeps pushing, we're on the right track now, Iraq is retreating and we shouldn't let up. Today the Egyptians[,] the French and the Russians all said we got what we wanted, we don't need a new resolution. Secretary Powell[,] in your sound bite[,] said[:] wrong[,] we need it more than ever. I agree completely with Colin.

President Bush in his speech last week, and I'm not here to speak for the administration, I'm not part of it, but I read it very carefully, President Bush in his speech ... I'm not criticizing him, I thought it was a good speech and I had called on this program and elsewhere for a policy of going to the UN [–] not, not necessarily to get their approval but to go through the process. So I'm glad they've done that. But what President Bush said was that (Saddam's) violated 16 resolutions, it's not just about weapons of mass destruction, it's about a lot of other things and he listed a lot of other issue[s] he violated, sanctions, the oil embargo, cheating, there's some human rights issues he raised, so there's a lot of different issues in there.

These are only a few of the many excerpts one could select from the interview to clearly establish the point that Bush adopted a strategy Fuerth, Holbrooke and Gore strongly recommended. A more extensive collection of similar statements by leading Democrats is included in Appendices 3.1 and 3.2, all of which reinforce the same central *Gore-war* theme. This evidence should dispel the popular myths that neoconservatives were largely responsible for Iraq policy, or that a few ideologues in the administration were powerful enough to con everyone else into endorsing pre-emptive unilateralism. In fact, most of the case evidence confirms the exact opposite point.

Not only did Holbrooke support the policy adopted by the president, he admitted after the war to having serious reservations about the Bush–Blair decision to seek a second resolution before the invasion. The time and effort invested in trying to negotiate a second resolution, Holbrooke argued,

> was a serious mistake in terms of presenting America's case to the world. Instead of spending the last weeks and months making clear to the world why Saddam was an international outlaw who violated resolutions, we should have just gone ahead with war ... I would support the process that uses maximum force at the outset. I have lived through wars in which a gradual escalation did not work. I have come to the conclusion that once you *are* engaged, you have to *be* engaged ... Our goal should be to strengthen the UN but not put it ahead of [our] own national interests.[39]

Several important points should be obvious from Holbrooke's comments. First, his opposition to a second resolution does not automatically preclude the possibility that Holbrooke might have advised Gore to negotiate a second

[38] Holbrooke 2002b.   [39] Holbrooke quoted in Schiff 2003.

resolution anyway (consistent with the commitment in UNSCR 1441 to "consider" this option), but French officials were unlikely to change their positions regarding a threat of force or timeline for inspections. Consequently, the same dilemmas would have prevailed. In light of what we know about Holbrooke's (and Fuerth's and Lieberman's) views on Iraq and US foreign policy, the far less plausible (*Gore-peace*) counterfactual is that they would have advised Gore to remain committed to multilateral consensus and, in essence, concede US security to the French position. But why would Gore have accepted the French interpretation as the best approach, despite the high political costs of losing credibility after 9/11, instead of following the advice he would almost certainly have received from his top advisers? Now, had France been persuaded by a less threatening and more diplomatically astute Gore-Holbrooke team to sign onto a second resolution with a clear threat of military force, then we still would have ended up with intervention – Saddam could not comply with UNSCR 1441 (see Chapter 8), and further inspections would simply have revealed additional (and increasingly more damaging) evidence of material breach.

What clearly emerges from any balanced assessment of Holbrooke's statements is that he (like Fuerth and Gore) strongly endorsed Bush's strategy not because its success was obvious, but because no one (including neoconservatives and unilateralists) had a better alternative. Once you issue a clear threat tied to "serious consequences," as Holbrooke repeatedly explained when dealing with Milosevic and Hussein in the 1990s, it is very difficult to back down. This would undermine perceptions of Washington's resolve in this and other instances and raise serious concerns with allies in the Middle East who were hoping the United States would deal with the Iraq impasse once and for all (see Chapter 7).

Academic advisers

Graham Allison – nuclear threat

According to Bill Turque's (2000: 56) biography of Gore,[40] the vice president was "inspired" by Graham Allison's work and often consulted him on important foreign policy matters. Allison, assistant secretary of defense under Clinton, had been writing extensively on the threat from WMD and nuclear proliferation, publishing a major book on the subject in 2004.[41] When Allison was dean of the John F. Kennedy School at Harvard, he admitted in interviews that Gore was "very interested in nuclear questions." With Allison as a primary source for policy advice on WMD, Gore would have been less inclined to downplay or ignore the significance of proliferation in the context of Iraq.

[40] Turque 2000.   [41] Allison 2004.

Bruce Jentelson – "tough love multilateralism"

Jentelson's "tough love multilateralism" (TLM) is essentially a minor, almost insignificant variation on the assertive multilateralism theme.[42] The piece, published after the war but most likely written during the 2002–2003 crisis, argues that UN engagement often requires an implicit (or explicit) threat from the United States that Washington will act with others if possible – and alone if necessary – to protect US security and national interests. This approach to strategic coercion is often required to kick-start the multilateral process, and it was certainly a strategy adopted by Bush and Blair in the Iraq case (Harvey 2004). But Jentelson's version of this well established argument has a long tradition in international relations theory and the literature on coercive diplomacy – the policy logically flows from experiences in Bosnia (1995), Iraq (1998) and Kosovo (1998). TLM, however, does not represent the other end of the policy spectrum that would have moved the United States and UK away from the path followed by Bush and Blair in 2002–2003 – it essentially encompasses the exact same approach. There is nothing in Jentelson's version of assertive multilateralism that would have recommended making the same series of multilateral decisions in 2002–2003 except the final decision to invade after the French demanded the removal of the military threat, presumably the cornerstone of TLM. Despite Jentelson's efforts to draw a pretty straightforward distinction between his policy prescriptions and the pre-emptive unilateral alternative endorsed by neoconservatives, he fails to draw out any relevant difference between his advice and the approach that was actually adopted by Bush and Blair. In the end, they followed Jentelson's recommendations.

Policy advisers – Ashton Carter and William Perry

Two other advisers Gore would likely have consulted on Iraq policy, Ashton Carter and former National Security Adviser William Perry, co-authored a book entitled *Preventive Defense*. The purpose of the book was to provide the basic outlines of a "security strategy for the 21st century."[43] Again, the strategy they recommend is virtually indistinguishable from George W. Bush's 2001 United States National Security Strategy. The 2001 USNSS recommends preventing threats before they emerge, but it is a theme that was just as apparent in Clinton's 1999 USNSS. Only those dedicated to parsing specific words and phrases would be able to identify minor policy differences, but the larger themes, objectives and intentions remained consistent across administrations.

---

[42] Jentelson 2003.   [43] Carter and Perry 1999.

Conclusions

Once again, as with Appendix 2.1, all of the quotes included in this chapter's Appendices are consistent with evidence supporting *Gore-war* (category C from Figure 1.1).[44] There is very little one can find in these speeches, editorials or scholarly articles (or any other work produced by these officials) that would produce a profile of an administration committed to pursuing a completely different path than the one Bush and Blair selected. There is no *Gore-peace* (category A) evidence to be found in any of these statements. More importantly, even if the list of potential advisers is expanded to include other Democrats who expressed clearly dissenting opinions on the need to deal with Iraq (Dennis Kucinich, Edward Kennedy) there is no reason to expect their positions would have carried any more weight than the opinions of advisers Gore was clearly planning to hire. It is unlikely anyone on this list (or an expanded list) would have had a stronger influence on Gore's position than Leon Fuerth, Richard Holbrooke or Joe Lieberman. Almost every other senior Democrat at the time was on the same page with respect to the ideal strategy for dealing with Hussein. In fact, there is no evidence that any potential member of Gore's national security team expressed serious reservations about the threat from Saddam, the imperative to get inspectors back into Iraq (after 9/11), the need for congressional authorization to use force, the wisdom of deploying troops to the region to establish credibility, and the need for a strong UN resolution outlining a final reckoning with Saddam if he failed to comply. I have found no statements by any prospective adviser who argued that a second resolution beyond UNSCR 1441 was absolutely required to justify intervention, or who recommended conceding to France's demands to take the timeline and military options off the table in order to extend inspections indefinitely. And none of Gore's actual or prospective advisers are on record questioning the general (as distinct from Cheney's distorted) views on Iraq's WMD and links to terrorism (as distinct from links to Al-Qaeda or 9/11). Everything they wrote prior to the war consistently conveyed support for the UN-based multilateral strategy that Bush, Blair and Powell selected – they too found it appealing because it rejected the more dangerous alternative recommended by neoconservatives in the Bush administration. Without exception, Gore's most senior advisers shared primarily hawkish views on the application of coercive threats and the use of military deployments to reinforce credibility and resolve, no doubt positions that were informed by their experiences during the Bosnia and Kosovo campaigns in the previous decade.

The real challenge when trying to confirm any counterfactual claim, especially one suggesting that Bush and Blair received widespread support for their

---

[44] For a large collection of video recordings of very hawkish speeches on Iraq's threat, WMD, ties to terrorism and the need for military force (including speeches by Bill Clinton, Al Gore, Madeleine Albright, Sandy Berger, John Kerry, and others), please see: www.brianakira. wordpress.com/2008/02/03/clinton-kerry-gore-call-for-war-against-saddams-iraq.

policies from senior Democrats, is that many of these same Democrats are claiming today that all they were trying to do was provide the president with the bargaining leverage he needed to deal with the UN and Saddam. But it is the simple fact that they felt compelled to do so that represents the key counterfactual point supporting the analysis. Once a decision is made to support Bush's and Blair's multilateral strategy, all related decisions to succeed in the implementation of that strategy make sense, which is why they too received widespread support (e.g., congressional authorization; deployment of troops; draconian inspections).

Of course, many of those who supported the president may not have fully appreciated the implications of their actions or the potential ripple effects of issuing coercive threats that Saddam did not believe. And they may regret the fact that they supported a policy that led to war. But they did, and would have done the same thing – for the same reasons – in support of Gore's multilateral strategy. Fuerth, Albright, Berger and Holbrooke endorsed the same approach when they were in power and had no qualms about applying US military force to achieve similar objectives – they certainly made many of the same arguments. There is no compelling reason why they would have formed different impressions of the utility of US military force in 2003, two years after 9/11.

Appendix 3.1

Speeches and policy statements on Iraq

Al Gore's foreign policy advisers

1991 to 2003

Note: among the more relevant quotes appearing below are excerpts from speeches delivered by senior Democratic senators justifying their support for the joint House and Senate resolution that authorized the president to use force to disarm Iraq. Given space constraints, the selected excerpts, while informative with respect to the comparative counterfactual analysis, represent only a small fraction of the entire collection of full speeches delivered from October 8 through October 10. These speeches offer very strong endorsement of the resolution and convey a very clear picture of the widespread consensus on the threat from Saddam and his WMD programs. Readers are therefore encouraged to review the collection of speeches to fully understand the powerful consensus on WMD intelligence.

Joe Lieberman (2000 vice presidential candidate)

• (October 7, 2002) "[W]e have evidence of meetings between Iraqi officials and leaders of al Qaeda, and testimony that Iraqi agents helped train al Qaeda operatives to use chemical and biological weapons. We also know that al Qaeda leaders have been, and are now, harbored in Iraq. Having reached the conclusion

I have about the clear and present danger Saddam represents to the US, I want to give the president a limited but strong mandate to act against Saddam."[45]

Leon Fuerth (senior national security adviser to Gore)

• (2000) "With respect to Saddam, both sides have come to the same understanding: As long as he is in power, he is a menace. To be fair, however, Saddam is a legacy bequeathed to the United States by the administration of former President George Bush, which had a sword at Saddam's throat at the end of the Gulf War but elected not to use it. Once there was peace, and once the United States moved into the post-Cold War period, there were many constraints upon America's freedom of action. One must understand these limitations in terms of the attitudes of the other members of the coalition and the attitudes of countries in the region, like Saudi Arabia, upon whose cooperation Washington depends. These things have tended to place some limits on the extent to which the United States might otherwise exercise power."[46]

• (2000) "The United States looks forward to the time when the people of Iraq are free of Saddam, and Baghdad's relations with Washington begin to improve. The United States has continued to maintain the box in which it flies missions and attacks Iraq when Iraq attacks the United States. Washington struggles with some of its best friends to maintain the sanctions, and President Bill Clinton's administration has also begun to work more closely with the Iraqi opposition. Vice President Al Gore wrote to the opposition recently, saying that he looks forward to meeting with them, and his staff is currently working on such a meeting."[47]

• (2000) "With Saddam, the issue will be settled in time with persistence and determination. The Iraqi leader is well hedged in, for his position and power acts as a protection. It would take an unusually cruel assault on Iraq as a whole to dislodge him by use of pure military force. The United States will have to bide its time and work toward circumstances in which Saddam ultimately conspires to bring about his own downfall. Peace is not safe while he is still in power."[48]

• (January 4, 2002) "America's choices are not limited to attack or neglect. There can be an interim program for Iraq. We should reheat the demand for international inspectors and return to the Security Council for 'smart' sanctions.

---

[45] Lieberman 2002. Congressional Record, V. 148, Pt. 14, October 2, 2002 to October 9, 2002, p. 19213
[46] Fuerth and Zoellick 2000.   [47] Fuerth and Zoellick 2000.
[48] Fuerth and Zoellick 2000. On May 19, 2000, Leon Fuerth, national security adviser to Vice President Al Gore, and Robert Zoellick, a foreign policy adviser to Texas governor George W. Bush, addressed The Washington Institute's annual Soref Symposium.

We should take the position that if Mr. Hussein blocks inspection of facilities suspected of being used for manufacturing weapons of mass destruction, the United States will destroy those sites."[49]

• (March 20, 2003) "The US had the right to resume military operations against Iraq under existing Security Council resolutions because Saddam Hussein was patently in breach of his commitments."[50]

Richard Holbrooke (likely choice for secretary of state)

• (November 1999) "Let's be clear about what the UN isn't. The United Nations was never intended to be – nor will it ever be – some sort of world government. It will never make foreign policy decisions for the United States, nor will it ever lead our troops in combat. It will never replace the institutions or individuals in our country, who[,] in fulfillment of their constitutional obligations to the people[,] make these decisions. The President, the Secretary of State, the Secretary of Defense, as well as the entire national security team, along with both houses of Congress, make our decisions. They, and they alone, not the UN, determine our national policy."[51]

• (January 11, 2001) "Saddam Hussein's activities continue to be unacceptable and, in my view, dangerous to the region and, indeed, to the world, not only because he possesses the potential for weapons of mass destruction but because of the very nature of his regime."[52]

• (January 11, 2001) "(Saddam's) willingness to be cruel internally is not unique in the world, but the combination of that and his willingness to export his problems makes him a clear and present danger at all times."[53]

• (January 11, 2001) The Bush administration "will have to deal with this problem, which we inherited from our predecessors and they now inherit from us."[54]

• (September 17, 2002) "Disorganized and full of disarray, the President straightened all that out with a beautifully crafted, beautifully delivered speech a week ago at the UN where he didn't change his positions an inch. Within a week Saddam Hussein blinked, he backed off to the extent of this letter … that's in a week. The United States is now on the right track, whatever your goal, because Saddam has made this gesture. But I certainly agree with Secretary Powell that it's not enough and there needs to be an embodying Security Council resolution as we move forward. I think Saddam Hussein

[49] Fuerth 2002a.   [50] Fuerth 2003.
[51] Holbrooke 1999.   [52] Richard Holbrooke quoted in Aita 2001.
[53] Aita 2001.   [54] Aita 2001.

is far away the most dangerous person in leadership in the world today and removing him, which is not related to September 11th, is a legitimate goal just as removing Milosevic was a legitimate goal and you and I spent a lot more time in Milosevic than Iraq."[55]

Additional excerpts from Holbrooke interview with Charlie Rose

• (September 17, 2002) "We are going into an intense Security Council phase so let's have your viewers understand the way it goes. It goes recalling 16 security resolutions, then you list them, finding that Iraq has violated all of them. UN Security Council determines that he's in violation, then the UN resolution demands that he lets in the UN inspectors called UNMOVIC, that's Hans Blix. And Blix is now starting his discussion this afternoon and this evening with the Iraqis. And then comes the critical issue, does the resolution contain, at the end of it, a statement that if he's not complying with this resolution and the previous resolutions, the Security Council authorizes whatever means are necessary to enforce. That is the issue that Colin Powell is here in New York working on right now and he's making headway."[56]

"I don't think if it's one resolution or two is the governing issue. What is the governing issue is that the US keeps pushing, we're on the right track now, Iraq is retreating and we shouldn't let up. Today the Egyptians, the French and the Russians all said we got what we wanted, we don't need a new resolution. Secretary Powell, in your sound bite, said, 'wrong, we need it more than ever.' I agree completely with Colin."

"If a total capitulation on inspection, by which I mean air tight, anytime, anywhere, no notice, inspections would be sufficient as the next step[;] we're on a different path and that is something that the administration has intentionally kept ambiguous and I think they're right to be ambiguous for the time being. But bear in mind that three weeks ago the Vice President of the US, Dick Cheney[,] said inspections aren't worth anything and they'll be another fraud, where Secretary Powell continues to stress inspection. I have no problem with this creative ambiguity for right now. Because Colin is doing his job here in New York and Dick Cheney is issuing the stronger message. But sooner or later, sooner or later the administration will have to make clear if they'll accept anything short of regime change."

"President Bush in his speech last week, and I'm not here to speak for the administration, I'm not part of it, but I read it very carefully, President Bush in his speech … I'm not criticizing him, I thought it was a good speech and I had called, I had called on this program and elsewhere for a policy of going to the UN not, not necessarily to get their approval but to go through the process. So I'm glad they've done that. But what President Bush said was that he's violated 16 res[olutions], it's not just about weapons of mass destruction, it's about a lot of other things and he listed a lot of other issues

---

[55] Holbrooke 2002b.   [56] Holbrooke 2002b.

he violated – sanctions, the oil embargo, cheating, there's some human rights issues he raised, so there's a lot of different issues in there."

"I was debating Larry Eagleburger the night of the speech and Larry[,] who had been very critical of the administration, now said he was 90% in agreement with President Bush. I was the democrat defending the President, Larry being critical. So I was wondering to myself as I was listening to this: well, Larry, I'm glad that you changed your position. But why did you change your position when President Bush didn't change his, simply presented it in a very coherent, articulate and well crafted way[?]"

"Larry's position, I was just making the point that the president was picking up support from people like Larry, who now reverses himself without the president changing positions. That's high politics and he deserves praise for that[;] obviously, I'm not here to speak on his behalf but we can all recognize a skilful diplomatic move and Colin Powell has done an excellent job of following up here in New York."

"President Bush straightened out both those problems in the last ten days so now we can clean away the debris of process and focus on the goal, which is regime change on the one hand, or[,] as you attribute to Kissinger, inspection on the other."

"Whatever happened 12 years ago, there's going to be another vote. The Democrats are now trying to figure out – and my understanding is now they're having intense meetings, I've talked to many of them on the phone – they're trying to figure out how they can best support the President and be responsible to their conscience. It's very difficult to have a vote like this, an up and down vote on something like this, in the heat of the final weeks of an election campaign, but it looks like they may have to do this. Many of my friends in the democratic house, caucus and senate would like to push this over until after the election but the White House doesn't want to do that so they're in a dilemma."

"The democrats are not going to repeat mistake[s] of 1991, they're going to vote for it. Hillary on Meet the Press was very clear on this and remember that in 1998[,] President Clinton endorsed a resolution put forth by Senator Daschle and Senator Lott calling for regime change, and Tim Russert put the resolution on the screen and she recognized it immediately and said 'of course I support that, it was my husband's language.'"

"Nothing is certain. The undertaking of a vast military operation on the premise it will be a success is always a gamble. Now let me be clear, I believe we will succeed militarily, I think with Saddam's forces at 1/3 of the size they were 12 years ago, our force is stronger, and with much stronger, better precision guided munitions and missiles and high incident of defection among the Iraqis, every day now American and British forces are taking down anti aircraft systems in the no fly zone … I don't want to use a word like cake walk, that's too contemptuous to the men and women who risk their lives, but I think the odds heavily favour us in a military conflict. But we can't do it alone, we need the Turks, we need the British, we need the support of at least one or two Arab states in the region and there is the post period."

"[The President's] got Saddam backing up diplomatically now, his box is getting smaller[;] it's a tremendous achievement for one week of diplomacy after a summer of disarray, he should be encouraged and[,] frankly[,] he should be supported by all Americans[,] Democrat or Republican, in the phase that is now going on just 15 blocks from where we're sitting now."

Senator Sam Nunn (possible pick for secretary of defense)[57]

• (April 5, 2004) Nunn voted against Operation Desert Storm in 1991. This was an interview long after the war, so there is some question that his views of Iraq would be affected by the absence of WMD and the declining state of Iraq. But, when responding to a question about the authorization to use force, he made these comments:

> I would have been in favor of the Biden-Lugar approach, which they dropped before actually having a vote on it. That approach would have mandated that the President take steps, more steps than he took by far, to get our allies involved.

Like the Levin amendment, the purpose was to get Bush to approach the UN first to gain a strong resolution and then come back to Congress. The fear was that Bush would use the authorization to endorse and justify unilateral preemption in this and other cases. But the resolution was used to get a unanimous resolution endorsing serious consequences. Nunn stated:

> Now, in terms of Iraq, several mistakes. One good thing, I think Bush did what Clinton should have done in 1998; he basically used enough military force to get – or threatened military force to the extent he got [–] the inspectors back in, the UN inspectors.

So Nunn would have supported threat of force and deployment of troops to force compliance, but he too would have been stuck with the prospects of demanding from Saddam something he could not provide. The inspectors could have been given more time but the same conclusions would have created the same impressions of failure. It is hard to see how a defense secretary, after deploying troops to the region, would be able to sustain the view to give inspectors more time when facing Gore, Lieberman, Holbrooke and Fuerth. Even if he succeeded, it would have been impossible to arrive at the clear conclusions he would have been hoping for.

Sam Nunn on "axis of evil"[58]

• (January 31, 2002) *Question from Margaret Warner, PBS*: Senator Nunn, did you agree with what he did ... [?] What did you make of what he did[,] essentially equating nations that sponsor terror and nations that are seeking weapons of mass destruction?

---

[57] Interview with Senator Sam Nunn conducted by Graham Allison. See www.jfklibrary.org/Events-and-Awards/Forums.aspx?p=2&f=2004.

[58] www.pbs.org/newshour/bb/congress/jan-june02/agenda_1-31.html.

Nunn: I think that's exactly the right message. And I agree with Bush's concept on that. I would agree more with the way he approached it today to make it generic and let the slipper fit whatever shoe it really fits rather than singling out countries.

Sam Nunn after authorization of force[59]

• (October 22, 2002) "The headlines each day again remind us of our vulnerability here at home with the sniper attacks and danger abroad in the cases of Iraq and North Korea ... Nuclear, biological, and chemical weapons, materials, and know-how are becoming more widely available to both rogue states and terrorists. Some people have called this the 'democratization' of weapons of mass destruction. Ordinarily, we think of democratization as a good thing. Democratization in the area of nuclear, biological and chemical weapons, however, means giving more people the power to find them, build them, and use them for destruction. Two examples before us today are Iraq and North Korea, each posing unique and dangerous challenges. There are many differences between the two, and the Bush Administration is correct, in my view, to proceed with these differences in mind, but the common denominator is the danger of nuclear development leading to nuclear use. When we combine the growing availability of nuclear, biological and chemical weapons with the growing anger and hatred it would take to use them, we have a much higher probability of catastrophic terrorism – with effects that would make the attacks of September 11th look like a warning shot."

The implicit linkages between Iraq's WMD and terrorism (and 9/11) are apparent from this quote.

Wesley Clark (possible secretary of defense)

• (September 26, 2002) "There's no question that Saddam Hussein is a threat ... Yes, he has chemical and biological weapons. He's had those for a long time. But the United States right now is on a very much different defensive posture than we were before September 11th of 2001."[60]

• (September 26, 2002) "He is, as far as we know, actively pursuing nuclear capabilities, though he doesn't have nuclear warheads yet. If he were to acquire nuclear weapons, I think our friends in the region would face greatly increased risks[,] as would we. Saddam might use these weapons as a deterrent while launching attacks against Israel or his other neighbors."[61]

[59] Nunn 2002.
[60] Wesley Clark Testimony – see House Armed Services Committee Hearing on US Policy Toward Iraq, September 26, 2002.
[61] Wesley Clark Testimony – see House Armed Services Committee Hearing on US Policy Toward Iraq, September 26, 2002.

• (September 26, 2002) "Now, Saddam has been pursuing nuclear weapons and we've been living with this risk for over 20 years. He does not have the weapons now as best we can determine. He might have the weapons in a year or two if the control for the highly-enriched uranium and other fissionable materials broke down. I think his best opportunity would have been to go to his friend Slobodan Milosevic and ask for those materials during the time of the Kosovo campaign, since there was active collusion between the Serbs and the Iraqis, but apparently if he asked for them he didn't get them because the Serbs have turned them over for us."[62]

• (September 26, 2002) "If he can't get the highly-enriched uranium, then it might take him five years or more to go through a centrifuge process or gaseous diffusion process to enrich the uranium, but the situation is not stable. The UN weapons inspectors who, however ineffective they might have been and there's some degree of difference of opinion on that, nevertheless provided assistance in impeding his development programs. They've been absent for four years, and the sanction regime designed to restrict his access to weapons materials and resources has been continuously eroded, and therefore the situation is not stable."[63]

• (September 26, 2002) "The problem of Iraq is not a problem that can be postponed indefinitely, and of course Saddam's current efforts themselves are violations of international law as expressed in the UN resolutions. Our President has emphasized the urgency of eliminating these weapons and weapons programs. I strongly support his efforts to encourage the United Nations to act on this problem and in taking this to the United Nations, the president's clear determination to act if the United States can't – excuse me, if the United Nations can't – provides strong leverage for undergirding ongoing diplomatic efforts."[64]

Appendix 3.2

Statements and speeches by other prospective Gore advisers

Madeline Albright

• (March 16, 1997) "Consider that Iraq admitted producing chemical and biological warfare agents before the Gulf War that were sufficiently lethal to kill every man, woman and child on earth ... Consider that Iraq has yet to provide convincing evidence that it has destroyed all of these weapons ... Consider that Iraq admitted loading many of those agents into missile warheads before

[62] Wesley Clark Testimony – see House Armed Services Committee Hearing on US Policy Toward Iraq, September 26, 2002.
[63] Wesley Clark Testimony – see House Armed Services Committee Hearing on US Policy Toward Iraq, September 26, 2002.
[64] Wesley Clark Testimony – see House Armed Services Committee Hearing on US Policy Toward Iraq, September 26, 2002.

the war ... Consider that Iraq retains more than 7500 nuclear scientists and technicians, as well as technical documents related to the production of nuclear weapons ... Consider that Iraq has been caught trying to smuggle in missile guidance instruments ... And consider that, according to Ambassador Ekeus, UNSCOM has not been able to account for all the missiles Iraq acquired over the years. In fact, Ekeus believes it is highly likely that Iraq retains an operational SCUD missile force, probably with chemical or biological weapons to go with it ... When I was a professor, I taught that you have to consider all possibilities. As Secretary of State, I have to deal in the realm of reality and probability. And the evidence is overwhelming that Saddam Hussein's intentions will never be peaceful."[65]

• (1998) "Iraq is a long way from [the] USA but what happens there matters a great deal here. For the risks that the leaders of a rogue state will use nuclear, chemical or biological weapons against us or our allies is the greatest security threat we face."[66]

• (1998) "Over the past six-and-a-half years, UN inspectors and monitors, backed by sanctions and the threat of force, have kept Iraq in a strategic box, limiting the regime's capabilities but not ending Saddam Hussein's efforts to defy the will of the world. Saddam's goal is to have it both ways – to achieve a lifting of UN sanctions while retaining and enhancing Iraq's weapons of mass destruction programs. We cannot, we must not and we will not let him succeed. In recent months, he has attempted to dictate the terms and conditions of UN inspections and denied access to important suspect sites. These flagrant acts of obstruction pose a profound threat to the international security and peace."[67]

• (1998) "After the Gulf War, Iraq was directed by the Security Council to declare its weapons of mass destruction and delivery systems, destroy them and never build them again. UNSCOM was to verify the declarations and the destruction, inspect to be sure of the truth and monitor to prevent the rebuilding of weapons. To accomplish all that, UN inspectors must have unrestricted access to locations, people, and documents that may be related to weapons of mass destruction programs. But as UNSCOM's chairman, Richard Butler, has made very clear, Iraq's interference is making it impossible for the commission to fulfill its mandate."[68]

• (1998) "As President Clinton affirmed last night, Iraq cannot continue to defy UN Security Council resolutions or to act in contempt of the community of nations. We cannot allow Saddam Hussein once again to brandish weapons of mass destruction and use them to intimidate Iraq's neighbors and threaten the

---

[65] See Albright 1997. The speech was said nine months before Operation Desert Fox.
[66] Albright 1998.   [67] Albright 1998.   [68] Albright 1998.

world. Over the next few days, I will be explaining the American position to leaders in the countries I visit, while *making it clear that in confronting the clear and present danger posed by Iraqi lawlessness, the diplomatic string is running out*" (emphasis added).[69]

• (1998) "There was bipartisan support for a very loud and clear message to be delivered. I think that we have also made quite clear, as ha[ve] Russia and other members of the Security Council[,] that it's necessary to have unfettered and unconditional access to the sites so that we can – we, the international community – can be assured that UNSCOM can carry out its mission."[70]

• (1998) "I think the issue that is important for us is that we are determined, all of us, to have unfettered, unconditional access."[71]

• (1998) "I think that Saddam needs to get a message here, one way or another, about the fact that he cannot defy the will of the international community and threaten all those around him. I believe that the message is beginning to take hold. I think that you have to analyze how they say it and what they say. But there has been remarkable unity in the international community behind the idea that he has to abide by the Security Council resolutions, and that he has to provide unfettered, unconditional access to all the sites."[72]

• (1998) "First of all, we are not seeking a [new] resolution. We have made very clear that we have the authority to use military force, and we are not seeking a resolution."[73]

• (1998) "I think [UNSCOM] Chairman Butler has done a remarkable job all these months, in terms of speaking on behalf of the international community and trying to do his work. I think that he makes his statements very clearly, and I think he was speaking about the dangers of chemical and biological weapons, and making clear how important it is for them to have unfettered and unconditional access. So I think that he has done and is doing a remarkable job. We obviously support his work, and we agree with the fact that, under the present conditions, he cannot fulfill his mandate, and that that is not acceptable."[74]

• (1998) "Well, we have said this, that it is our preference, as it is in all conditions, to do everything multilaterally and to act in concert with others. But I am not going anywhere to seek support; I am going to explain our position. And while we prefer always to go multilaterally and have as much support as possible, we are prepared to go unilaterally."[75]

• (February 1998 press conference on Desert Fox) "But the evidence is strong that Iraq continues to hide prohibited weapons and materials. There remains a

[69] Albright 1998.   [70] Albright 1998.   [71] Albright 1998.
[72] Albright 1998.   [73] Albright 1998.   [74] Albright 1998.   [75] Albright 1998.

critical gap between the number of weapons we know Iraq produced and the amount we can confirm were destroyed. There is only one way to learn the truth: UNSCOM's inspectors must have free, unfettered and unconditional access to people, documents and facilities in Iraq. That is what we're demanding, and that demand has been echoed repeatedly by the UN Security Council and by the world."[76]

• (October 8, 1998) Willingness to defy absence of multilateral consensus over Kosovo: "One of the keys to good diplomacy is knowing when diplomacy has reached its limits, and we are rapidly approaching that point now. I have asked Ambassador Holbrooke to return to Belgrade to convey a very clear and simple message to President Milosevic: he must comply in a manner that is both durable and verifiable, with the longstanding political humanitarian and military demands of the international community, or face the gravest consequences. I believe it is time for the [NATO] alliance to move to the next phase of its decision making: to take the difficult but necessary decision to authorise military force if Milosevic does not comply."[77]

Note: Albright, Holbrooke, Cohen and Clinton were willing to ignore the absence of consensus in favour of military action, based on intelligence that did not clearly establish an imminent threat and that, after the war, was shown to be seriously exaggerated.

• (1999) "Hussein has chosen to spend his money on building weapons of mass destruction and palaces for his cronies … There has never been an embargo against food and medicine. It's just that Hussein has just not chosen to spend his money on that. Instead, he has chosen to spend his money on building weapons of mass destruction, and palaces for his cronies."[78]

Madeleine Albright interview with Charlie Rose

• (2002) "We have a responsibility to act abroad as the only superpower and yet clearly it creates a backlash, so that is a real problem."[79] *Albright went on in the interview to recommend a continuation of the inspections.*

• (2002) "I don't believe anymore that we have a unilateral foreign policy, but I'm concerned about the unidimensional aspect of it, and that we are not concerned visibly about the same kind of problems that the other countries are."[80] *She was referring here to the general impression that the US does not demonstrate a clear*

---

[76] See Appendices 3.1 and 3.2. Secretary of State Madeleine Albright, Secretary of Defense Bill Cohen, and National Security Adviser Sandy Berger elaborated on US goals in Iraq during an appearance on February 18 at Ohio State University. The discussion was broadcast live worldwide by the Cable News Network (CNN) both on television and radio.

[77] See BBCNews.com 1998.   [78] Albright 1999.   [79] Albright 2009.

[80] Albright 2009.

enough willingness to deal with the economic and related problems in developing
countries (poverty, AIDS, infectious diseases, crime, corruption).

• (2002) "I applaud what the administration has done in terms of going to
the UN and ... trying to get support. If that is to continue in the face of[,]
let's say[,] the inspectors saying nothing's there, then the US is going to have
to come forward with the evidence that we think the inspectors are wrong or
that Saddam is lying and that we need other countries' support on the basis of
X fact."[81]

• (2002) "I think there's some sense of pleasure and respect that the President
went to the General Assembly and gave what I thought was a very good speech.
That they have gone to the Security Council ... I think it is worth going through
the process of looking at what the inspectors have to say because it ultimately
gets more international support for the United States if we do follow out that
diplomatic string."

• (2002) "I do believe that he [Saddam Hussein] is capable of reconstructing,
reconstituting and I have no faith in him whatsoever, but I think that in many
ways it is important to keep him in this strategic box and to choose out time in
a way that does not distract from other activities and that does have more international support because we need it."

Note: Of course, once France rejects the use of military force, keeping him in this
strategic box is no longer an option. Containment, disarmament and regime
change all fail if the United States concedes on this point.

• (2002) "I want to make clear, I hold no brief from Saddam Hussein, I think
he is a liar, I think Tariq Aziz is a liar, I think the no-fly zone bombing works to
a great extent and I think we need to know better what an action in Iraq would
bring."

Sandy Berger (Clinton's national security adviser)

• (February 18, 2002) "We want to resolve this peacefully, but there are some
things worth fighting for. And those include fighting aggression, fighting
people who threaten their neighbors, and fighting to make this world a safer
and more secure place for my children and for yours. But it must be a peaceful
solution that establishes the right of the UN inspectors to go in the country
wherever they believe they have to go to get rid of his weapons of mass destruction. Now, the alternatives some have suggested[,] that we should basically
turn away; we should close our eyes to this effort to create a safe haven for
weapons of mass destruction. But imagine the consequences if Saddam fails

---

[81] Albright 2009.

to comply and we fail to act. Saddam will be emboldened, believing the international community has lost its will. *He will rebuild his arsenal of weapons of mass destruction. And some day, some way, I am certain, he will use that arsenal again, as he has ten times since 1983.* So the best result would be to get them back in. If they got back in and they were given access to all parts of the country, we would hasten the day when we were able to say that this country has no more weapons of mass destruction. Now, if he keeps them out or he says there are certain places you can't go – it's a pretty good tip-off that that's where he doesn't want them to go – then we can try to accomplish militarily what we are not able to do on the ground; that is, we can try to reduce his weapons of mass destruction threat significantly through a military action and reduce his capacity to threaten his neighbors. It is, in a sense, trying to do to some degree, but by military means, what the inspectors are being deprived of doing on the ground. So they have been effective. It would be better if they got back. If they can't get back, we will have to try to accomplish the same objective in a different way."[82]

Richard N. Gardner

• (2002) On the unanimous passage of UNSCR 1441: "It's enormously important. It is a historic day. It is a great success for the United States, for the president, for Secretary of State Colin Powell, for our ambassador to the United Nations, John Negroponte, for UN Secretary General Kofi Annan, whose support for a unanimous resolution was continuous and strong, and for head UN inspector Hans Blix, who went before the council and was very explicit that he wanted a strong resolution backed by the threat of force. The tremendous value of this resolution is that it averts any need and temptation for the United States to go to war now on its own without any international legitimacy or support. This way we are going to give inspections a try. It gives a chance to disarm Saddam Hussein peacefully. But if that fails, the US still has the freedom to act. If it does act, after a material breach by Saddam of the inspection regime, it will do so with a great deal more international support than it had before."[83] Further on in the document, Gardner states:

> The French, and indeed, other members of the Security Council[,] have passed this resolution, which says Iraq has been in material breach, and which says that any further refusal to implement this new unanimously passed resolution would be a new material breach, with serious consequences. And if Hans Blix comes back with a persuasive story of non-cooperation, how could the Security Council refuse to act?
>
> If they should decide not to act, and Russia casts a veto, for instance, but everyone else is in favor of action, then the United States will act, this time

---

[82] See Appendices 3.1 and 3.2.   [83] Richard Gardner quoted in Gwertzman 2002.

without a new UN resolution but with a great deal of legitimacy. In my view, we have the authority to act now, under resolutions 678 and 687. But we have rightly decided to stay our hand. We will be in a much stronger position if we act after a clear violation than if the Security Council doesn't act in the face of such evidence. But I think there is a chance it will, and this conveys a strong message to Saddam, who must be very shocked and surprised by the outcome of the vote.

Hans Blix told me that he planned to go to Baghdad with an advance team 10 days after a resolution was passed. Within 30 days, Saddam has to declare everything he has – all his weapons of mass destruction, as well as dual-use facilities where they might be producing chemical or biological agents, allegedly for some non-weapons purpose.

In 45 days, the inspections will begin and 60 days thereafter, which takes us to February 21, there has to be a report back to the Security Council by the inspection leaders on how it is going. They have to report back earlier if they encounter opposition.

Hans Blix very clearly has quoted Defense Secretary Donald Rumsfeld, who said that "the absence of evidence is not the evidence of absence." Just because they haven't found anything doesn't mean it doesn't exist. Blix said the burden of proof is on Saddam to prove he doesn't have anything.

My expectation is that while all this is going on, the United States will continue its military buildup in the countries around Iraq.

The pressure on Saddam by the international community and his neighbors via the threat of force and inspectors will be enormous. The risk of going to war right away without any international sanction, without making one more try to solve the problem peacefully through inspections, would have been much more risky than what we are doing now.

I blame the French and the Russians [for the length of negotiations]. They have been mischievous on Iraq for years. They have important economic interests. The Russians are owed something like $7 billion or $8 billion by Iraq. They and the French have contracts already signed to sell things to Iraq. They also are waiting to go in with their oil companies. They always put their short term interests ahead of their long term interests of disarmament.

Putin and Chirac have a lot of reasons to play ball with us. A veto would have torn the relationship. And maybe behind the scenes we have given them some assurances that some of their economic concerns will be taken care of. I have no way of knowing, but I am guessing. Also, the French and Russians had to demonstrate they would not be pushed around by the United States. I am sure Chirac is taking credit. You will see articles in Le Monde on what a great success this was for France. The United States made it explicit that it would not press the trigger. We're going to wait until the inspectors go, and if there is a breach, it will be for the Security Council to discuss it. But as Colin Powell said rightfully, we will not be handcuffed if the Council fails to act … We gave the French assurances that the United States will go the multilateral way for a while and will not act unilaterally. But we also said that if they fail to accept their responsibility, we will not give up our right to act. It took a while to work that detail out.[84]

- (November 1, 2002) "We have the right to use force because there has clearly been a material breach" of past Council resolutions by Iraq. "No administration is going to allow the French to take away from us a right we clearly have."[85]

Robert E. Hunter

- (2002a) "Today, there is equal confidence of prevailing militarily against Iraq. But this time, the belief is founded: The US defeated Iraq 11 years ago and since then America's military strength has risen dramatically while Iraq's has surely gone down. As in the case of Vietnam in 1964, we have not yet sufficiently sorted out the 'why' of attacking Iraq, at least not enough for the American people – or our friends and allies abroad – to understand. Yes, Saddam Hussein has earned his villain's stripes, and Iraq, the region and the world would be better off without him. But deposing him does not guarantee that Iraq, under new leaders, would not continue to seek nuclear weapons – the threat that really matters. Perhaps those who support invading Iraq are right that deterrence would have no value; perhaps even intrusive inspections, imposed on Iraq with a gun at its head, would fail to cleanse it of mass-destruction weapons. But such courses should be explored while they are options, not historians' conjecture ... The Middle East and Southwest Asia can no longer be treated as separate islands of isolated threats and challenges. Long-term victory is not just about defeating Iraq or wiping up what is left of Al Qaeda. It is also about 'nation-building,' preventing conflict over Kashmir, fulfilling America's ineluctable destiny to lead Israel and the Palestinians to peace, building policies to inhibit the spread of mass-destruction weapons and to deal with them if they do, drawing Iran out of its isolation, and promoting political, economic and social reform in so many societies over so many years. All these matters are in play as we think about war with Iraq."[86]

- (2002b) Positive prediction/assessment of war effort: "Despite UN consideration of a new inspections regime for Iraq, the odds still favor war to disarm the country and change the regime in Baghdad. That will determine the US role in the world more profoundly even than Sept. 11. Sept. 11 spawned a US war on global terrorism and major efforts to tighten homeland security. But it did not fundamentally alter the way the outside world works. By contrast, defeating Iraq – which US forces could do, even if acting alone – would thrust the United States into commitments abroad that must last years if not decades and, in the process, would transform global politics. If he moves to war, President Bush will

---

[84] Gwertzman 2002.   [85] Preston 2002.   [86] Hunter 2002a.

have the support of Congress and most, if not all, of the European allies. Russia and China will try to exact a price, but will go along. And most of the unknowns in the 'fog of war' could also break our way … Victory in Iraq might not lead to the overthrow of Gen. Pervez Musharraf in Pakistan, with its nuclear weapons, or of friendly governments in Jordan or Morocco. Israel might not be drawn into the conflict and inflame the Arab 'street.' And Israel might not suffer terrible casualties during Saddam Hussein's death throes, including from chemical or biological weapons, which surely he will try to use. The United States also would face choices that will shape its role in the region for at least a generation. It could reapply itself to settling the Israeli-Palestinian conflict, embracing the view that it will become easier with Mr. Hussein out of the way. Moreover, after victory, the United States must decide how to use its radically enhanced power and position in the Persian Gulf. Some argue that Washington would have less need to contain Iran and could support its president, Mohammad Khatami, in facing down the clerical relics of the Iranian revolution. Others argue that the United States should either make Iran another Cuba or strike militarily, beginning with Iran's nuclear reactor, while US combat forces remain nearby. With Iraq as the world's second-largest oil repository, occupying it could break OPEC's ability to set global oil prices. But the United States would be expected to create a new energy structure that would provide widespread benefits, both an opportunity and a burden. More broadly, the United States will need to decide whether Iraq is the exception or the rule. Will it have acted out of necessity against the growing threat of nuclear weapons in the hands of a psychopathic killer, or intended to become the arbiter of other nations' behavior, regularly backing its judgments with military power? Will the United States begin acting alone as a rule, or will it use its renewed record of resolve to re-energize alliances and promote international cooperation for democratic reform, peaceful change and the rule of law?"[87]

• (2002c) "While the world waits to see whether Saddam Hussein will comply with UN demands, there is no doubt that President Bush will succeed – either through successful inspections or through war – in guaranteeing that Iraq will be cleansed of weapons of mass destruction and the means of making them. But the post-crisis course of US policy in the Middle East is far from clear, and with it major elements of global politics for years to come. *During the past several months, President Bush has mobilized sufficient opinion – both at home and abroad – to support the use of military power, thereby forestalling the emergence of a major threat to security. Thus, at least in this one instance, the newly proclaimed US doctrine of pre-emption has been validated: Iraq will be disarmed, to almost universal satisfaction.* But Bush's forging of a broad international political

[87] Hunter 2002b.

coalition, implicitly if not formally sanctioning war if need be to disarm Iraq, also bears hard upon the United States. America is now responsible, not just for choosing the means to achieve this goal, but also for dealing decisively with the aftermath. This most important political-military venture since the last gasp of the Cold War has already sealed America's fate as permanent power in the Middle East. It is also confirming the requirements of US leadership on a much broader canvass and far beyond military power as an instrument of influence (emphasis added).[88]

• (2003) "The United Nations has been underscored in US public perceptions as critical to provide legitimacy for US military actions, especially a discretionary war. Even more important, there is increasing concern the United States is eroding some of its most precious assets by asserting it can make a pre-emptive war without a UN resolution."[89]

Joseph Nye

• (October 21, 2002) Additional support for policy adopted and endorsed by Powell, Blair and Bush to approach Congress and UN for UNSCR 1441: "The debate over whether the US should go to war with Iraq is often cast as one between hawks who urge the prompt use of force and doves who oppose it. But a third position – let us call it that of owls – makes more sense. Owls would use force to back up the United National Security Council resolutions violated by Saddam Hussein but take the time necessary to develop a broad, multilateral coalition. Now that the US Congress has authorised the use of force, the crucial choice is between hawks and owls. So owls argue that the best way to reduce the risks is to gain the legitimacy of multilateral approval and assistance, both when going in and after getting there. That is why multilateral action does not simply amount to letting others determine the interests of the US. It is instead the best way to pursue the country's interests."[90]

James P. Rubin (President Clinton's state department spokesman)

• (July 11, 2002) "Ten years after the Gulf War and Saddam is still there and still continues to stockpile weapons of mass destruction. Now there are suggestions he is working with Al-Qaeda, which means the very terrorists who attacked the United States last September may now have access to chemical and biological weapons."[91]

[88] Hunter 2002c.   [89] Hunter 2003.   [90] Nye 2002.   [91] Rubin 2002.

4

Domestic and congressional politics

This chapter explores the powerful political motivations that inspired officials in Washington, regardless of political affiliation, to shape the post-9/11 and Iraq WMD contexts. The objective is to highlight the significant role leaders in the Democratic Party played in constructing public perceptions of the Iraq threat. Further, the significant bipartisan consensus that characterized relevant debates during this time period will reveal the power of prevailing perceptions regarding Saddam, Iraq, WMD, and ultimately the appropriate strategies for tackling such important foreign policy issues.

Among the most relevant political speeches are those delivered by every prominent Democratic senator in October 2002 justifying their strong endorsement of the resolution authorizing the president to use 'all necessary means' to force Saddam's compliance.[1] The same group of senators would have been in power had Gore been elected president in 2000 and would have faced identical domestic pressures after 9/11 to craft similar speeches on Iraq. In fact, as noted earlier, the speeches read much like those delivered by many of the same senators in 1998 when voting 98–0 in support of the Iraq Liberation Act. There was really only one dominant perspective on the Iraq threat at the time, and neoconservatives were *not* relevant to establishing that standard point of view.

The very strong endorsement President Bush and Prime Minister Blair received for their multilateral strategy – from both liberals and conservatives in Congress and the British Parliament, respectively – says a great deal about the kind of support Gore would very likely have received for pursuing the same assertive multilateral strategy to return UN inspectors. Obviously, not all Republicans would have supported Gore's push to authorize force in an effort to bolster negotiating leverage at the UN, but it is very likely there would have been more Republican support for Gore than there was Democratic support for Bush, and the latter was remarkably substantial. Further, there is simply no logical reason why these same Democrats would have taken a different stance had Gore played the same diplomatic cards. Almost everyone at the time understood the imperative of mounting a credible threat to (1) engage UN Security

---

[1] www.georgewbush-whitehouse.archives.gov/news/releases/2002/10/20021002–2.html.

Council members to seriously consider a new, unanimous resolution, and (2) force Saddam to re-admit inspectors with unfettered access to suspected WMD sites. Many of the same Democrats supported the identical coercive strategy against Slobodan Milosevic in the 1995 (Bosnia) and 1998 (Kosovo) campaigns. The rest of the chapter examines more closely the different facets of support for Bush and Blair's strategy. As will be shown, both Democrats and Republicans were consistent – in statements, speeches, and actions – in reinforcing the prevailing perceptions regarding this and other policy options.

Democratic support for authorization

Several important points emerge from the entire record of statements on Iraq (see Appendix 3.1). First, there was widespread bipartisan support for the view that Saddam's WMD posed a serious threat, and that he had developed, deployed, used and was hiding proscribed weapons from inspectors that constituted a threat to US interests; some questioned the extent to which the WMD capabilities posed an imminent risk, but all agreed there was a threat. This is the fairest interpretation of the record.

Second, there was unanimous consensus on the need to get inspectors back into Iraq, approach the UN for another strong resolution, and convey a commitment to follow through if Saddam did not comply. The push against the neocons' preference for unilateralism was not simply Powell and Blair's battle – the rejection of unilateralism was apparent in the Senate and House in a joint resolution passed on July 18, 2002, which made it clear that there was no agreement that Congress should be bypassed as it was when Clinton authorized air strikes in 1998 during Operation Desert Fox. Congress pressured the White House to have a full debate and vote, because many Democrats and Republicans were concerned about the signals coming from Cheney and others threatening to bypass congressional and UN authorization.

> *Mr. SPECTER*: Mr. President, I have sought recognition, as noted, to discuss the pending resolution. At the outset, I commend the President for coming to Congress. Originally the position had been articulated by the White House that congressional authority was not necessary. The President, as Commander in Chief, has the authority under the Constitution to act in cases of emergency. But if there is time for discussion, deliberation, and debate, then in my view it is a matter for the Congress. Senator Harkin and I introduced a resolution on July 18 of this year calling for the President to come to Congress before using military force.[2]

An identical resolution was introduced in the House calling on Congress to "consider and vote on a resolution authorizing the use of force by the United

---

[2] Specter 2002.

States Armed Forces against Iraq before such force is deployed against Iraq." The resolution was passed on July 18, 2002 (S.J. RES. 41), very early in the process, to ensure the president rejected the call by hard-line neoconservatives to bypass Congress and rely on previous congressional and UN resolutions.

Kerry's October 2002 authorization speech exemplifies the coercive diplomatic logic that underpinned the Democrats' support:[3]

> When I vote to give the President of the United States the authority to use force, if necessary, to disarm Saddam Hussein, it is because I believe that a deadly arsenal of weapons of mass destruction in his hands is a threat, and a grave threat, to our security and that of our allies in the Persian Gulf region. I will vote yes.
>
> As the President made clear earlier this week, "Approving this resolution does not mean that military action is imminent or unavoidable." It means "America speaks with one voice."
>
> Let me be clear, the vote I will give to the President is for one reason and one reason only: *To disarm Iraq of weapons of mass destruction, if we cannot accomplish that objective through new, tough weapons inspections in joint concert with our allies.* (Emphasis added)
>
> In giving the President this authority, I expect him to fulfill the commitments he has made to the American people in recent days – *to work with the United Nations Security Council to adopt a new resolution setting out tough and immediate inspection requirements, and to act with our allies at our side if we have to disarm Saddam Hussein by force.* If he fails to do so, I will be among the first to speak out. (Emphasis added)
>
> In voting to grant the President the authority, I am not giving him carte blanche to run roughshod over every country that poses or may pose some kind of potential threat to the United States. Every nation has the right to act preemptively, if it faces an imminent and grave threat, for its self-defense under the standards of law. The threat we face today with Iraq does not meet that test yet. I emphasize "yet." Yes, it is grave because of the deadliness of Saddam Hussein's arsenal and the very high probability that he might use these weapons one day if not disarmed. But it is not imminent, and no one in the CIA, no intelligence briefing we have had suggests it is imminent. None of our intelligence reports suggest that he is about to launch an attack.

Kerry, like many others who voted for authorization, was trying to establish a strong argument against the unilateralist-neocon alternative to bypass the UN in favor of relying on existing resolutions. Authorization, in other words, was viewed as the best way to *control* Cheney and the neocons, and to challenge the case for an imminent threat that might provide unilateralists with their *casus belli.* The relevant point to Kerry's argument is that you don't need an imminent

---

[3] www.frwebgate.access.gpo.gov/cgi-bin/getpage.cgi?dbname=2002_record&page=
S10233&position=all.

threat to endorse the multilateral strategy Kerry (and Powell, Blair and Gore) were recommending. Kerry's speech goes on to express the need to *limit* the president's authority to invade Iraq alone, again, and to control unilateral pre-emption while dealing with Iraq through the UN.

> The argument for going to war against Iraq is rooted in enforcement of the international community's demand that he disarm. It is not rooted in the doctrine of preemption. Nor is the grant of authority in this resolution an acknowledgment that Congress accepts or agrees with the President's new strategic doctrine of preemption. Just the opposite. This resolution clearly limits the authority given to the President to use force in Iraq, and Iraq only, and for the specific purpose of defending the United States against the threat posed by Iraq and enforcing relevant Security Council resolutions.

These same arguments were made by Al Gore in two of his major speeches in 2002 (see Chapter 2). The path selected by the president, in other words, *was* the approach Kerry (and Gore) recommended. Democrats saw authorization as a vote in favor of multilateral inspections and UN diplomacy. But Kerry also understood that the only way to succeed multilaterally was to demonstrate credibility and resolve to act alone if necessary.

> The administration must continue its efforts to build support at the United Nations for a new, unfettered, unconditional weapons inspection regime. If we can eliminate the threat posed by Iraq's weapons of mass destruction through inspections, whenever, wherever, and however we want them, including in palaces – and I am highly skeptical, given the full record, given their past practices, that we can necessarily achieve that – then we have an obligation to try that as the first course of action before we expend American lives in any further effort.

When asked in May 2003 whether this was the right decision, Kerry responded:

> I would have preferred if we had given diplomacy a greater opportunity, but I think it was the right decision to disarm Saddam Hussein, and when the president made the decision, I supported him, and I support the fact that we did disarm him.[4]

The congressional authorization produced strong support for both the President's use of force, and the dozens of letters by the Democratic leadership in the Senate and House reaffirming their commitment to respond to Iraq's WMD threat confirm this. These leaders were not forced by the president to arrive at these conclusions – their conclusions were instrumental in forming the policy

---

[4] Democratic Candidates Debate in Columbia SC May 3, 2003: – www.washingtonpost.com/ ac2/wp-dyn?pagename=article&node=&contentId=A16686–2003May5&notFound=true.

recommendations they persuaded the president to adopt, much to the dismay of neoconservatives. As Kagan (2006) explains:[5]

> Twenty-nine Democratic senators voted in the fall of 2002 to author-ize the invasion of Iraq. There isn't enough room on this page to list the Democratic foreign policy experts and former officials, including those from the top ranks of the Clinton administration, who supported the war publicly and privately – some of whom even signed letters calling for the removal of Saddam Hussein. Nor is there any need to list the many liberal, and conservative, columnists on this and other editorial pages around the country who supported the war, or the many prominent journalists who provided the reporting that helped convince so many that the war was necessary.

The widespread bipartisan consensus on how to deal with the Iraq problem was considerably more obvious than is typically revealed in standard neoconist accounts. Unfortunately, everyone involved in the crisis from 2002–2003 now has an interest in distancing themselves from this history and their role in deci-sions that led to war.

Moreover, the bipartisan consensus was not new to the 2003 debates – Clinton's secretary of defense, UN ambassador, national security adviser, secre-tary of state, press secretary and President Clinton himself made the exact same claims about Saddam Hussein (*before* inspectors left) and after seven years of inspections from 1991 to 1998.

Sandy Berger – Clinton's national security adviser (1998)

As Sandy Berger stated in 1998:

> If, at some point, Saddam Hussein were to decide to allow UNSCOM back in and to cooperate with it fully, that would be a welcome development. I think it is a highly unlikely development. But the fact of the matter is, UNSCOM has been ineffective for some time … We've learned from previous episodes that the longer the time between CNN reporting that we're thinking about acting and actually acting, the more time Saddam Hussein has to disperse his forces, *the more time he has to move things that we would like not to be moved. And, therefore, the element of surprise here, of tactical surprise, was extremely important* … what the United States says matters in the world. And the credibility of our word, and the fact that we will carry out what we say we will do, is important. (Emphasis added)[6]

Every senior member of the Clinton administration, including Al Gore, con-cluded that Saddam was defying UNSCOM and preventing inspectors from

---

[5] Kagan 2006.   [6] Berger 1998.

doing their job. But the depth of this consensus has never been fully engaged in the neoconist literature.

Republican support for assertive multilateralism

Democrats in Congress were not the only ones who rejected the unilateral pre-emption option in favor of the multilateral approach endorsed by Bush and Blair. Senior Republicans – including key members of George H. W. Bush's national security team, James Baker and Brent Scowcroft – were very vocal in the press about the strategy they thought Bush and Blair should adopt in the crucial period between 2002 and 2003. Their strong preference for the multilateral approach to the problem was based on the same basic principles guiding Al Gore – Iraq is an important, but not imminent threat, and the distorted intelligence pushed by Cheney and prominent neoconservatives was not credible enough to justify unilateralism.[7] These positions were articulated months before Bush decided to go back to Congress for authorization and back to the UN for another resolution – therefore, their contributions should be understood in this context.

Baker and Scowcroft were not issuing anti-war tirades – they were offering strong recommendations for an alternative path they believed the Bush administration should take. Their key piece of advice was to reject the neocons' preference for pre-emptive unilateralism that would marginalize key allies and undermine Washington's ability to fight the larger war on terror.

James Baker – former secretary of state (George H. W. Bush administration)

As Baker explains:

> While there may be little evidence that Iraq has ties to Al Qaeda or to the attacks of Sept. 11, there is no question that its present government, under Saddam Hussein, is an outlaw regime, is in violation of United Nations Security Council resolutions, is embarked upon a program of developing weapons of mass destruction and is a threat to peace and stability, both in the Middle East and, because of the risk of proliferation of these weapons, in other parts of the globe.[8]

As with Gore's recommendations, Baker's view does not require an imminent threat from Saddam, and prioritizes Afghanistan and the war against Al-Qaeda.

---

[7] The obvious division between senior Republicans inside and outside of Congress, on the one hand, and leading neoconservatives and unilateralists on the other, was well known and understood by the media at the time. See Purdum and Tyler 2002.

[8] Baker 2002.

Based on this interpretation of the problem(s), Baker proceeds to recommend essentially the same strategy endorsed by Al Gore:

> Peace-loving nations have a moral responsibility to fight against the development and proliferation of weapons of mass destruction by rogues like Saddam Hussein. We owe it to our children and grandchildren to do so, and leading that fight is, and must continue to be, an important foreign policy priority for America. And thus regime change in Iraq is the policy of the current administration, just as it was the policy of its predecessor. That being the case, *the issue for policymakers to resolve is not whether to use military force to achieve this, but how to go about it.* (Emphasis added)[9]

Baker also rejects the notion that previous strategies (containment, sanctions, covert action, support for the Iraqi National Congress, no-fly zones, etc.) have successfully addressed the problem or hold any promise in the future:

> Covert action has been tried before and failed every time. Iraqi opposition groups are not strong enough to get the job done. It will not happen through internal revolt, either of the army or the civilian population. We would have to be extremely lucky to take out the top leadership through insertion into Iraq of a small rapid-strike force. And this last approach carries significant political risks for the administration, as President Jimmy Carter found out in April 1980 ... The only realistic way to effect regime change in Iraq is through the application of military force, including sufficient ground troops to occupy the country (including Baghdad), depose the current leadership and install a successor government. Anyone who thinks we can effect regime change in Iraq with anything less than this is simply not realistic.

Baker was acknowledging the need to sustain a policy of regime change through military force – there was no alternative. But the most important question for Baker was how to achieve this outcome with maximum benefits and with fewer risks of losing international support and legitimacy – both essential to American security interests and to fighting the larger war against terrorism. As he goes on to explain:

> Unless we do it in the right way, there will be costs to other American foreign policy interests, including our relationships with practically all other Arab countries (and even many of our customary allies in Europe and elsewhere) and perhaps even to our top foreign policy priority, the war on terrorism.[10]

The interests at stake here, Baker argued, go well beyond Iraq, which is the same argument put forward by almost everyone: multilateralism and UN endorsement of a new, stronger resolution was essential to American security:

> So how should we proceed to effect regime change in Iraq? *Although the United States could certainly succeed, we should try our best not to have to go*

[9] Baker 2002.   [10] Baker 2002.

it alone, and the president should reject the advice of those who counsel doing
so. The costs in all areas will be much greater, as will the political risks, both
domestic and international, if we end up going it alone or with only one
or two other countries. The president should do his best to stop his advisers and their surrogates from playing out their differences publicly and try
to get everybody on the same page. *The United States should advocate the*
adoption by the United Nations Security Council of a simple and straightfor-
ward resolution requiring that Iraq submit to intrusive inspections anytime,
anywhere, with no exceptions, and authorizing all necessary means to enforce
it. Although it is technically true that the United Nations already has suffi-
cient legal authority to deal with Iraq, the failure to act when Saddam Hussein
ejected the inspectors has weakened that authority. Seeking new authorization
now is necessary, politically and practically, and will help build international
support. (Emphasis added)

Some will argue [here Baker is referring to the arguments by Cheney,
Rumsfeld, Wolfowitz, Pearle, Feith, Kagan, Kristol, Woolsey and other
neocons], as was done in 1990, *that going for United Nations authority and*
not getting it will weaken our case. I disagree. By proposing to proceed in
such a way, we will be doing the right thing, both politically and substan-
tively. We will occupy the moral high ground and put the burden of supporting an outlaw regime and proliferation of weapons of mass destruction
on any countries that vote no. History will be an unkind judge for those
who prefer to do business rather than to do the right thing. And even if
the administration fails in the Security Council, it is still free – citing Iraq's
flouting of the international community's resolutions and perhaps Article
51 of the United Nations Charter, which guarantees a nation's right to self-
defense – to weigh the costs versus the benefit of going forward alone.
(Emphasis added)

Baker is directly challenging the view being defended by those in Bush administration pushing the unilateral route. His position was clear: even the *attempt*
by Washington to approach the UN for a new resolution would be a sufficient
expression of the administration's commitment to the important principles of
multilateralism, allowing them to then move forward based on congressional
endorsement and existing UN resolutions.

Others will argue that this approach would give Saddam Hussein a way out
because he might agree and then begin the "cheat-and-retreat" tactics he
used during the first inspection regime. And so we must not be deterred.
The first time he resorts to these tactics, we should apply whatever means are
necessary to change the regime. And the international community must know
during the Security Council debate that this will be our policy. (Emphasis
added)

There are no differences at all between the approach Baker was recommending
here and the one Bush and Blair adopted. The only significant difference was

the failure of the administration to heed Baker's warnings regarding post-war reconstruction.[11]

Brent Scowcroft: former national security adviser for President George H. W. Bush

Brent Scowcroft, much like James Baker and Al Gore, dismissed the imminent threat claims and recommended the same multilateral, UN approach to the crisis backed by a coercive military threat:[12]

> It is beyond dispute that Saddam Hussein is a menace. He terrorizes and brutalizes his own people. He has launched war on two of his neighbors. He devotes enormous effort to rebuilding his military forces and equipping them with weapons of mass destruction. We will all be better off when he is gone. That said, we need to think through this issue very carefully. *We need to analyze the relationship between Iraq and our other pressing priorities – notably the war on terrorism – as well as the best strategy and tactics available were we to move to change the regime in Baghdad.* (Emphasis added)

Like many others, Scowcroft is essentially linking US interests in Iraq with the imperative to deal with the larger war on terror. He rejects the links between Hussein and Al-Qaeda and warns against fabricating such links – exaggerations undermine the larger case against Iraq:

> [T]here is scant evidence to tie Saddam to terrorist organizations, and even less to the Sept. 11 attacks. Indeed Saddam's goals have little in common with the terrorists who threaten us, and there is little incentive for him to make common cause with them. He is unlikely to risk his investment in weapons of mass destruction, much less his country, by handing such weapons to terrorists who would use them for their own purposes and leave Baghdad as the return address. Threatening to use these weapons for blackmail – much less their actual use – would open him and his entire regime to a devastating response by the US. While Saddam is thoroughly evil, he is above all a power-hungry survivor.[13]

Scowcroft assumed Saddam was too rational to risk this kind of attack, but these same assumptions about Saddam's rationality were directly responsible for promoting suspicions about Saddam's WMD programs – how could such a rational leader sustain the myth that he retained WMD if these suspicions would almost

---

[11] Baker (2002) argues that "If we are to change the regime in Iraq, we will have to occupy the country militarily. The costs of doing so, politically, economically and in terms of casualties, could be great. They will be lessened if the president brings together an international coalition behind the effort. Doing so would also help in achieving the continuing support of the American people, a necessary prerequisite for any successful foreign policy."

[12] Scowcroft 2002.   [13] Scowcroft 2002.

certainly lead to a devastating invasion? The answer is that Saddam never expected the invasion that unfolded, and honestly believed that the WMD myth protected him against an attack from regional enemies, including Iran (see Chapter 8 for more details on these misperceptions).

> In any event, we should be pressing the United Nations Security Council to insist on an effective no-notice inspection regime for Iraq – anytime, any-where, no permission required. On this point, senior administration officials have opined that Saddam Hussein would never agree to such an inspection regime. But if he did, inspections would serve to keep him off balance and under close observation, even if all his weapons of mass destruction capabil-ities were not uncovered. And if he refused, his rejection could provide the persuasive *casus belli* which many claim we do not now have. Compelling evidence that Saddam had acquired nuclear-weapons capability could have a similar effect.[14]

Scowcroft, like Gore, Baker, Holbrooke, Blair and others, was arguing for a new UN resolution on a draconian inspections regime with no qualifiers – he too was demanding absolute compliance that would justify the application of force if not forthcoming.

Democrats and Republicans in sync on Iraq

Washington politics is geared toward highlighting differences over major pol-icy initiatives – the entire political system is driven by a compulsion to generate policy debates, divisions and distinctions to exploit political gain. It is rare that a major foreign policy generates the kind of consensus that emerged from 2002–2003 both inside Washington and across the general public (see Chapter 5). With respect to making the case for bipartisan consensus, consider Berger's (2004) comments in his *Foreign Affairs* piece:[15]

> The foreign policy debate in this year's presidential election is as much about means as it is about ends. Most Democrats agree with President Bush that the fight against terrorism and the spread of weapons of mass destruction (WMD) must be top global priorities, that the war in Afghanistan was neces-sary and just, and that Saddam Hussein's Iraq posed a threat that needed to be dealt with in one form or another … The real "clash of civilizations" is taking place within Washington. Considering the open differences between Secretary of State Colin Powell and Secretary of Defense Donald Rumsfeld, it is even playing out within the Bush administration itself … It is a battle fought between liberal internationalists in both parties who believe that our strength is usually greatest when we work in concert with allies in defense of shared values and interests, versus those who seem to believe that the United States should go it alone – or not go it at all.

[14] Scowcroft 2002.   [15] Berger 2004.

Now compare this with leading Republican Senator Chuck Hagel's outline of the principles of a "Republican" foreign policy:[16]

> The United States' long-term security interests are connected to alliances, coalitions, and international institutions. A Republican foreign policy must view alliances and international institutions as extensions of our influence, not as constraints on our power. No single country, including the United States with all its vast military and economic power, can successfully meet the challenges of the twenty-first century alone. Winning the war on terrorism, for example, will require a seamless network of relationships … The United States must therefore help strengthen global institutions and alliances, beginning with the United Nations and NATO. Like all institutions, the UN has its limitations. It needs reform. Too often, the UN, especially the General Assembly, succumbs to the worst forms of political posturing and irresponsible action. But the UN is more relevant today than it has ever been. The global challenges of terrorism, proliferation of weapons of mass destruction, hunger, disease, and poverty require multilateral responses and initiatives.

The point here is not simply to describe these opinions – it is to provide evidence that leading Democrats and Republicans *shared* these opinions and perceptions. The same pressures that emerged throughout this period in American history to produce consensus around the wisdom of applying assertive multilateralism would almost certainly have played out with a president responsible for campaigning on that very policy. The only group rejecting key elements of the consensus were neoconservatives and unilateralists in the Bush administration, who rejected UN multilateralism.

The Levin amendment

Where debate in Congress did exist, its substance was not between those in favor of *war* or *peace* (or between hawks and doves) but rather between those in favor of giving the president the authorization to use force *with* or *without* another UN resolution.

Most legislators who rejected authorization (e.g., Carl Levin) did so not because they rejected the prospects of using military force or because they challenged the WMD case against Saddam, but because they were hoping to get UN multilateral endorsement first.[17] The Levin amendment recommended authorization to deploy US Armed Forces

---

[16] Hagel 2004.

[17] There were other reasons for the Democrats' opposition that had little to do with their support for some anti-war position that challenged the generally accepted intelligence on Iraq's WMD. Some of those opposed to authorization were fearful that Saddam might actually use his stockpiles of biological or chemical weapons against US troops who lacked sufficient protection. Others opposed authorization because Rumsfeld did not demonstrate adequate

pursuant to a new resolution of the United Nations Security Council, to destroy, remove, or render harmless Iraq's weapons of mass destruction, nuclear weapons-usable material, long-range ballistic missiles, and related facilities, and for other purposes ... This joint resolution may be cited as the "Multilateral Use of Force Authorization Act of 2002."[18]

Levin simply wanted to make sure Washington had UN support *before* authorizing force. The president could either return to Congress should Saddam fail to live up to the mandate outlined in the new resolution, or he could return to Congress for authorization should the UN fail to live up to its stated obligation to disarm Iraq as stipulated in many previous resolutions. But it is important to understand what this amendment was not about – it was not about rejecting the WMD consensus or making a strong, principled case against war. The amendment was essentially a minor adjustment to the sequence and timing of the coercive strategy everyone agreed was essential for success. But critics like Carl Levin and Robert Byrd were justifiably concerned with statements by Cheney and prominent neoconservatives who were pushing for unilateral pre-emption. "This is the Tonkin Gulf resolution all over again," Byrd argued. "Let us stop, look and listen. Let us not give this president or any president unchecked power. Remember the Constitution." Obviously, a large number of the twenty-one senators who voted against authorization breathed a huge sigh of relief when Bush declared his intention to negotiate another resolution, and were even happier when Powell and Blair successfully negotiated a unanimous UN resolution threatening 'serious consequences' – the major concerns expressed by Levin and other Democrats to 'multilateralize' the process were effectively resolved.

In fact, Levin himself clearly prescribed, at the time, to the standard and prevailing interpretation of the Iraq threat. Consider other elements of the Levin amendment that speak to the consensus on WMD:

> (2.4) Iraq continues to develop weapons of mass destruction, in violation of its commitments under United Nations Security Council Resolution 687 (1991) and subsequent resolutions, and the regime of Saddam Hussein has used weapons of mass destruction against its own people and other nations.
>
> (2.5) The development of weapons of mass destruction by Iraq is a threat to the United States, to the friends and allies of the United States in the Middle East, and to international peace and security.

commitment to intervene with a sufficiently large military force for successful post-war reconstruction. But most Democrats, like Levin, were opposed because of concerns that neoconservatives and unilateralists would intervene without any UN endorsement. None of these critics seriously questioned the generally accepted consensus on the Iraqi threat, nor did they reject the core principles underlying a need for a coercive military threat to force compliance with UN disarmament resolutions.

[18] *Congressional Record* (Senate) 2002a.

In essence, the amendment was designed to assuage concerns that Bush and Cheney would use authorization to bypass the UN en route to a pre-emptive unilateral invasion – which did not happen. The amendment went on to read that Congress:

> (3.2) urges the United Nations Security Council to adopt promptly a resolution that –
>
> (A) demands that Iraq provide immediate, unconditional, and unrestricted access of the United Nations weapons inspectors so that Iraq's weapons of mass destruction, nuclear weapons-usable material, ballistic missiles with a range in excess of 150 kilometers, and related facilities are destroyed, removed, or rendered harmless; and
> (B) authorizes the use of necessary and appropriate military force by member states of the United Nations to enforce such resolution in the event that the Government of Iraq refuses to comply;
>
> (3.3) affirms that, under international law and the United Nations Charter, the United States has at all times the inherent right to use military force in self-defense.

This is precisely what the president, secretary of state, and British prime minister accomplished by successfully negotiating UNSCR 1441, the very resolution critics in the Senate were demanding. Understanding these details is crucial to appreciating the nature and scope of the domestic political consensus driving policy from 2002 to 2003. Levin's amendment lost 75–24. But those who rejected the amendment were not unilateralists – they were multilateralists who rationally argued that you cannot tie important US security decisions to the veto power of any single member of the council. It made more sense to use congressional authorization first to enhance Washington's bargaining leverage when negotiating a new UN mandate to reinstate coercive inspections. Tom Daschle drew attention to this argument when he stressed the critical importance of speaking with "one voice at this critical moment."[19] Almost everyone supported the president's approach once it became clear that he used the authorization to go back to the UN. Neoconservatives lost this battle.

With respect to exploring interesting counterfactual arguments, consider this one – had the Levin amendment succeeded, Bush would have gone to the UN first, without deploying troops to the region and without any bargaining leverage to negotiate a new, stronger UN mandate. If the negotiations failed, Congress would then have been forced to grant authorization in the face of the UNSC's refusal to compel Saddam to disarm. As the amendment stipulated:

> Before the authority granted in subsection (a) is exercised, the President shall make available to the Speaker of the House of Representatives and

---

[19] Daschle 2002.

the President pro tempore of the Senate his determination that the United States has used appropriate diplomatic and other peaceful means to obtain compliance by Iraq with a resolution of the United Nations Security Council described in section 3(2) and that those efforts have not been and are not likely to be successful in obtaining such compliance.

The president could easily have demonstrated a commitment to negotiate a new resolution, and the failure would have confirmed to most members of Congress that the UN was incapable of resolving the impasse multilaterally. Ironically, had Levin's amendment succeeded, Levin would have been responsible for a strategy that would have produced a decidedly more unilateralist approach to the Iraq crisis. Even if Bush (or Gore) had accepted Levin's amendment and still achieved the same UNSCR 1441 resolution before authorization, the evidence of compliance would never have been sufficient to resolve the inspections impasse (see Chapter 8), meaning the outcome would not have been appreciably different.

Comparing Operation Desert Fox (1998) to Operation Iraqi Freedom (2002)

Comparing the speeches in favor of the 1998 Iraq Liberation Act and Operation Desert Fox (ODF) during the Clinton administration with those delivered in favor of the October 2002 authorization (and Operation Iraqi Freedom – OIF) reveals several facts that are relevant to the comparative counterfactual exercise.[20] First, the general content of the speeches was virtually identical; both sets of speeches made reference to the same WMD threats. One need only compare the speeches in October 2002 delivered by senior Democrats, including John Kerry, Joe Lieberman and Tom Daschle (see Appendix 3.1) with the content of the Iraq Liberation Act, which arrived at the following consensus:

> 1998 ILA: Expresses the sense of the Congress that once the Saddam Hussein regime is removed from power in Iraq, the United States should support Iraq's *transition to democracy* by providing humanitarian assistance to the Iraqi people and *democracy transition* assistance to Iraqi parties and movements with *democratic goals*, including convening Iraq's foreign creditors to develop a multilateral response to the foreign debt incurred by the Hussein regime.[21]

In fact, it was President Clinton who delivered one of the strongest cases against Hussein's regime, and in favor of regime change, prior to the passage of the ILA and Operation Desert Fox.[22]

The main difference is that the military actions in 1998 were not endorsed by Congress or a new UN resolution declaring Iraq in material breach and

---

[20] GovTrack 2002a. Full text and video of speeches in the Senate and House.
[21] *Iraq Liberation Act* 1998.
[22] Mylroie 1998. See also Clinton's statement to Joint Chiefs of Staff in 1998 in Clinton (1998a).

threatening 'serious consequences.' Moreover, the 1998 operation occurred at the very end of eight years of UNSCOM inspections, whereas OIF was launched in the context of a four-year absence of inspectors.

Now, if Clinton, Gore, Holbrooke, Albright, Kerry, Fuerth (and many others) firmly believed in 1998 that the United States had the right (indeed, obligation) to attack Iraq without congressional or UN approval, why would these same leaders be opposed to attacking Iraq after 9/11, with congressional support *and* a new, unanimously endorsed UN resolution? The only way for some alternative *Gore-peace* counterfactual scenario to make sense is to provide a set of auxiliary hypotheses (or assumptions) that explain why Gore would have rejected these pressures, focused on others, and promoted a different solution he did not reveal in the 2000 campaign or in his 2002 speeches on Iraq. On balance, such a case is very weak.

The two dominant forces that pushed the country down the path to war had nothing to do with individuals or ideology – 9/11 and the reality of US power were largely responsible.[23] The 9/11 attacks created a set of conditions that transformed the views of most people in 2002–2003 – it created a policy spectrum that became considerably more narrow, with the exception of neo-conservatives and staunch unilateralists in the administration who adopted non-mainstream, marginalized views on how to handle Iraq. As Gordon (2006) correctly concludes, it was a combination of 'vulnerability' and 'power' that established priorities for Iraq policy. When the post-war operation shifted to a focus on *democratization*, neoconist observers mistakenly assumed this insidious goal was part of the neoconservatives' plan from the outset, forgetting the substance of the speeches at the time. Those in favor of authorization did not justify their support in terms of democratization, because their priorities focused mostly on disarmament. The shift to democratization was the product of the foreign policy and intelligence failures that produced the miscalculations (that is, the failure to find the WMD everyone expected Saddam was hiding), and not the result of some strategic doctrine or grand strategy on the part of neoconservatives. Clear consensus on the seriousness of the WMD threat is indisputable, and this general consensus (which rejected much of the Pentagon's distorted intelligence on Iraq's WMD) was sufficient after 9/11 to compel leaders to support authorization. Even retired Army General Norman Schwartzkopf, commander of US ground forces in Operation Desert Storm in 1991, stated as late as August 18, 2002: "If we invade Iraq and the regime is very close to falling, I'm very, very concerned that the Iraqis will, in fact, use weapons of mass destruction."[24] The differences over the WMD record did

---

[23] Gordon (2006) provides one of the best accounts of the far more complex account of the ideologies that existed and changed throughout this period, and the consistency in the Democratic and Republican views on the best way to handle Iraq.

[24] *San Francisco Chronicle* 2002.

not amount to anything approaching serious reservations that credibly challenged the overall record or provide a plausible policy alternative. Nothing in the Gore team's speeches or statements would reveal a preference for an alternative course of action. Not a single prominent Democratic leader at the time was opposed to the key foreign policy moves to get inspectors back in.

Democratic endorsement of other controversial 'Republican' security policies

The degree of bipartisan support for the policies Bush adopted is repeatedly overlooked by neoconists. Also absent from conventional accounts of the Bush administration is the post-9/11 bipartisan consensus on security policies more generally – agreement did not begin or end with the Iraq crisis. Consider, for example, the strong support Democrats provided in favor of the Patriot Act or the use of "enhanced interrogation techniques" for Guantanamo prisoners.[25]

The Patriot Act

The Iraq war is not the only initiative pegged to the Bush administration by a majority of Democrats, who have conveniently forgotten their endorsement of bills before both the House and Senate. The House voted 357 in favor, 66 opposed (83 percent) in support of the Patriot Act.[26] Among Democrats, 145 voted in favor (versus 62 against) of the measures included in the bill. The Senate voted 98–1 in favor of the Patriot Act – virtually unanimous support, with a 48–1 margin of support from Democrats.

Enhanced interrogations

Democrats on all key foreign policy and intelligence committees were briefed on the CIA's enhanced interrogation techniques, but they now have a strong interest in distancing themselves from that support despite evidence to the contrary. Notwithstanding her assurances that she was never briefed by the CIA on waterboarding, for example, Speaker of the House Nancy Pelosi prevented the launch of a congressional investigation to determine what she knew and when she knew it. The 2009 Nancy Pelosi media frenzy is a perfect illustration of how the facts of bipartisan consensus slowly dissipate over time when the public and media become less enthusiastic about the original legislation. Former CIA Director Porter Goss offered the following comment on Pelosi's assertions that she was never briefed:

> A disturbing epidemic of amnesia seems to be plaguing my former colleagues on Capitol Hill … Today, I am slack-jawed to read that members

---

[25] Warrick and Eggen 2007.   [26] GovTrack 2002a.

claim to have not understood that the techniques on which they were briefed were to actually be employed; or that specific techniques such as "waterboarding" were never mentioned. It must be hard for most Americans of common sense to imagine how a member of Congress can forget being told about the interrogations of Sept. 11 mastermind Khalid Sheik Mohammed. In that case, though, perhaps it is not amnesia but political expedience. Let me be clear. It is my recollection that ... the chairs and the ranking minority members of the House and Senate intelligence committees, known as the Gang of Four, were briefed that the CIA was holding and interrogating high-value terrorists – we understood what the CIA was doing; we gave the CIA our bipartisan support; we gave the CIA funding to carry out its activities ... On a bipartisan basis, we asked if the CIA needed more support from Congress to carry out its mission against al-Qaeda. I do not recall a single objection from my colleagues.[27]

Obama's choice for CIA Director, Leon Panetta (former senior adviser to Clinton), also defended the CIA's version of the 'truth' about briefing Pelosi on waterboarding.[28] The fact that these interrogation techniques received bipartisan support in a post-9/11 world is not surprising, nor is the support Bush received for his Iraq policy. Of course, the concerted effort by senior Democrats to revise history in an effort to distance themselves from these policies is also not very surprising.

Conclusions: Gore-war versus Gore-peace revisited

Obviously, if there was a completely different 'Democratic' option to the one Bush and Blair adopted, or the one Gore, Holbrooke, Fuerth and others recommended at the time, it certainly wasn't articulated by leading Democrats. In light of this widespread bipartisan consensus, there is no reason to expect Gore's team would have come up with an approach that received as much support with the same probability of success. The coercive diplomatic value of assertive multilateralism was a policy Gore endorsed throughout his political career. The approach also stood the best chance of strengthening the Clinton–Gore policy of containment with the fewest political risks.

Neoconists have consistently (perhaps intentionally) misinterpreted the substance of the domestic political debates throughout this period. They have also ignored (or completely misunderstood) the content of congressional speeches endorsing authorization. These errors have led to a seriously flawed representation of the case history, which also explains the popularity of neoconism. But the facts surrounding these political debates should speak for themselves – the

---

[27] Goss 2009.
[28] Virtually all major media outlets covered the story of CIA Director Panetta's criticisms of Pelosi for creating the impression that Democrats were out of the loop on waterboarding. See: Kane 2009; Klein 2009; Rowley 2009.

evidence clearly establishes the truth behind the options Bush and Blair were considering at the time, the same facts and circumstances that Gore's team would have faced had they been in power.

With respect to the October 2002 authorization, the House voted 296–133 in favor of the resolution, followed by the Senate's 77–23 vote the next day.[29] There are several important reasons why strong bipartisan support for the Iraq war resolution was inevitable, regardless of whether Bush or Gore was in the White House defending it.

First, almost everyone in Washington understood how important it was to provide the president with the bargaining leverage he needed to persuade members of the UN Security Council to endorse UNSCR 1441. A threat to deal with a serious problem 'alone if necessary' (Gore 2002a) is often a prerequisite for kick-starting multilateral diplomacy (Harvey 2004). A strong, credible threat backed by congressional and UN authorization was viewed at the time as the best hope for managing the disarmament crisis multilaterally and *peacefully*. In fact, support for authorization made so much sense that John Kerry and Hillary Clinton continued to defend their vote throughout their election campaigns in 2004 and 2008, respectively – they justified their decision with references to the logic of coercive diplomacy.[30] During the 2004 campaign, John Kerry was asked:

> *Interviewer*: You've been saying that you voted to authorize the president, President Bush, to threaten the use of force in Iraq. In fact, as Senator Graham pointed out, you voted to authorize the use of force at President Bush's discretion. To some it may seem that you're trying to get out of a vote that's now unpopular with many in the Democratic Party. Is that the way we should perceive it?
>
> *John Kerry*: Absolutely not. The vote is the vote. I voted to authorize, it was the right vote. And the reason I mentioned the threat is that we had to give life to the threat. If there wasn't a legitimate threat, Saddam Hussein was not going to allow inspectors in. If there hadn't been a vote, we would never have had inspectors. And if we hadn't voted the way we voted, we would not have been able to have a chance of going to the UN.

---

[29] Democrats supporting authorization: Baucus (D-MT); Bayh (D-IN); Biden (D-DE); Breaux (D-LA); Cantwell (D-WA); Carnahan (D-MO); Carper (D-DE); Cleland (D-GA); Clinton (D-NY); Daschle (D-SD); Dodd (D-CT); Dorgan (D-ND); Edwards (D-NC); Feinstein (D-CA); Harkin (D-IA); Hollings (D-SC); Johnson (D-SD); Kerry (D-MA); Kohl (D-WI); Landrieu (D-LA); Lieberman (D-CT); Lincoln (D-AR); Miller (D-GA); Nelson (D-FL); Nelson (D-NE); Reid (D-NV); Rockefeller (D-WV); Schumer (D-NY); Torricelli (D-NJ).

Democrats opposed to authorization: Akaka (D-HI); Bingaman (D-NM); Boxer (D-CA); Byrd (D-WV); Conrad (D-ND); Corzine (D-NJ); Dayton (D-MN); Durbin (D-IL); Feingold (D-WI); Graham (D-FL); Inouye (D-HI); Kennedy (D-MA); Leahy (D-VT); Levin (D-MI); Mikulski (D-MD); Murray (D-WA); Reed (D-RI); Sarbanes (D-MD); Stabenow (D-MI); Wellstone (D-MN); Wyden (D-OR).

[30] Kerry 2003b. The comments were made at the Congressional Black Caucus Institute debate, September 9, 2003.

As Democratic Senator Jay Rockefeller (2002) explained:

> Any headway we are making to get Saddam Hussein to disarm has not occurred in a vacuum. UN members did not just suddenly decide to debate a new resolution forcing Iraq to disarm. Saddam Hussein did not just suddenly decide to reinvite UN inspectors and to remove the roadblocks that had hindered their efforts in the past. Progress is occurring because the President told the United Nations General Assembly that if the UN is not prepared to enforce its resolution on Iraqi disarmament, the United States will be forced to act.[31]
>
> At this point, America's best opportunity to move the United Nations and Iraq to a peaceful resolution of this crisis is by making clear that the United States is prepared to act on our own, if necessary, as one nation, indivisible. Sometimes, the rest of the world looks to America not just for the diversity of our debate, or the vitality of our ideals, but for the firm resolve that the world's leader must demonstrate if intractable global problems are to be solved – and dangerous ones at that. So that is the context in which I am approaching this vote.[32]

The subsequent deployment by the United States and UK of close to 200,000 troops to Kuwait and Qatar, they argued, established the credibility of the US–UK threat and provided the requisite demonstration of resolve to carry through with military action if compliance from the Iraqi regime was not forthcoming. The overall approach was praised by Hans Blix and Jacques Chirac, who both explicitly acknowledged that the troop deployment was responsible for whatever successes UNMOVIC experienced (see the discussion of coercive diplomacy in Chapter 9 for more on this).[33] But once that resolution was passed, this perfectly reasonable (multilaterally and domestically supported) strategy set both the United States and UK down a path to war that became difficult to alter.

Second, had President Gore approached Congress in 2002 for a similar resolution (likely, given Gore's clear preference for coercive multilateralism), there is no logical reason why the resolution would have failed. In fact, support from Democrats would likely have been even stronger without reluctant senators like Levin and Byrd expressing concerns about neocons using authorization to justify a unilateral pre-emptive war. Gore would not have raised any of these concerns given his commitment to liberal internationalism. The speeches delivered in the House and Senate in October 2002 authorizing the use of force

---

[31] *Congressional Record* 2002b; 20454. The position of Rockefeller was clear and yet President Obama still managed to get his vote wrong in a speech on the Iraq war. This is the problem with the power of neoconism and assumptions we have about the past based on popular opinion and myth rather than facts and evidence.

[32] *Congressional Record* 2002b.

[33] Hans Blix stated at the time, "I have never complained about your military pressure. I think it's a good thing." Quoted in Woodward 2004: 254.

were largely indistinguishable from those delivered in 1998 in support of the Iraq Liberation Act, and each year's set of speeches made reference to identical concerns about Iraq's expanding WMD programs. Both the 1998 Act and 2003 authorization were framed in terms of American security, a clear threat from Iraq's WMD (everyone was wrong in 1998, as well), the linkage between American security and the spread of freedom and democracy, and preventive diplomacy to deal with mounting threats before they escalated out of control. On the Iraq file, in other words, the positions expressed by both Democrats and Republicans in Congress throughout the Clinton and Bush administrations were in sync. A Democratic Gore presidency, therefore, could have expected the same (if not more) bipartisan support than was received by a Republican Bush presidency.

Third, the failure to anticipate 9/11, which at the time was viewed by many as the most significant intelligence blunder in decades, revealed the very high political costs of *underestimating* threats – the Central Intelligence Agency, Federal Bureau of Investigation, National Security Agency and Pentagon were all criticized for stove-piping intelligence information and for missing (ignoring) too many signals that prevented them from connecting a sufficient number of dots. These lessons, which were later confirmed by a very popular bipartisan 9/11 Commission report, encouraged the government, intelligence communities and Congress to err on the side of actively searching for and 'imagining' (overestimating) the next security threats, including those coming from Iraq. Had the Democrats in Congress refused to authorize 'all necessary means' in 2002 to enforce Saddam's compliance, it would have reinforced public perceptions of Democratic weaknesses on the central election issue: security and defense. In light of the overwhelming evidence from speeches and statements by Gore and his team, covered in the previous two chapters, there is no reason to believe a Democratic administration would have failed to appreciate the post-9/11 realities and associated political pressures.

Finally, overreacting to the WMD threat was far less risky (in the short term) than under-reacting to a threat everyone acknowledged was real. This is not to suggest that a majority of Congress was persuaded by the Pentagon's distorted interpretation of the intelligence, but their concerns, as expressed in almost every single speech delivered in October, were more than sufficient to support the multilateral approach adopted by the president. The political risks of inaction were far greater than the risks of following the strategy that ultimately set the stage for war. And at the final stage, in March 2003, the risks of the status quo (endless inspections despite the threat of military force) were greater than the risks of war, as long as the public believed the war was launched in the interest of their security. The fact that George Bush *won* the 2004 presidential election (with a larger segment of the popular vote than 2000 and additional seats in the House), despite being wrong about WMD stockpiles in Iraq confirms this point. In essence, the Republicans were given credit for erring on the side of American security even though everyone got the intelligence so very wrong. Obviously, support for Bush plummeted over the years, but a Democratic administration would have exploited (and benefited from) the same domestic imperatives in 2002–2003 to prioritize public safety. Gore's record on Iraq does not support the view that he (or his advisers) would have been more willing to accept the high political costs of downplaying or doing nothing on Iraq after 9/11, demonstrating inaction on enforcing compliance after the passage of UNSCR 1441, or doing nothing after France rejected any and all military options for disarming Iraq in favor of extending inspections indefinitely. With respect to indefinite inspections, the US government (not France, Germany, Russia or China) would have suffered the burden of paying for the extended deployment of 200,000 troops in theater. Again, this situation would have amounted to another impossible position for a president leading into the 2004 presidential campaign.

With respect to Gore's preferences, despite the enormous political risks involved in opposing so many of his colleagues in 1991, not to mention the potential effects on his future prospects within the party, Gore supported the war. Since that vote, Gore and his advisers have consistently delivered speeches on foreign policy and Iraq that include reference to this vote (and the fact that he was one of only a few Democrats to make what he regarded as the right decision at the time) – Gore wears that vote as a badge of honor. Now, consider the political context Gore would have faced in 2003 – more significant support among Democrats, a strongly worded congressional resolution granting the president the authority to use force, a strong UN mandate (above and beyond the mandate already provided by the UN in 1991 and several subsequent UN resolutions) and a belief that the US had the legal authority to follow through if the UN did not endorse a new resolution. The *Gore-peace* counterfactual, which implies that he would have dismissed all of this in favor of the status quo or endless inspections, is simply not supported by existing evidence.

Neoconist critics might argue that I am conflating the notion that Democrats were unable to block the administration's plans for war with the notion that, had they been in charge, they would have chosen war at the expense of splintering their own camp. But the argument here is not that Gore would have pushed the war option at the risk of splintering his own party. My point is that the UN-based strategy at the heart of assertive multilateralism would have been endorsed by most Democrats as a solid liberal internationalist approach to constructive engagement and cooperative security. This was the best hope for disarming Iraq. But the same interim decisions required to see this policy through would have driven the country closer to, not further from, war.

5

American intelligence failures and miscalculations

Threat manipulation, distortions and exaggerations

In line with a central premise of the *Gore-peace* counterfactual, neoconists have consistently argued that exaggerated intelligence estimates and threat distortions were directly responsible for generating support for the Iraq war. A Gore administration would likely not have engaged in this kind of threat rhetoric and would have endorsed the generally accepted (non-distorted) impressions of the WMD threat when crafting policy responses. More importantly, a Gore administration would have excluded out-of-power neocons who would not have had access to or control over the selective release of intelligence necessary to engage in the manipulation that led to congressional authorization. The following chapter challenges this standard account of history.

Neoconism clearly asserts that intelligence on Iraq's WMD was intentionally manipulated by White House and Pentagon officials to obtain the domestic (congressional) and international (UN) support required to justify invasion. Of all pre-war intelligence estimates the Bush administration is accused of exaggerating, neoconists typically focus on the following three items: (1) operational linkages between Saddam and Al-Qaeda leading to 9/11; (2) Saddam's attempted acquisition of aluminum tubes used in centrifuge enrichment programs; and (3) the attempted purchase of uranium yellowcake from Africa. All three intelligence estimates were shown after the war to be largely baseless and seriously flawed, but these errors, according to neoconists, were known to administration officials yet nonetheless ignored. Congressional leaders, the argument goes, inadvertently relied on these false estimates to defend their support for the October 2002 authorization. And since authorization was a crucial step toward war, the war itself can be blamed on these distortions and on those who were responsible for their fabrication.

This version of the case history is particularly appealing to neoconists for obvious reasons – the fewer and more identifiable the intelligence errors, the easier it is to track and apportion blame. Assigning extraordinary causal weight to these three intelligence errors, rather than so many others compiled over a decade of data gathering and intelligence assessments, biases the case in favor of neoconism by buttressing the first-image 'leadership' theory of intelligence manipulation and war. By focusing on a small, manageable (and more controllable) part of the intelligence failure record, all we really need for proof are examples of prominent neocons spinning these specific estimates.

But what are the implications for neoconism if these three intelligence estimates were irrelevant to the positions articulated and defended by most participants at the time? What if these items were largely unrelated to the rationales offered by those on both sides of the aisle who supported the president's decisions at each stage? If institutional and structural impediments to intelligence collection were far more significant and difficult to control, or if the scope of intelligence errors were considerably more entrenched across both Democratic and Republican administrations (a product of failed inspections, years of deception and strategic ambiguity practiced by Saddam Hussein, and the absence of inspectors from 1998), or if there were other societal, political, institutional, diplomatic and strategic factors that explain the bipartisan support both Clinton and Bush received for their Iraq policies, then the choices would not be related to distinct *leadership* qualities of the president or the ideological idiosyncrasies (neoconservatism) of a few individuals in the Bush administration. In sum, if the causes and scope of intelligence errors were systemic, *structural* and considerably more entrenched, then these findings would pose a serious challenge to a central part of the neoconist story.

Now, with respect to assessing the popular neoconist claims regarding a direct causal relationship between congressional authorization and politically manipulated intelligence on aluminum tubes, uranium and Al-Qaeda, the key methodological questions are these: what collection of specific historical facts would we need to observe in order to confirm or disconfirm this central claim, and how should we interpret this evidence in light of the logical arguments stipulated in 'leadership' (intelligence manipulation) versus '*structural*' (intelligence failure) theories of the war? More specifically, how many officials (Democrats, Republicans, neoconservatives, UNSCOM or UNMOVIC inspectors, members of the Labour and Conservative parties in Britain, etc.) accepted what proportion of the hundreds of intelligence estimates, compiled over a decade of US–UK–UN inspections, with what degree of confidence? Were these general impressions, suspicions and concerns sufficient to endorse the Bush administration's UN-based strategy at each stage? And, more importantly, how relevant were aluminum tubes, uranium and Al-Qaeda links when compared with everything else the regime was suspected of hiding?

One straightforward method for answering these questions is to track (through, for example, process tracing and content analysis) any reference to these three items in congressional debates on the resolution authorizing the use of military force (from congressional records, October 8–10, 2002).[1] Speeches defending a vote to deploy military troops are very risky, career-defining

---

[1] www.gpoaccess.gov/crecord/index.html.

moments that often establish (or kill) political legacies. The content of these speeches arguably constitutes the best case these officials can extract from all available evidence and intelligence to defend one of the most important votes they will ever cast. Logically, we would expect these officials to highlight in their speeches the most relevant information, data and intelligence they believe is crucial to establishing their case. Any indication that uranium, aluminum tubes or operational links between Iraq, Al-Qaeda and 9/11 were largely *absent* from these speeches, or completely ignored altogether, would raise serious doubts about this crucial part of neoconist accounts of history – such an absence would indicate they were obviously *not* necessary for selling the war.

A total of fifty-two senators gave seventy-six speeches to defend their vote. Only nine made reference to uranium or aluminum tubes – six were Democrats, three of whom opposed authorization (Robert Byrd – WV, Bob Graham – FL and Ted Kennedy – MA), and three supported the president (Joe Lieberman – CT, Joe Biden – DE and Byron Dorgan – ND). The remaining three senators who made reference to these items were Republicans (Susan Collins – ME, Kay Bailey Hutchison – KY and Olympia Snowe – ME). Leaving aside the three Democrats who opposed authorization (they dismissed these intelligence estimates based on alternative interpretations included in the full National Intelligence Estimate and its appendices), there were a total of only six out of forty-nine senators who made references to these items. This hardly constitutes anything approaching compelling empirical evidence that these distortions were necessary to obtain congressional authorization or to successfully 'sell' the war. In fact, a significant majority of Republican senators considered these three items to be irrelevant to the case they were making, obviously because the case *without* these distortions was more than sufficient to justify their vote.

Moreover, both sides of the debate over the relevance of these three estimates were voiced in the October speeches – Senators Byrd, Leahy and Kennedy, for example, issued very strong statements *against* the aluminum tube story and links to Al-Qaeda. Such dissenting views were not hidden from congressional debates and were clearly articulated by those who opposed authorization in the absence of a new UN resolution. The disagreement between the CIA and Department of Energy (DOE) over the relevance of aluminum tubes was also raised – the 2002 National Intelligence Estimate noted that "all intelligence experts agree … these tubes could be used in a centrifuge enrichment program," but the DOE did not believe this was true in this particular case, because there was no corroborating evidence from other parts of an Iraqi nuclear program. The DOE concluded, therefore, that the tubes were likely intended for conventional rockets. The point is that the CIA-DOE debate was recognized in speeches surrounding authorization, but the critics' arguments failed to convince most Democrats to shift their vote, for a simple reason – these distorted intelligence items were marginal to the larger WMD picture and threat.

With respect to references to Al-Qaeda – fifteen out of the twenty-nine Democrats who voted in favor of authorization made references to Al-Qaeda, but none of them accepted the distorted claims regarding *operational* linkages associated with the planning and execution of 9/11. Joe Biden and Hillary Clinton delivered speeches that actually downplayed the operational links between Al-Qaeda and Iraq, but, like almost everyone else, defended the view that Saddam's links to terrorism in the Middle East were serious enough (sufficient, along with everything else on record) to justify authorization. Ironically, Joe Lieberman (Gore's choice for vice president) was one of the few Democrats who raised the possibility of stronger links between Iraq regime officials and Al-Qaeda, but even he didn't come close to claiming a connection between Saddam and 9/11. Not one of the remaining twenty-two Democrats who voted in favor of the resolution authorizing force made *any* reference to Al-Qaeda or Saddam-9/11 linkages – their support did not depend on that distortion. The reason for highlighting the absence of Democratic references to these items is to defend the counterfactual argument that Democrats would have supported Gore's push for authorization *without relying on these distortions*.

In fact, many of the speeches acknowledged the heated debate the CIA and state department were having with the Pentagon on Iraq–Al-Qaeda links. George Tenet, Colin Powell and Tony Blair, for example, warned Bush against accepting (or issuing) the distorted Pentagon claims being pushed by Douglas Feith's office (undersecretary of defense for policy).[2] Powell and Blair endorsed the more qualified (but generally supported) estimates regarding some second-level communication between Iraqi officials and Al-Qaeda regarding a non-aggression pact. But they both encouraged the president to focus on the largely substantiated linkages between the regime and other well known terrorist groups. Using distorted claims about Al-Qaeda, they argued, could jeopardize other parts of the case against Saddam by raising questions about the administration's credibility on other estimates. There was no need, in other words, to prove Mohammed Atta met with Iraqi intelligence officials in Prague (the CIA confirmed that Atta was in Virginia at the time), because the regime's links to other terrorist organizations were threatening enough, along with everything else on record, to justify the approach Bush, Powell and Blair were recommending.

A few neoconist scholars who endorse the distorted intelligence argument (e.g., Kellett Cramer 2007: 524) agree that members of Congress were not necessarily persuaded by inflated threats but voted for the resolution because they were afraid of violating the norm of 'militarized patriotism' – "The norm to be patriotic trumped politicians' rational judgment on the merits of the case." With respect to the primary motivation of most of Congress at the time, however, Kellett Cramer seriously overstates their case. These officials voted for authorization to provide the president with the bargaining leverage he needed to

[2] Tenet 2007.

approach the UN for a strong multilateral resolution, which made perfect sense at the time. They understood that successful coercion required a clear demonstration of resolve through the deployment of troops backed by congressional authorization to act alone if the international community failed to address the problem. Most legislators believed at the time that this strategy stood the best chance of resolving the crisis without having to actually resort to military force. This is a much stronger interpretation of the motivations driving reasonably intelligent people in Congress, far more plausible than the alternative view that members of Congress were pressured into war by a public duped by neocons' inflated threats, despite their better judgements. Again, distorted threats were not necessary for the authorization vote to make perfect sense.

These are not insignificant findings – they reveal serious errors with neoconist accounts of history. Fabricated intelligence did not appear to play a major role in persuading Democrats in Congress to support authorization or the president's Iraq strategy. The record disconfirms the standard assumption that an 'imminent threat' based on these distorted intelligence estimates was *necessary* for congressional support – it was not. None of these speeches drew direct linkages between Saddam and 9/11, except for those who dismissed the claims as silly, a position shared by senior members of Tony Blair's administration and, of course, Al Gore. With respect to additional evidence disconfirming the necessity of threat inflation, consider the fact that none of these distortions played a role in the 98–0 vote in favor of the 1998 Iraq Liberation Act and subsequent bombing campaign – indeed, the speeches delivered in the Senate endorsing the ILA looked very similar to those delivered in October 2002. Distorted intelligence about these three items was essentially irrelevant.

Neoconists, therefore, are faced with a difficult dilemma – if it is appropriate to quote Cheney's references to aluminum tubes to explain his push for unilateral pre-emption, then the absence of these distortions in the speeches defending authorization should be acknowledged when explaining the course of events. These exaggerations may have been relevant to defending Cheney's preferred strategy, but the evidence clearly shows that they were not necessary to support the policy Bush, Blair and Powell adopted, which Gore, Holbrooke and many others defended. Gore's national security team would not have been persuaded or pressured by the WMD distortions exploited by Cheney and Wolfowitz; Congress would not have relied on them to support authorization; and the key elements in the path-dependent set of decisions leading to war would have remained the same.

Structural/institutional explanations for intelligence failures – not leadership

A more relevant approach to linking intelligence errors with decisions surrounding Iraq should focus on structural and institutional impediments to intelligence collection that were far more serious, widespread and difficult to control. The three intelligence estimates described above represent only a small fraction of the hundreds of estimates on various parts of Iraq's WMD programs. This much larger collection of estimates was documented in thousands of pages of US, UK, UN and EU documents – they did not suddenly appear in March 2003. Almost *all* of these estimates were shown after the war to be equally flawed, for many of the same reasons, including the absence of human intelligence on the ground in Iraq, the departure of inspectors in 1998, and the decisions by Saddam Hussein to practice *strategic ambiguity* and *deterrence by deception* to enhance his own regional security (see Chapter 8). Acknowledging the true scope and scale of the intelligence errors at the time is essential to understanding what happened.

Obviously there were many debates in the intelligence community on specific items – e.g., the Department of Energy rejected the CIA's claims regarding aluminum tubes; the CIA and state department rejected the Pentagon's assessment of operational links between Iraq and Al-Qaeda. It is also true that in the interest of generating support for a policy the administration deemed essential, a more balanced and nuanced interpretation of the intelligence did not always emerge. But the balance in question was never between, on the one hand, the WMD case the administration was making and, on the other, some alternative, dissenting view that Saddam had nothing. Rather, the debate consisted of how much relative weight should be assigned to specific items, like operational links to Al-Qaeda or aluminum tubes, in the context of a general consensus that Saddam had, or was developing, some level of WMD. No one in the government (or international community) came close to making the argument that the regime was clean, for one simple reason – there was no way to arrive at that conclusion in the absence of UN inspectors, or in the absence of a UN inspections report defending that conclusion. Neither UNSCOM nor UNMOVIC ever came close to producing such a report. On the contrary, the March 6, 2003 report by chief weapons inspector Hans Blix, in the final stages of the crisis, included 175 pages of "unresolved disarmament issues" related to Iraq's proscribed weapons programs. However, it's important to appreciate the fact that the estimates outlined in Blix's report (which were clearly *not* manipulated by neoconservatives) were equally flawed.[3] For reasons outlined in more detail in Chapter 9, there was no way for Blix to establish the truth, because the proof he needed (and the evidence UNSCR 1441 demanded) no longer existed – the documents inspectors required for proof of compliance had long since been destroyed, ironically because Saddam was motivated by the ongoing threat of sanctions to remove all evidence of WMD programs, including proof that he had already destroyed proscribed weapons.

---

[3] www.un.org/Depts/unmovic/SC7asdelivered.htm.

In light of the evidence from speeches and statements collected in Appendices 2.1 and 3.1, the prevailing perception and widespread consensus at the time, based on reasonable assessments of the findings from a decade of inspections and intelligence reports, was that Iraq's WMD programs posed a threat to the United States and its allies – whether it was serious, imminent or potentially dangerous was a matter of dispute, but the general consensus that something had to be done was apparent, despite disagreements on specific intelligence estimates. Many of those who rejected one or more of the three estimates noted earlier still *supported* the tactics central to the president's overall strategy. Most officials on both sides of the aisle believed enough of the intelligence to support the president's decision to get inspectors back in, and that decision, once made, added to the momentum for war (see Chapter 9). These important choices set the stage (and parameters) for making subsequent decisions later on regarding how to interpret the success and failure of inspections, whether to extend inspections for another few weeks or months, and what to do in the face of further evidence of non-compliance.

To illustrate how difficult a challenge it would be to dismiss as complete non-sense the entire intelligence record compiled by 2003, consider the following two pieces of information any official could have offered to raise serious public concerns about Iraq, and how difficult it would be for any politician after 9/11 to dismiss, downplay or refute this evidence. In an October 22, 2001 interview on CNN, Dr. Khidhir Hamza (a former Iraqi nuclear scientist for 20 years) stated:

> Saddam has a whole range of weapons of mass destruction, nuclear, biological and chemical. According to German intelligence estimates, we expect him to have three nuclear weapons by 2005. So, the window will close by 2005, and we expect him then to be a lot more aggressive with his neighbours and encouraging terrorism, and using biological weapons. Now he's using them through surrogates like al Qaeda, but we expect he'll use them more aggressively then.[4]

In 2002, Al-Qaeda operatives issued the following directive on one of the group's websites:

> We have not reached parity with them. We have the right to kill 4 million Americans – 2 million of them children – and to exile twice as many and wound and cripple hundreds of thousands. Furthermore, it is our right to fight them with chemical and biological weapons, so as to afflict them with the fatal maladies that have afflicted the Muslims because of the [Americans'] chemical and biological weapons.[5]

---

[4] Hamza 2001.   [5] Middle East Media Research Institute 2002.

After the war, with the help of the Iraq Survey Group's complete and unfettered access throughout Iraq, these claims were proven to be exaggerations, but there had previously been no easy way for critics of the war to credibly and consistently defend their position. These quotations are only two of thousands of similar statements, compiled over the previous decade, used by officials in Washington when forming their own opinions on Iraq's WMD and when defending those opinions in public. In the absence of inspectors, and in the context of 9/11, there was no way to prove these statements wrong, and no political incentive to do so. All political benefits pointed to accepting the threat as serious enough to address, and those who downplayed the threat were routinely criticized for pre-9/11 thinking. As Bush argued:

> Some have said we must not act until the threat is imminent. Since when have terrorists and tyrants announced their intentions, politely putting us on notice before they strike? If this threat is permitted to fully and suddenly emerge, all actions, all words, and all recriminations would come too late. Trusting in the sanity and restraint of Saddam Hussein is not a strategy, and it is not an option.[6]

There were certainly suspicions raised about some of the evidence, and a few tried hard to raise these suspicions in public as often as possible, but critics of the war simply could not compete with the prevailing position. The problem with trying to mount a sufficiently potent voice for skeptics was explained by Zbigniew Brzezinski, former national security adviser to President Jimmy Carter. Referring to a White House meeting held on Monday February 3, 2003 involving former defense secretaries and secretaries of states (Robert McNamara, Madeleine Albright, William Webster [CIA] and Henry Kissinger), Brzezinski recalls:

> They didn't go into any of the evidence, but they very specifically made it clear that this is not assertion, this is not hypothesis, this was actual knowledge … Your doubts, honestly, tend to shrink when three people whom you respect, whom you trust, whom you have known for years, tell you they know … What it means when they say they know … there is certain data that leads to the conclusion that this is a fact. It's not something which is just loose talk … I felt, at that particular moment, maybe reassured is the wrong word. I felt more inclined to say to myself, "Well, if they know, it must be so."[7]

Again, when it comes to competing narratives (imminent threat, serious threat or no threat), the more plausible narratives after 9/11 are those that overestimate the threats, because these interpretations are more believable in light of previous Iraqi behavior, and, politically, much safer to endorse or exploit in the context

---

[6] Bush 2003.   [7] Brzezinsky quoted in Deyoung 2007: 446.

of the 9/11 Commission. Many of those present at the White House briefing on Iraq were vocal critics of the Bush administration's unilateralist tendencies, but they supported the multilateral track based on the intelligence to which they had access when they were in power. In other words, based on the intelligence they found credible, the approach the government was taking to deal with the problem was appropriate. Agreement on various aspects of the WMD threat may have varied, but almost everyone (except for neocons and unilateralists) accepted the multilateral approach as prudent for resolving the Iraq disarmament impasse. Support for the UN-based strategy was strong even among the war's most vocal critics. Consider the sentiments expressed by UNSCOM inspector Scott Ritter in his 2002 interview on CNN:[8]

> RITTER: We approached the weapons inspections the way that for instance a forensic crime scene investigator approaches a crime – forensically. And we always uncovered every lie the Iraqis told us. They didn't get away with anything.
>
> INTERVIEWER: But when you say you always uncovered every lie that Iraq told you, it means that Iraq didn't fully cooperate by any stretch of the imagination.
>
> RITTER: I have never said that Iraq was fully cooperating and when I make an assessment about Iraq's disarmament level, it has nothing to do with what Iraq has declared. I do not trust them. I take nothing they say at face value, it is based upon the hard work of weapons inspectors who have verified that Iraq has been disarmed through their own independent sources.
>
> INTERVIEWER: So you don't believe that Iraq has any weapons of mass destruction at the moment, or are you not sure?
>
> RITTER: I would say it is a difficult case to make, based on my experience, and if you are going to make that case, back it up with fact.
>
> INTERVIEWER: Is the current debate about the re-entry of weapons inspectors something you believe is directly linked to Washington's decision on whether or not to attack Iraq?
>
> RITTER: I believe Washington, DC is using the concept of inspections as a political foil to justify war. America doesn't want the inspectors to return. *The best way to stop war is to get the inspectors back in. I believe it should be the policy of the United Nations to get the inspectors back in.* (Emphasis added)

Ritter's comments provide additional evidence that accepting the three intelligence distortions noted earlier was not necessary to support the policy Bush adopted. And Ritter was making these arguments in the midst of heated debates in the United States over the two policy options. Like Powell, Blair, Baker, Scowcroft and Gore, Ritter saw the *absence* of inspectors as the unilateralists' and neocons' best hope for war; if inspectors returned, he believed, they

---

[8] Ritter 2002.

would force Saddam to provide the necessary information to confirm the status of the remaining 5–10 per cent of the WMD remaining in the country. Ritter, like everyone else, overestimated the threat by relying on mistaken assumptions about what was likely still in place when inspectors left in 1998.[9]

Of course, Ritter may have reversed his 1998 position in 2002–2003, but even he had problems defending his revised estimates when challenged by reporters:[10]

> INTERVIEWER: In 1998, you said Saddam had "not nearly disarmed." Now you say he doesn't have weapons of mass destruction (WMD). Why did you change your mind?
>
> RITTER: I have never given Iraq a clean bill of health! Never! Never! I've said that no one has backed up any allegations that Iraq has reconstituted WMD capability with anything that remotely resembles substantive fact. To say that Saddam's doing it is in total disregard to the fact that if he gets caught he's a dead man and he knows it. Deterrence has been adequate in the absence of inspectors but this is not a situation that can succeed in the long term. *In the long term you have to get inspectors back in.* (Emphasis added)

Ritter essentially confirms the nature of the dilemma (we just don't know) and the related risks and threats. He recommends the return of inspectors as the best hope to disarm Iraq and avoid war. But, like everyone else, Ritter failed to appreciate the coercive diplomatic dilemma associated with demanding the proof of disarmament Saddam was unable or unwilling to provide – the proof of disarmament demanded by UNSCR 1441 was destroyed along with the regime's WMD. Ritter underestimated the powerful role Saddam's mistakes, misperceptions and miscalculations would play (see Chapter 8) in sustaining everyone's suspicions, including Hans Blix's (as he noted in his February 2003 report to the UN):

> During the period of time covered by the present report, Iraq could have made greater efforts to find any remaining proscribed items or provide cred-ible evidence showing the absence of such items. The results in terms of dis-armament have been very limited so far. The destruction of missiles, which is an important operation, has not yet begun. Iraq could have made full use of the declaration, which was submitted on 7 December. It is hard to under-stand why a number of the measures, which are now being taken, could not have been initiated earlier. If they had been taken earlier, they might have borne fruit by now. It is only by the middle of January and thereafter that Iraq has taken a number of steps, which have the potential of resulting either in the presentation for destruction of stocks or items that are proscribed or

---

[9]   See Appendix of Ritter's 1999 book *Endgame* for a list of proscribed weapons he mistakenly believed Saddam retained.

[10]   Calabresi 2002.

the presentation of relevant evidence solving long-standing unresolved disarmament issues.[11]

These lingering suspicions and long list of unresolved disarmament issues itemized in Blix's 'cluster document' have nothing to do with neoconservative or unilateralist distortions. The problem was that it was almost impossible for anyone (including Blix) to prove anything without documentation and evidence. This was the central problem Blix acknowledged in every one of his reports to the UN and it was the prevailing dilemma that drove decision-making throughout this crisis. A few dissenting voices, no matter how committed they were to their views, were competing with an overwhelming consensus that Saddam continued to hide proscribed weapons that needed to be uncovered.

The absence of politically motivated intelligence failures?

The common neoconist accusation that most of the intelligence on Iraq's WMD programs was intentionally (and knowingly) exaggerated for political reasons has not been confirmed by any of the major bipartisan commissions established in the United States and UK to review the case evidence. As head of the Iraq Survey Group, David Kay admitted as much in his January 2004 interim report to Congress: "Let me begin by saying, we were almost all wrong, and I certainly include myself here. It turns out that we were all wrong … and that is most disturbing."[12] With respect to questions about politically motivated intelligence, Kay concluded: "I deeply think that is a wrong explanation." He explained that "innumerable analysts" made these mistakes and he was given no indication by anyone he interviewed that they felt pressure to spin the intelligence. As Kay explains, "Almost in a perverse way, I wish it had been undue influence, because we know how to correct that. The fact that it wasn't tells me that we've got a much more fundamental problem of understanding what went wrong." The very same conclusions appeared in the final report by the bipartisan Senate Select Committee on Intelligence:[13]

> Conclusion 83. The Committee did not find any evidence that Administration officials attempted to coerce, influence or pressure analysts to change their judgments related to Iraq's weapons of mass destruction capabilities.

> Conclusion 84. The Committee found no evidence that the Vice President's visits to the Central Intelligence Agency were attempts to pressure analysts, were perceived as intended to pressure analysts by those who participated in

---

[11] UNMOVIC 2003: 13. See United Nations Monitoring, Verification and Inspection Commission 2003a.
[12] David Kay ISG interim report to Congress – see Kay 2004.
[13] Senate Select Committee on Intelligence on the US 2004: 284–5.

the briefings on Iraq's weapons of mass destruction programs, or did pressure analysts to change their assessments.

The UK's Robb-Silberman Commission concluded:[14]

> These are serious errors. But these errors stem from poor tradecraft and poor management. The Commission found no evidence of political pressure to influence the Intelligence Community's pre-war assessments of Iraq's weapons programs. As we discuss in detail in the body of our report, analysts universally asserted that in no instance did political pressure cause them to skew or alter any of their analytical judgments. We conclude that it was the paucity of intelligence and poor analytical tradecraft, rather than political pressure, that produced the inaccurate pre-war intelligence assessments.

All of these reports revealed structural problems associated with the institutions and organizations responsible for collecting intelligence – the conclusions did not support the view that leaders intentionally distorted intelligence to support a political or ideological agenda. The same general WMD claims were endorsed by both the Clinton and Bush administrations. There is no evidence that Gore or any member of his national security team formed different opinions based on different intelligence estimates. The same dilemma would have applied had Bush or Gore accepted the most benign interpretation of available intelligence, or accepted the views put forward by the most skeptical of intelligence analysts, such as:

- the IAEA's assessment of Iraq's nuclear program;
- Scott Ritter's assessment of the biological threats;
- the Department of Energy's conclusions on aluminum tubes;
- Ambassador Joe Wilson's views on African yellowcakes (uranium);
- the CIA/state department/UK assessment of Iraq–Al-Qaeda linkages.

Even if these conservative estimates are accepted, the president is left with hundreds of other items from dozens of other major reports that provided details of weapons the Iraqi regime failed to account for.

Sixteen words that didn't start a war?

In addition to the three items neoconists typically reference in their minimalist interpretation of intelligence failures during the Bush administration, several critics have also highlighted the dangerous, war-mongering effects of Bush's

---

[14] Robb and Silberman 2005: 50–1.

January 28, 2003 State of the Union address, which included the following six-teen words:[15]

> The British Government has learned that Saddam Hussein recently sought significant quantities of uranium from Africa.

Neoconists continue to cite these sixteen words as if they were singularly respon-sible for persuading the public and Congress to endorse the war. The sentence was so powerful, they argue, that it alone was sufficient to convince legislators that Iraq was on the verge of reconstituting its nuclear weapons program. The irony of relying so heavily on the relevance of these sixteen cherry-picked words is consistently overlooked by these critics – they appear to be guilty of the same crime they ascribe to neoconservatives by using exaggerations and distortions to defend their version of history.

Leaving aside the fact that one of the sixteen words, 'sought', does not mean 'obtained', there are several obvious problems with this common argument. First, the January 2003 speech came almost four months *after* congressional author-ization (October 2002) and the deployment of US and UK troops to the region. And, as the evidence described earlier in this chapter clearly shows, African uranium and aluminum tubes were not referenced by most of those who voted in favor of authorization – the British estimates had no apparent impact on this support. Second, most members of Congress were bright enough to understand that the acquisition of this material constitutes nothing more than a very prelim-inary stage in the process of developing a nuclear weapon, let alone deploying and ultimately launching a nuclear tipped ballistic missile with a range sufficient enough to threaten the United States or its European allies. The nuclear case, even with the UK estimate, was always the weakest part of the overall risk and threat assessments.

Third, news that Saddam "sought" uranium from Africa was not a particu-larly earth-shattering revelation capable of instantly transforming opinions – it was just one more item from a long list of WMD that Saddam may have pos-sessed that was probably disconcerting to some, but benign to others. Even if the nuclear file was the most important issue for some Congress members, the nuclear threat threshold would still vary from person to person. Some in Congress might have been sufficiently threatened by evidence that Saddam was still interested in reconstituting his nuclear program at some future point in time. For others, passing the threshold would require evidence Saddam continued to hide rudimentary parts of his largely dismantled nuclear program – some-thing the Iraq Survey Group confirmed after the war. And some would prefer to support authorization based exclusively on proof that he actually acquired the material and technology or, worse, deployed a nuclear tipped ballistic missile.

---

[15] www.washingtonpost.com/wp-srv/onpolitics/transcripts/bushtext_012803.html.

With these caveats in mind, the emphasis on the 'power' of these sixteen words seems more than a little silly.

Fourth, why would critics assign so much relevance to sixteen words about an *attempt* to purchase uranium that *could be* used in centrifuge programs? Why do these qualified estimates deserve any more recognition for influencing perceptions or determining preferences than the remaining 5,322 words in the same speech? In fact, one did not have to rely on these sixteen words to be concerned about Saddam's WMD or his nuclear intentions. Consider the following examples of statements issued by other influential participants, most of which appeared before Bush's 2003 speech:

> Deploring the fact that Iraq has not provided an accurate, full, final, and complete disclosure, as required by resolution 687 (1991), of all aspects of its programs to develop weapons of mass destruction and ballistic missiles with a range greater than 150 kilometers, and of all holdings of such weapons, their components and production facilities and locations, *as well as all other nuclear programs, including any which it claims are for purposes not related to nuclear-weapons-usable material.* (UNSCR 1441, emphasis added)
>
> The recent inspection find in the private home of a scientist of a box of some 3,000 pages of documents, *much of it relating to the laser enrichment of uranium*[,] support[s] a concern that has long existed that documents might be distributed to the homes of private individuals ... we cannot help but think that the case might not be isolated and that such placements of documents is deliberate to make discovery difficult and to seek to shield documents by placing them in private homes. (Blix 2003c, emphasis added)
>
> The last UN weapons inspectors left Iraq in October of 1998. We are confident that Saddam Hussein retained some stockpiles of chemical and biological weapons, and that he has since embarked on a crash course to build up his chemical and biological warfare capability. Intelligence reports also indicate that he is seeking nuclear weapons, but has not yet achieved nuclear capability. (Robert Byrd, October 2002)[16]
>
> [Saddam] is, as far as we know, actively pursuing nuclear capabilities, though he doesn't have nuclear warheads yet. If he were to acquire nuclear weapons, I think our friends in the region would face greatly increased risks[,] as would we. Saddam might use these weapons as a deterrent while launching attacks against Israel or his other neighbors ... Saddam has been pursing nuclear weapons and we've been living with this risk for over 20 years. He does not have the weapons now as best we can determine. He might have the weapons in a year or two if the control for the highly-enriched uranium and other fissionable materials broke down. I think his best opportunity would have been to go to his friend Slobodan Milosevic and ask for those materials during the time of the Kosovo campaign, since there

---

[16] www.gpoaccess.gov/crecord/index.html.

was active collusion between the Serbs and the Iraqis, but apparently if he asked for them he didn't get them because the Serbs have turned them over for us … If he can't get the highly-enriched uranium, then it might take him five years or more to go through a centrifuge process or gaseous diffusion process to enrich the uranium, but the situation is not stable. The UN weapons inspectors who, however ineffective they might have been and there's some degree of difference of opinion on that, nevertheless provided assistance in impeding his development programs. They've [the UN inspectors] been absent for four years, and the sanction regime designed to restrict his access to weapons materials and resources has been continuously eroded, and therefore the situation is not stable. (General Wesley Clark Testimony – House Armed Services Committee Hearing on US Policy toward Iraq, September 26, 2002)[17]

We know that he is doing everything he can to build nuclear weapons, and we know that each day he gets closer to achieving that goal. (John Edwards, explaining his October 10, 2002 vote to authorize the use of force against Iraq)[18]

There is unmistakable evidence that Saddam Hussein is working aggressively to develop nuclear weapons and will likely have nuclear weapons within the next five years … We also should remember we have always underestimated the progress Saddam has made in development of weapons of mass destruction. (Jay Rockefeller, explaining his October 10, 2002 vote to authorize the use of force against Iraq)[19]

Reports indicate that biological, chemical and nuclear programs continue a pace and may be back to pre-Gulf War status. (Bob Graham, December 5, 2001)[20]

[T]his is a man who has used poison gas on his own people and on his neighbors repeatedly. He's trying to get ballistic missiles, nuclear weapons, chemical and biological weapons. He could be a mass murderer of the first order of magnitude. We are not going to allow that to happen. We are going to win this confrontation. (Vice President Al Gore – ABC News' "Special Report," December 16, 1998)[21]

Consider that Iraq retains more than 7500 nuclear scientists and technicians, as well as technical documents related to the production of nuclear weapons … Consider that Iraq has been caught trying to smuggle in missile guidance instruments. (Madeleine Albright, March 16, 1997)[22]

Clinton's 1998 letter to Congress defending Operation Desert Fox also makes reference to Saddam's *nuclear* ambitions no fewer than eight times in the same

[17] www.drudgereportarchives.com/data/2004/01/15/20040115_165004_mattwc.htm.
[18] www.gpoaccess.gov/crecord/index.html.
[19] www.gpoaccess.gov/crecord/index.html.
[20] Text of a letter to Bush signed by several US Senators quoted in Norman Podhoretz (2007: 154).
[21] www.en.wikiquote.org/wiki/Iraq_and_weapons_of_mass_destruction.
[22] www.fas.org/news/iraq/1997/03/bmd970327b.htm.

letter – an entire section of the letter is devoted to describing the details of intelligence on Saddam's nuclear weapons program.[23] There are dozens of other references to nuclear material and programs included in Appendices 3.1 and 3.2. To suggest that sixteen words from Bush's 2003 State of the Union address were crucial to the outcome simply ignores the thousands of words issued over the previous decade in dozens of other reports. Anyone concerned about Saddam's nuclear programs could ignore Bush's sixteen words (or the entire speech, for that matter) and focus on any of the following:

(1) 85,000 words in Blix's 175-page 'cluster document' outlining all remaining "unresolved disarmament issues," which was published on March 6, 2003 – a few weeks before the war;[24]

(2) 1,408 words in the 2003 summary of Blix's 175-page report published by the Department of State;[25]

(3) 4,926 words from Tony Blair's March 18, 2003 speech to British Parliament before the vote on Iraq;[26]

(4) 5,600 words from Hans Blix's February 2003 UNMOVIC report;[27]

(5) 8,743 words from Hans Blix's January 2003 UNMOVIC report;[28]

(6) 2,083 words from the October 16, 2002 authorization to use military force;[29]

(7) 800 words in Tony Blair's foreword to the 2002 official UK dossier on Iraq's WMD;[30]

(8) 15,660 words from the main 2002 UK dossier on Iraq's WMD;[31]

(9) 2,684 words in UNSCR 1441 (2002), including reference to the need for Iraq to provide "a complete declaration of all aspects of its programmes to develop chemical, biological and nuclear weapons, including chemical, biological and nuclear programmes it claims are for purposes not related to weapons production or material."[32] What follows is a brief, 129-word

---

[23] Clinton 1999a.

[24] United Nations Monitoring, Verification and Inspection Commission 2003b.

[25] US Department of State (Office of the Spokesman) 2003: "This fact sheet carefully reviews UNMOVIC's report (the 'cluster document') delivered on March 7 before the UN Security Council concerning the Iraqi government and its refusal to carry out full and complete disarmament of its weapons of mass destruction." Among the many lessons Gore's state department would have picked up from this is the pattern of deception. This multilaterally endorsed document would constitute more than sufficient proof that Saddam was continuing to deceive inspectors and would have been evidence that any president and cabinet would have confronted.

[26] Blair 2003.

[27] A complete collection of UNMOVIC reports can be found here: www.unmovic.org.

[28] For copies of UNMOVIC's February and March 2003 reports to the UN Security Council, see www.unmovic.org.

[29] *Congressional Record* 2002c.   [30] Government of the United Kingdom 2002.

[31] Government of the United Kingdom 1998.

[32] United Nations Security Council 2002.

summary of Hans Blix's briefing to the UN Security Council on Iraq's declaration:

> During the period 1991–1998, Iraq submitted many declarations called full, final and complete. Regrettably, much in these declarations proved inaccurate or incomplete or was unsupported or contradicted by evidence. In such cases, no confidence can arise that proscribed programmes or items have been eliminated. Such was the situation at the end of 1998 … To these question marks, nearly four years without any inspection activity have been added. In resolution 1441 [2002], Iraq was given an opportunity to provide a fresh declaration and to make it verifiable to the inspecting authorities by submitting supporting evidence … The overall impression is that not much new significant information has been provided in the part of Iraq's Declaration, which relates to proscribed weapons programmes, nor has much new supporting documentation or other evidence been submitted.[33]

(10)　3,312 words from UNSCOM's 1998 Report to the UN *before* the departure of weapons inspectors;[34]

(11)　3,993 words in the UK's 2002 assessment of containment policy and options for dealing with Iraq;[35]

(12)　5,817 words from the 2002 National Intelligence Estimate;[36]

(13)　2,060 words in President Clinton's December 16, 1998 defense of Operation Desert Fox to the Joint Chiefs of Staff;[37]

(14)　And more.[38]

Of particular importance is Hans Blix's 175-page "cluster document" detailing unresolved disarmament issues. No one writing on intelligence errors leading to the Iraq war should do so without reviewing this report. It was sufficiently compelling (and disconcerting) to be cited by Colin Powell in his own UN address as a must read for anyone interested in understanding the nature of the threat. Among the many interesting claims in Blix's compendium was the following 21-word claim: UNMOVIC "cannot discount the possibility that Iraq has developed mobile-production facilities or that it has production equipment at other hidden sites."[39] Colin Powell was obviously not the only official to raise what turned out to be exaggerated concerns about Iraq's mobile labs.

---

[33] For copies of UNMOVIC's February and March 2003 reports to the UN Security Council, see www.unmovic.org.

[34] United Nations Special Commission 1998.

[35] Government of the United Kingdom 2002.

[36] Central Intelligence Agency 2002b.　　[37] Clinton 1998c.

[38] For a complete collection of US and UK government papers and official intelligence reports, statements and documents, see: www.iraqwatch.org/government/Index_US_CIA.htm and www.iraqwatch.org/government/Index_UK.htm. For Australian, German and other European documents, see: www.iraqwatch.org/government.

[39] United Nations Monitoring, Verification and Inspection Commission 2003b.

Overestimating the devastating effects of Bush's sixteen words is not the only exaggeration neoconists are fond of repeating in support of their thesis. Consider the following examples of other exaggerated causal claims.

According to Powers (2007), "without Curveball and without the aluminium tubes, Colin Powell would have been left standing in front of the UN with nothing[.]"[40] Nothing? Powers spends no time working through any of the material included in the above list of documents and reports, and completely ignores the content of a decade of other UN and national intelligence documents. Neoconists consistently underestimate (or ignore) the enormity of the intelligence errors in order to create the impression that only a few exaggerations (e.g., sixteen words) were sufficient to take the country to war.

According to Ambassador Joe Wilson (2004), "uranium was not discussed. It would be a tragedy to think that we went to war over a conversation in which uranium was not discussed because the Niger official was sufficiently sophisticated to think that perhaps he might have wanted to discuss uranium at some later date."[41] It is beyond arrogant for Wilson to believe that he was at the center of the storm – that this single piece of intelligence derived from his one conversation about uranium with a Nigerian official, selected from thousands of other estimates compiled in dozens of intelligence reports over a decade, was essential to the government's case for war.

James Risen's (2006: 110) manuscript is described as "the explosive book on the abuse of power of the Bush administration."[42] In Chapter 5, entitled "Skeptics and Zealots," Risen recounts a conversation between a senior CIA officer and the chief of the Counterproliferation Division of the Directorate of Operations, "the unit within the CIA that was supposed to be in charge of recruiting spies and collecting intelligence on WMD in Iraq and other countries." According to Risen, "the division chief admitted during the conversation that the agency 'didn't have much intelligence on Iraq WMD. There were a lot of people who said we *didn't have enough intelligence*'" (Risen 2006, emphasis added). But Risen misses the central dilemma – without inspectors in Iraq for four years, and Blix's inability to prove Hussein destroyed the weapons he had, the CIA "didn't have enough intelligence" to establish the truth one way or the other. Saddam was unable or unwilling to satisfy the demands laid out in UNSCR 1441 or any other unanimous UN resolution passed since 1991 (see Chapter 8). Critics like Risen look at these admissions as evidence of an absence of intelligence on WMD, but it also confirmed the absence of any proof that Saddam destroyed the weapons – Blix was convinced Hussein could provide such proof if he was willing to do so. These lingering suspicions and the absence of clarity explain the policies that propelled the United States and UK closer to war at each stage. The problem, as Risen (2006: 89) explains, is that, "in the year before the 2003 war, the CIA

---

[40] Powers 2007.   [41] Wilson 2004.   [42] Risen 2006.

had one case officer spying from inside Baghdad." Conspicuously absent from Risen's book are quotes from any intelligence officer who came close to arguing that the entire WMD case was as wrong as it turned out to be – all they could say for sure was that they "didn't have enough intelligence."

Risen (2006: 107) quotes a former Iraqi nuclear scientist, Saad Tawfiq, who claimed to have told US officials that Saddam didn't have weapons: "They didn't listen. I told them there were no weapons." But almost every single Iraqi official was saying the exact same thing at the time. It is not clear why Risen thinks this source is any more crucial than others to make this point. The problem neither Risen or Tawfiq seem to understand is that, despite the absence of WMD, the Iraqi regime did not (or could not) provide the proof demanded by UN officials. In the absence of definitive proof that the weapons listed in Blix's reports had been destroyed, the only plausible interpretation was that, for whatever reasons, Saddam chose to retain proscribed weapons. This was an irresolvable impasse, especially when Saddam initially rejected UN demands for unfettered access to sites and to former scientists. No one at the time believed the truth – that he had nothing – because the intelligence errors were so extensive, entrenched and, for many reasons, inevitable.

Cyclical nature of intelligence failures

Major intelligence errors typically re-emerge from a combination of bureaucratic and organizational pressures designed to fix the last mistake (Barger 2004; Betts 1978, 2002 and 2004; Cooper and Brown 2005; Diamond 2008; Jervis 1986 and 1987; Kissinger 2004).[43] As former CIA Director George Tenet admits, "the remedy for one so-called intelligence failure can help set the stage for another."[44] The failure to imagine new and more serious terrorist threats after the Cold War, or, more specifically, to connect Al-Qaeda to flight schools in Florida, set the stage for 9/11. These lessons, confirmed in the bipartisan 9/11 Commission report, encouraged government officials, intelligence communities and Congress to err on the side of 'imagining' (*overestimating*) the next security threats, including those coming from Iraq. Research on the phenomenon of loss aversion and prospect theory provide useful insights on these problems (Kahneman and Tversky 1979 and 1992; Kahneman *et al.* 1982; Tetlock and Mellers 2002).[45] We tend to exaggerate probabilities associated with threats (and risk) we perceive as unfamiliar and uncontrollable (e.g., terrorism), and typically underestimate the risks and probabilities of familiar threats we believe we can control (e.g.,

---

[43] For an excellent treatment of the cyclical nature of intelligence failures, see Betts (1978). See also Knorr 1983.
[44] Tenet 2007: 332.
[45] Kahneman and Tversky 1979 and 1992; Kahneman *et al.* 1982; Tetlock and Mellers 2002.

driving without a seat belt; drinking; gambling). Humans are notoriously bad at correctly estimating risks and probabilities.

Even the most conservative (minimalist) interpretation of intelligence on Iraq's WMD would lead to the same conclusions: Saddam did not account for a large portion of his chemical and biological weapons program. There was virtually unanimous consensus on this point. The main question framing the entire WMD dilemma was this: why would Saddam spend so much time and effort challenging the United Nations Special Commission (UNSCOM), and then the United Nations Monitoring, Verification and Inspection Commission (UNMOVIC), if he had absolutely nothing to hide?

Overestimating a threat is a logical reaction to underestimating the previous threat, and recommendations from the 9/11 Commission to deal with the 'failure of imagination' involved institutionalizing the imagination of failure – to make it the job of governments to err on the side of over-interpreting, not underestimating, threats. And both parties understood the post-9/11 challenge of gaining political points for their commitment to public security. This also explains why Democrats shifted to the right on security matters, as revealed by their statements in Appendices 2.1, 3.1 and 3.2.

Dueling National Intelligence Estimates

The 2001 National Intelligence Estimate (NIE) on Iraq's WMD was peppered with the following caveats: Iraq "*probably* continued at least low-level theoretical R&D on nuclear weapons technologies," "Baghdad *may* be attempting to acquire materials that could aid in reconstructing its nuclear weapons program" and "We are concerned that Iraq *may* again be producing biological warfare agents."[46] Many of these qualifiers were deleted in the updated 2002 NIE: Iraq "has chemical and biological warfare agents" and is "reconstituting its nuclear program;" "all key aspects (research & development, production, weaponization) of Iraq's offensive biological weapons program are active and most elements are larger and more advanced than they were before the gulf war."[47] Senior intelligence officials offer the following defense of the updated 2002 report:

> Contrary to popular misconceptions, the NIE also gives full voice to those agencies that wanted to express alternative views. Dissenting opinions are not relegated to footnotes and, indeed, often appear in boxes with special

[46] Central Intelligence Agency 2002a. According to Ivo H. Daalder and James M. Lindsay, "with respect to chemical weapons, the Defense Intelligence Agency concluded even as late as September 2002 that 'there is no reliable information on whether Iraq is producing and stockpiling chemical weapons, or where Iraq has – or will – establish its chemical warfare agent production facilities.'" See Daalder and Lindsay 2003. www.tpmcafe.talkingpoints-memo.com/2005/10/26/excerpt_america_unbound.

[47] www.fas.org/irp/congress/2003_cr/h072103.html.

coloured background to make them stand out. These make up an unprecedented 16 pages of the ninety-page NIE.[48]

CIA Director Tenet (2007: 330) readily admits now that the "nuance was lost" in the five-page summary of key findings, and he goes on to point out that very few decision-makers actually read the entire ninety-page report. The Democrats and Republicans who voted to authorize the use of force had made up their minds long before the publication of a five-page summary attached to an updated NIE; the many speeches they delivered in previous years confirm this important point. Tenet goes on to note that "the judgements [the CIA] delivered in the NIE on Iraq's chemical, biological and nuclear weapons program were consistent with the ones we had given to the Clinton administration."[49] Further, he states that:

> The absence of evidence and linear thinking, and Iraq's extensive efforts to conceal illicit procurement of proscribed components, told us that a deceptive regime could and would easily surprise us. It was never a question of a known imminent threat; it was about an unwillingness to risk surprise ... In many ways we were prisoners of our own history.[50]

The clear consensus, with or without the caveats in the five-page NIE summary, was more than sufficient to raise serious security concerns after 9/11. The larger case did not depend entirely on the CIA's NIE but also on the Pentagon's intelligence estimates, the DCI-chaired National Foreign Intelligence Board, the Defense Intelligence Agency, the Department of State's Bureau of Intelligence and Research (INR), the National Security Agency, the Department of Energy, the National Imagery and Mapping Agency, and *every* UK and UN report from UNSCOM and UNMOVIC over the previous decade.

Anyone looking for reasons to be worried about Iraq could easily ignore speeches by Bush, Cheney or Rumsfeld and focus instead on those delivered by Clinton (Bill or Hillary), Gore and Kerry; they could ignore the 2002 NIE and read intelligence reports published over the previous ten years; or they could simply read the reports by UNMOVIC's chief weapons inspector, Hans Blix, or UNSCOM's inspector, Scott Ritter (one of the war's strongest critics) – please see Appendix 7.1 for relevant quotes.

With all of this in mind, a decision by President Bush (or Gore) to extend inspections by a few more weeks (or even months) could not have resolved the perceived problem. Remember, it took two years for the Iraq Survey Group (ISG), with the benefit of unfettered access to the entire country, to produce its final report. Obviously the ISG uncovered no evidence of WMD stockpiles,

---

[48] Tenet 2007: 327. As Daalder and Lindsay (2003: 156) point out, "these footnotes, of course, were not technical asides. They represented fundamental judgements, by the most qualified people, about the nature of the threat facing the nation and thus about whether war, especially preventive war, would be a justifiable response."
[49] Tenet 2007: 330.   [50] Tenet 2007: 329–30.

but they did find information and material, intentionally hidden by the regime, that would have constituted 'material breach' if uncovered by UNMOVIC. This would have been the worst possible combination of facts and assumptions: a prevailing WMD consensus, ongoing suspicions reinforced by years of non-compliance, additional evidence of material breach, and a strong UNSC resolution (1441) threatening 'serious consequences.' The problem, again, was that the international community was demanding evidence Saddam either could not or would not provide.

Most reasonably informed neoconists will concede that the 2002 NIE reflected doubts within the intelligence community about the interpretation and reliability of the evidence for Iraqi WMD programs. The problem, they argue, is that the relevant portions of the NIE that were declassified and released to the public omitted those doubts. However, we also know that congressional leaders, particularly those on key intelligence and foreign affairs committees, had complete access to the full report. Many of these caveats and qualifiers were explicitly noted in congressional speeches surrounding the authorization vote – the doubts about the WMD case were well debated. Notwithstanding these caveats, however, the WMD case was sufficiently worrisome to generate strong support in favor of authorization.

Consider the statements by Senator Rockefeller, Vice Chair of the Senate Intelligence Committee and the leading Democratic voice on intelligence matters. When defending his vote to support the October resolution, Rockefeller issued the following statement:

> September 11 changed America. It made us realize we must deal differently with the very real threat of terrorism, whether it comes from shadowy groups operating in the mountains of Afghanistan or in 70 other countries around the world, including our own.
>
> There has been some debate over how "imminent" a threat Iraq poses. I do believe that Iraq poses an imminent threat, but I also believe that after September 11, that question is increasingly outdated.
>
> It is in the nature of these weapons that he has[,] and the way they are targeted against civilian populations, that documented capability and demonstrated intent may be the only warning we get. To insist on further evidence could put some of our fellow Americans at risk. Can we afford to take that chance? I do not think we can.

Of course, like many Democrats (and Republicans) at the time, Rockefeller changed his position after the war:

> [Iraq] had nothing to do with Osama bin Laden, it had nothing to do with al-Qaida, it had nothing to do with September 11, which [the president] managed to mention three or four times and infer three or four more times … It's sort of amazing that a president could stand up before hundreds of millions of Americans and say that and come back to 9/11 – somehow

figuring that it clicks a button, that everybody grows more patriotic and more patient. Well, maybe that's good p.r. work, which it isn't, but it's not the way that a commander in chief executes a war. And that's his responsibility in this case.[51]

Despite Rockefeller's revised 2005 position, his 2002 speech clearly expressed concerns about the general link between 9/11, globalized terrorism, Saddam's support to terrorist organizations, and the WMD–terrorism nexus; all were common themes embedded in many of the speeches delivered in support of authorization. The tendency for politicians to distance themselves from these statements is not surprising, but these transformations should have absolutely no bearing on the evidence required for evaluating competing counterfactuals.

Neoconists are also likely to argue that the doubts included in the 2001 CIA report were absent from the 2002 NIE due to intense pressure on the CIA from White House officials (particularly Cheney) who made repeated visits to CIA headquarters to harangue analysts to produce results that would support war. Such highly unusual and improper pressure, they will argue, would not have occurred in a Gore administration – an NIE produced in a Gore administration would likely have better reflected the professional judgment of intelligence analysts, not the political imperatives of justifying a war. But these observations are logically consistent with the counterfactual argument being defended throughout this book. The UN-based, congressionally endorsed multilateral policy recommended by Gore in 2002 was firmly rooted in his rejection of the imminent threat claims. As explained in Chapters 2 and 3, that level of threat was obviously not required for the policies endorsed by Congress and the path ultimately selected by Bush, Blair and Powell. The intelligence reports on Iraq's WMD produced during the Clinton administration (without distortions by neoconservatives and unilateralists) were more than sufficient to justify the 98–0 vote in the Senate in favor of the Iraq Liberation Act, as well as the 1998 Iraq bombing campaign. The intelligence estimates Gore would have accepted, based on the professional judgements of unpressured intelligence officials (the application of such pressure was also proven after the war to be largely inaccurate) would have been sufficient to begin the same path-dependent series of decisions to reinvigorate coercive inspections that were responsible for pushing the country closer to war. It is also very likely that Gore would have retained the same CIA director – if George W. Bush kept George Tenet, why wouldn't Gore, Holbrooke and Lieberman? The argument here is not that these estimates alone would have been sufficient to take us directly to war; the point is that the generally accepted estimates would, nevertheless, have justified the series of rational decisions that, when combined, made war more likely.

[51] Hayes 2005.

Summary: comparative plausibility as a determinant of WMD consensus

For American and British officials, the debate over Iraq's WMD was never about whether the intelligence definitively established the presence or absence of stockpiles of WMD – it was always about which one of the following two arguments was more convincing based on generally accepted intelligence at the time: (1) Saddam's regime *did not* use the billions of dollars he siphoned from a corrupt oil-for-food program to continue to develop his WMD program during the four-year absence of inspectors from 1998 to 2002, and did not retain *any* of the weapons listed in Hans Blix's reports to the United Nations; or (2) that Saddam *did* retain the proscribed weapons cited in every UN resolution and report since 1991, and continued in the absence of UN inspectors to spend billions to develop (and hide) a range of WMD programs that threatened the US and its allies. Every member of the UN Security Council (including the war's strongest critics, France, Russia and China) unanimously endorsed the second interpretation when they passed UNSCR 1441 in November 2002. No American politician at the time came close to defending the first argument.

Given the choice, the more plausible interpretation of accepted intelligence will always be the one exploited by political officials, which explains the bipartisan consensus on Iraq's WMD. It just made more sense in light of the entire record since 1991. As Tenet explains:

> To conclude that Saddam was not pursuing WMD in 2002 our analysis would have had to ignore years and years of intelligence that pointed in the direction of active programs and continuing evidence of aggressive attempts on Iraq's part to conceal its activities ... In retrospect we got it wrong partly because the truth was so implausible ... *We had no previous experience with a country that did not possess such weapons but pretended that it did.* (Emphasis added)[52]

Accepting the more plausible interpretation created the most appealing political strategy. These same plausible interpretations of intelligence were also included in *all* UNSCRs – including UNSCR 1441, which declared Iraq in material breach – and they were present in all other intelligence reports discussed earlier. Policy on Iraq was guided by this general interpretation.

"Failure of imagination," take II

Much like the 9/11 error, the main problem before the Iraq war was a 'failure of imagination.' The possibility that Saddam was actually bluffing (or, as it turned out, intentionally recreating the illusion of his WMD program to deter Iran – see

---

[52] Tenet 2007: 331.

Chapter 8) was never considered, because it was simply too far-fetched to assume he would be so reckless. Paradoxically, the US and UK decision not to underestimate their opponent (by assuming he could not possibly be this foolish) is usually the most prudent strategy: 'never underestimate your enemy.' In this case, however, the more prudent assumptions regarding Saddam's 'rationality' turned out to be a serious error.

These mistaken assessments were not fabricated to further some warped neoconservative agenda, they were shared by Al Gore and his key advisers, and by every leading Democratic senator at the time that served on prominent intelligence and foreign affairs committees. In hindsight, the failure to re-interpret Saddam's behavior was a serious mistake, but there is no evidence any of these individuals ever contemplated the possibility the intelligence was so completely wrong. The WMD threat would have been exploited by Gore for the same post-9/11 security maximizing reasons: defending the 'obvious' interpretation was the only winnable political strategy. There was no alternative *Gore-peace* interpretation of intelligence that would have produced a strategy so fundamentally different from the one Gore and his team outlined in 2002. Nor was there a different course of action that would have provided the same political returns without incurring the same or greater political costs. Clinton and Gore calculated the costs and benefits of alternatives in 1998 and arrived at the identical conclusions prior to Operation Desert Fox, when *they* were responsible for misinterpreting Saddam's intentions and miscalculating the scope of the WMD threat.

There were consistent signals that reinforced the plausibility of the accepted intelligence. The initial letter from Foreign Minister Sabi rejecting the new UN resolution created more suspicions. And, in hindsight, the following statement by Aziz was obviously a mistake, because it reinforced the US–UK assumption that inspections were unacceptable to a regime retaining proscribed weapons:

> This proposal of the United States [for a new Security Council resolution] is unacceptable ... The standing resolutions of the Security Council concerning the inspections are valid and they are enough for the perfect performance by the inspectors of their job ... Only the United States is unhappy [with the outcome of the Vienna discussions] because ... [they] are afraid that when the inspectors come to Iraq, in the end they will tell the world that Iraq doesn't have any weapons of mass destruction. (October 2, 2002)[53]

The more plausible WMD case was not only reinforced by speeches from Iraqi officials – it was directly connected to the ongoing deception uncovered by UNMOVIC, suspicions formed over the previous ten years, and the absence of inspectors since 1998. Every time Saddam refused to comply with any UN requirements, these suspicions were reinforced. But the later in the crisis this

---

[53] Acronym Institute 2002.

happened, the more worrisome Saddam's challenges became, because they raised the question of why he would be doing this if he had nothing to hide. The closer to war, the less rational Saddam's strategy would have become, and the less plausible the view that he was doing this without having any weapons. The more convinced the US–UK became that their threats were clear and credible, the more suspicious Saddam's refusal to cooperate. The truth – that he had nothing – became increasingly more difficult to defend even for those who had strong doubts about the WMD threat. *The reality of WMD became less important than the relative plausibility of competing accounts of Saddam's behavior.* Paradoxically, the more inaccurate the WMD intelligence, the more suspicion was raised when full, complete and unconditional compliance was not forthcoming, because it made the truth (that he had nothing) so implausible.

The same view was fully endorsed by Tony Blair in his final speech to the British parliament before receiving authorization – he called the alternative interpretation "palpably absurd."[54] As Richard Betts (2007: 606) explains, "the fact of being wrong is not in itself evidence of mistakes that could have been avoided or that show dereliction." Russell (2004: 147) concurs with Betts' analysis:

> The language used to describe intelligence estimates as objective reflections of available evidence has led in some cases to a misunderstanding of the role of intelligence in supporting the decision to go to war in Iraq. Saying that the estimate that identified the threats was either "right" or "wrong" ignores the probabilistic nature of intelligence assessments and the necessary subjective elements that make them useful to policymakers. By making this clear in the case of Iraq, we can separate the crucial question of how policy should be decided in the face of increased uncertainty and even more elusive enemies than have been faced in the past. Only then does it make sense to say how intelligence can be made more useful, leaving behind the misguided question of whether the intelligence community was right or wrong on Iraq.

The fact remains that some estimates and conclusions were simply more plausible (probable) than alternatives, and the more plausible case typically gets the most attention and support. The serious threat interpretation of Iraqi intelligence was always likely to be so much stronger than any of the views put forward by skeptics. As predicted, the intelligence errors associated with Iraq can be linked to attempts to fix the intelligence errors that led to 9/11 – the "failure of imagination" in assessing the threat from Al-Qaeda resulted in an overestimation of the threat derived from Saddam's WMD.

[54] www.guardian.co.uk/politics/2003/mar/18/foreignpolicy.iraq1.

Plausibility, consensus and common decision pathologies

Studies on intelligence failures in Iraq (as distinct from neoconists' work on intelligence distortions) consistently discuss the effects of a number of psychological pathologies, all of which explain the consensus emerging from the more plausible arguments and estimates (Betts 2007; Fukuyama 2003; Jervis 2006; Phythian 2006; Pollack 2004; Russell 2004; Tenet 2007).[55] These findings are supported by other major reports on intelligence errors in Iraq.[56] Among the patterned errors revealed in these works, the following encompass a sample of the decision pathologies relevant to explaining the Iraq case: groupthink and politically motivated conformity; over-learning from previous cases; using inappropriate analogies of the past to interpret present circumstances; absence of human intelligence on the ground to revise outdated estimates; worst-case-scenario misinterpretations of communications between Iraqi officials; a failure of imagination to appreciate Saddam's real security interests and intentions; overvaluing the relevance of a single source; cognitive closure, bolstering and motivational errors; analytical problems tied to assumption-driven intelligence; absence of devil's advocate or red team; and so on. In his review of the major reports on intelligence failures after the war, Jervis (2006: 14) points out:

> The reports are clearly correct to note that many of the IC's [intelligence community] judgments were stated with excessive certainty: while the preponderance of evidence indicated that Iraq had WMD, it was not sufficient to prove it beyond reasonable doubt. In effect, the IC should have said that the evidence was good enough to convict Saddam in a civil suit, but not in criminal prosecution.

Two points should be noted. First, all available intelligence estimates, even those that included caveats and qualifiers, were more than sufficient to support the policy of getting inspectors back into Iraq with a strong mandate and an explicit military threat. Second, consider the dilemma facing the United States and UK in the context of having enough evidence for a civil suit – the case against Saddam became stronger as time went on, following additional deceptions uncovered by UNMOVIC. Wouldn't anyone in a civil trial do their best to

---

[55] Betts 2007; Fukuyama 2003; Jervis 2006; Phythian 2006; Pollack 2004; Robb and Silberman 2005; Russell 2004; Senate Select Committee on Intelligence on the US 2004; Tenet 2007; Review of Intelligence on Weapons of Mass Destruction (Report of a Committee of Privy Councilors to the House of Commons – the Butler Report). See www.archive2.official-documents.co.uk/document/deps/hc/hc898/898.pdf.

[56] See Senate Select Committee on Intelligence on the US 2004; Review of Intelligence on Weapons of Mass Destruction (Report of a Committee of Privy Councilors to the House of Commons – the Butler Report) (see www.archive2.official-documents.co.uk/document/deps/hc/hc898/898.pdf); Robb and Silberman 2005. www.globalsecurity.org/intell/library/reports/2005/wmd_report_31mar2005.pdf.

provide the judge and jury with every piece of available evidence they needed to establish their innocence? Why would Saddam, in the context of a civil trial, continue to raise suspicions? There is no question from Blix's reports that Saddam failed (or refused) to do this. When one considers the stakes, the only reasonable interpretations were these: (1) Saddam was completely misreading US and UK intentions and did not believe they were serious about invading, or (2) he was hiding something. Most people believed (2), because the alternative miscalculation by Saddam was so unlikely.

Jervis does acknowledge that in some cases there were correctives to specific errors – like the reliance on a single informant (Curveball), or the mistaken belief that aluminum tubes were meant for a nuclear program. But inspectors were unable to interview senior leadership, and even if they were, it was not likely they would have provided the same information the Iraq Survey Group was able to uncover through months of interrogation after the war. Jervis highlights the problems:

> [N]o general alternative explanations for Saddam's behavior were offered. There were no "Red Teams" to attack the prevailing views; no analyses commissioned from Devil's Advocates; no papers that weighed competing possibilities ... Most strikingly, no one proposed a view close to that we now believe to be true [except for Kucinich]. This was a serious failure, but one that needs to be placed in context. No observers outside the government, including opponents of the war, proposed serious alternatives, and no one, including analysts in the Arab world, provided a description of Saddam's motives and behavior that was close to what we now think is correct. There is no reason to think that any alternative would have been seen as highly credible had it been proposed, and indeed it is hard to argue that any alternative fit the available evidence better than the prevailing one. (2006: 15–16)

These are points neoconists consistently ignore in their accounts of the Iraq war. The dilemma facing US and UK decision-makers at the time is obvious today – the only way to get the evidence required to begin to formulate this alternative hypothesis was to compile the information from documents and interviews that only became available after the war. In other words, the plausibility of the alternative hypothesis was a prerequisite for crafting the alternative, *Gore-peace* path. Again, the problem was not unlike the *failure of imagination* that explains 9/11, but in this case it was not the failure to imagine the enormity of the threat or the possibility of flying a plane into buildings. Regarding Iraq, it was a failure to imagine that Saddam could be so reckless, or that all of our intelligence was wrong. With respect to comparative plausibility, Jervis (2006: 42) sums up the dilemma:

> The fundamental reason for the intelligence failures in Iraq was that the assumptions and inferences were reasonable, much more so than the alternatives. This is recognized by the WMD Commission and the Butler Report,

although they shy away from the full implications. Saddam had vigorously pursued WMD in the past (and had used chemical weapons to good effect), had major incentives to rebuild his programs, had funds, skilled technicians, and a good procurement network at his disposal, and had no other apparent reason to deceive and hinder the inspectors. In fact, even if there had been no errors in analytic tradecraft I believe that the best-supported conclusion was that Saddam was actively pursuing all kinds of WMD, and probably had some on hand. The judgment should have been expressed with much less certainty, the limitations on direct evidence should have been stressed, and the grounds for reaching the assessments should have been explicated. But while it would be nice to believe that better analysis would have led to a fundamentally different conclusion, I do not think this is the case … If before the war someone had produced the post-war Duelfer Report, I am sure that she would have been praised for her imagination, but would not have come close to persuading. Even now, the report is hard to believe. To take one example, who would have believed that the reason why Saddam's scientists would not account for much of the missing anthrax was that they feared his anger if he learned that they had dumped it near one of his palaces? Did it make any sense that "by late 2002 Saddam had persuaded himself … that the United States would not attack Iraq because it already had achieved its objectives of establishing a military presence in the region"?

Jervis (2006: 1, 44–5, 46) arrives at the following conclusions:

Confirmation bias was rampant, alternative hypotheses were not tested, and negative evidence was ignored. Although the opportunities to do better are many, the prospects for adequate reform are dim … Being strongly influenced by plausibility can be criticized as being closed-minded or assumption-driven. But this is a powerful and legitimate habit of the mind, necessary for making sense of a complex and contradictory world, and it is responsible for many correct as well as incorrect inferences … Despite the many errors, most of the IC's general conclusions, although wrong, *were reasonable*. Indeed the Flood Report "acknowledges that it is doubtful that better process would have changed the fundamental judgments about the existence of WMD". (Emphasis added)

Assuming a rigorous analytical approach was taken to provide a more balanced interpretation of the intelligence, it may have been possible to push marginal items (Al-Qaeda links and aluminum tubes) to the side, but the revised estimates would not have had a major effect on the direction of policy. Despite Jervis' excellent discussion of intelligence failures, he still believes Gore would not have gone to war, a counterfactual conclusion that does not flow from his analysis. Jervis provides no evidence beyond his simple counterfactual assertion to explain how and why the structural impediments plaguing the Bush (and Clinton) administration(s) would have been corrected by Gore's team.

Comparative plausibility: interpreting communications between Iraqi officials

After the war, Kevin M. Woods, James R. Lacey and Williamson Murray (2006b) produced a comprehensive report on the Iraqi regime's thinking about US–UK pre-war actions.[57] The report's findings are addressed in more detail in Chapter 8, but they are useful here to gain a better understanding of how US and UK (and UN) suspicions were informed by Saddam's misperceptions, and vice versa. The Joint Forces Command team that conducted the Iraqi Perspectives Project interviewed over 100 Iraqi military and political leaders and reviewed hundreds of thousands of Iraqi documents recovered after the invasion. The findings reveal how seriously flawed assumptions based on poor intelligence (and wishful thinking) fueled a set of misperceptions on the Iraqi side that, in turn, reinforced the intelligence assumptions Washington and London used when measuring Iraqi compliance. These mutually reinforcing strategic errors explain, for example, why US and UK officials misinterpreted the exchange between Iraqi officials regarding anthrax:

> *Ironically, it now appears that some of the actions resulting from Saddam's new policy of cooperation actually helped solidify the coalition's case for war.* Over the years, Western intelligence services had obtained many internal Iraqi communications, among them a 1996 memorandum from the director of the Iraqi Intelligence Service directing all subordinates to *"insure that there is no equipment, materials, research, studies, or books related to manufacturing of the prohibited weapons (chemical, biological, nuclear, and missiles) in your site"*. And when UN inspectors went to these research and storage locations, they inevitably discovered lingering evidence of WMD-related programs. (Emphasis added)
>
> In 2002, therefore, when the United States intercepted a message between two Iraqi Republican Guard Corps commanders discussing the removal of the words "nerve agents" from "the wireless instructions," or learned of instructions to "search the area surrounding the headquarters camp and [the unit] for any chemical agents, make sure the area is free of chemical containers, and write a report on it," *US analysts viewed this information through the prism of a decade of prior deceit. They had no way of knowing that this time the information reflected the regime's attempt to ensure it was in compliance with UN resolutions. What was meant to prevent suspicion thus ended up heightening it.* The tidbit about removing the term "nerve agents" from radio instructions was prominently cited as an example of Iraqi bad faith by US Secretary of State Colin Powell in his February 5, 2003, statement to the UN. (Emphasis added)
>
> *Powell's UN Statement*: Just a few weeks ago, we intercepted communications between two commanders in Iraq's Second Republican Guard Corps.

---

[57] Woods *et al.* 2006b. The far more comprehensive final report can be found here: Woods *et al.* 2006a.

One commander is going to be giving an instruction to the other. You will hear as this unfolds that what he wants to communicate to the other guy, he wants to make sure the other guy hears clearly, to the point of repeating it so that it gets written down and completely understood. Listen. Let's review a few selected items of this conversation. Two officers talking to each other on the radio want to make sure that nothing is misunderstood: "Remove. Remove. The expression, the expression, I got it." "Nerve agents. Nerve agents. Wherever it comes up." "Got it." "Wherever it comes up." "In the wireless instructions, in the instructions." "Correction. No. In the wireless instructions." "Wireless. I got it." Why does he repeat it that way? Why is he so forceful in making sure this is understood? And why did he focus on wireless instructions? Because the senior officer is concerned that somebody might be listening. Well, somebody was. "Nerve agents. Stop talking about it. They are listening to us. Don't give any evidence that we have these horrible agents." Well, we know that they do. And this kind of conversation confirms it.

Powell was not the only one who believed these exchanges 'confirmed it.' There was very little ammunition available for skeptics to make the other case – no compelling evidence, in other words, to defend the truth about these exchanges. Like the larger WMD dilemma, the interpretation of this exchange comes down to a question of comparative plausibility. Just imagine, for the sake of illustrating the point, two US intelligence officers briefing senior White House or congressional staff after 9/11 on the meaning of these communications: one claiming they confirm the same behavior consistent with the kind of deceptions the regime had engaged in for years, the other officer recommending a much higher standard for rendering judgements about this intelligence and concluding the communications were more benign, revealing a clear commitment by Iraqi officials to disarm in line with UNSCR 1441. Given the choice, which of the two interpretations are likely to be accepted by political officials concerned about their security credentials in a post-9/11 world and facing the recommendations from the 9/11 Commission report regarding the failure of imagination and the costs of underestimating threats?

Conclusions: *Gore-war* versus *Gore-peace* revisited

Gore's team of advisers would almost certainly have succumbed to the same structural impediments to accurate WMD intelligence that plagued both the Clinton and Bush administrations. They would have included in their calculations the political costs to US credibility of issuing all previous threats and backing off at the last minute – the costs to US influence in the region (after acquiring tacit support from other regional players), the costs to American influence in Europe (after receiving support from most European powers), and the political costs approaching the first post-9/11 mid-term (2002) and US presidential (2004) campaigns and elections. It is reasonable to expect that these advisers would have looked at the costs to US interests more generally and the effects this diplomatic defeat would have had on containment, sanctions and inspections. Perhaps the most important costs were those associated with sustaining the status quo, at the end of the crisis, when the president was asked by France to continue the deployment of a few hundred thousand troops in the region but without an explicit military threat or timeline tied to a second resolution. Finally, Gore's team would also have considered the costs to the reputation of the United States and resolve as these relate to other, potential crises with aspiring nuclear states (Iran, Libya, North Korea). Recall that the central problem confounding Washington's capacity to deter (and compel) both Saddam and Milosevic was their assumption that casualty aversion virtually guarantees a reluctant administration prone to avoiding war and the loss of US troops. This perception would have been reinforced had US and UK leaders conceded to France's demands.

Bill Clinton sums up the case for going back to the UN in 2002 with a strong defense of the administration's WMD case, derived from intelligence gathered in 1998 during the Clinton–Gore administration:

> When I left office, there was a substantial amount of biological and chemical material unaccounted for. That is, at the end of the first Gulf War, we knew what he had. We knew what was destroyed in all the inspection processes and that was a lot. And then we bombed with the British for four days in 1998. We might have gotten it all; we might have gotten half of it; we might have gotten none of it. But we didn't know. So I thought it was prudent for the president to go to the UN and for the UN to say you got to let these inspectors in, and this time if you don't cooperate the penalty could be regime change, not just continued sanctions. (July 22, 2003)[58]

There is no reason to believe Gore's team would have formed a different set of impressions, as they repeatedly made clear in their own statements on WMD. It is important to note that Gore was once a serious WMD skeptic – in 1991 he challenged Bush senior's estimates on Iraq's WMD and was convinced that the case for Iraq possessing an advanced nuclear program was largely unsubstantiated.[59] Gore was wrong in 1991. In fact, the biggest intelligence error revealed in the first years of the Clinton administration was that the United States had seriously underestimated the advanced nature of Iraq's nuclear program. As Gordon and Trainor (2006: 131) point out: "For years, the intelligence agencies had been assailed for failing to anticipate threats, from nuclear tests by India and Pakistan to the Al-Qaeda attacks on the United States (many of them). There was a powerful incentive to make sure that they were not caught short again."[60] As one would expect after these errors, Gore changed his position in every speech he delivered on Iraq throughout the remainder of his political career,

---

[58] Quoted in Kagan and Kristol 2003.
[59] Kengor 1997. See pp. 16–18 for Gore's evolving views on Iraq and Saddam Hussein.
[60] Gordon and Trainor 2006.

firmly defending the general consensus that Saddam's WMD programs posed a serious threat to the United States and its allies. The costs of underestimating intelligence on Iraq's WMD in 2003, again, would have been compounded by the 9/11 attacks.

Gore's decision in 2002 to support the president's policy, precisely because it rejected the neocons' alternative, would have been regarded by President Gore as the only winning political strategy, with very high prospects of receiving public and bipartisan political support. The purpose here is not to present a definitive account of exactly what Gore would have done, but to compare the relative strengths of two alternative counterfactual claims. But any alternative path would have to be defended with reference to the facts. The historical record of intelligence consensus over the past decade, and the views expressed by Gore and his advisers, strongly supports the *Gore-war* counterfactual. Unless we can demonstrate that intelligence failures did not apply to Gore or his advisers, or provide some theory for why Gore would have resolved these structural deficiencies, or explain why Gore would have raised serious questions about the WMD consensus, then it is difficult to support *Gore-peace*.

In the final analysis, however, the plausibility of the *Gore-war* counterfactual does rest on the guiding assumption that another major intelligence failure, the one leading to the 9/11 attacks, also occurred (or was inevitable). This is an important point, because many of the pressures that arguably compelled Bush to follow the path he did would have been less likely without the security imperatives produced by the 9/11 attacks. If the attacks did not take place, the path-dependent momentum toward war would have been largely absent. But those who raise this point are making a pretty significant concession that if 9/11 *did* occur under a Gore presidency, it is entirely conceivable his team would have seen the wisdom in returning inspectors and the logic of other moves in the path to war. Ideology, once again, would have been irrelevant.

In any case, the extent to which the 9/11 attacks influenced the decisions and strategy raises legitimate questions worthy of another carefully constructed counterfactual analysis. It is beyond the scope of this exercise to produce another book exploring both sides of this debate, but, with respect to Gore's ability to prevent 9/11, it is useful to consider Richard A. Clarke's (2004) skepticism. In both his testimony to the 9/11 Commission and his memoirs, the former White House adviser on security and counterterrorism laid the blame for 9/11 squarely on both the Clinton *and* Bush administrations.[61] Clarke provides no evidence in the book suggesting that Al Gore, unlike other members of Clinton's national security team, shared the author's concerns about key security gaps. And, as explained in more detail in Chapter 6, there is no evidence from Gore's formal recommendations as chair of Clinton's White House Commission on Aviation Safety and Security that hint of any serious commitment to address the

---

[61] Clarke 2004.

type of terrorist threats associated with the failures surrounding 9/11.[62] Gore's reports did not include recommendations to prevent passengers from carrying box-cutters onto the flight or prohibiting flight schools from training students to fly but not land passenger jets. Experiencing security failures is a prerequisite for identifying where the most serious security gaps are. Gore did *not* prioritize counterterrorism in any of his campaign speeches and provided no indication whatsoever that a major overhaul of the CIA or intelligence gathering procedures was a priority for his administration.

Of course, it is possible that an administration willing to take the CIA's warnings in the summer of 2001 more seriously might have succeeded in preventing the attacks, but the question then is whether a Gore administration would have been inclined to do so – and what evidence would we need to confirm or disconfirm that assertion? With respect to relevant evidence, for example, it's important to recall the following facts: (1) Clinton's national security adviser, Sandy Berger, refused on several occasions to follow through on actionable intelligence from the CIA regarding bin Laden's whereabouts because of concerns about civilian casualties; (2) Bush retained Clinton's CIA director, George Tenet, so the probability was quite high that Gore would have extended Tenet's term (and accepted the CIA director's pre-9/11 approach to counterterrorism and post-9/11 impressions of Iraq's WMD); (3) 9/11 hijackers attacked New York, a city with a very large Democratic support base, suggesting that Al-Qaeda did not differentiate between Democrats and Republicans when planning the 9/11 attacks; (4) the planning for 9/11 was well underway prior to the Bush administration, and many of the key organizational problems identified by the 9/11 Commission were structural impediments that would have remained in a Gore administration – after all, it was the *Democratic* chair of the Senate Intelligence Committee, Bob Graham (D-FL), who acknowledged the structural (and bipartisan) errors prior to 9/11:[63]

> [U]nfortunately because the information was not placed in the right hands or was distributed to too many places, there wasn't a single point of contact for analysis and reporting of what was going on … We failed to put the puzzle together before the horrific event.

It is entirely conceivable (indeed highly probable) that the 2003 Iraq war would not have happened in either a Bush or Gore administration had the 9/11 attacks been prevented, but neoconists are unlikely to concede the point that, in the context of 9/11, Gore's team would have been more inclined to make the same decisions on the path to war.

---

[62] White House Commission on Aviation Safety and Security Final Report to President Clinton. Submitted by Vice President Al Gore, Chairman, February 12, 1997, www.fas.org/irp/threat/212fin~1.html.

[63] Quoted in Vasquez 2003.

6

Societal pressures and public opinion

The preceding four chapters have outlined the leadership, domestic political and organizational factors that privileged some options over others and combined to reinforce the utility of key decisions on the path to war. But there are several societal and international (Chapter 7) pressures that should also be considered when evaluating the relative strengths of *Gore-war* and *Gore-peace* counterfactuals. Of course, these 'structural' variables, like the organizational impediments described in the previous chapter, are less amenable to significant alterations over time and, by extension, are much more likely to encourage continuity across administrations. The broader the level of analysis, the more structured the variables, and the more likely they are to induce consistent priorities and patterned behavior from one leader to the next.

For example, polling on public approval of Bush's Iraq strategy from 2002 to 2003 was consistently above 60 percent, the highest polling numbers since the peak after 9/11 (see Figure 6.1).

The public was certainly not calling for war during this period, but a significant majority of Americans clearly supported the various decisions and overall strategy the Bush administration implemented to get inspectors back into Iraq. Support ranged between 60 and 70 percent across all major media outlets from December 2002 through March 2003 (Figure 6.1). These very high numbers indicate solid support from both Republicans and Democrats in the general public. Any president pursuing the same UN-endorsed, multilateral strategy would have received similarly high public approval ratings, and there is no reason to believe Al Gore would have been any less inclined to understand (and exploit) the positive political benefits from the same UN-based approach to a lingering foreign policy problem. Several other polls conducted throughout the 2002–2003 time frame (many compiled by the American Enterprise Institute) produced the exact same results.[1] Christie's (2006) research on the interaction between public support for the president's strategy and mass media coverage is useful here.[2] The author reviews agenda-setting and agenda-building models, tracking the interaction of public opinion, public policy and media coverage. Two periods are studied, April–May 2003 and April–May 2004, which

---

[1] Bowman 2008.   [2] Christie 2006.

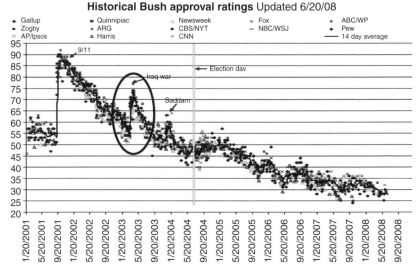

Figure 6.1 Historical Bush approval ratings (the data in Figure 6.1 represents all polling on presidential job approval ratings throughout the first few years of George W. Bush's administration. Public opinions were compiled by leading media and polling organizations listed at the top of the graph. The data also include a fourteen-day moving average to illustrate trends in overall approval ratings. The spike in approval from February through March, 2003, is particularly relevant to highlighting the American public's endorsement of the approach adopted by Bush and Blair).
Sources: www.washingtonmonthly.com/blogphotos/Blog_Bush_Approval_May_2004.jpg; www.hist.umn.edu/~ruggles/Approval.htm.

respectively corresponded to high and low public support. The author found that the strategy implemented by Bush and Blair, including efforts to assemble a coalition to disarm Iraq, accounted for the high public and media support before the war.

In addition to healthy overall-job approval ratings, Bush's specific Iraq strategy to approach Congress and the UN also garnered substantial support from the American public in both the lead up to war and in the initial post-invasion stages. In a series of polls compiled by the American Enterprise Institute, support for Bush's multilateral strategy rarely dips below 60 percent (see Figure 6.2).[3]

---

[3] In those cases in which Bush's approval ratings fell below 60 percent, these polls were typically conducted during earlier periods when the public (and many in Washington) were concerned that neoconservatives would succeed in pushing Bush down the unilateralist path. However, approval began to rise considerably and consistently over 60 percent when the president endorsed the UN multilateral path. These findings directly challenge an important

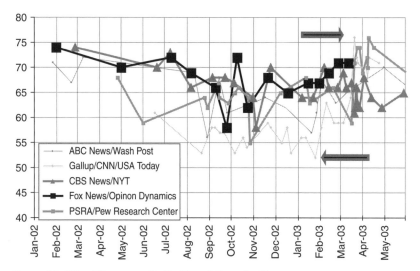

Figure 6.2 US public support for Bush's multilateral military strategy

In the three-month period leading to the March, 2003 invasion (January–March 2003) the public became generally *more* supportive of the president and the possibility of military intervention in Iraq. Slight increases in approval were seen across most polls during this time period. In January of 2003, approval tracked by ABC News/*Washington Post* stood at 57% before rising to 67% in February and remaining high right up until military action – a 65% approval rating was registered on March 9, 2003. Just as the plan was being implemented approval hit its highest mark at 70% in April 2003. The Gallup/CNN poll similarly showed significant increases in approval during the crucial three months before intervention. Approval hit a low of 52% in January 2003 (see lower arrow) before jumping substantially in March 2003, with a 64% approval rating being registered on March 15 and a 76% rating on March 20 (see upper arrow) – just as the president's multilateral plan was being implemented. Support in the CBS poll stood at 64% in January 2003 before climbing to 70% on February 6, 2003 after which approval averaged 64.7% for the month of March 2003. Data from the Fox News poll also showed an increase in support for the president over the three-month span, with 67% approval in January 2003 followed by 71% approval in both February and March 2003. Finally, the PSRA/*Newsweek* poll

part of the threat inflation literature which continues to mistakenly argue that support for unilateralism increased as exaggerated threats pushed by neoconservative took hold. In reality, these threats failed to convince the public that unilateralism was the best policy. Those responsible for inflating the threat did *not* present a strong enough case to convince the public to see the wisdom of unilateral prevention.

showed support at 63% in January 2003, followed by a low of 56% on March 16, 2003 before a spike to 71% on March 20 2003 and a high of 76% in April 2003.

Further, the average approval rating for each poll remains consistently above 60%. The highest single rating (76% in both the Gallup/CNN and PSRA/ Newsweek respectively) occurred around the time military intervention was taking place (March–April 2003); in other words, the highest approval ratings for Bush's Iraq strategy occurred just as his assertive multilateral approach was being implemented. This is consistent with the polls cited earlier indicating the public's preference for a multilateral, UN-backed solution to the Iraqi threat. By delivering such a solution, the Bush administration was able to benefit from strong public approval. The key question then becomes: why would a Gore administration eschew a politically popular strategy, particularly when that strategy is the one Gore himself (along with his advisers) had been consistently advocating?

Similar public support can be found in the AEI data for other aspects of the assertive multilateral approach adopted by Bush and Blair. In a set of polls conducted by PSRA/Newsweek in late 2002, 86% of respondents considered it 'important' (either 'very' or 'somewhat') that President Bush receive congressional approval prior to military intervention in Iraq. Similarly, 87% considered it important for the United States to receive support from their major European allies. Finally, 83.25% indicated it was important for the president to achieve support from the UN. In many ways, each question corresponds to a step in the assertive multilateral process – each of which was ultimately satisfied by President Bush. Again, the neoconservative strategy (to bypass Congress, bypass the UN, and go it alone with or without the support of the UK and other allies) was clearly rejected by the American public. Instead, the American people overwhelmingly supported the multilateral approach being advocated by Powell, Gore, and other prominent Democrats and Republicans.

The forum of public opinion is yet another venue in which neoconservatives lost key debates over how best to deal with the Iraqi threat. For instance, there is clear evidence that the strategy of returning to, and gaining support from the UNSC, was strongly endorsed by the public at the time. In a poll conducted by PSRA/Newsweek on January 3–6 and January 16–17 of 2003, respondents were asked whether they would support US military action given three potential scenarios: (1) support from the UNSC; (2) support from one or two major allies; or (3) unilateral action by the United States. The responses can be seen in Figure 6.3.

These numbers (taken just three months prior to war) indicate a clear rejection of the unilateral approach being advocated by neoconservatives. Indeed, by almost two to one (61% to 32.5%) the American public stated it would *oppose* a unilateral American intervention. Conversely, an overwhelming majority (82% to 13.5%) indicated they would *support* a multilateral, UNSC-supported intervention. Indeed, the fact that the public endorsed the strategy indicates that they generally perceived the president as adopting their preferred approach to

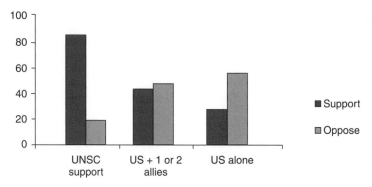

Figure 6.3 Conditions determining US public support for military action

the problem, and subsequently assigned very high approval of the job Bush was doing more generally and in Iraq.

Throughout most of the 1990s, Democratic polling typically produced a roughly fifty-fifty split on the question of whether or not to attack Iraq. In light of the fact that these polls were taken before 9/11, these numbers suggest pretty strong support for a controversial policy. Of course, there is a difference between polls asking directly about invasion and those designed to extract opinions about specific foreign policy initiatives and approaches. Americans tend to favor working with allies over doing things unilaterally, and definitely prefer to work through coalitions backed by UN endorsement. With these patterns in mind, most of the polling during this period clearly shows that once neoconservatives lost the central debate over the wisdom of going back to the UN, public support for the president's multilateral strategy increased and remained high. Given the choice between these two strategies, the American (and British) public obviously preferred multilateral diplomacy and, only if necessary, a coalition of the willing to enforce disarmament.

Critics in the neoconist camp will point to the prominent role Bush and his advisers played in shaping the context within which threats were sold to the American public. The 'constructed political context' argument has already been addressed in detail in Chapter 2, but it raises other relevant questions about why political officials shape context – what motivates or inspires political leaders to select one or another narrative? Is the shaping of political context essentially a top-down phenomenon in which leaders mold public perceptions to serve their interests? Or do leaders respond to what they perceive to be strong preferences held by a majority of the public? How would Gore's team have shaped the post-9/11, Afghanistan or Iraq context, and why? Would Gore have been less inclined, for example, to appreciate heightened public fears of WMD proliferation and terrorism after 9/11, or less likely to pursue a policy that conveyed to the American public his clear commitment to address those threats? Would the context shaped by Gore have been sufficiently different to change the course of history? Finally, what historical evidence would we need to compile to establish the point that Gore's team would have shaped a different context in competition with his Republican opponents, who would almost certainly have been exploiting public fears of terrorism and Iraq's WMD program to reinforce their security credentials?

Context is certainly sculpted by political leaders, but it is shaped for reasons that are common in American politics, regardless of political affiliation. Obviously Al Gore and George Bush are different people, but their similarities as American politicians confronting enormous foreign policy challenges are relevant when thinking about how context would have been formed.

Now, consider the political 'context' within which Gore would have found himself in 2002. He and other former Clinton administration officials (some of whom would have been selected for Gore's national security team) would almost certainly have been held responsible for the 9/11 failure and for seriously *underestimating* the Al-Qaeda threat. For Gore to follow this failure with any indication that he was underestimating the Iraqi threat as well (a threat he himself helped to foment) would have been viewed by everyone as dangerously irresponsible. The political costs of such a strategy would have been very high – Republicans would have jumped at the opportunity to exploit Gore's foreign policy failure(s) at the height of the mid-term election campaign. Gore would also have been assigned direct responsibility for the four-year absence of inspectors in Iraq who left in 1998 prior to Operation Desert Fox. The thought of constructing an alternative narrative in which the Iraqi threat is downplayed or ignored was simply not a credible option for Gore, and there is no evidence that any of his advisers were inclined to encourage him to do so. Neoconism fails by comparison.

Gore's position as chair of Clinton's White House Commission on Aviation Safety and Security would not have helped Gore's case and would have made him particularly vulnerable to Republican attacks.[4] His critics would almost certainly have highlighted his failures in this regard with direct quotes from a dissenting report written by Victoria Cummock, a member of Gore's aviation security commission, a senior member of the FAA Security Baseline Work Group, president of the Families of Pan Am 103/Lockerbie and a widow of one of the victims of the Lockerbie bombing (John Binning Cummock). She offered the following conclusions in her critique of Gore's final recommendations to the president:

> It is after much thoughtful consideration and with a very heavy heart that I register my dissent with the final report of the White House Commission on

---

[4] Gore 1997.

Aviation Safety and Security. Sadly, the overall emphasis of the recommendations reflects a clear commitment to *the enhancement of aviation at the expense of the Commission's mandate of enhancing aviation safety and security*. Clearly, as a nation we have the capability to do all three, but sadly as a Commission have not had the moral courage nor will to do so. (Emphasis added)

History has proven the aviation industry's lack of sincerity and willingness to address safety and security on behalf of their customers by continually citing misleading safety statistics as their rationale for inaction. Valid statistics compare apples to apples, yet repeatedly we are inundated with apple to orange comparisons by the industry.

… In summary, the final report contains no specific call to action, no commitments to address aviation safety and security system-wide by mandating the deployment of current technology and training, with actionable timetables and budgets. Later attempts to track these recommendations will result in problems with differing agency interpretations, misunderstandings, and outright opposition to implementation by individuals and/or organizations who oppose the specific recommendations.

Of all security related committees or commissions in Washington, this one was perhaps most responsible for a "failure of imagination." The word 'cockpit' was referenced only twice in the Commission's entire report and never in relation to protecting the cockpit from hijackers who may be carrying box-cutters or other weapons. The only contemporary reference to terrorism was the Lockerbie attack, a traditional (and outdated) interpretation of the threat from terrorists. The point is that Gore would have been considerably more vulnerable to criticism for underestimating the threat and more inclined to appreciate the importance of avoiding the same mistake with the Iraq WMD threat. His team would not have deserved all of the blame for 9/11, but they would have been more closely linked than Bush's to the errors responsible for the intelligence failure.

Explaining Bush's high public approval ratings

Rallying around the flag

The rally-around-the-flag effect, in which public approval of and support for the president spikes in times of crisis, suggests that Gore would have had overwhelming public support in pursuing an Al-Qaeda-focused response to 9/11. But this also explains why Gore would have received support (not to mention a good deal of motivation and incentive) for resolving the lingering Iraq WMD problem as well, and he would have used the rallying effects to obtain support (in Congress) to push a multilateral approach to the problem. There is nothing inherent in the rallying phenomenon that precludes or privileges one or another foreign policy option – it simply means that the president tends to receive widespread public and congressional support for the options he selects in times of crisis. By logical implication, a rallying effect does *not* discount the strong incentives for Gore to exploit the situation in support of a multilaterally endorsed approach to get inspectors back in, receiving congressional authorization, and getting a strong UN resolution backed by coercive threats. That is precisely what Bush did, and there is no reason why Gore would have missed an opportunity to generate the same increase in public approval ratings with the same strategy.

Media complicity

Another major component of the standard neoconist version of history suggests that only a few journalists (e.g., Judith Miller of the *New York Times*) and media outlets (e.g., Fox News) were responsible for sustaining the false impression of Iraq's threat and for pushing public support for the president's policies. But the intelligence case against the Iraqi regime was never seriously challenged by any major media outlet – none of the reporting raised serious questions and never produced anything approaching a major critique of the generally accepted WMD case. There were a few reports challenging some minor elements of the intelligence case (e.g., operational linkages between Iraq and Al-Qaeda, uranium purchases from Africa, aluminum tubes), but the most plausible interpretation of a decade of intelligence gathering, the interpretation accepted by most members of Congress, was also the one covered by the mainstream press and accepted by the majority of American citizens, regardless of political affiliation. It was the same media story pushed by all national papers and news broadcast throughout the George H.W. Bush and Bill Clinton administrations. And it would have been the same media story during a Gore administration.

Space constraints preclude a very detailed listing of articles reinforcing the standard view, just as it would be difficult to include all of the speeches and statements by those who supported the president's strategy. Unfortunately, journalists, much like politicians, now have an incentive to distance themselves from the facts surrounding their coverage of Iraq's WMD by shifting the blame to the 'distorted' and 'exaggerated' coverage of a few of their colleagues – Judith Miller was among the more obvious targets of scapegoating in this regard. But just as George W. Bush does not deserve credit for singlehandedly creating the illusions of Saddam's WMD, neither does Judith Miller. Kagan (2005) cites a large collection of obvious examples from domestic and international print and broadcast media with alarming headlines, editorials and investigative reports about Saddam's WMD published during the Clinton administration, from 1998–2000, long before 9/11 and the ascendency of neoconservatives to the White House.[5] The structural problems confounding the media's coverage of WMD mirrored

---

[5] Kagan 2005a.

those plaguing the intelligence community – no sources or assets on the ground in Iraq since 1998. Many of these reports relied on information obtained from sources in the Clinton administration, data based on several WMD reports compiled by the CIA,[6] and other UN reports on Iraq's WMD program published by UNSCOM.[7]

Neoconists and other Bush administration critics are fond of citing a few examples of articles that raised legitimate questions about specific intelligence items, but these stories did not amount to anything approaching a sustained challenge to the generally accepted WMD case against the Iraqi regime – there was no plausible alternative to the mainstream view, because it required occupation to produce the definitive evidence needed to support that alternative. There is no reason to expect media coverage in a Gore administration would have been different, since every member of Gore's national security team fully endorsed the previous intelligence estimates they would have used to inform the media.

The media's role in sustaining and reinforcing the WMD consensus was only one dimension of the media's complicity – the major outlets also strongly supported President Bush's strategy when it became clear that he was following the approach recommended by Powell, Blair and a large group of distinguished senior Democrats and Republicans in Washington. Consistent with the kind of coverage the Bush administration received after obtaining congressional authorization and returning to the UN for a strong resolution, the *New York Times* published an editorial in November 2002 entitled "A Unified Message to Iraq" describing the unanimous passage of UN resolution 1441 as a "well-deserved triumph."[8] The editorial also commended the president for the tactics and strategies he used to mount a credible coercive diplomatic threat, tactics considered necessary for a multilateral solution:

> This is a well-deserved triumph for President Bush, a tribute to eight weeks of patient but determined and coercive American diplomacy. Mr. Bush and his aides believe that by threatening unilateral action they have forced the world to pay attention to a danger that had been allowed to fester. Once the alarm was raised, administration officials say, they were in a position to produce a draft acceptable to all the council's 5 permanent and 10 elected members, yet strong enough to involve rigorous and thorough weapons inspections, backed by a clear threat of military force … If Baghdad violates any of these provisions, Washington should insist that the Security Council enforce its decision. Only if the council fails to approve the serious consequences it now invokes – generally understood to be military measures – should Washington consider acting alone.

---

[6] Please refer to multiple intelligence reports compiled by the CIA: www.cia.gov/library/reports/archived-reports-1/index.html.
[7] United Nations Special Commission 1998.   [8] *New York Times* 2002.

In addition to support for Bush's team and policies, similar editorials also commended Powell for his impressive diplomatic coup and praised the team for applying coercive diplomacy by threatening "serious consequences." All major US newspapers (the *New York Times*, the *Chicago Tribune*, the *LA Times*, the *Washington Post*) were virtually unanimous in their praise for the UN speech and subsequent efforts by Powell in the UN.

Some of the best work on the role of the media during this period confirms the prevalence of these general patterns. Enée's (2008) review of editorials published by the *New York Times* and *Washington Post* clearly illustrates the print media's complicity in reinforcing the WMD claims by consistently repeating a substantial list of facts (and speculations) regarding Saddam's reconstitution of his WMD programs.[9] Howard Kurtz, the *Washington Post's* media critic, discovered that "from August 2002 until the war was launched in March of 2003 there were about 140 front page pieces in the *Washington Post* making the administration's case for war. But there was only a handful of stories that ran on the front page that made the opposite case. Or, if not making the opposite case, raised questions."[10] Walter Pincus explains the problem in these terms: "More and more the media become, I think, common carriers of administration statements and critics of the administration. We've sort of given up being independent on our own."[11] Perhaps the most comprehensive treatment of the media's complicity in reporting WMD intelligence is Bill Moyers' PBS special on the subject:[12]

> What the conservative media did was easy to fathom; they had been cheerleaders for the White House from the beginning and were simply continuing to rally the public behind the President – no questions asked. How mainstream journalists suspended skepticism and scrutiny remains an issue of significance that the media has not satisfactorily explored. How the administration marketed the war to the American people has been well covered,

---

[9] Enée 2008. As the author notes, "A quick search through the *Times* archives before 2001 produces such headlines as: *Iraq Has Network of Outside Help on Arms, Experts Say* (November 1998), *US Says Iraq Aided Production of Chemical Weapons in Sudan* (August 1998), *Iraq Suspected of Secret Germ War Effort* (February 2000), *Signs of Iraqi Arms Buildup Bedevil US Administration* (February 2000), *Flight Tests Show Iraq Has Resumed a Missile Program* (July 2000) … As for the *Post's* archives: *Iraqi Work Toward A-Bomb Reported* (September 1998), 'Of all the booby traps left behind by the Clinton administration, none is more dangerous – or more urgent – than the situation in Iraq. Over the last year, Mr. Clinton and his team quietly avoided dealing with, or calling attention to, the almost complete unraveling of a decade's efforts to isolate the regime of Saddam Hussein and prevent it from rebuilding its weapons of mass destruction. That leaves President Bush to confront a dismaying panorama in the Persian Gulf,' including 'intelligence photos that show the reconstruction of factories long suspected of producing chemical and biological weapons' (January 29th, 2001 Editorial). Many such stories appeared before and after the Clinton administration bombed Iraq for four days in late 1998."

[10] Howard Kurtz quoted in Moyers 2008.   [11] Moyers 2008.   [12] Moyers 2008.

but critical questions remain: How and why did the press buy it, and what does it say about the role of journalists in helping the public sort out fact from propaganda?

The most relevant point to emerge from studies of media complicity is not simply that the media pushed the same line as the administration, but the fact that the media, regardless of type or political leanings, collectively failed to uncover anything approaching the final truth about Saddam's WMD. Moyers' claim that it was the "conservative media" alone that was responsible for defending the standard WMD line is a serious misreading of the case history – with the exception of a few marginalized voices, almost all of the media shared the same views. Moreover, US and British media were not the only ones endorsing the 'administration's' position on WMD. Again, excluding the distortions coming out of the Pentagon, everyone shared the same mistaken impression as to the nature of the threat from Saddam, including the UN and its chief inspector Hans Blix (please refer to Chapters 2–5). As it turned out, everyone was wrong about the larger WMD case, regardless of ideological persuasion.

The main problem with Moyers' coverage of media complicity is that, while generally correct, it suffers from the same weaknesses that plague much of the neoconist literature – rather than focusing on the very large number of intelligence errors and the structural and organizational impediments in the media that precluded efforts to correct them, excessive attention is devoted to the media's role in pushing a few select intelligence errors and distortions about, for example, Niger yellowcakes, aluminum tubes and operational linkages between Iraq and Al-Qaeda. Moyers' reference to journalist Bob Simon's (*60 Minutes*) interpretation of the media's errors exemplifies the nature of the problem:

> I mean we knew things or suspected things that perhaps the Washington press corps could not suspect. For example, the absurdity of putting up a connection between Saddam Hussein and Al Qaeda. Saddam ... was a total control freak. To introduce a wild card like Al Qaeda in any sense was just something he would not do. So I just didn't believe it for an instant.

There are at least two problems with the central point Moyers and Simon are making here. First, Simon was not the only person in Washington completely rejecting claims about operational linkages between Iraq and Al-Qaeda, or Iraq and 9/11. Such links were systematically rejected by Colin Powell, George Tenet and Tony Blair (for many of the reasons outlined in Chapter 5). The notion that these links were generally accepted (and explicitly endorsed) by everyone at the time simply misses too much of the relevant history and domestic political debates during this period. These links may have been exaggerated by neoconservatives and unilateralists to generate support for unilateralism, but they were not generally substantiated. Second, both Moyers and Simon mistakenly assume that these intelligence distortions were more responsible than thousands of other WMD-related estimates for the path to war. But if these items were largely irrelevant to the support Bush and Blair received for their approach to the crisis, as demonstrated in Chapter 5, then Moyers' and Simon's focus on media complicity in pushing these particular distortions is equally irrelevant to understand the causes of the war. The real cause of media complicity, which also explains the larger collection of intelligence errors, is structural in nature and not a function of leadership or a neoconservative ideology. Moyers, like other neoconists, is guilty of selectively cherry-picking the intelligence distortions when making his case for the media's mistakes, but inadvertently ignores so much of the larger intelligence consensus (and errors) that collectively served to justify the decisions that led to war. Contrary to Moyers' conclusions, even if the media forcefully challenged the administration on these particular intelligence estimates, the effects would have been negligible with respect to the war. These distortions, especially those related to Iraqi–Al-Qaeda links, did not determine the support Bush received for authorization or any other aspects of the strategy adopted to force Saddam to disarm.

Third, Moyers' assumptions about the relative importance of these particular intelligence estimates also biases his interpretation of what the solution would have been – the fewer and more manageable the number of intelligence errors that could have been corrected, the easier it would have been for the media to change the course of history, and the more blame the media deserves for its failure to stop the war. But if the intelligence errors were considerably more numerous, entrenched and difficult to correct, then blame for the course of events must shift to these other factors – a point that critics of the Bush administration are loath to accept.

The collective failure of the US (and British) media was a product of the same basic problem confronting intelligence communities – the most plausible interpretation of Saddam's behavior was privileged over an alternative story that was simply too absurd to fathom. In the absence of inspectors on the ground with the capacity to generate an alternative intelligence story, or investigative reporters on the ground with alternative intelligence gathering capabilities to challenge the general views, it was easier to play up the 'fears' associated with WMD than to challenge the historical record. The key to uncovering the truth behind the regime's behavior was revealed through hundreds of transcripts from interviews with Hussein and his advisers. The truth about the onset of hostilities in 2003 requires a thorough understanding of how and why Saddam Hussein and senior members of his regime misunderstood the predicament they were in, misperceived the threats they faced and miscalculated the utility of strategic ambiguity surrounding their WMD programs. The mutually reinforcing effects of these mistakes, when combined with the intelligence errors by the United States and UK, are explored in more detail in Chapter 8.

Conclusions: *Gore-war* versus *Gore-peace* revisited

In keeping with the counterfactual exercise, the most important consideration is of course evaluating how or what would have been different had Al Gore become president in 2000. Gore would certainly have been a different type of leader, but the relevant counterfactual question is whether these differences would have had a substantial effect on the outcomes. For example, how might we interpret the potential role of Gore's communications skills on public approval? Logically, had Gore been a more successful communicator than Bush (a likely scenario) he would have been more successful at explaining US policy to the public, thus receiving even higher public approval for his multilateral strategy to return inspectors.

Consider, for example, the nature of public opinion in 2002. With 9/11 weighing heavily on the public psyche, Americans generally favored hard-line policies on matters related to national security. This is reflected in the high approval ratings garnered by President Bush for his handling of Iraq during this time period. Given the added security incentives of a post-9/11 world, there is no reason to believe President Gore would have significantly altered his established foreign policy stance. Instead, he would have used the same rally-around-the-flag effects that helped the Bush administration in order to pursue the same multilateral solution to the Iraq impasse. Of course, public approval of the war eventually declined to some of the lowest levels for a sitting president, but these opinions shifted as casualties mounted and as the Iraq Survey Group failed to uncover WMD stockpiles – they declined *after* the war, for good reason. But strong public support for the president's strategy *before* the war is relevant to assessing the two competing counterfactuals.

With respect to media complicity, the most important counterfactual point emerging from relevant research is that the media's coverage would not have appreciably changed if Gore's team had been in power – as mentioned, the Clinton–Gore administration was largely responsible for reinforcing the mainstream interpretation of Saddam's WMD threat that ultimately helped to shape the media's preferred narrative. There is no logical reason, therefore, why officials in a Gore administration would challenge media reports that contributed to strengthening the case Gore himself was making. A policy favoring congressional authorization, deployment of troops to the region, a unanimous UN resolution and a new rigorous inspections regime, all perfectly reasonable and rational policies, requires evidence that Saddam poses a threat – if the media was willing to push the WMD case, so much the better.

Obviously, members of the Bush administration did very little (if anything) to challenge exaggerated media reports on Saddam's WMD (and some were responsible for exploiting these myths). However, there is no documented illustration of a Clinton administration official challenging similar reports during the 1990s either, because they served the Iraq policies that Clinton and Gore endorsed at the time – it helped the Clinton administration make the case for sanctions, containment and the bombing of Iraq in 1998. If the strategy was considered by Clinton–Gore and Bush–Cheney to be useful, there is no reason the same strategy would have been rejected by Gore–Lieberman to defend the policy of getting inspectors back into Iraq.

With respect to domestic factors and societal pressures, then, a thorough and balanced assessment of the relevant historical facts strongly supports general continuity as opposed to significant change between the factual (Bush) and counterfactual (Gore) realities. That is, the nature of the domestic context in the United States in late 2002/early 2003 was such that a hypothetical President Gore would have likely pursued (and been compelled to pursue) many of the same, or similar, policies than did actual President Bush. Similarly, the media's complicity in promoting standard interpretations of Iraq's WMD threat would have continued, and been just as beneficial to President Gore as they were to President Bush. Again, this is not an assertion based on blind hypothesizing, but rather a careful conclusion premised on the available historical facts regarding the relevant structural variables combined with Al Gore's known policy legacy and policy preferences.

7

International politics, global WMD consensus and UN power balancing

The evidence from preceding chapters reveals serious weaknesses with standard neoconist accounts of the Iraq war. When exposed to the facts, the conventional account emerges as an excessively simplistic take on American leadership, domestic politics, US–UK intelligence failures, media coverage and public opinion. So much of what is relevant to telling the whole story is excluded in traditional narratives, no doubt because many aspects of the historical record directly challenge accepted wisdom. As it turns out, the truth is so much more interesting than the story of a few ideologues in the Bush administration – clearly, they were not solely responsible for transforming the direction of American foreign and security policy after 9/11. Moreover, they did not have the intellectual prowess, political authority or negotiating skills to manipulate the preferences, perceptions and priorities of so many other very intelligent people in Washington, including a significant majority of both political parties, members of whom served on key congressional foreign policy and intelligence committees that authorized the use of force, and a majority of the American public (between 60 to 70 percent) who consistently supported Bush's handling of the Iraq crisis from 2002 to 2003.

But problems with the most widely accepted account of the Iraq war are not limited to simplistic historical portrayals of American leadership or domestic politics during this period – neoconism also assumes that these same powerful ideologues managed, through sheer willpower and political skills, to shift the focus of an entire international community to accommodate the neocons' Iraq policy. Consider the list of world leaders whose perceptions and priorities, neoconists believe, were successfully manipulated to serve a misguided agenda: Tony Blair and a significant majority of British parliamentarians from both major parties who supported the war effort; Prime Minister John Howard of Australia and a majority of the Australian parliament; leaders from almost every European government excluding France, Germany and Belgium; every member of the UN Security Council (including France, Russia and China), which unanimously endorsed UN Security Council Resolution 1441 (a clear summary of the global intelligence consensus on Iraq's "material breach," failure to disarm chemical and biological weapons programs and suspicions about "nuclear facilities"); and a significant majority of Iraqi citizens who, despite being threatened with death, voted in the democratic elections at the center of the Bush-neocon empire-building scheme.[1] Space constraints preclude a more detailed list of world leaders and senior military officials scammed by Bush, Cheney and their neocon team.

The alternative interpretation – that perhaps these leaders were compelled to act for strategic reasons directly associated with their own independent assessments of Iraq's WMD threat, or their country's national security interests, or because they endorsed a very rational (and popular) UN-based multilateral path to disarmament – is never seriously considered within the neoconist framework. Of particular note is the manner in which the Blair administration arrived at its policy stance – a careful, balanced assessment of available intelligence followed by a reasonable and rational appraisal of national interests culminated in the strong endorsement of assertive multilateralism through coercive diplomacy. As we will see, the internal debate in the UK involved explicit *rejections* of many standard neocon arguments – far from manipulation, neocons appear to have had little to no traction with this important ally. But just as the domestic political battles in the United States and elsewhere were far more complex than neoconists acknowledge, the *international* politics that played out during this period were equally complicated, nuanced and considerably more interesting.

For example, standard accounts of the war consistently overlook the scope of international consensus on Iraq's WMD that informed intelligence estimates in other capitals, a consensus that was expressed most vividly in the content of UNSCR 1441. Neoconists also miss the significance of the seven weeks of diplomatic negotiations and bargaining invested in crafting the final version of the new resolution. They also rarely acknowledge the consensus among world leaders (including some of the war's strongest critics, such as French President Jacques Chirac and UNMOVIC's Hans Blix) praising the initial deployment of US and UK troops as essential to the credibility of the coercive threats responsible for whatever successes UNMOVIC managed to obtain during this period. In addition to ignoring the importance of these facts, neoconism also fails to appreciate the relevance of negotiations surrounding the two proposals, put forward by the UK and Canada, respectively,

---

[1] Had a majority of Iraqis viewed Bush's policies in the same light as they are portrayed by the strongest neoconist critics of the administration, I doubt they would have wanted to participate in democratic elections at the center of the neocons' diabolical scheme, especially while being shot at. If the invasion was viewed by a significant majority of Iraqi citizens as a reprehensible and unacceptable thrust into the Middle East to control Iraq – or Iraqi oil – most of them would have been far less enthusiastic about risking their lives to elect officials largely viewed as pre-selected by the US invader. On the other hand, had Iraqis interpreted the US–UK invasion through the prism of the historical account I am portraying in this book then it is easier to understand why Iraqis viewed the entire democratization project as legitimate and worthy of the risk and sacrifice.

to prolong inspections. These details are not only relevant to weighing the relative strengths of competing counterfactual claims, they are crucial to providing historically accurate accounts of why negotiations over a second resolution ultimately failed. Each of these points is addressed in more detail below.

Global consensus on WMD

As noted in Chapter 5, the global consensus on Iraq's WMD threat was fundamentally connected to the relative plausibility of two mutually exclusive interpretations of Iraq's behavior: that Saddam *did* or *did not* retain the proscribed weapons cited in every UN resolution and report since 1991, and continued, in the absence of UN inspectors since 1998, to spend billions of dollars to develop (and hide) a range of WMD programs that were sufficient to threaten the United States and its allies.[2]

Every member of the UN Security Council (including the war's strongest critics, France, Russia and China) unanimously endorsed the view that he did retain proscribed weapons when they passed UNSCR 1441 in November, 2002 – they agreed that Saddam did not disarm in line with previous resolutions, and failed to provide credible documentation that such disarmament had taken place. No official at the time came close to defending the more optimistic interpretation. In addition to the fact that intelligence reports from the UK and Germany, from 1991 through 1998, reinforced the same suspicions, Hans Blix also directly contributed to the WMD myth by re-producing 'mixed' reports that consistently expressed serious concerns about unaccounted-for weapons – in the end, he was just as wrong as everyone else. All of these misperceptions were encouraged by Saddam every time he refused admission to a site, demanded some exception to a UN resolution's mandate, or refused un-monitored interviews with his WMD scientists. The result was a widespread international consensus in 2003 that Saddam retained proscribed weapons – again, this was the only reasonable interpretation of a decade of intelligence on the regime's behavior. These impressions may seem absurd today, but they made a lot of sense in 2002–2003 after a four-year absence of inspectors and no documented proof of disarmament demanded by UNSCR 1441. Cognitive biases, formed over a decade of failed inspections and systematic deception by the Iraqi regime, explain part of the problem, as do post-9/11 imperatives to avoid underestimating future security threats.[3] A

---

[2] United Nations Monitoring, Verification and Inspection Commission 2003b.
[3] For an excellent discussion of cognitive biases and other psychological and organizational biases and pathologies that played out during the Iraq crisis, see Jervis 2006.

more detailed assessment of the Iraqi regime's errors and miscalculations will follow in Chapter 8.

UNSCR 1441 and all related UN resolutions on Iraq should be read in their entirety to acquire a crystal clear impression of the perceptions and assumptions guiding the global consensus on Iraq's WMD. A brief, cursory review of these documents would remove any doubts that the international community endorsed the more pessimistic view. This is precisely why all previous resolutions were cited in UNSCR 1441, why coercive inspections were required and demanded by the Security Council, and why so many suspected WMD programs and materials were outlined in Hans Blix's March 6, 2003 'cluster document.'[4] There is no way one could review this entire record and conclude that it was only neoconservatives and unilateralists who assumed Saddam retained proscribed weapons. Consider the opinions of IAEA spokesperson Melissa Fleming (September 29, 2002): "We're certainly aware of what happened [in Iraq] last time ... But we uncovered Iraq's secret nuclear programme and we dismantled it. If we get unfettered access, we will be successful again."[5] The working assumption under which everyone functioned was that a rigid inspections regime would uncover proscribed WMD.

Dismissing WMD concerns as delusions held and perpetuated by only a few Bush administration officials distorts too much of this history – the only way to understand what happened is to appreciate the widespread consensus that prevailed. As President Jacques Chirac pointed out on October 16, 2002:

> What is at stake is how to answer the potential threat Iraq represents with the risk of proliferation of WMD. Baghdad's regime did use such weapons in the past. Today, a number of indications lead us to believe that for the past four years, in the absence of international inspectors, this country [Iraq] has continued armament programs. Proliferation of WMD constitutes a threat for the planet at large. Our security depends on our capacity to deal collectively with this major risk. On this topic, no more than on others, our policy is not to spare Iraq: we have always called for the strict implementation of UN resolutions ... The immediate unfettered and unconditional access of inspectors to all sites is the indispensable guarantee of efficiency and credibility of UN inspections. This demand is explicitly written in all existing resolutions.[6]

Everyone – including Chirac, one of the war's strongest critics – believed Saddam's WMD programs posed a threat to the international community, so they endorsed the UN-based multilateral approach to inspections and disarmament. In fact, as Rivkin and Casey (2003) point out, "France unwittingly

---

[4] United Nations Monitoring, Verification and Inspection Commission 2003b.
[5] FoxNews.com 2002. See also Acronym Institute 2002.   [6] Chirac 2002.

revealed just how effective Hussein's *strategic ambiguity* program was when its US ambassador announced shortly after the war began that his country would support the coalition if the Iraqi leader used any weapons of mass destruction" (emphasis added).[7] Other strong critics of the war were equally convinced of the WMD problem – consider Gerhardt Schroeder's statement on February 13, 2003:

> *There are indications that Iraq might be capable of producing other weapons of mass destruction* ... Iraq must cooperate comprehensively and actively with the UN Security Council and the weapons inspectors. We need absolute clarity about Iraqi weapons of mass destruction, and, if they exist, their final destruction ... [T]he power to decide about the progress made by the inspectors and about all consequences rests with the UN Security Council ... [T]he decisive instrument for the abolition of prohibited Iraqi armament programmes is and remains an effective inspection and verification regime. It must be expanded and intensified in line with the requirements. (Emphasis added)[8]

Clear evidence of a widespread, global (multi-party) consensus on Saddam's WMD can be found everywhere.

John Howard, prime minister of Australia, September 9, 2002:[9]

> There's no doubt, on the evidence of the intelligence material presented to us, that not only does Iraq possess chemical and biological weapons, but Iraq also has not abandoned her nuclear aspirations.

Tom Scheiffer, Australian UN ambassador, September 9, 2002:[10]

> No American President can be comfortable with the proposition that these weapons might be developed and then distributed to those who would detonate a nuclear device in New York or Sydney harbour.

Anders Fogh Rasmussen, prime minister of Denmark (EU president), October 1, 2002:[11]

> Europe and the United States must stand together in ... preventing tyrannical and irresponsible regimes ... [from] having weapons of mass destruction ... Iraq is ruled by such a regime ... The United Nations must live up to its responsibility to stop the spreading of the weapons of mass destruction. It will be too late when the toxic gases have ... spread over one of our cities.

---

[7] Rivkin and Casey 2003.   [8] Schroeder 2003.   [9] Quoted in Acronym Institute 2002.
[10] Quoted in Acronym Institute 2002.   [11] See Acronym Institute 2002.

Jack Straw, UK foreign secretary, September 25, 2002:[12]

> The objective which we seek is the disarmament of the Saddam Hussein regime. It may be that a consequence of that process will be regime change, but in terms of the objective it is disarmament.

Hans Blix (UNMOVIC chair) interview with the Associated Press, August 17, 2002:[13]

> I'm not assuming at all that the Iraqis have retained weapons of mass destruction. At the same time, it would evidently be naïve of me to conclude that they don't. If inspectors are allowed in, and if they are given really unfettered access with no delays, etc., then I think this might play an important role and we would be eager to do that and to help toward a non-belligerent solution ... Inspections cannot guarantee 100 percent that there are not underground facilities, hidden, but even the United States cannot guarantee that there is not some anthrax around somewhere in the US. You cannot give a 100 percent guarantee of that kind.

These widespread suspicions explain why UNSCR 1441 received unanimous consent. Logically, if France, Russia and China believed Saddam had nothing to hide, or that the Iraqi regime had been successfully disarmed through sanctions and inspections, then it would make absolutely no sense for these leaders to endorse the content of 1441. If they believed Saddam's regime was clean, then it would have been a catastrophic miscalculation on their part to declare Iraq in material breach in 2002 if it was not, or to demand Saddam comply with disarmament obligations if he had no weapons stockpiles to dismantle, or to demand proof he destroyed these weapons when he had no proof to provide (ironically because it was destroyed along with proscribed weapons to prevent inspectors from uncovering *any* evidence of WMD programs and prevent Washington from obtaining more ammunition to maintain UN sanctions). In other words, if France, Russia and China were prescient enough to know the truth about Saddam's WMD programs, then they would not have signed onto the content of UNSCR 1441, because there was no way for inspectors to demonstrate disarmament was working. Had these leaders understood the truth, they would have avoided any indication that they endorsed the US–UK story on Iraq's WMD or the need to inflict 'serious consequences' if Saddam failed to provide evidence of disarmament – as it happened, their support added a crucial piece to the US–UK justification for war.

Therefore, the only reasonable explanation for signing UNSCR 1441 is the signatories' strong conviction that Iraq was in material breach of previous disarmament obligations and retained WMD programs. They signed it, of course,

---

[12] Quoted in Acronym Institute 2002.   [13] Quoted in Acronym Institute 2002.

because they believed that a multilateral disarmament program stood the best chance of finding proscribed weapons, dismantling the WMD programs, and providing sufficient evidence of disarmament compliance to avoid a war. France, China and Russia also assumed Saddam would want to take advantage of this last opportunity to provide the evidence, demanded by UNSCR 1441, that he had actually destroyed many of the programs stipulated in Blix's 'cluster report.' Even Chinese Prime Minister Zhu Rongli demanded on September 25, 2002: "We request that Iraq comply with UN resolutions without any preconditions."[14] And these leaders calculated, based on their belief that Saddam retained proscribed weapons, that the best hope for disarming Saddam (given his reticence to comply in the past) would be to participate in a UN-based, coercive strategy that would (1) prevent the United States from engaging in unilateral pre-emption; (2) compel Saddam to disarm peacefully; (3) prolong the status quo by sustaining a very lucrative UN oil-for-food/ sanctions program; and, over the long term, (4) negotiate the lifting of sanctions to remove the remaining barriers to even more lucrative oil contracts with a then-disarmed Iraqi regime. This was the strategy France, Russia and China adopted, and it was a path firmly grounded in the conviction that Iraq retained proscribed WMD. There is no other, more plausible interpretation of their actions and preferences.

This widespread WMD consensus also explains international support for each of the key decisions in the sequence along the multilaterally endorsed path to war – i.e., obtaining US congressional and UK parliamentary authorization to use military force, deployment of troops to the region to enhance the credibility of the threat, a strong, unanimous UN resolution declaring Iraq in material breach, and the return of inspectors to Iraq with a tough, draconian mandate. For France, Germany, Russia and China, the risks of engaging the United States through the UN were much lower than the risks of declining the invitation to fix the WMD problem – this would have provided American neocons with the proof they needed to demonstrate the UN's failure and the need for pre-emptive unilateralism based on existing UN resolutions. French and Russian officials believed that by working through the UN they could constrain US and UK actions, but in the process they too signed onto a rigid inspections regime that, paradoxically, set the stage for war.

In essence, once UNSCR 1441 was unanimously endorsed, the inspections impasse constituted an irresolvable foreign policy dilemma for any US president or British prime minster, because diplomats on each side of the UN debate were applying different standards (constructs) for measuring 'success' and 'progress.' Transcripts of a January 31, 2003 meeting with Tony Blair, included in Alastair Campbell's memoirs (Campbell and Stott 2007: 660), clearly establish

---

[14] Quoted in Acronym Institute 2002.

the *"intellectual construct"* Blair wanted to use when framing the issue of UN inspections:[15]

> TB had also slept badly and was up and about, going over the same questions again and again, [he] kept saying we needed a clear intellectual construct[,] which was that 1441 focus should be on the cooperation issues, if the Iraqis didn't cooperate[,] Blix makes that clear repeatedly, we should say so and then we can go for a second resolution and action could follow. We had allowed the goalposts to be moved to the smoking gun issue, and instead it had to be about the inspections not getting cooperation.

For American and British officials, success meant full and complete compliance, and, in its absence, the only reasonable conclusion was that Saddam was hiding weapons the international community needed to find and destroy, with or without Saddam's help.

For France, Russia and China, on the other hand, success was defined by the absence of stockpiles. Paradoxically, the failure to locate stockpiles simply reinforced impressions in Washington and London that UN inspectors were incapable of doing their job – again, the alternative interpretation (i.e., Saddam had nothing and was seriously miscalculating) was not plausible. The dangerous paradox unfolding here was revealed in comments by Bush's press secretary, Ari Fleischer, on December 2, 2002:

> If Saddam Hussein indicates that he has weapons of mass destruction and that he is violating United Nations resolutions, then we will know that Saddam Hussein again deceived the world. If he declared he has none, then we will know that Saddam Hussein is once again misleading the world.[16]

Ironically, it would have been far better for Saddam had inspectors uncovered stockpiles of WMD – this would at least have demonstrated real progress on disarmament. Finding none was a problem because it was interpreted as a failure of inspections rather than the absence of WMD. The worst outcome for Saddam was the one that prevailed – inspectors slowly uncovered additional evidence of deception and proscribed weapons material that reinforced suspicions, and since they found no stockpiles, it raised concerns that inspections were failing.

In the context of these irreconcilable differences, France's final declaration, rejecting any military options to resolve the Iraq crisis, seriously damaged the credibility of the US–UK threat and put American and British officials in a very difficult position. As Blair (2010: 432) explains in his memoirs, "when I look back and reread all the documents and the memories flood back to me of all those agonized and agonizing meetings, calls and deliberations, I know that there was never any way Britain was not going to be with the US at that moment, once we went down the UN route and Saddam was in breach." For reasons

---

[15] Alastair Campbell was Tony Blair's Chief of Staff. See Campbell and Stott 2007.
[16] Fleischer 2003.

covered in Chapters 2, 3, 4 and 9, the costs and risks of war at this point in the crisis became more acceptable than the costs and risks of inaction and the status quo – retaining hundreds of thousands of troops in theater with no purpose or coercive diplomatic effect was unacceptable.

UNMOVIC updates by Hans Blix – reinforcing the global consensus on Iraq's WMD

Perhaps the most revealing entry in Hans Blix's (2004: 259) book about his Iraq experience is this one: "The UN and the world had succeeded in disarming Iraq without knowing it."[17] Blix did not know the truth in March 2003, and judging by his 175-page collection of unaccounted-for weapons, there was really no way for Blix to uncover the truth. As we now know, there were no weapons of mass destruction to uncover and no way for any inspector to produce a report confirming Iraq was free of WMD. The problem from the beginning, as he states in his book, is that "[t]here could be no presumption of innocence in the case of Iraq" (Blix 2004: 128). He adds, "no one … could guarantee that Iraq was without any weapons of mass destruction … Presumably it was an awareness of this circumstance that led the US and UK governments to claim certainty that the weapons existed" (Blix 2004: 270).

In his January 27 report to the UN, Blix concluded, "Iraq appears not to have come to a genuine acceptance – not even today – of the disarmament, which was demanded of it and which it needs to carry out to win the confidence of the world and to live in peace."[18] Other disconcerting observations from the report are included in Appendix 7.1. There are essentially two ways to interpret and use Hans Blix's periodic (and mixed) inspections updates: (1) to confirm the absence of any evidence of WMD stockpiles, or (2) to confirm the absence of clear evidence of Iraqi compliance. This was always the main problem with the inspections regime – the reports would never successfully resolve the disarmament impasse or address lingering suspicions. Hans Blix's reports directly contributed to the problem because, as it turns out, he was just as wrong as everyone else. UNSCR 1441 required nothing less than full and complete compliance and demanded from Saddam all necessary documentation to confirm the location of WMD (or clear proof he destroyed the weapons) – but no such evidence existed, and the information that did exist was hidden from inspectors to accommodate strategic ambiguity and deterrence by deception (see Chapter 8).

Blix constantly reminded Iraqi officials (and the UN Security Council) that UNMOVIC's standards for measuring compliance could not (and should not) be defined in terms of UNMOVIC's success at uncovering evidence of proscribed

---

[17] Blix 2004.   [18] www.un.org/Depts/unmovic/Bx27.htm.

WMD programs (which directly contradicted France's preferred approach to the problem). The more reasonable and widely accepted standard, which Blix repeatedly used, was whether he found clear evidence of proactive compliance, consistent with what South African or, more recently, Libyan officials did when dismantling their WMD programs. Officials in these states proactively accompanied inspectors to places where proscribed weapons systems, materials and files were located, or took it upon themselves to provide clear proof that these weapons were dismantled or destroyed. This form of compliance was not forthcoming in Iraq, something Blix pointed out in every one of his reports. The burden of proof, Blix demanded, was on Saddam Hussein to provide clear evidence that the WMD listed in his reports had been retained.[19] This is an important point to consider when interpreting the context of Blix's statements. A quick glance through such statements (Appendix 7.1) could easily have provided US and UK officials with all the ammunition they needed to conclude inspections were failing to uncover the weapons Blix was looking for, but his reports to the UN were never definitive enough. No one in Washington or Britain came close to concluding that evidence of partial compliance on 'process' was sufficient. In one briefing to the UNSC, Hans Blix issued the following statement:[20]

> Mr. President: In my earlier briefings, I have noted that significant outstanding issues of substance were listed in two Security Council documents from early 1999 (S/1999/94 and S/1999/356) and should be well known to Iraq. I referred, as examples, to the issues of anthrax, the nerve agent VX and long-range missiles, and said that such issues "deserve to be taken seriously by Iraq rather than being brushed aside" … *The declaration submitted by Iraq on 7 December last year, despite its large volume, missed the opportunity to provide the fresh material and evidence needed to respond to the open questions. This is perhaps the most important problem we are facing. Although I can understand that it may not be easy for Iraq in all cases to provide the evidence needed, it is not the task of the inspectors to find it. Iraq itself must squarely tackle this task and avoid belittling the questions.* (Emphasis added)

The briefing went on to state:

> We have now commenced the process of destroying approximately 50 litres of mustard gas declared by Iraq that was being kept under UNMOVIC seal at the Muthanna site. One-third of the quantity has already been destroyed. The laboratory quantity of thiodiglycol, a mustard gas precursor, which we found at another site, has also been destroyed.

---

[19]   United Nations Monitoring, Verification and Inspection Commission 2003b.
[20]   Blix 2003b.

The question inevitably raised by those seriously concerned about Iraq's WMD was whether this was the entire stockpile or simply an amount judged by the regime to be sufficient to appease inspectors – a strategy commonly used by Hussein throughout the 1990s. Under the current inspections regime, there was no way to persuasively challenge the plausibility of these suspicions. According to Blix's briefing, UNMOVIC consisted of over 250 staff members from about sixty countries – including 100 inspectors, fifteen IAEA inspectors, fifty aircrew and sixty-five support staff. One way Saddam could have played the public relations game more effectively (had he honestly been committed to proving he had no WMD) would have been to demand a much larger inspections group filming their inspections for public release. Why not ask for 500 or 1,000 inspectors? The answers to these questions, revealed through hundreds of interviews with Saddam and former regime officials, are discussed in detail in Chapter 8. But these nagging questions were explicitly raised by Blix himself in his January 2003 report to the UN:[21]

> Information provided by Member States tells us about the movement and concealment of missiles and chemical weapons and mobile units for biological weapons production. We shall certainly follow up any credible leads given to us and report what we might find as well as any denial of access.
>
> So far we have reported on the recent find of a small number of empty 122 mm warheads for chemical weapons. Iraq declared that it appointed a commission of inquiry to look for more. *Fine. Why not extend the search to other items? Declare what may be found and destroy it under our supervision?* (Emphasis added)
>
> When we have urged our Iraqi counterparts to present more evidence, *we have all too often met the response that there are no more documents. All existing relevant documents have been presented, we are told. All documents relating to the biological weapons programme were destroyed together with the weapons.* (Emphasis added)
>
> *However, Iraq has all the archives of the Government and its various departments, institutions and mechanisms. It should have budgetary documents, requests for funds and reports on how they have been used. It should also have letters of credit and bills of lading, reports on production and losses of material.* (Emphasis added)
>
> In response to a recent UNMOVIC request for a number of specific documents, the only new documents Iraq provided was a ledger of 193 pages which Iraq stated included all imports from 1983 to 1990 by the Technical and Scientific Importation Division, the importing authority for the biological weapons programme. Potentially, it might help to clear some open issues.

We now know that Blix's suspicions (and overestimations of the threat) turned out to be just as wrong as US and UK approximations. The problem is that many

[21] Blix 2003a.

of the documents proving the destruction of Iraq's weapons were actually eradicated by regime officials. Yet these lingering suspicions were raised in all of Blix's reports, because it was inconceivable to Blix that the alternative interpretation (that he had nothing) was plausible. Like everyone else, Blix never considered the possibility that Saddam was simply creating the very dangerous illusion about his WMD capabilities to address what he mistakenly viewed as more serious regional threats from Iran and Israel. Nor did it occur to Blix that Saddam did not see the US–UK threat as credible, despite the mobilization of hundreds of thousands of troops to the region. Had Blix (or others) correctly surmised that Saddam did not believe the US–UK coalition would attack, it would have been easier to contemplate the possibility that Saddam was practicing strategic ambiguity for other reasons.

Hans Blix was also more inclined to believe at the time that a government so committed to keeping records would also have retained evidence of disarmament operations. The absence of these records implied to Blix that disarmament had not taken place, which emerged as the more plausible explanation for why they would be keeping these records from inspectors. If Blix had accepted the Iraqi explanation – that they destroyed the documents to get rid of evidence they thought would hurt them (which turned out to be closer to the truth than anyone believed at the time) then Blix would certainly not have raised these suspicions in such a crucial report – nor continued to do so in every one of his reports, including those in February and March 2003.

As Blix continued to raise these questions, he consequently reinforced suspicions and strengthened impressions of deception. The longer it took Saddam to comply, despite the deployment of troops to the region, the more convinced US and UK officials became that their interpretation of his actions was right. It was impossible for anyone to really understand his intentions until after the war, and after hundreds of interviews with key Iraqi officials. The paradox this presented was even more pronounced when one considers the logic of coercive diplomacy and momentum. The more convinced the United States and UK became that their military threats and ultimatums were credible and resolute, the more difficult it was for them to believe Saddam misread their signals. Why, at the eleventh hour – following authorization by Congress and the British Parliament, a unanimous UN resolution threatening serious consequences and the deployment of hundreds of thousands of American and British troops to the region – would a regime with nothing to hide continue to defy Blix's demands?

No one at the time (including Blix) understood why Saddam would want to create the WMD illusion to protect his state from an attack by Iran. But why would they? US–UK intelligence found no evidence of an impending attack by Iran, so there would have been no reason to acknowledge the depths of Hussein's misplaced concerns about his neighbor. Anyone interpreting Saddam's behavior as anything but an effort to hide proscribed weapons would have been considered irresponsible after 9/11. What rationale would Saddam have had to create the myth of WMD in light of the consequences and the high probability of a US–UK invasion?

Britain's position on WMD, Al-Qaeda and multilateral inspections

Neoconist models almost never include references to Tony Blair's role in the crisis or the fact that the same WMD consensus prevailed in Britain – obviously, no one in Blair's administration could be regarded as a neoconservative ideologue. Either neoconists' explanations are incomplete or neocons were so powerful in their persuasiveness that they managed to convince Blair to risk his career and reputation to fight their war. Again, the latter account simply misses too much of what went on at the time, and it mistakenly assigns superhuman coercive power to ideologues who actually lost key debates throughout the crisis. As Blair explained on September 6, 2002:[22]

> In the end, Britain is a sovereign nation. Britain decides its own policy and although I back America, I would never back America if I thought they were doing something wrong. If I thought that [the United States was] … committing military action in a way that was wrong, I would not support it. But I have never found that, and I don't expect to find it in the future.

Blair, like Bush (and Gore), was just as convinced about Iraq's WMD threat:[23]

> It is high time we sorted out Saddam's weapons of mass destruction. In the post 9/11 world, it is no longer tenable for a brutal dictator like Saddam Hussein to be allowed to develop weapons of mass destruction with impunity while at the same time defying the will of the international community. We have no alternative other than to act.

And to questions from journalists about why he appeared to be so committed to Iraq and so focused on that particular crisis, Blair responded:

> This is about Saddam and WMD. He's had them in the past and he's used them in the past. All the evidence suggests he is continuing to develop them, and all the time he is defying the UN. I simply don't think that this is something we can ignore.[24]

Blair consistently repeated these same concerns throughout his tenure as prime minster, and, contrary to neoconist assumptions, his views were not based on ideologically motivated interpretations forced upon him by US or UK intelligence officials.

With respect to additional evidence confirming Blair's WMD convictions, nowhere in Alastair Campbell's 793-page memoir does Blair's former chief of

---

[22] BBCNews.com 2002.　　[23] Quoted in Coughlin 2006: 231–2.
[24] Quoted in Coughlin 2006: 232.

staff come close to suggesting anyone on the prime minister's national security team believed the general (as distinct from the neocons' distorted) case against Saddam was wrong.[25] These conclusions were firm and unequivocal. The debate was never about whether or not Saddam had WMD, but whether he retained sufficient weaponry that needed to be dismantled. That imperative alone was sufficient to get inspectors back into the country.

Consider the entry by Campbell (Campbell and Stott 2007: 655) for Wednesday, January 15, 2003: in a discussion of war planning, "TB pressed on whether Saddam would use chemical or biological weapons. They said they were buried so he might not be able to activate them quickly, but that was the reason Franks had gone for the doctrine of overwhelming force."[26] Two weeks later, in his Thursday, January 30 entry, Campbell describes Blair's concerns about Saddam using WMD while the prime minister outlined worst-case scenarios after invasion: "He then laid out potential problems on the way – e.g., Saddam uses WMD, attacks Israel, destroys oil wells, or there is a major civil unrest."[27] It is pretty clear from this entry and other evidence from the war planning meetings described in Gordon and Trainor (2006) that UK military planners not only believed Saddam retained WMD but was capable of using them – the alternative view that he had nothing was never considered.[28]

Tony Blair's crucial role in the 'multilateral' inspections strategy

Bush understood very early in the crisis that Tony Blair was an essential piece of the overall strategy for resolving the Iraq impasse – Blair was a very popular European leader who brought more credibility to the multilateral policy and provided an eloquent defense of the approach. Powell desperately needed Blair as an ally to withstand the pressure from neocons pushing for a pre-emptive, unilateral invasion. Coughlin (2006: 237) recounts the pressure Blair directed at Bush to reject unilateralism in favor of returning to the UN for a new resolution.[29] In a letter from Blair to Bush dated July 2002, the prime minster explained that, in the absence of UN support, he would be unable to contribute to the effort: "the UN was useful as a way of dealing with the matter rather than a means of avoiding it."[30] A strong effort by Washington to obtain UN support would make it much easier for Blair to address his own domestic pressures. As Blair's senior aide explains:

> We knew that Bush was committed to regime change, but that was not something we could support publically for all kinds of reasons. So far as we were concerned, there was a smart way and a dumb way of doing it, and we

---

[25] Campbell and Stott 2007.   [26] Campbell and Stott 2007.
[27] Campbell and Stott 2007: 659.   [28] Gordon and Trainor 2006.
[29] Coughlin 2006.   [30] Coughlin 2006.

believed the smart way of doing it was through the UN. There was still no sense then that we were going to storm into Iraq.[31]

Bush understood Blair's predicament and adjusted his policy accordingly. In fact, one senior Bush administration official was quoted as saying, "when ideas were being put forward, if someone said we are doing this because it is important to Blair, then people sat up and took notice. His name topped our allies list. No one else came close."[32] So when Bush delivered his UN speech committing the country to another round of UN negotiations on another resolution, both Tony Blair and British Foreign Secretary Jack Straw considered it to be one of their most important diplomatic achievements.

At this point, British officials understood that they were not dealing with a singularly committed administration absolutely committed to fighting a unilateral war. The multilateral effort also made it much easier for Blair to recruit other European powers to sign on to the coercive diplomatic strategy. Unofficial multilateral support grew to include several Middle East allies.[33] As Gordon and Trainor (2006: 111) point out:

> As for Egypt, the government was officially opposed to the war. Unofficially, it planned to give US warships access to the Suez Canal and accepted that the United States would fire cruise missiles from the Red Sea. Franks wanted more. The US, he said, could base refuelling tankers at the Cairo West airfield.[34]
>
> *General Franks – speaking with General Mosley (the air war commander):* Let me put pressure on the Egyptians now. I want to get Mubarak more pregnant. Give me the entire package so I can run it through.
>
> Franks' trip to Kuwait went well. The Kuwaitis rolled out the red carpet for him. The Kuwaitis told Franks that Saddam had built man-made lakes to hide his WMD and that weapons were hidden in the Haditha Dam.

Support from Germany (among the war's strongest critics), Jordan, Saudi Arabia and many other states in the region followed, the details of which are outlined in Harvey (2004) and Gordon and Trainor (2006: 123):[35]

> At CENTCOM's headquarters in Qatar, US intelligence officers received a hot tip from one of the unlikeliest sources. Two German agents in Baghdad obtained Saddam's latest plans for defending the capital ... But the German government had cooperated to a limited extent with the US military's war preparation. In Germany, German troops helped guard US bases, freeing up more of Scott Wallace's V Corps to deploy for the war. The German soldiers

---

[31] Coughlin 2006: 239.   [32] Coughlin 2006: 241.   [33] Harvey 2004.

[34] Gordon and Trainor 2006.

[35] Gordon and Trainor 2006. Harvey (2004) also provides a complete list of support from many states that claimed to be opposed but nevertheless facilitated the US–UK (NATO) war effort.

at McKiernan's Camp Delta who operated equipment that was designed
to detect and clean up a potential chemical or biological weapons attack
were another example ... Moreover, Germany had given the Turkish military Patriot antimissile interceptors, a move intended to protect the Turks
against an Iraqi missile attack, but which the Bush administration hopes
would make Ankara more receptive to the idea of opening a Northern front.
In the Red Sea and the Gulf of Aden, German ships guarded the sea lanes
on behalf of Franks' CENTCOM ... in effect the Germans were safeguard-
ing the waterways the United States was using to build up its forces in the
Persian Gulf.

As the authors conclude, "the German decision to provide the Americans with
Saddam's secret plan for protecting his capital was not a defensive precaution but
an act that facilitated CENTCOM's US-led invasion to topple Saddam's regime"
(Gordon and Trainor 2006). Many similar acts by other states that were ostensibly 'opposed' to the war effort are important – but rarely acknowledged – parts
of the multilateralism surrounding the Iraq war. Consider the following statement by Saudi ambassador Prince Bandar bin Sultan in a meeting with Bush on
November 15, 2002:

> Now Mr. President, we want to hear from you directly on your serious
> intention regarding this subject so we can adjust and coordinate so we
> can make the right policy decisions ... Now tell us what you are going
> to do. If you have serious intention, we will not hesitate in giving you
> the right facilities that our two military people can then implement and
> discuss in order to support American military action or campaign ... We
> also expect Saudi Arabia to play a major role in shaping the regime that
> will emerge not only in Iraq but in the region after the fall of Saddam
> Hussein.[36]

The Vilnius letter, signed by eight European leaders "standing alongside the US"
and supporting its approach to Iraq, was viewed by Blair's team as "a rare PR
hit."[37] Both Bush and Blair exploited these multilateral endorsements as a crucial part of their efforts to pressure the UN beyond just its relations with Iraq –
they were meant to convey credible, post-9/11 signals to Libya, Iran and North
Korea.

Comparative plausibility and the UK case for war

As was the case with speeches delivered in the US Congress in October 2002
supporting authorization, in Tony Blair's final speech to parliament there were
no references to neocons' distorted claims about aluminum tubes, uranium
yellowcakes or Iraq–Al-Qaeda–9/11 linkages. These exaggerations were not

---

[36] Quoted in Woodward 2004: 229–30.   [37] Campbell and Stott 2007: 658

required for Blair to make what he believed at the time to be his strongest case for war and the most important speech of his career. Blair's address to the House of Commons on the eve of war, March 18, 2003, reveals how confident Blair was in the more *plausible* interpretation:[38]

> Indeed, we are asked to believe that after seven years of obstruction and non-compliance, finally resulting in the inspectors' leaving in 1998 – seven years in which he hid his programme and built it up, even when the inspectors were there in Iraq – when they had left, he voluntarily decided to do what he had consistently refused to do under coercion.
>
> When the inspectors left in 1998, they left unaccounted for 10,000 litres of anthrax; a far-reaching VX nerve agent programme; up to 6,500 chemical munitions; at least 80 tonnes of mustard gas, and possibly more than 10 times that amount; unquantifiable amounts of sarin, botulinum toxin and a host of other biological poisons; and an entire Scud missile programme.
>
> On 7 March, the inspectors published a remarkable document. It is 173 pages long, and details all the unanswered questions about Iraq's weapons of mass destruction. It lists 29 different areas in which the inspectors have been unable to obtain information. On VX, for example, it says, "Documentation available to Unmovic suggests that Iraq at least had had far reaching plans to weaponise VX." On mustard gas, it says, "Mustard constituted an important part ... of Iraq's CW arsenal ... 550 mustard-filled shells and up to 450 mustard-filled aerial bombs unaccounted for ... additional uncertainty ... with respect to over 6,500 aerial bombs, corresponding to approximately 1,000 tons of agent, predominantly mustard." On biological weapons, the inspectors' report states, "Based on unaccounted-for growth media, Iraq's potential production of anthrax could have been in the range of about 15,000 to 25,000 litres ... Based on all the available evidence, the strong presumption is that about 10,000 litres of anthrax was not destroyed and may still exist."
>
> *We are asked now seriously to accept that in the last few years – contrary to all history, contrary to all intelligence – Saddam decided unilaterally to destroy those weapons. I say that such a claim is palpably absurd.* (Emphasis added)

With respect to the comparative plausibility of competing explanations for Saddam's behavior (threat versus no threat), the case against Iraq was a pretty easy one to make, notwithstanding how wrong it turned out to be – trying to reject this interpretation, a necessary prerequisite for selecting an alternative path away from war, was an almost impossible challenge for skeptics. No one at the time was making this case, including Hans Blix, who issued the following admission one month *after* the war (May 2003):

> Little progress was made in the solution of outstanding issues ... the long list of proscribed items unaccounted for and as such resulting in unresolved

---

[38] Blair 2003.

disarmament issues was not shortened either by the inspections or by Iraqi declarations and documentation.[39]

Doubts, assumptions and suspicions about Saddam's failure to comply were widely shared – in fact, Blix appeared to actually look forward to finally getting some answers once full and complete compliance was possible through occupation.

The final vote in the UK Parliament was 412 for, 149 against. These numbers are not insignificant – they represent a left-of-center party winning on the basis of defending an essentially multilateral approach to the problem that ultimately set the country on a path to war. What was so interesting was the description of Tony Blair's speech as described by Campbell (Campbell and Stott 2007: 681) on Tuesday, March 18 before the vote in the UK Parliament:[40]

> TB's speech in the House was one of his best. Very serious, full of real argument, confronting the points of difficulty and we felt it moving our way. He did a brilliant put-down to the Liberal Democrats, which helped the mood behind him.

Blair also understood the escalatory implications of coercive diplomacy. It is very difficult to come back once these statements and threats are issued – especially when France declares their intention to strip the military option off the table, thereby killing any hope for a second UN resolution.

Campbell (Campbell and Stott 2007: 671) recounted a question he asked Blair on the eve of war, as well as Blair's response: "if at the end of this (Blair) was history before his time, was this really worth sacrificing everything? He said it is always worth doing what you think is the right thing to do. Iraq is a real problem, Saddam is a real problem, for us as much as anyone, and it's been ignored too long."[41] This sentiment captures the perception of the Iraqi threat that drove US–UK policies forward. At the final hour, with mixed reports from Blix, the intelligence on WMD was sufficient to convince Blair that war was justified, despite the political costs and risks. There is no reason why Blair's position would have been different with Gore, Lieberman and Holbrooke in power. Arguably, the most significant difference would have been the higher probability that agreement on the UN process would have occurred much earlier without Gore or Blair having to worry about neocons pushing a unilateralist alternative.

Downing Street memos[42]

The Downing Street memos were written by senior officials serving on Blair's national security and foreign policy teams, usually commenting on: British strategies for dealing with neoconservatives in the Bush administration; the

---

[39] www.un.org/News/Press/docs/2003/sc7777.doc.htm.
[40] Campbell and Stott 2007.   [41] Campbell and Stott 2007.   [42] Straw 2002.

imperative to convince Bush to reject pre-emptive unilateralism by returning to the UN to restart multilateral inspections; the government's position
on exaggerated links to Al-Qaeda; the scope and nature of the WMD threats
they were dealing with; and the wisdom of applying coercive military threats
to force Saddam to comply with UN obligations. The relevant memos included
exchanges involving David Manning (foreign policy adviser), Richard Dearlove
(chief of MI6), Eliza Manningham-Buller (deputy chief of MI5), Jack Straw (foreign secretary) and Geoff Hoon (minister of defence). The memos include some
of the clearest statements by UK officials on record outlining their understanding of the crisis, their interpretation of the evidence against Saddam, and their
policy preferences regarding the appropriate method for disarming the regime.
It becomes evident upon reading that their views were entirely consistent with
Powell's and in sync with the liberal internationalist policy endorsed by Gore in
his 2002 speeches on Iraq.

The memos also clearly acknowledge the division in Washington between
the State Department (Colin Powell), the Pentagon (Donald Rumsfeld, Paul
Wolfowitz and Douglas Feith) and the Vice President's office (Dick Cheney). The
facts revealed by the Downing Street memos are particularly relevant for assessing competing counterfactuals because they highlight the UK's interpretation of
the central divisions in Washington between unilateralists and multilateralists,
as well as the British disdain for those in the Bush administration who were trying to establish Iraq–Al-Qaeda–9/11 linkages. Exaggerating these links would
detract from the main project, British officials argued, because it would intro-
duce weak claims into an otherwise strong case against Saddam for his material
breach of UN resolutions – the same position Powell was defending in exchanges
with Cheney. A more detailed account of the content of these memos is crucial
for understanding the role they played in the policies adopted by Bush and Blair.

Collectively, the memos essentially outline the parameters of the UK's policy preferences and the reasoning they used to convince Bush of the utility of
the UN approach. They understood it would be an uphill battle, but nonetheless considered it essential to protect the bilateral relationship and to address
pressures from other European states and the British public. The UK team was
convinced the UN approach would work to disarm Iraq via a legitimate application of force. Four of the more important and controversial memos will be
discussed below.

Memo 1
Date: March 14, 2002
From: David Manning (UK foreign policy adviser)
To: Prime Minister Tony Blair

Manning describes his impressions in this memo of Washington's Iraq policy, based on a dinner meeting with Condoleezza Rice (US national security
adviser) and a lunch meeting with Rice's National Security Council team.

> We spent a long time at dinner on Iraq. It is clear that Bush is grateful for
> your support and has registered that you are getting flak. I said that you
> would not budge in your support for regime change but you had to manage
> a press, a Parliament and a public opinion that was very different than any-
> thing in the States. And you would not budge either in your insistence that,
> if we pursued regime change, it must be very carefully done and produce the
> right result. Failure was not an option.

The memo confirms the importance Bush placed on obtaining Blair's
support – this, in turn, gave the UK team significant influence (with Powell's
support) when trying to shift Bush's preferences toward the UN strategy. Bush
came to understand the domestic political predicament Blair was facing and
went to great lengths to accommodate his concerns, including accepting his
request to negotiate a second resolution. Manning describes his impressions
of the administration's movement away from a rigid commitment to regime
change:

> Condi's enthusiasm for regime change is undimmed. But there were some
> signs, since we last spoke, of greater awareness of the practical difficulties
> and political risks ... From what she said, Bush has yet to find the answers
> to the big questions: how to persuade international opinion that military
> action against Iraq is necessary and justified; what value to put on the
> exiled Iraqi opposition; how to coordinate a US/allied military campaign
> with internal opposition (assuming there is any); what happens on the
> morning after?

There is a clear sense from this memo that US officials had begun to understand
the domestic political realities Blair was facing:

> Bush will want to pick your brains. He will also want to hear whether he can
> expect coalition support. *I told Condi that we realised that the Administration
> could go it alone if it chose. But if it wanted company, it would have to take
> account of the concerns of its potential coalition partners. In particular: the Un
> [sic] dimension. The issue of the weapons inspectors must be handled in a way
> that would persuade European and wider opinion that the US was conscious
> of the international framework, and the insistence of many countries on the
> need for a legal base. Renewed refused [sic] by Saddam to accept unfettered
> inspections would be a powerful argument*; the paramount importance of
> tackling Israel/Palestine. Unless we did, we could find ourselves bombing
> Iraq and losing the Gulf. (Emphasis added)

Bush's team did come to appreciate the wisdom of Blair's UN-based coercive
diplomatic strategy and accepted the UK view that the approach stood the best
chance of resolving the crisis peacefully:

> No doubt we need to keep a sense of perspective. *But my talks with Condi
> convinced me that Bush wants to hear you [sic] views on Iraq before taking*

decisions. He also wants your support. He is still smarting from the comments by other European leaders on his Iraq policy. *This gives you real influence: on the public relations strategy; on the UN and weapons inspections; and on US planning for any military campaign. This could be critically important.* I think there is a real risk that the Administration underestimates the difficulties. They may agree that failure isn't an option, but this does not mean that they will avoid it. (Emphasis added)

Manning was right. Bush prioritized Blair's support and, as a result, accepted the UK's position on key strategic decisions associated with implementing the multilateral strategy.

Memo 2
Date: March 22, 2002
From: Peter Ricketts (political director, UK Foreign and Commonwealth Office)
To: Jack Straw (UK foreign secretary)

This memo speaks directly to challenging the neoconservative narrative being touted by Cheney, Rumsfeld and other prominent neocon advisers. It highlights the commonality of US and UK interests, and emphasizes the potential for Blair to influence the president's outlook on the impasse:

> By sharing Bush's broad objective the Prime Minister can help shape how it is defined, and the approach to achieving it. In the process, he can bring home to Bush the realities which will be less evident from Washington. He can help Bush make good decisions by telling him things his own machine probably isn't. (Emphasis added)

This is the approach Blair adopted and used to great success in the next several weeks. Bush was persuaded to see the international and diplomatic "realities" that highlighted the need to approach the crisis multilaterally:

> First, the THREAT. *The truth is that what has changed is not the pace of Saddam Hussein's WMD programmes, but our tolerance of them post-11 September. This is not something we need to be defensive about, but attempts to claim otherwise publicly will increase scepticism about our case.* I am relieved that you decided to postpone publication of the unclassified document. My meeting yesterday showed that there is more work to do to ensure that the figures are accurate and consistent with those of the US. *But even the best survey of Iraq's WMD programmes will not show much advance in recent years on the nuclear, missile or CW/BW fronts: the programmes are extremely worrying but have not, as far as we know, been stepped up.* (Emphasis added)

UK officials believed there was a sufficient enough threat tied to Iraq's WMD, and this was even more pressing after 9/11. The memo also clarifies the view that the WMD threat was "extremely worrying" but had not been stepped up. This is a common theme in all of the UK memos that helped to form Blair's policy preference in talks with Bush – the generally accepted (non-distorted) threat was *sufficient* to take the UN route, and the UN route was essential for UK support:

> US scrambling to establish a link between Iraq and Al Qaida is so far frankly unconvincing. To get public and Parliamentary support for military operations, we have to be convincing that: the threat is so serious/imminent that it is worth sending our troops to die for; it is qualitatively different from the threat posed by other proliferators who are closer to achieving nuclear capability (including Iran) … We can make the case on qualitative difference[:] only Iraq has attacked a neighbour, used CW and fired missiles against Israel. The overall strategy needs to include re-doubled efforts to tackle other proliferators, including Iran, in other ways (the UK/French ideas on greater IAEA activity are helpful here). *But we are still left with a problem of bringing public opinion to accept the imminence of a threat from Iraq. This is something the Prime Minister and President need to have a frank discussion about.* (Emphasis added)
>
> *As with the fight against (Osama Bin-laden) Bush would do well to depersonalise the objective – focus on elimination of WMD, and show that he is serious about UN Inspectors as the first choice means of achieving that (it is win/win for him: either Saddam against all the odds allows Inspectors to operate freely, in which case we can further hobble his WMD programmes, or he blocks/hinders, and we are on stronger ground for switching to other methods).* (Emphasis added)

This is a crucial memo because, together with previous exchanges, it clearly establishes the view held by UK officials that links to Al-Qaeda were not required to justify the approach they were endorsing. The Al-Qaeda threat and purported operational linkages to the Iraqi regime were, in the minds of most UK and US officials, too weak to be taken seriously and created more challenges than they resolved. This same point was shared by George Tenet and Colin Powell in their debates with Cheney.

The memo to Manning was referring to the intelligence being highlighted by the National Security Agency (NSA), Vice President Cheney and the Pentagon – the links to Al-Qaeda were being interpreted and exaggerated to fit the policy of unilateral pre-emption. Tenet and Powell shared the UK concerns and, with Blair's support, convinced Bush that the best policy was not unilateralism but multilateral coercion through the UN. The memo was not a sweeping rejection of the concept of dealing with Iraq's WMD threat – it was simply a rejection of this particular part of the intelligence record being manipulated by Cheney, the Pentagon and neoconservatives in the administration. As Campbell (Campbell and Stott 2007: 669) points out in his Thursday, February 27 entry:

> TB felt we had to be pushing on two main arguments – the moral case, and the reason why the threat was real and current, not because he could whack missiles off at London but because he could tie up with terrorists

and others with a vested interest in damaging us and our interests. *But we should understate rather than overstate* a point I made on the conference call. The Americans' saying there was a direct link (to Al-Qaeda) was *counterproductive*. Far better to be saying this was a possibility and one we were determined to ensure never came about. (Emphasis added)[43]

Blair is essentially saying more is less and less is more. The key point is that the overall case regarding links between Saddam and terrorism, and the larger WMD case against Iraq, compiled from years of intelligence – the case everyone (including critics of the war) could agree on without *any* reference to exaggerated intelligence being pushed by neoconservatives – was the case Blair believed should form the core of the arguments against Saddam. The exception in the UK's case was the suggestion in one report that Saddam had the capability to deploy and use his WMD in a very short period of time. And this was the same general case that was winning the day in Washington and clearly emerges from a review of the speeches delivered in Congress supporting authorization (see Chapter 4).

Memo 3
Date: March 25, 2002
From: Jack Straw (UK foreign secretary)
To: Tony Blair

The memo was composed for Blair in preparation for his visit to Crawford, Texas to meet President Bush and his national security team:

> On whether any military action would require a fresh UNSC mandate (Desert Fox did not). The US are [*sic*] likely to oppose any idea of a fresh mandate. On the other side, the weight of legal advice here is that a fresh mandate may well be required. *There is no doubt that a new UNSCR would transform the climate in the [Parliamentary Labour Party]* (emphasis added). Whilst that (a new mandate) is very unlikely, given the US's position, a draft resolution against military action with 13 in favour (or handsitting) and two vetoes against could play very badly here … A legal justification is a necessary but far from sufficient pre-condition for military action. We have also to answer the big question – what will this action achieve? There seems to be a larger hole in this than on anything. *Most of the assessments from the US have assumed regime change as a means of eliminating Iraq's WMD threat. But none has satisfactorily answered how that regime change is to be secured, and how there can be any certainty that the replacement regime will be better.* (Emphasis added)

Although expectations were not high for a new resolution and fresh mandate, the UK team was hopeful they could persuade Bush to see the importance of at

---

[43] Campbell and Stott 2007.

least negotiating towards a new resolution. Obviously the team was very pleased when Powell managed to get unanimous endorsement of UNSCR 1441 declaring Iraq in material breach and threatening "serious consequences." This was exactly what Blair and his team were hoping for. And, with respect to moving the administration on regime change, Bush officials were persuaded in the end to issue a final ultimatum requesting the removal of Saddam, his sons and senior members of his staff – *leadership* change rather than *regime* change was the preferred strategy, another victory for the UK and another defeat for Cheney and the neocons.

Memo 4
Date: July 23, 2002
From: Matthew Rycroft (private secretary to Tony Blair, advising on foreign affairs)
To: David Manning (UK foreign policy adviser)
cc: national security team (defence secretary, foreign secretary, attorney general).

This memo helps to highlight the divide between unilateralists (who favoured bypassing the UN) and those who believed another UNSC resolution was necessary to provide a legal justification for war. The UK was strongly committed to the latter, and British officials were largely successful in helping to convince the Bush administration of the same.

> C [Sir Richard Dearlove, Director of MI6] reported on his recent talks in Washington. There was a perceptible shift in attitude. Military action was now seen as inevitable. *Bush wanted to remove Saddam, through military action, justified by the conjunction of terrorism and WMD. But the intelligence and facts were being fixed around the policy. The NSC had no patience with the UN route, and no enthusiasm for publishing material on the Iraqi regime's record.* There was little discussion in Washington of the aftermath after military action. (Emphasis added)
>
> The Foreign Secretary said he would discuss this with Colin Powell this week. It seemed clear that Bush had made up his mind to take military action, even if the timing was not yet decided. But the case was thin. *Saddam was not threatening his neighbours, and his WMD capability was less than that of Libya, North Korea or Iran. We should work up a plan for an ultimatum to Saddam to allow back in the UN weapons inspectors. This would also help with the legal justification for the use of force.* (Emphasis added)

Based on these optimistic impressions of Iraq's WMD programs and the related threat, the officials recommended rejecting the distorted estimates, and the unilateralist policy such estimates were designed to support, in favor of returning to the UN for an ultimatum to force Saddam to allow inspectors back into the country – again, *consistent* with the policy path strongly endorsed by Tony Blair and Al Gore, and the one Bush ultimately adopted.

With respect to the central legal arguments UK officials were debating, the memo goes on to explain:

> There were three possible legal bases: self-defence, humanitarian intervention, or UNSC authorisation. The first and second could not be the base in this case. Relying on UNSCR 1205 of three years ago would be difficult. The situation might of course change.
>
> *The Prime Minister said that it would make a big difference politically and legally if Saddam refused to allow in the UN inspectors. Regime change and WMD were linked in the sense that it was the regime that was producing the WMD.* There were different strategies for dealing with Libya and Iran. If the political context were right, people would support regime change. The two key issues were whether the military plan worked and whether we had the political strategy to give the military plan the space to work. (Emphasis added)

The battle was never between those in favor of war and peace; it was between those favoring unilateral pre-emption, on the one hand, and, on the other, almost everyone else who preferred a multilaterally endorsed UN route. The neocons lost this crucially important battle to the British, realists, moderates and liberal internationalists. From this point on, the policy that was adopted, and the consequences that flowed from efforts to make the policy work, were direct products of this UN/multilateral approach.

International diplomacy and negotiations: UNSCR 1441

Appreciating the true significance of a UN resolution requires more than simply reading it – the contents are given added meaning when viewed in the context of the battles that were won and lost during negotiations over wording. These details are often neglected in standard neoconist accounts. The drafting stage for the new resolution on Iraq was expected to last two weeks but it actually required seven weeks to complete. Debates over the final wording were prolonged because both sides wanted a multilateral agreement that served their unilateral self-interests. In view of the fact that both sides invested so much time and effort in the process, the final product of these negotiations is essentially the best outcome both sides could get to protect their respective interests.

From the point of view of France, Russia and China, UNSCR 1441 represents the most watered down version of the WMD picture they could negotiate – the best version they could work out in their attempt to prevent the United States and UK from making a strong case for war. Despite their efforts to challenge Washington's claims regarding Iraq's flagrant violation (material breach) of all previous UN resolutions, the final draft of the resolution is a damning indictment of the Iraqi regime and a clear case for the seriousness of the WMD threat.

Apparently, if anyone in these negotiations was convinced that Saddam's WMD stockpiles were a myth, they failed miserably to persuade others to accept that view. The US–UK position on Iraq's WMD prevailed, and France, Russia and China endorsed that interpretation when they signed the resolution.

Among the many debates over the words to include in the resolution, the most important centered on the question of whether Saddam would be in further material breach of his UN obligations if he delivered a false declaration on the status of his WMD *and/or* failed to cooperate by providing UN inspectors with unconditional, immediate and unfettered access to all suspected WMD sites. Powell preferred the more straightforward 'or' mandate to determine the conditions under which "serious consequences" would follow, but France's Foreign Minister, Dominique de Villepin, argued in favor of using the word 'and' as a way of raising the standards for determining further material breach.[44] Powell conceded on this point, but both he and Blair forcefully argued later in the process that Saddam had clearly violated both conditions.

Of course, there were other important reasons the negotiations over UNSCR 1441 required seven weeks, including the extended debate over the precise requirements for a second resolution authorizing force. This time, Colin Powell and UK Foreign Affairs Minister Jack Straw won the debate – the final wording did *not* require a second resolution, only an agreement to "consider" one. This was viewed by US and UK officials as a significant diplomatic coup, a victory both Blair and Straw highlighted during the most recent British government inquiry into events leading up to the Iraq war.[45] As Straw points out in his testimony, if all sides agreed that UNSCR 1441 was only the first step of a two-stage process, "negotiations would have been over in a week. They just would have." Straw's (2010: 42) testimony goes on to explain:

> People would have said, "Okay, we all accept all these resolutions could have happened already. We all accept that Iraq continues to be in material breach, we have all said so time and again. We agree that we should get the inspectors back in and we also agree that a final decision on anything else that follows from that, serious consequences, anything else, should come back to the Security Council for decision." That would have been dead easy and it would have been over. There has to be a reason, Sir Lawrence, why these negotiations began in late September and went on intensively, night and day, for six weeks, and the reason was that, because of the Americans', so called red line, and indeed our own, that we believed that Saddam had had enough final opportunities to be given just one more.[46]

---

[44] Woodward (2004: 223) devotes a good part of his book on the war to events surrounding the seven-week debate with France over the wording of the new UNSCR 1441 resolution.

[45] Please see video at: www.iraqinquiry.org.uk.

[46] www.iraqinquiry.org.uk/media/44940/100208pm-straw.pdf.

Sir Jeffrey Greenstock (British ambassador to the UN and heavily involved in UN negotiations) agreed with this interpretation of UNSCR 1441 as it related to the need for a second resolution:

> The French were very difficult throughout the negotiations for 1441 and, frankly, I was surprised that they voted for it, as it did not contain their bottom line, which was that the UN retain control over the whole process. I suppose they calculated that it was not in their interest to cross the US over a state like Iraq that they knew to be unsavoury.[47]

Powell and Straw firmly believed they had persuaded France, Russia and China to accept their draft in which the military threat to impose "serious consequences" would not be tied to a second resolution, and would not require another round of debate to determine whether military force should be used "to secure international peace and security." As mentioned, the US–UK team successfully negotiated the exclusion of the word "decide" (in paragraph 12) and replaced it with the word "consider:"

> 12. Decides to convene immediately upon receipt of a report in accordance with paragraphs 4 or 11 above, in order to *consider* the situation and the need for full compliance with all of the relevant Council resolutions in order to secure international peace and security. (Emphasis added)

The diplomatic coup was discussed at other points during the UK's Iraq Inquiry:[48]

> *Sir Lawrence Freedman*: Then you make a point very strongly in your statement and this has been confirmed by Sir Jeremy Greenstock that you did not believe that military action thereafter, in the event of noncompliance, would depend on a second resolution. It would be desirable but it wasn't dependent on that. We are not, today, going into the legal arguments on that. Sir Jeremy's basic contention was that he had got the Americans and British into a comparable position as before Desert Fox in December 1998. So I think that's quite important, that your understanding, at least of the position, was that it wasn't absolutely essential to have a second resolution.
>
> *Right Honourable Jack Straw*: I was not in any doubt about that and neither was Jeremy Greenstock, and for very good reasons, which is that there had been talk by the French and Germans of a draft which would have required a second resolution, but they never tabled it. We tabled a draft, which, as I set out in this memorandum, and which Sir Jeremy Greenstock confirms in his memorandum, was aimed to be self-contained, in the sense that, if very important conditions were met through failures by the Saddam regime, that of itself would provide sufficient authority for military action, and no doubt

---

[47] Coughlin 2006: 260. Con interviewed Sir Jeffrey Greenstock, British Ambassador to the UN, who was heavily involved in the crisis.

[48] www.iraqinquiry.org.uk.

the next time we will get into the wording of the resolution, which, as I say in this memorandum, I can virtually recite in my sleep, but there are reasons why in OP12 we use the language that we do, and serious consequences are mentioned in OP13 and so on. For sure, we wanted a second resolution after that.

France's Foreign Minister de Villepin believed he successfully negotiated a resolution that meant no automatic war, but the United States and UK believed they took seven weeks to successfully negotiate a resolution that required no second resolution – only a commitment to consider one. France got what they wanted – no automatic war *and* a subsequent decision by the United States and UK to return to the UNSC to negotiate a second resolution, consistent with their obligation to "consider" the option. However, when French officials decided, in the context of the second round of negotiations, to exclude any reference to a strict timeline or a military solution, this put US and UK officials in a very difficult, irresolvable position – the status quo (endless inspections without a military threat despite the deployment of hundreds of thousands of troops in theater) was not acceptable. Far too much had been invested, and too many explicit threats issued, to accept this outcome.

International diplomacy and negotiations over a second resolution

US and UK suspicions continued to mount each time UNMOVIC Chief Hans Blix tabled yet another mixed report. Despite it being Saddam's last chance to comply, he failed to satisfy the demands of UNSCR 1441 regarding unconditional and unfettered access, and the absence of proactive cooperation (the term Blix used to describe what he would have preferred to see from the regime) simply reconfirmed suspicions that Iraqi officials continued to hide proscribed WMD.

Blair and other UK officials invested considerable time and effort into convincing Bush's team to begin negotiations on a second resolution, despite the strong reservations expressed by Cheney and neoconservatives. Once again, the latter group lost this key debate. Bush's determination to keep Britain in the coalition was far more important to him than support from neocons, so he decided to return to the UN for another round of negotiations. As the push for a second resolution kicked in, there were essentially two approaches put forward – the strategy endorsed by Britain and Canada was to extend inspections by a specific timeframe (from two weeks to a month), backed by the threat of military force; and the alternative approach, recommended by France, to extend inspections without a timeline and without a threat of military force. In fact, French officials made it very clear that they would not move forward with a second resolution if a military threat was included.

Once Hans Blix tabled his 'cluster document' detailing all outstanding, unaccounted for WMD (March 6), the British government recommended using

March 17 as the ten-day deadline for Iraq to produce all remaining documents pertaining to the location of WMD programs or clear proof of their destruction. On March 7, French officials rejected the inclusion of any reference to timelines or military threat: "France will not allow a resolution to pass that authorizes the automatic use of force" (Dominique de Villepin).[49] UK Foreign Minister Jack Straw responded to the French decree with this quip: "It may take time to fabricate further falsehoods, but the truth takes only seconds to tell."[50] Secretary of State Colin Powell added his own critique of the French position: "Some people, in my judgment, simply do not want to see the facts clearly."[51]

Notwithstanding France's reservations, Canada's Foreign Minister Bill Graham described the British proposal as "a positive step."[52] In an effort to establish a compromise, Canadian officials recommended using March 31 as the new deadline, but at no point in these deliberations did any Canadian official suggest removing the military threat. The problem, however, with the UK and Canadian proposals to extend inspections by either two weeks or a month, respectively, is that both proposals were destined to fail.

The futility of Canadian and British compromises on extending inspections

The Canadian government's position on Iraq's WMD was clearly outlined by Canada's UN ambassador, Paul Heinbecker, in several speeches to the United Nations – on October 16, 2002; February 9, 2003; March 11, 2003; and March 26, 2003 (please see Appendix 7.1).[53] It is absolutely clear from the content of these statements that Canadian officials, like everyone else, firmly believed Saddam posed a serious threat to international security, was in material breach of existing UN resolutions, and had failed to provide the required information on the status of proscribed weapons listed in Blix's reports. Canadian officials were thus equally responsible for reinforcing conventional views about Saddam's WMD.

---

[49] Quoted in Knox 2003.   [50] Knox 2003.   [51] Knox 2003.   [52] Knox 2003.

[53] Statement by Ambassador Paul Heinbecker, Permanent Representative of Canada to the United Nations Security Council Open Debate on the Situation in Iraq. New York, October 16, 2002: – www.heinbecker.ca/Speeches/UN_speeches/oct%2016%202002.pdf; Statement Given by H.E Paul Heinbecker, Ambassador of Canada to the United Nations at the UNSC Open Debate on the Situation Between Iraq and Kuwait, March 11, 2003: www.heinbecker. ca/Speeches/UN_speeches/Statement-March11–2003-situation-between-Iraq-Kuwait. pdf; Statement Given by H.E Paul Heinbecker, Ambassador of Canada to the United Nations at the UNSC Open Debate on the Situation Between Iraq and Kuwait, March 26, 2003: www.heinbecker.ca/Speeches/UN_speeches/mar%2026%202003.pdf; Statement by Ambassador Paul Heinbecker to the United Nations Security Council, March 27, 2003: www.heinbecker.ca/Speeches/UNSecCouncilStatement-Mar27–03.pdf; Statement Given by H.E Paul Heinbecker, Ambassador of Canada to the United Nations at the UNSC Open Debate on the Situation Between Iraq and Kuwait, February 19, 2003: www.heinbecker.ca/ Speeches/UN_speeches/february%2018%202003.pdf.

It is also clear from Heinbecker's speeches that Canadian officials supported the US–UK approach to the crisis, including the "useful" deployment of troops to the region to enhance the credibility of the military threat. When negotiations over the second resolution began, Heinbecker crafted what he believed was the perfect compromise between the British and French positions:

> Both sides have a point: An open-ended inspection process would relieve the pressure on the Iraqis to disarm. A truncated inspection process would leave doubt that war was a last resort. The focus should be put back upon disarmament, on substance, not on process – e.g., the disposition of the VX gas and precursors, etc.
>
> The Iraqis should be left in no doubt exactly what is demanded of them on substance, not just on process, i.e., no wiggle room.
>
> Hence the need for a deadline for substantial cooperation, for example, March 28, which would (1) be near-term enough to keep the pressure on the Iraqis to disarm, (2) nonetheless afford sufficient time for judgments to be made whether the Iraqis were cooperating on substance in disarming and/or providing persuasive and credible evidence that weapons have already been destroyed, as claimed.

Heinbecker believed the Canadian proposal satisfied the French and German position to extend inspections beyond March 17 (the deadline stipulated in the UK proposal), and would determine whether Iraq was willing to provide "credible" evidence that weapons had been destroyed.

But there are several reasons why extending inspections would not have worked. First, extending inspections would not have resolved the deadlock simply because Saddam did not retain the documents required by UNSCR 1441 to prove he had destroyed the proscribed material. Second, Saddam and his senior advisers were working under a set of false assumptions about US and UK intentions – they did not believe the invasion threat (see Chapter 8). Why would another month of inspections convince Saddam of the credibility of the US–UK threat? And, with respect to the French declaration rejecting any attempt to retain the military option, why would Saddam be more likely to comply with UNSCR 1441 without a credible threat to worry about? Third, despite strong suspicions to the contrary, there were no stockpiles of WMD to uncover and, therefore, no evidence to demonstrate successful inspections and disarmament. An additional few weeks or a month would not have resolved these fundamental issues, and would not have produced a final report from Blix declaring the regime clean. How would UNMOVIC inspectors accomplish in two weeks (or one month) what it took the Iraq Survey Group a full two years to conclude, while ISG inspectors had absolute control over the entire country?

Fourth, whatever evidence UNMOVIC would uncover through extended inspections would have revealed additional proof of material breach and deception, but no clear evidence of stockpiles – the worst possible outcome for those opposed to invasion. David Kay's interim report to Congress provided the following list of examples of material breach of UNSCR 1441:[54]

> We have discovered dozens of WMD-related program activities and significant amounts of equipment that Iraq concealed from the United Nations during the inspections that began in late 2002. The discovery of these deliberate concealment efforts have come about both through the admissions of Iraqi scientists and officials concerning information they deliberately withheld and through physical evidence of equipment and activities that ISG has discovered that should have been declared to the UN. Let me just give you a few examples of these concealment efforts, some of which I will elaborate on later:
>
> - A clandestine network of laboratories and safehouses within the Iraqi Intelligence Service that contained equipment subject to UN monitoring and suitable for continuing CBW research.
> - A prison laboratory complex, possibly used in human testing of BW agents, that Iraqi officials working to prepare for UN inspections were explicitly ordered not to declare to the UN.
> - Reference strains of biological organisms concealed in a scientist's home, one of which can be used to produce biological weapons.
> - New research on BW-applicable agents, Brucella and Congo Crimean Hemorrhagic Fever (CCHF), and continuing work on ricin and aflatoxin were not declared to the UN.
> - Documents and equipment, hidden in scientists' homes, that would have been useful in resuming uranium enrichment by centrifuge and electromagnetic isotope separation (EMIS).
> - A line of UAVs not fully declared at an undeclared production facility and an admission that they had tested one of their declared UAVs out to a range of 500 km, 350 km beyond the permissible limit.
> - Continuing covert capability to manufacture fuel propellant useful only for prohibited SCUD variant missiles, a capability that was maintained at least until the end of 2001 and that cooperating Iraqi scientists have said they were told to conceal from the UN.
> - Plans and advanced design work for new long-range missiles with ranges up to at least 1,000 km – well beyond the 150 km range limit imposed by the UN. Missiles of a 1000 km range would have allowed Iraq to threaten targets throughout the Middle East, including Ankara, Cairo, and Abu Dhabi.
> - Clandestine attempts between late 1999 and 2002 to obtain from North Korea technology related to 1,300 km range ballistic missiles – probably the No Dong – 300 km range anti-ship cruise missiles, and other prohibited military equipment.

[54] Kay 2003.

In addition to the discovery of extensive concealment efforts, we have been faced with a systematic sanitization of documentary and computer evidence in a wide range of offices, laboratories, and companies suspected of WMD work. The pattern of these efforts to erase evidence – hard drives destroyed, specific files burned, equipment cleaned of all traces of use – are ones of deliberate, rather than random, acts.

Consider Kay's conclusions:

In my judgment, based on the work that has been done to this point of the Iraq Survey Group, and in fact, that I reported to you in October, Iraq was in clear violation of the terms of [UN] Resolution 1441. Resolution 1441 required that Iraq report all of its activities – one last chance to come clean about what it had. We have discovered hundreds of cases, based on both documents, physical evidence and the testimony of Iraqis, of activities that were prohibited under the initial UN Resolution 687 and that should have been reported under 1441, with Iraqi testimony that not only did they not tell the UN about this, they were instructed not to do it and they hid material.

Had inspections been extended in line with either the Canadian or British compromise, inspectors would have continued to uncover minor infractions of material breach (like those listed above). The problem is that uncovering further proof of deception and material breach at this late stage in the crisis would have been far more disturbing, because it would have confirmed Saddam's reluctance, despite the threat of war, to comply with clear demands and would have reinforced suspicions that he must be hiding something significant – why else would he risk war and death? The international community was essentially facing an irresolvable paradox in which war could only be avoided if Saddam provided proof of disarmament, which didn't exist, and the only way to find the required evidence that would have prevented war was after invasion and occupation.

The reason Washington rejected the Canadian compromise was explained by State Department spokesman Richard Boucher – it "only procrastinates":[55]

Our goal is also to focus peoples' minds on the facts of the matter, to focus peoples' minds on where we are, how long it's been since 1991 when the council set its first deadline of 45 days for Iraq to disarm. We've now gone over 4,200 days. The council has said nine times that Iraq was in material breach. We've said 11 times that that would result in serious consequences. The question that faces us now is when are we going to mean it?

Rivkin and Casey (2003) capture another important reason why extending inspections was bound to fail:[56]

---

[55] Voice of America News 2003.   [56] Rivkin and Casey 2003.

Inspections agreements – no matter how coercive – never could have worked because they never addressed the fundamental issue: Hussein's desire to preserve WMD ambiguity in order to preserve Iraq's perceived influence and power. Removing that ambiguity would have removed Hussein's ability to bully, bluster and blackmail the world. Perversely, UN Resolution 1441's poorly implemented inspection protocols fed the worst fears of both sides. Iraq's perfunctory compliance and deceitful history guaranteed that the United States would distrust the UN's lackluster assurances of compliance. By contrast, Iraq's desire to be feared guaranteed that it would always manufacture just enough ambiguity to preserve its aura of menace. The inspectors' tortured attempts to appear even handed succeeded only in generating even greater ambiguities about both Iraq's willingness to comply and the weapons in its possession. And Secretary of State Colin L. Powell's dramatic yet desperate presentation before the UN Security Council was harshly attacked by critics who maintained that, yes, America's WMD evidence was inconclusively ambiguous.

Strategic ambiguity could not be removed by inspections, because the regime's strategy was based on several fundamentally mistaken assumptions (discussed in more detail in the next chapter):

(1) the US–UK coalition would not invade;
(2) any attack would be limited to air strikes with no invading forces approaching Baghdad;
(3) Iran was a bigger threat than the United States and UK;
(4) the Iraqi military was capable of holding off an invading force (headed for Baghdad) long enough to make the conflict too costly to sustain;
(5) the United States and UK could not sustain the number of casualties the Iraqi military was capable of generating; and
(6) France and Russia were strong enough to prevent a US–UK invasion by simply rejecting the call for a second resolution backed by a military threat.

Extending inspections would do very little to correct these serious misperceptions – in fact, a decision at the eleventh hour to concede to a British, Canadian or French demand to extend inspections would simply have reinforced Saddam's suspicions regarding the absence of resolve on the part of Western leaders.

Ironically, had Heinbecker's compromise been accepted by the United States, it would have put Canada in a very difficult position of having to support an intervention, because inspections were bound to fail for all of the reasons outlined above. Like many participants, Heinbecker is now trying hard to distance himself (and the Canadian government) from any indication that they supported the WMD case against Iraq. But there is nothing in Heinbecker's (or the Canadian government's) official speeches indicating serious reservations about that threat. In fact, had Heinbecker honestly believed at the time that Saddam did not pose a threat, or had no WMD to worry about or dismantle, then

Canada's decision to push the Heinbecker compromise would have been a huge strategic blunder that could have dragged the country into the Iraq war. Since the regime did not have weapons to uncover, or documented proof that they had been destroyed, there was no evidence to demonstrate any of the disarmament "successes" Heinbecker and others were hoping to find. If Washington accepted the Canadian compromise, it would have been very difficult for Canadian officials to then decline the US–UK request to help the coalition impose serious consequences for Saddam's failures.

Furthermore, with respect to relevant counterfactual points emerging from these facts, it was widely known at the time that Prime Minister Jean Chrétien openly supported Gore's candidacy, so it is certainly not unreasonable to expect that Gore would have received more support from Heinbecker and Ottawa for the same policies, as was the case with Canadian support for Clinton and Gore when they went to war with Iraq in 1998. Consider Canadian Foreign Affairs Minister Lloyd Axworthy's statement of support for Operation Desert Fox on December 8, 1998:[57]

> Perhaps the greatest challenge that we face is the proliferation of nuclear, chemical and biological weapons of mass destruction. The impact of these weapons is indisputable. Yet the non-proliferation regime we have constructed to counter this threat is in jeopardy. The dangers come from several sources: Iraq, Libya and Sudan remain risks in developing chemical and biological weapons. Illicit transfers of nuclear, chemical and biological weapon grade materials or know-how pose a very real threat to us all.

The fact is that everyone in Canada, including Heinbecker and Foreign Affairs Minister Bill Graham, believed that Saddam retained proscribed WMD. The only logical reason Canadian officials wanted to extend inspections was their strong suspicions that WMD (or proof of their destruction) could actually be uncovered. Everyone in favor of extending inspections assumed that with enough time, inspectors would uncover the programs everyone believed he was hiding, thereby demonstrating sufficient success to prevent war. Paradoxically, war became more likely precisely because there were no WMD for inspectors to uncover. There was, in essence, no way to satisfy the Canadian (or any other) compromise.

When no WMD were found after the war, Heinbecker, like many of those who participated in these events, began to construct his own revisionist historical accounts of the crisis. In April, 2004, Heinbecker wrote the following in Canada's national newspaper, the *Globe and Mail*:[58]

---

[57] The statement was delivered in support of the bombing campaign in Operation Desert Fox. See Canadian Minister of Foreign Affairs to the North Atlantic Council Meeting, December 8, 1998: www.nato.int/docu/speech/1998/s981208i.htm.

[58] Heinbecker 2004.

The substance of the compromise consisted of setting a series of tests of Iraqi co-operation, on a pass-or-fail basis, and a limited time frame within which to assess results ... Few were persuaded by the "intelligence" presented to the UN Security Council and to the world by the US Secretary of State and the director of the CIA. There is little doubt that it would have been in everyone's interests, especially Washington's, to have accepted the compromise.

Heinbecker's counterfactual argument fails to acknowledge the significant problems plaguing the Canadian compromise (listed above) – his 'solution' would not have resolved the disarmament impasse, would not have uncovered the WMD material everyone suspected Saddam retained, would not have corrected the misperceptions driving Iraq policy, and, as a result, would very likely have dragged Canada into the war once the compromise failed. In truth, Heinbecker should consider himself very lucky not to have been blessed with the diplomatic skills required to persuade the UK and United States to accept his compromise.

The former ambassador goes on in the same article to make the following claim:

[T]he Iraq war demonstrates the limits of intelligence. The US administration and others made intelligence pivotal to their decision-making. The Canadian government used it as one input among many. One government is embarrassed and the other is not. Time, and enquiries, will tell whether the intelligence in the United States and Britain was just catastrophically bad, politically manipulated or both. The Canadian analysis was better ... We should not shrink from disagreeing with US administrations when they are wrong any more than we should shrink from agreeing with them when they are right. We should call them as we see them. We did so on Iraq, and we have been vindicated.

It is astounding that, within a year of making several major speeches to the UN defending the exact opposite arguments (see Appendix 7.1), Heinbecker is now prepared to completely ignore his legacy of previous statements in order to distance himself from the role he and Canadian officials played in events leading to war. He was directly responsible, through his speeches, for reinforcing the WMD consensus, and he relied on the exact same intelligence he now dismisses as embarrassing, catastrophically bad and politically manipulated. Nowhere in any of the speeches he delivered during this crucial period did Heinbecker come anywhere close to making the points he raised in the *Globe* piece, and he is now comfortably removed from any responsibility for Canadian security. He never once explicitly questioned the generally accepted intelligence, never once stated that the United States had no basis for intervening, never once questioned the reference to nuclear programs in UNSCR 1441 or the conclusion that Iraq was in material breach of existing UN resolutions. In fact, Heinbecker's speeches to the UN were no different from speeches being made by Bush, Blair, or US and British legislators on both sides of the aisle. Heinbecker also acknowledges that the placement of coercive US and UK troops in the region was *"indispensable"* to getting Iraq to comply, so he too was giving credit where he thought credit was due and blaming Saddam (not the United States) for the impasse.[59] Yet critics today claim the deployment was among the most important enabling conditions that created the path-dependent momentum to war; Heinbecker was in favor of this approach, because it stood the best chance of forcing Saddam to dismantle the WMD programs everyone, including Heinbecker, believed he had.

If Heinbecker honestly believed in 2002–2003 what he wrote in 2004, then he had an obligation to the Canadian people and UN to raise these concerns as explicitly and publically as possible back then. The speeches he delivered not only failed to do so but in fact achieved the exact opposite effect – reinforcing consensus on Saddam's WMD. Missing in Heinbecker's analysis is any reference to what ISG inspectors uncovered through hundreds of interviews with Saddam and his senior advisers after the war, and how Iraq's mistakes reinforced Western (and Heinbecker's) suspicions.

France's rejection of a timeline backed by a threat of military force

The United States was not the only UN Security Council member to reject the Canadian compromise. While the United States rejected the proposal because there was no indication that an extension would resolve the impasse, France rejected the compromise because it retained the threat of military force. Chirac did acknowledge that a delay of thirty days "would allow weapons inspectors to determine whether an impasse had been reached," but both Chirac and de Villepin remained steadfastly against the attachment of a deadline backed by a threat of military force.[60] However, if this option were stripped from the overall strategy, the costs to the United States of sustaining such a large deployment in theater, with no relevant role in the diplomacy, was unacceptable. Conceding on this issue would have been very costly for any president or prime minister – it would have amounted to accepting a French veto over a congressional resolution authorizing force and a UN resolution authorizing "serious consequences" in a post-9/11 environment. Krauthammer offers a compelling counterfactual description of the circumstances that would likely have followed a decision by US officials to accept France's demands:

> The troop deployment was itself unsustainable. Upon its withdrawal, the collapse of the sanctions regime would have continued, resulting in a re-energized and relegitimized regime headed by Saddam (and ultimately,

---

[59] Statement Given by H.E. Paul Heinbecker, Ambassador of Canada to the United Nations at the UNSC Open Debate on the Situation Between Iraq and Kuwait, March 11, 2003: www.heinbecker.ca/Speeches/UN_speeches/Statement-March11–2003-situation-between-Iraq-Kuwait.pdf.

[60] Kopp 2003.

even worse, by his sons) that was increasingly Islamicizing its Ba'athi ideology, re-arming and renewing WMD programs, and extending its connections with terror groups.[61]

Ironically, France's decision to reject the military option increased the probability of war for several reasons. It convinced Saddam the US–UK would not attack, while simultaneously threatening to produce a status quo that was politically untenable for any president. It would have been very expensive to sustain the deployment through summer, would damage US–UK credibility in this and future cases with other aspiring WMD powers, and would do nothing to address lingering suspicions regarding WMD. The French declaration simply reconfirmed US–UK suspicions that France was not serious about threatening military force to ensure the success of inspections. This would also have confirmed to Saddam that US and UK leaders were not serious about regime change.

Conclusions: *Gore-war* versus *Gore-peace* revisited

As this chapter has outlined, the international politics associated with the Iraq war were far more complex, nuanced and interesting than is commonly acknowledged in standard neoconist accounts. Far from an elaborate and diabolical 'hoodwinking' of the international community by a set of neoconservative confidence men, the story reveals repeated and rational (albeit eventually disastrous) errors by national governments from around the world – errors that had very little to do with neoconservative interpretations, arguments or distortions. Global consensus on Iraq's WMD, the content of Hans Blix's reports, the UK rejection of intelligence distortions, and the negotiations at the UN over a first and second UNSC resolution – all of these factors highlight the interconnected and incremental nature of the international community's response to the Iraqi threat. As outlined in earlier chapters, there is no reason to believe a Gore administration would have challenged the WMD case, nor would a Gore presidency have altered the interpretation of Blix's reports and their troubling conclusions. As for the UK's stance, a Gore administration would have been staunchly committed to the assertive multilateralism that was the clear preference of Blair and his team from the beginning. As per the counterfactual exercise.

It is most useful to reflect on Gore's ability to influence international diplomacy, such as negotiations at the UN, and what these differences might have meant for the outcome of the impasse. For example, is there anything Gore's team could (or would) have done differently to alter the views of French, Russian and Chinese officials during negotiations over the first or second resolutions? Without neocons or pre-emptive unilateralism to worry about, would French

[61] Krauthammer 2004.

officials have been less threatened by a Democratic administration? Would Chirac have been more likely to join a coalition of the willing if they were dealing with Gore, as they did in 1998 when they joined Clinton–Gore to bomb Kosovo? With respect to assessing competing counterfactual claims about the effects of international politics on a Gore administration and vice versa, these are important questions to consider.

In this context, it is important to note that Richard Holbrooke (Gore's likely choice for secretary of state) was not in favor of a second resolution. Based on the "serious consequences" threatened in UNSCR 1441, and all previous resolutions and congressional authorization, Holbrooke believed the United States was right to invade and was left with no choice once France rejected the inclusion of a timeline and military threat in the second resolution (see Appendix 3.1). Holbrooke and Lieberman would have calculated the same risks and costs at the final stage, and there is no evidence Gore would have challenged their views or rejected their advice. The costs of maintaining the status quo – that is, endless inspections without a clear timeline or a military threat – would have been too high for any president, but even higher for a Democratic president leading into the first post-9/11 presidential election campaign.

France had no incentive to sign onto a second resolution – the US–UK occupation of Iraq would jeopardize the significant economic benefits from the preferred treatment French oil companies had been receiving from a corrupt UN oil-for-food program (Harvey 2004). It is conceivable that French officials would have been more inclined to trust a Gore administration, but it is unlikely Russia or China would have changed their views. Even with a slightly higher probability of receiving French support, there are no compelling reasons to believe a larger coalition would have succeeded in persuading Saddam to correct his mistaken assumptions about Western intentions or improve the regime's understanding of the US–UK post-9/11 resolve to fix the WMD problem. Saddam had his own reasons for maintaining a strategically ambiguous posture on his regime's WMD programs, and there was very little the international community could have done to correct the misperceptions that guided his poor strategic calculations.

Gore's team would also have faced the same pressure to defend the US interpretation of non-compliance, because that was the core of what Washington, London and the UN (Blix) were demanding. The failure to find stockpiles would not have been the benchmark for measuring success. Had Gore accepted the French demand to take the military option off the table, he too would have been faced with the prospect of covering the costs of sustaining the deployment of hundreds of thousands of troops (through summer) without any relevant coercive role for the military to play. Democrats would be just as likely to criticize Gore for taking such a weak stance after issuing so many earlier explicit coercive threats, after receiving authorization from Congress and after obtaining unanimous UN consensus to impose serious consequences. Even if Gore and Holbrooke were inclined to accept either the Canadian or British proposals to extend inspections for a short period, these actions would not have resolved the key disarmament impasse. There is no logical or political reason why Gore's team would have overlooked the enormous political consequences to US credibility for this and similar cases.

Support from the UK and Australia would have remained very strong, but Gore and Holbrooke could have applied superior diplomatic skills to generate additional help from other European powers. With respect to these counterfactual assertions, consider Busby's (2003: 60) observations:[62]

> Had US diplomacy been better, it is conceivable that Schroeder would have felt less inclined to rule out German support for any UN-sanctioned military action against Iraq. In that instance, the French, feeling isolated, might have consented to authorization of military force, particularly if inspectors had been given more time. However, choices of rhetoric and policy on both sides – from comments about Old Europe to comparisons of Bush with Hitler – foreclosed compromise.

These insults would have been less likely with a Gore presidency, but better multilateral diplomacy in the tradition of liberal internationalism does not automatically produce a peaceful outcome – all other factors associated with the Iraq crisis must be considered to appreciate the nature of the dilemma and the path-dependent momentum to war. Moreover, key structural features of US and European domestic politics reinforced differences that would not have been easily resolved with a Democratic president. As Busby (2003: 1) points out:[63]

> Materialist and cultural arguments miss or minimize the ways in which differences in "domestic" decision-making processes shape which interests and values exercise influence in political life. These internal institutions establish constraints on European and American decision-makers in international fora that may exacerbate differences between us.

The pandering to domestic constituencies in Europe that thrive on anti-Americanism would not have dissolved had Gore been president – they were just as pronounced in 1998 when Clinton and Gore initiated attacks against Milosevic and Hussein. "Certain structural qualities of the US and European political systems," Busby (2003: 29) explains, "hinder cooperation and thereby reinforce differences in both material conditions and values." These value differences would have been just as significant regardless of the domestic political makeup of Washington under a different leader.[64]

---

[62] Busby 2003.   [63] Busby 2003.
[64] "The Iraq crisis of 2002–03," Banchoff (2004) writes, "revealed a deep value conflict between the US and its EU allies around the principle of unilateralism. In the run-up to the war, different views of the legitimate use of force in international relations divided the US from the European Commission and the EU's two leading member states, France and Germany."

Gore and Holbrooke would have learned a great deal about the application of coercive threats from a decade of interaction with leaders in Iraq, Bosnia and Kosovo – strong, credible, coercive threats work when backed by a clear threat of military retaliation and the resolve to carry through if compliance with demands is not forthcoming. On the other hand, weak threats are more likely to encourage defiance and produce the very behavior the threats were designed to prevent (Harvey 2006). The lessons from military and coercive diplomatic victories in Bosnia and Kosovo would certainly have been relevant to Gore's risk assessment in the final stages of the crisis in March 2003.

The preference for a more assertive form of multilateralism was shared by Gore's key advisers, many of whom were based in the Council on Foreign Relations. The council's Middle East director, Rachael Bronson, acknowledged that clear and credible threats, including the threat to act unilaterally, is a prerequisite for multilateral actions.[65] The administration, she argued, needs "to show it is committed to go unilaterally." As Bronson explains:

> I think they are doing that quite well. Part of what will motivate other Security Council members is the desire to appear to be restraining the US, or at least, shaping how the US acts. The only way we are going to get them to go along with us is to show a commitment to unilateralism. At the same time, and this may seem to contradict what I said just now, is that the administration has to work within the multilateral framework. That is, they need to show that they did follow the rules of resolution 1441, let the inspectors go in, waited for their report to the Security Council, did everything as they had promised in the resolution, and then decided that we still needed to invade. This will make it much more likely for others to join us. So, in a bizarre way, they need to be acting unilaterally within a multilateral context. I don't think any of this is about what the inspectors find, but how well America can convince others that we made a good faith effort, but that at the end of the day, we just don't believe the Iraqis are complying. We have to make some sort of case that they are not only in material breach, but have been over time, and are so now, repeatedly. I think the administration should be able to do this.

These observations are common in the literature on coercive diplomacy and are not exclusive to the minds of neocons bent on world domination. Gore would have calculated the benefits of obtaining a strong, unanimous resolution in the form of UNSCR 1441, and this objective first required strong, bipartisan domestic political support from Congress for unilateral action. There was a strategic logic to the approach taken – although it came with certain risks, it achieved a conservable degree of multilateral cooperation that would have been impossible in its absence.

---

[65] Bronson 2002.

The neoconist case in favor of *Gore-peace* typically conflates the multilateralism that would have been necessary to prevent war in 2003 (essentially a US–UK commitment to UNSC *consensus* or *unanimity* – France's version of multilateralism) with the kind of multilateralism Gore and Holbrooke consistently (and explicitly) defended in every one of their statements and speeches on multilateralism, the UN and US foreign policy. They have always maintained that US interests will not be guided exclusively by multilateral consensus. The last of many Gore statements on this (see Appendix 2.1) was in the 2002 Council on Foreign Relations speech: "The Administration in which I served looked at the challenges we faced in the world and said we wished to tackle these with others, if possible; alone, if we must."[66] Liberal internationalism, assertive multilateralism and forward engagement do *not* (and never have) commit(ted) the United States to a grand strategy of multilateral consensus or UN unanimity – no US president has ever made such a commitment, for obvious reasons; this commitment would essentially give France, Russia and China a veto over US foreign and security policy. If Gore did accept this broader version of multilateralism, he would never have sanctioned or defended the 1998 Kosovo and Iraq bombing campaigns.

On the other hand, Gore's commitment to expanding the size of the coalition would have been strong – there is no reason to believe his team would have failed to achieve at least the same multilateral endorsements from major allies, the same European support from those who signed the Vilnius letter and the same clandestine endorsement from Arab allies. Had Gore accepted the Canadian compromise, he would likely have benefited from a stronger Canadian contribution to the war effort as well – beyond the substantial assistance the United States already received from the Canadian navy through Operation Apollo (Harvey 2004).

The term 'multilateralism' is rarely attached to a foreign policy initiative because leaders have satisfied (or failed to satisfy) some clearly articulated international legal standard or benchmark. Usually, the term is applied for political reasons, because multilateralism is in the eye of the beholder. Kosovo was described by Democrats in 1998 as a multilateral operation, despite not having UN support. It was an acceptable enough coalition of the willing to constitute and justify the 'multilateral' imprimatur. Republicans criticized Clinton's Kosovo campaign at the time because they viewed the military operation as setting a dangerous precedent for unilateral action driven by a liberal internationalist predilection for humanitarianism. None of this, they argued, was in the national interest. In 1998, Democrats defended the Operation Desert Fox bombing campaign against Iraq without congressional endorsement or a UN resolution – they referenced previous UN resolutions demanding compliance,

---

[66] www.cfr.org/publication/4343/commentary_on_the_war_against_terror.html.

which served as sufficient justification to attack. Many of the same Democratic leaders who defended the Clinton–Gore policies in Iraq have since characterized the 2003 war in Iraq as unilateral pre-emption despite congressional authorization, a larger coalition of the willing led by the US–UK and most European states, support from Saudi Arabia and Jordan, and a UN resolution threatening "serious consequences."

Appendix 7.1

Internationally endorsed WMD suspicions

Hans Blix (chief UN weapons inspector)

• (January 27, 2003) "Iraq appears not to have come to a genuine acceptance – not even today – of the disarmament, which was demanded of it and which it needs to carry out to win the confidence of the world and to live in peace."

"The nerve agent VX is one of the most toxic ever developed."

"13,000 chemical bombs were dropped by the Iraqi Air Force between 1983 and 1988, while Iraq has declared that 19,500 bombs were consumed during this period. Thus, there is a discrepancy of 6,500 bombs. The amount of chemical agent in these bombs would be in the order of about 1,000 tonnes."

"The recent inspection find in the private home of a scientist of a box of some 3,000 pages of documents, much of it relating to the laser enrichment of uranium support a concern that has long existed that documents might be distributed to the homes of private individuals … we cannot help but think that the case might not be isolated and that such placements of documents is deliberate to make discovery difficult and to seek to shield documents by placing them in private homes."

"I have mentioned the issue of anthrax to the Council on previous occasions and I come back to it as it is an important one. Iraq has declared that it produced about 8,500 litres of this biological warfare agent, which it states it unilaterally destroyed in the summer of 1991. Iraq has provided little evidence for this production and no convincing evidence for its destruction. There are strong indications that Iraq produced more anthrax than it declared, and that at least some of this was retained after the declared destruction date. It might still exist. Either it should be found and be destroyed under UNMOVIC supervision or else convincing evidence should be produced to show that it was, indeed, destroyed in 1991."[67]

---

[67] See Blix 2003a.

Hans Blix (chief UN weapons inspector report)

• (March 6, 2003) "One bottleneck for Tabun production is the availability of precursors. Iraq may have retained up to 191 tonnes of NaCN [potassium cyanide] and up to 140 tonnes of DMA.HCl [dimethylamine hydrochloride]."

"In total, at least 300 to 350 R-400 and R-400A bombs remained unaccounted for by UNSCOM."

"A document submitted by Iraq in February 2003 outlining the production of Clostridium perfringens [gas gangrene], did not add any detail to previous Iraqi declarations. No evidence to support the declared destruction of the agent was provided."

"Based on its estimate of the amounts of various types of media unaccounted for, UNSCOM estimated that the quantities of additional undeclared agent that potentially could have been produced were: 3,000–11,000 litres of botulinum toxin, 6,000–16,000 litres of anthrax, up to 5,600 litres of Clostridium perfringens, and a significant quantity of an unknown bacterial agent."

"There are 550 Mustard filled shells and up to 450 mustard filled aerial bombs unaccounted for since 1998. The mustard filled shells account for a couple of tonnes of agent while the aerial bombs account for approximately 70 tons."[68]

Paul Heinbecker (Canada's UN ambassador)

• (October 16, 2002) "Regrettably, given the record of the past eleven years, world opinion has learned to be sceptical of the assurances provided by the government of Iraq. Instead of progress, we have seen only obstruction and a failure to comply fully with Security Council resolutions. That is why Canada fully supports correct efforts to seek a new and unambiguous resolution. That resolution should spell out what is required of the government of Iraq: immediate, unconditional and unrestricted access to all sites for UNMOVIC weapons inspectors."[69]

---

[68] See United Nations Monitoring, Verification and Inspection Commission 2003b.

[69] Collection of quotes from ambassador Paul Heinbecker taken from the following online documents – Statement by Ambassador Paul Heinbecker, Permanent Representative of Canada to the United Nations Security Council Open Debate on the Situation in Iraq. New York, October 16, 2002: www.heinbecker.ca/Speeches/UN_speeches/oct%2016%20 2002.pdf; Statement Given by H.E. Paul Heinbecker, Ambassador of Canada to the United Nations at the UNSC Open Debate on the Situation Between Iraq and Kuwait, March 11, 2003: www.heinbecker.ca/Speeches/UN_speeches/Statement-March11–2003-situation-between-Iraq-Kuwait.pdf; Statement Given by H.E. Paul Heinbecker, Ambassador of Canada to the United Nations at the UNSC Open Debate on the Situation Between Iraq and Kuwait, March 26, 2003: www.heinbecker.ca/Speeches/UN_speeches/mar%2026%202003. pdf; Statement by Ambassador Paul Heinbecker to the United Nations Security Council,

"Equally, *it must leave no doubt that Iraq will face serious consequences should it fail once again to fully comply with decisions of the Security Council, acting on behalf of the international community*" (emphasis added).

"The Council should adopt a new and unambiguous resolution that lays out the terms for compliance against which the Council itself will bear the responsibility of measuring Iraq's response."

• (February 19, 2003) "No one wants war. But people also know Saddam Hussein's record of massive human rights abuse only too well. And people know that, armed with weapons of mass destruction, he is a major threat to international peace and security in the region. Since the UNSCOM inspectors withdrew in 1998, we have no evidence that Iraq has disposed of weapons of mass destruction. *In fact, we have reason to fear the opposite*" (emphasis added).

"As UNSCOM and UNMOVIC have both reported, there are still major weapons unaccounted for and essential questions unanswered, especially in regard to biological and chemical weapons and missiles."

"That is why the Council decided, unanimously, in UN Security Resolution 1441 that Iraq be given one last chance to answer these questions convincingly and to cooperate with the inspectors in disarming itself voluntarily, actively and transparently."

"While we may be seeing the beginning of the kind of cooperation that should have been forthcoming years ago, this cooperation remains last minute, process-oriented and grudging. As Chief Inspector Blix told this Council January 27, Saddam Hussein clearly has still not fully accepted his obligation to disarm. *Recent cooperation from Baghdad has come only in response to intense international pressure, including the deliberate and useful build up of US and UK military forces in the region*" (emphasis added).

"*The job of the inspectors is to verify Iraq's disarmament, not to search out weapons of mass destruction on their own. More time for the inspectors, or even an intensified inspection process as suggested by some, could be useful but only if Iraq decides to cooperate fully, actively and transparently, beginning now. The decision is Iraq's to make*" (emphasis added).

"The world simply must have the answers to the as yet unanswered questions[,] especially about the disposition of VX gas, anthrax and botulinum. In order to

March 27, 2003: www.heinbecker.ca/Speeches/UNSecCouncilStatement-Mar27–03.pdf; Statement Given by H.E. Paul Heinbecker, Ambassador of Canada to the United Nations at the UNSC Open Debate on the Situation Between Iraq and Kuwait, February 19, 2003: www.heinbecker.ca/Speeches/UN_speeches/february%2018%202003.pdf.

spell out clearly to Iraq what is expected of it, and within what timelines, we suggest that the Council direct the inspectors: to lay out the list of key remaining disarmament tasks immediately and to establish those on which evidence of Iraqi compliance is most urgently required."

"The Council should also establish an early deadline for Iraqi compliance. This process would provide the Council the basis on which to assess Iraqi compliance."

"More importantly, it would allow the Security Council and the international community to judge whether Iraq is cooperating on substance and not just on process. Everyone understands what disarmament looks like. The case study of South Africa is often cited because that country took the decision to get out of the business of weapons of mass destruction and did so with determination, transparency and purpose."

• (March 11, 2003) "If Iraq has nothing to hide, it has nothing to fear from facilitating private meetings of its scientists and officials with weapons inspectors outside of Iraq. We still do not have the answers we need to crucial questions about Iraq's past chemical and biological weapons production and of its residual capabilities and programs, now."

"We are [sic] yet to see the evidence that would convince us that Iraq no longer possesses or intends to reacquire weapons of mass destruction. We still fear that the opposite may be true. The Government of Canada believes that a message of absolute clarity and urgency needs to be sent from this Council to the Iraqi Government as to what is required of it and by when."

"[T]he Council should ask Dr. Blix to bring forward the program of work urgently, within a week, including the list of key remaining disarmament tasks that the Government of Iraq must perform. Dr. Blix should establish the priorities among those tasks, particularly the biological and chemical weapons priorities, especially concerning bulk quantities of anthrax, the disposition of the chemical agent VX and evidence regarding chemical weapons shells, bombs and other munitions."

"We believe, therefore, that the Council should set a deadline of three weeks for Iraq to demonstrate conclusively that it is implementing these tasks and is cooperating actively and effectively on substance, on real disarmament, and not only on process."

"To keep the pressure on Iraq, the Council should consider authorizing member states now to eventually use all necessary means to force compliance, unless, on the basis of on-going inspectors' reports, it concludes that the Government of Iraq is complying."

Appendix 7.2

Tony Blair's foreword to UK WMD dossier

In recent months, I have been increasingly alarmed by the evidence from inside Iraq that despite sanctions, despite the damage done to his capability in the past, despite the UN Security Council Resolutions expressly outlawing it, and despite his denials, Saddam Hussein is continuing to develop WMD, and with them the ability to inflict real damage upon the region, and the stability of the world.

… I and other Ministers have been briefed in detail on the intelligence and are satisfied as to its authority.

… What I believe the assessed intelligence has established beyond doubt is that Saddam has continued to produce chemical and biological weapons, that he continues in his efforts to develop nuclear weapons, and that he has been able to extend the range of his ballistic missile programme. I also believe that, as stated in the document, Saddam will now do his utmost to try to conceal his weapons from UN inspectors.

… The picture presented to me by the JIC in recent months has become more[,] not less[,] worrying. It is clear that, despite sanctions, the policy of containment has not worked sufficiently well to prevent Saddam from developing these weapons. I am in no doubt that the threat is serious and current, that he has made progress on WMD, and that he has to be stopped.

… And the document discloses that his military planning allows for some of the WMD to be ready within 45 minutes of an order to use them. I am quite clear that Saddam will go to extreme lengths, indeed has already done so, to hide these weapons and avoid giving them up.

… The case I make is that the UN Resolutions demanding he stops his WMD programme are being flouted; that since the inspectors left four years ago he has continued with this programme; that the inspectors must be allowed back in to do their job properly; and that if he refuses, or if he makes it impossible for them to do their job, as he has done in the past, the international community will have to act. I believe that faced with the information available to me, the UK Government has been right to support the demands that this issue be confronted and dealt with. We must ensure that he does not get to use the weapons he has, or get hold of the weapons he wants.[70]

---

[70] Government of the United Kingdom 2002.

8

Hussein's mistakes, miscalculations and misperceptions

It should be clear to anyone exposed to all relevant facts from this case that American, British and UN (UNSCOM and UNMOVIC) intelligence estimates on Saddam's WMD programs were seriously flawed (see Chapter 5) – as were dozens of major intelligence reports produced by Germany, France, Russia, and almost every think tank and organization with a mandate to track global WMD proliferation. Everyone overestimated the threat(s) from the Iraqi regime, and no one at the time issued definitive statements on record that came close to what turned out to be the truth. But these serious errors account for only half of the mistakes that were directly responsible for the decisions leading to the 2003 war. The Iraqi regime, not surprisingly, was also plagued by serious intelligence errors and prone to making bad decisions based on dangerous strategic miscalculations. The effects of these mutually reinforcing misperceptions were aptly described by Tenet (2007):

> I did not think he was bluffing, either. With the quality of UN inspections growing weaker over time, the political will to maintain sanctions fading, and Saddam's coffers ballooning through the Oil-for-Food program, I had little doubt in my own mind what Saddam was up to. I believed he had WMD and I said so. From then on, after UNSCOM's departure, we had to rely more on analysis and extrapolation of more nuanced technical data ... Yet Saddam gave us little reason to believe that he had changed his stripes ... [He] was a fool for not understanding, especially after 9/11, that the United States was not going to risk underestimating his WMD capabilities as we had done once before ... Before the war, we didn't understand he was bluffing, and he didn't understand that we were not.[1]

It is impossible to fully appreciate the causes of the Iraq war without acknowledging the role and impact of Saddam's mistakes. Critics of US and UK decision-making will immediately demand a higher standard for Western intelligence, but it would have been irresponsible for intelligence officials to completely ignore signals coming out of Iraq or to assume Saddam was making a series of dangerous miscalculations and strategic blunders. Clearly, Western intelligence

[1] Tenet 2007: 331–3.

communities should have given serious thought to the possibility that Saddam had nothing substantial to hide, but it was, for obvious reasons, not the best time in American history for any official in Washington to reject the combined intelligence on Saddam's WMD that had been compiled over the previous decade. This alternative assessment – i.e., that Saddam was foolish enough to fabricate the myth of his regime's WMD capabilities because of an irrational and largely unsubstantiated fear of an attack from Iran – was not a credible interpretation of his behavior. Never underestimating your opponent's sanity or intelligence is usually the first rule leaders are cautioned to follow during any crisis. In this context, downplaying the threat from Saddam's WMD would have been viewed by almost everyone as reckless and irresponsible.

Everyone was understandably focused on avoiding the type of intelligence failures that produced 9/11 (underestimating your opponent), but the pressure to correctly anticipate the next security threat led to the exact opposite problem – overestimating threats by failing to imagine the possibility that Saddam actually had nothing worthy of major concern. Critics who claim today that the more benign interpretation of the threat was obvious at the time can only support this position by ignoring too much of the case history. American and British foreign policy blunders, intelligence errors and miscalculations explain the decisions that led to war, but Saddam's strategic errors are inexorably connected to Washington's working assumptions (Betts 2004 and 2007; Fukuyama 2003; Jervis 2006; Maoz 2009; Pillar 2006; Phythian 2006; Pollack 2004; Russell 2004; Tenet 2007). It is impossible to fully appreciate the origins of one set of errors without understanding the other side's mistakes or how these interdependent misperceptions reinforced assumptions and moves on both sides.

Research in the fields of political psychology and misperception theory can be tapped to help explain why Saddam was so prone to making so many dangerous miscalculations.[2] A large number of decision-making pathologies and cognitive biases commonly described in the literature played a role in this case, including, for example: cognitive dissonance, cognitive closure, motivational biases, inappropriate use of history, bolstering, discounting alternatives, cognitive distortion, groupthink, confirmation bias, loss aversion and probability neglect. Yet, despite the combined effects of so many serious pathologies, research applying cognitive and misperception models to Hussein has been completely overlooked in neoconist accounts.

Ironically, Hussein's dictatorial rule over his generals, key advisers and virtually every other part of Iraq's military and political establishment gave the Iraqi leader absolute control to shape the state's perceptions, priorities and foreign policy strategies. Such a high level of centralized control logically implies that the Iraqi regime would be a far better candidate for leadership models and an idiosyncratic level of analysis when explaining Iraq's actions. By logical

---

[2] Jervis 1976; Vertzberger 1990.

implication, Iraq's policy preferences were more likely to be expressions of its leader's personality, prejudices, psychological predispositions and leadership style. Despite the fact that decision-making authority and influence is far more widely dispersed in Western political systems, neoconism tends to reverse this standard interpretation by assigning more explanatory relevance to leadership models when discussing the United States and Britain. Almost no comparable weight is assigned to these same variables when discussing Iraq's decisions, and mistakes. But the more significant the mistakes by Saddam, the less compelling the claim that Bush's errors were solely responsible for the war.

James Risen's (2006) book on the Iraq war illustrates the typical problem with neoconist authors who ignore Saddam's role and responsibility.[3] By focusing entirely on the Bush administration's 'lies,' these accounts never acknowledge the important role the Iraqi regime played in reinforcing mistaken impressions. Risen references Saddam Hussein thirty times in his 232-page book without a single hint that Saddam's mistakes had anything to do with the consensus on his WMD programs or the strategic miscalculations that framed US and UK decision-making. The only reason one would discount Hussein's complicity (or the record of Democratic statements on Iraq's WMD) is the very strong conviction that the entire WMD intelligence record was fabricated by neoconservatives – why focus on Saddam's (or the Democrat's) role in the crisis if neocons had been planning to invade Iraq for years regardless of the truth? Everything else is simply a by-product of that diabolical scheme.

To illustrate the point, consider Risen's (2006: 130) assertion that, "according to CIA sources, most of the high-level members of Saddam Hussein's former regime who were captured by US forces after the invasion provided little useful information." In fact, most of Saddam's high-level advisers provided crucial information that was essential for understanding Iraq's errors. Only a neoconist bent on exclusively blaming the Bush administration could completely dismiss the mistakes revealed by thousands of pages of interview transcripts compiled by David Kay and Charles A. Duelfer (among many others), who were involved in the Iraq Survey Group and Iraqi Perspectives Project. Their important findings are described in more detail below.

Decision pathologies – Hussein's miscalculations

Based on extensive interviews with hundreds of Iraqi officials, the final reports of the Iraq Survey Group (ISG) and, more particularly, the Iraqi Perspectives Project (IPP) provide crucial insights into the regime's working assumptions throughout 2002–2003 (please see Appendix 8.1 for excerpts describing the IPP Scope Notes).[4] Understanding why Saddam and his advisers did what they

---

[3] Risen 2006.   [4] Duelfer 2004; see also Woods *et al.* 2006a.

did – and how their actions directly affected the actions and working assumptions of US and UK officials – is essential to appreciating the motivations for choices made throughout this period. If Saddam practiced strategic ambiguity to sustain the illusion of WMD in order to deter what he perceived as a more serious threat from Iran, or if he expected France and Russia to prevent the US–UK coalition from fighting without endorsement from a second UN resolution, or if he assumed Washington would rely on air strikes alone to avoid casualties from a ground invasion, then there may have been very little the UN or the Bush/Blair administrations could have done in the final stages (following the passage of UNSCR 1441) to improve the quality of his decision-making. Post-war transcripts of interviews with senior Iraqi officials (including Saddam Hussein and Tariq Aziz) can help resolve these important issues (Duelfer 2004; Gordon and Trainor 2006; Kay 2004; Rivkin and Casey 2003; Woods *et al.* 2006a).

Strategic ambiguity and deterrence by deception

Reports by the Iraq Survey Group (ISG) and Iraqi Perspectives Project (IPP) repeatedly raised the point that Saddam believed WMD were instrumental to the regime's survival.[5] As inspectors succeeded in uncovering and dismantling more of these programs, the illusion of WMD became more central to Saddam's calculations. George Piro, the senior FBI interrogator after Saddam's capture, asked the Iraqi leader the following question: "Why would you say something that suggests Iraq has WMD stocks when, as you say, you had been trying to convince the UN Security Council that Iraq had complied?" Saddam's reply encapsulates the logic underpinning his practice of *strategic ambiguity*:

> Mister George. You in America do not see the world that confronts Iraq. I must defend the Arab nation against the Persians and Israelis. The Persians have attacked regularly. They send missiles and infiltrations against us. If they believe we are weak, they will attack. And it is well known that both the Israelis and Persians have nuclear bombs and chemical bombs and the biological weapons. I made this speech to warn the Persians.[6]

As Charles Duelfer (2004: 24–5) explains in his final ISG report, Saddam saw specific utility in deliberately remaining ambiguous about his WMD:

> The former Regime viewed the four WMD areas (nuclear, chemical, biological, and missiles) differently. Differences between the views are explained by a complex web of historical military significance, level of prestige it afforded Iraq, capability as a deterrent or a coercive tool, and technical factors such as cost and difficulty of production. We would expect to see varying levels of attention to the four programs and varying efforts to prepare for, or engage in, actions to restart them. Saddam concluded that

---

[5] Duelfer 2004; see also Woods *et al.* 2006a.   [6] Quoted in Duelfer 2009: 407.

Iraq's use of CW prevented Iran, with its much greater population and tolerance for casualties, from completely overrunning Iraqi forces, according to former vice president Ramadan. Iraq used CW extensively in the Iran-Iraq war (1980–88) to repel the Iranian army. Iraq suffered from a quantitative imbalance between its conventional forces and those of Iran. Saddam's subordinates realized that the tactical use of WMD had beaten Iran … The former Regime also saw chemical weapons as a tool to control domestic unrest, in addition to their war-fighting role.[7]

Based on additional evidence compiled from interviews with former regime officials, including Tariq Aziz and Saddam Hussein, Rivkin and Casey (2003) pick up on the same themes in their summary of IPP findings:[8]

Since his first Gulf War defeat, Hussein deliberately created uncertainty regarding the true nature of his regime's weapons programs. Iraq would alternately cheat and retreat and then concede and mislead. At great cost, it defiantly chose sanctions over inspections. To guarantee that the perennially volatile region remained on edge, Hussein regularly threatened to engulf his enemies in a "sea of fire." No one knew what he was really trying to do. That was precisely his point.[9]

This behavior by Iraq's regime was completely rational. Hussein's calculated cultivation of WMD ambiguity is a tactic torn directly from the tough-minded Cold War game-theory scenarios of nuclear deterrence. Brilliantly crafted by defense analysts such as former Harvard economist Thomas Schelling and the Rand Corp.'s Herman Kahn, this literature stresses the strategic importance of "signaling" – that is, the critical behaviors potential combatants choose to display to either clarify or obscure their ultimate intentions. For years, "*strategic ambiguity*" worked very well for Hussein. His WMD ambiguity enhanced his survivability. (Emphasis added)[10]

In fact, WMD ambiguity was at the core of Iraq's strategy. Why? Because if it ever became unambiguously clear that Iraq had major initiatives underway in nuclear or bio-weapons, America, Israel and even Europe might intervene militarily. If, however, it ever became obvious that Iraq lacked the unconventional weaponry essential to inspiring fear and inflicting horrific damage, then the Kurds, Iranians and Saudis might lack appropriate respect for Hussein's imperial ambitions. Ambiguity thus kept the West at bay while keeping Hussein's neighbors and his people in line. A little rumor of anthrax or VX goes a long way.[11]

Ricks (2007: 15) also picks up on the implications of Saddam's ambiguous stance on WMD: "He got rid of his chemical and biological stocks, but wouldn't let international inspectors prove that he had done so, probably in order to intimidate his neighbours and citizens."[12] But Ricks and other neoconist critics

---

[7] Duelfer 2004.   [8] Rivkin and Casey 2003.   [9] Rivkin and Casey 2003.
[10] Rivkin and Casey 2003.   [11] Rivkin and Casey 2003.   [12] Ricks 2007.

acknowledge these mistakes without ever really connecting them to the perceptions formed in Washington and London, or to the decisions leading to war. The dilemma reveals the enormity of the intelligence challenges facing UNMOVIC inspector Hans Blix when determining Iraq's compliance with UNSCR 1441. Rivkin and Casey (2003) go on to make the following conclusions based on interview transcripts:

> To the very end of his brutal regime, Saddam Hussein behaved as if preserving WMD ambiguity and preserving his power were one and the same. If he did have active WMD programs, he could at any time have quietly invited in French, Russian and German technicians to help dispose of them. Word would have gotten around. Or, after Sept.11, he could have preemptively invited in UN inspectors as a prelude to lifting sanctions. Could he have done this without appearing weak? Yes. He could easily have preserved internal credibility by killing a few thousand more Kurds or chopping the ears off suspected dissidents. And regional balance-of-power issues could have been handled by a particularly brutal political assassination in Kuwait, for instance.[13]

Saddam compounded the errors associated with practicing strategic ambiguity by forbidding his weapons scientists from leaving the country. "The goal," Gordon and Trainor (2006: 118–19) point out in their definitive account of the invasion, "was to cooperate with the inspectors while preserving a measure of ambiguity about the ultimate disposition of Iraq's WMD – (this was) the 'deterrence by doubt' strategy discussed by Lieutenant General Raad Majid al-Hamdani, the II Republican Corps commander."[14] The decision to keep control over scientists prevented some obvious truths about the WMD program from being revealed to inspectors, truths that would have raised serious doubts about the extent of the threat. The absence of this information and the regime's unwillingness (or inability) to provide it were facts acknowledged in all three major UNMOVIC reports.

Strategic ambiguity also led to other decisions that proved in the end to be serious miscalculations. For example, instead of retaining at least some proof that the regime had actually destroyed the proscribed WMD listed in UN inspections reports, Saddam instructed his officials to wipe out both the weapons and relevant information pertaining to their destruction. He mistakenly believed that any WMD evidence uncovered by the UN teams would provide ammunition for the United States and UK to sustain the sanctions regime, and, worse, would confirm to potential enemies (Iran and Israel) the unambiguous status of his now limited capabilities (see below). This made it virtually impossible

---

[13] Rivkin and Casey 2003.   [14] Gordon and Trainor 2006: 118–19.

for UNMOVIC inspectors to satisfactorily conclude that the most important conditions stipulated in UNSCR 1441 had been met. The effects of this mistake would resonate throughout the crisis, because everyone, including Blix, assumed the weapons were hidden.

Of course, the most significant factor against Saddam's use of strategic ambiguity and deterrence by deception was the attack on 9/11. Coupled with the regime's failure to comply with demands stipulated in several previous UN resolutions, 9/11 made ambiguity far less acceptable to US and UK decision-makers for reasons covered in Chapters 2–7. This is not to suggest that 9/11 provided sufficient motivation to launch a pre-emptive invasion, but the lingering suspicions and doubts intentionally sustained by Saddam explain why returning to the UN to reinvigorate a dead inspections regime was inevitable, especially in light of the weaknesses with all available alternatives. It should be obvious even to neoconist critics of the Bush administration that Saddam's actions, at a minimum, provided the ammunition needed to make a very strong case for getting inspectors back into Iraq, obtaining congressional authorization to use force, and negotiating a strong, draconian UN resolution – all enabling conditions that created the momentum to war. In the end, strategic ambiguity was unsustainable, as Rivkin and Casey (2003) explain:

> There is no indication that those who have been critical of "regime change" as the most effective means for dealing with the threat posed by Saddam would have had the bureaucratic and political staying power of sustaining for years and even decades a policy of de facto international trusteeship, enforced by weapons inspectors, to be imposed over Iraq (as well as on other WMD-aspiring, rogue regimes). The notion that Western democracies can indefinitely sustain such a policy is inherently implausible … Not even a long-term inspection strategy could have stopped the full panoply of WMD-related activities. As was persuasively argued some months ago by the National Security Advisor, Condolezza [sic] Rice, experience amassed during the "de-nuclearization" of such countries as South Africa and Ukraine demonstrates that a prerequisite to a successful nuclear disarmament is a willing host regime that is prepared to give the international community an unrestricted access to its facilities and weapons installations and adopt a wide-range of confidence building measures. A rogue regime that is playing a shell game with inspectors can never be disarmed with any degree of confidence. Significantly, this concern was well recognized by the UN weapons inspectors; neither Hans Blix, nor any of his predecessors, have ever claimed that they were confident of their ability to disarm Iraq fully of its WMD.[15]

---

[15] Rivkin and Casey 2003.

Pollack (2004) is among only a small number of skeptics that reject the IPP claim that Saddam was pretending to have WMD to deal with Iran and Israel, or to enhance prestige in the region:[16]

> This explanation doesn't ring completely true either. It is certainly the case that Saddam garnered a great deal of admiration from Arabs of many countries by appearing to have such weapons, and that he aspired to dominate the Arab world. But this theory assumes that he was willing to incur severe penalties for the UN's belief that he still had WMD without reaping any tangible benefits from actually having them. If prestige had been more important to him than the lifting of the sanctions, it would have been more logical and more in keeping with his character to simply retain all his WMD capabilities.[17]

But there are at least two obvious problems with Pollack's argument. First, Saddam did not have the option of retaining WMD capabilities, because inspections and sanctions compelled him to disarm most of his programs, as the ISG confirmed. By logical implication, the only real option left was to sustain the myths surrounding these capabilities, as Saddam later admitted. We now know that he had little left, and we also know he was not complying with UNSCR 1441 (as Hans Blix confirmed), so ambiguity was obviously his preferred strategy. Second, Saddam did not believe his actions would incur severe penalties – he was convinced the United States would limit the attacks to air strikes in order to avoid casualties (especially without a second resolution), as Aziz confirmed when explaining Hussein's behavior. Third, Saddam was profiting from a corrupt oil-for-food program (as the Volker commission uncovered) by strategically distributing oil and other contracts to French, Russian and Chinese companies (as allowed under UNSCR 986). He was also winning the public relations battle. In his mind, the strategy of ambiguity was working, an important point that Pollack himself acknowledges:

> Saddam has always evinced much greater concern for his internal position than for his external status. He has made any number of highly foolish foreign-policy decisions – for example, invading Kuwait and then deciding to stick around and fight the US-led coalition – in response to domestic problems that he feared threatened his grip on power. The same forces may have been at work here; after all, ever since the Iran-Iraq war[,] WMD had been an important element of Saddam's strength within Iraq. He used them against the Kurds in the late 1980s, and during the revolts that broke out after the Gulf War, he sent signals that he might use them against both the Kurds and the Shiites. *He may have feared that if his internal adversaries realized that he no longer had the capability to use these weapons, they would try to move against him. In a similar vein, Saddam's standing among the Sunni*

---

[16] Pollack 2004.   [17] Pollack 2004.

elites who constituted his power base was linked to a great extent to his having made Iraq a regional power – which the elites saw as a product of Iraq's unconventional arsenal. Thus openly giving up his WMD could also have jeopardized his position with crucial supporters. (Emphasis added)[18]

In other words, 'strategic ambivalence' served well to address both internal and external enemies, but it was destined to fail as an approach to preventing war.

Saddam's overestimation of the Iranian threat

FBI agent George Piro interviewed Saddam almost every day after his capture; he was tasked with finding answers to puzzling questions about mythical WMD programs, the regime's ties to Al-Qaeda and other terrorist organizations, and why Saddam risked war with the United States rather than fully comply with UN resolutions and inspections. According to Piro, Saddam acknowledged that "most of the WMD had been destroyed by the UN inspectors in the '90s. And those that hadn't been destroyed by the inspectors were unilaterally destroyed by Iraq."[19] Saddam kept this secret in order to project an image of strength "because that was what kept him, in his mind, in power. That capability kept the Iranians away. It kept them from reinvading Iraq."[20] Saddam mistakenly believed Tehran was a bigger threat to his regime than Washington or London. He was convinced Iranian leaders wanted to annex southern Iraq and were capable, in the context of their relative freedom from sanctions and inspections, to advance their own WMD programs. FBI agent Piro was clear about this particular misperception when transcribing his notes from interviews with Saddam on June 11, 2004:[21]

> Hussein stated that Iran was Iraq's major threat due to their common border and believed Iran intended to annex Southern Iraq into Iran. The possibility of Iran trying to annex a portion of Southern Iraq was viewed by Hussein and Iraq as the most significant threat facing Iraq.
>
> … Even though Hussein claimed Iraq did not have WMD, the threat from Iran was the major factor as to why he did not allow the return of the UN inspectors. Hussein stated he was more concerned about Iran discovering Iraq's weaknesses and vulnerabilities than the repercussions of the United States for his refusal to allow UN inspectors back into Iraq. In his

---

[18] Pollack 2004.

[19] Pelley 2008. It was of course Iraq that invaded Iran in 1980, so the reference to Saddam's fears of Iran "re-invading" is unclear. It is likely the reference was to concerns Saddam had of another conflict with Iran – concerns that, although exaggerated, would have been partially justified in light of Iran's expanding military capabilities, Iraq's defeat in 1991, years of inspections and disarmament (ending in 1998), and economic sanctions.

[20] Pelley 2008.

[21] See US Department of Justice, Federal Bureau of Investigation 2009 – transcripts of interviews with Saddam Hussein and George Piro (June 2004). See also www.gwu.edu/~nsarchiv/NSAEBB/NSAEBB279/24.pdf.

opinion, the UN inspectors would have directly identified to the Iranians where to inflict maximum damage to Iraq. Hussein demonstrated this by pointing at the same effect as striking someone at the elbow or wrist, which would significantly disable the ability to use the arm. Hussein indicated he was angered when the United States struck Iraq in 1998. Hussein stated Iraq could have absorbed another United States strike for he viewed this as less of a threat than exposing themselves to Iran.

… Hussein further stated that Iran's weapons capabilities have increased dramatically, while Iraq's have been eliminated by the UN sanctions. The effects of this will be seen and felt in the future, as Iran's weapons capabilities will be a greater threat to Iraq and the region in the future. Hussein stated Iraq's weapons capabilities were a factor in the outcome of the Iraq-Iran war. Initially during the war, Iraq had missiles with a limited range of approximately 270 Kilometers, while Iran had no viable missile capability. The Iranians obtained long-range missiles from Libya which could strike deep into Iraq. The Iranians were the first to use the missiles, and struck Baghdad. Hussein claimed he warned the Iranians through a speech he gave, to cease these attacks. But Iranians again attacked Baghdad. Iraq's scientists came to him and advised him that they could increase the range of Iraq's missiles to also reach deep into Iran. Hussein directed them to do so. Iraq responded to Iran's attacks by striking Iran's capital, Tehran, with its own missiles.

… Hussein recognized that Iran continued to develop its weapons capabilities, to include WMD, while Iraq had lost its weapons capability due to the UN inspections and sanctions. Hussein was asked how Iraq would have dealt with the threat from Iran once the UN sanctions were lifted. Hussein replied Iraq would have been extremely vulnerable to an attack from Iran, and would have sought a security agreement with the United States to protect it from threats in the region. Hussein felt such an agreement would not only have benefited Iraq, but its neighbors, such as Saudi Arabia.

In essence, Saddam was convinced his WMD capabilities kept his regime safe from Iran, which also explains why Saddam ordered Iraqi ground forces to remain on the border with Iran for the entire sanctions period. The perceived need to deter Iran also explains why Saddam initially rejected UN inspections in 2002 – he was fearful that information about key strategic and military weaknesses would leak to the United States and Iran. These decisions were reasonable in light of Saddam's belief that Iran posed a serious threat, but they were dangerous miscalculations in a post-9/11 environment. His initial refusal to accept a new UN resolution or inspections simply fed already strong US–UK suspicions that he retained WMD.

In sum, Saddam simultaneously overestimated the threat from Iran *and* seriously underestimated the threat from the US–UK coalition. Unlike the Iranians, the Americans and British were actually amassing troops on Iraq's border in preparation for invasion and occupation. It made no sense to maintain the illusion of WMD to deter Tehran, because the more credible the threat was to Tehran, the more plausible the threat was to Washington that he retained proscribed WMD, and the more rational the policies adopted by Bush and Blair to deal with Iraq's WMD threat.

According to the same collection of unclassified reports by the US Joint Forces Command, Iran was not the only threat Saddam overestimated – Israel was also a major concern:[22]

> Ali Hassan al-Majid, known as "Chemical Ali" for his use of chemical weapons on Kurdish civilians in 1987, was convinced Iraq no longer possessed WMD but claims that many within Iraq's ruling circle never stopped believing that the weapons still existed. Even at the highest echelons of the regime, when it came to WMD there was always some element of doubt about the truth. According to Chemical Ali, Saddam was asked about the weapons during a meeting with members of the Revolutionary Command Council. He replied that Iraq did not have WMD but flatly rejected a suggestion that the regime remove all doubts to the contrary, going on to explain that such a declaration might encourage the Israelis to attack.

Of course, there is no way to independently confirm the existence of a pending plan by Iran or Israel to attack Iraq, but the assumption that they were more significant than the US–UK threat makes sense only if Saddam believed the US–UK troops would not be used, or, if used, would intervene in a way consistent with earlier efforts in 1991 or 1998. Saddam felt confident he could survive this kind of attack but never believed a full invasion, especially into Baghdad, was a possibility. The evidence confirming these mistaken assumptions is outlined below.

Limited intelligence on US domestic politics

US perceptions, domestic pressures and political imperatives to respond to any and all security threats after 9/11 predetermined a set of American foreign policies Saddam could not predict or fully grasp. The regime also failed to appreciate how their actions fed WMD suspicions that justified the US–UK strategy. George Piro (2008) describes many of Saddam's misperceptions about the United States in more detail:[23]

> He couldn't understand why we would re-elect our president every four years. In his opinion, it takes years to really understand the job and to be able to do it effectively. So every four years he was joking that he'd have to break in a new president ... He was relying on movies to get an insight into the American culture.

[22] The report was based on hundreds of detainee interviews, tens of thousands of pages of documents and transcripts involving former regime leaders over a two-year period. See Woods *et al.* 2006a.

[23] Pelley 2008.

Deulfer (2004: 33) makes a similar point in his ISG report:[24]

> Saddam's handling of Iraq's response to the 9/11 attacks probably reflects a lack of understanding of US politics and may explain why Baghdad failed to appreciate how profoundly US attitudes had changed following September 2001. Saddam's poor understanding of US attitudes contributed to flawed decision-making, according to Tariq Aziz.

While strategic ambiguity was becoming less acceptable to the United States and UK, Saddam was incapable of re-evaluating his insights about American post-9/11 fears to fully understand the implications of the domestic political debates playing out at the time. He failed to understand the sense of urgency US officials (on both sides of the aisle) felt to finally address Iraq's WMD threat, or the serious misperceptions in Washington regarding Iraqi WMD. Nor did Hussein appreciate the logic of coercive diplomacy, the political costs to the United States and UK of backing down after issuing credible threats, or his real proximity to war after the unanimous endorsement of UNSCR 1441. None of the requisite information that would have enhanced Saddam's capacity to consider the costs and risks of his actions (or how they were perceived in Washington) was available to him or members of his regime, a point so clearly noted by his chief adviser, Aziz. Saddam not only refused to collect and use relevant evidence and intelligence on the United States but admonished his chief advisers to leave these kinds of interpretations to him. In discussing this issue with his advisers in 1990, Saddam explained:

> America is a complicated country. Understanding it requires a politician's alertness that is beyond the intelligence community. Actually, I forbade the intelligence outfits from deducing from press and political analysis anything about America. I told them that [this] was not their specialty, because these organizations, when they are unable to find hard facts, start deducing from newspapers, which is what I already know. I said I don't want either intelligence organization [the Iraqi Intelligence Service or the General Military Intelligence Directorate] to give me analysis – that is my specialty ... We agree to continue on that basis ... which is what I used with the Iranians, some of it out of deduction and some of it through invention and connecting the dots, all without having hard evidence.[25]

The decision to prevent intelligence officials from processing easily accessible material to probe US or UK interests was a serious error in a regime already prone to generating information to confirm Saddam's preferences. If bolstering was a problem in the United States, it was certainly a major issue in a closed authoritarian regime as well. This stripped Saddam of access to intelligence that would have helped him and his advisers read how American officials were

---

[24] Duelfer 2004.   [25] Quoted in Woods *et al.* 2006b.

interpreting Saddam's actions, the fears they experienced after 9/11, their interpretation of UNSCR 1441, and the high risks of Saddam's policy of strategic
ambiguity.

Limited intelligence on US military plans

Saddam compounded the errors brought on by an absence of intelligence on
US domestic politics after 9/11 with a failure to appreciate the meaning of US
military plans and coercive strategies in the lead up to war. As Duelfer (2004:
32) explains:[26]

> Iraq derived much of its understanding of US military capabilities from
> television and the Internet, according to the former DGMI director. Iraq
> obtained only limited information about US military capabilities from its
> own intelligence assets, although they closely monitored the US buildup
> in Kuwait .... Saddam failed to understand the United States, its internal
> or foreign drivers, or what it saw as its interests in the Gulf region. Little
> short of the prospect of military action would get Saddam to focus on US
> policies. He told subordinates many times that following Desert Storm the
> United States had achieved all it wanted in the Gulf. He had no illusions
> about US military or technological capabilities, although he believed the
> United States would not invade Iraq because of exaggerated US fears of cas-
> ualties ... By late 2002 Saddam had persuaded himself, just as he did in 1991,
> that the United States would not attack Iraq because it already had achieved
> its objectives of establishing a military presence in the region, according to
> detainee interviews ... Some Iraqi leaders did not consider the United States
> to be a long-term enemy, but many knew little about the United States and
> less about its foreign policy formulation. Former advisors have also sug-
> gested that Saddam never concluded that the United States would attempt
> to overthrow him with an invasion.

Saddam essentially accepted the risks and costs of strategic ambiguity because
he was never convinced the US–UK coalition would launch a full-fledged invasion that included occupation of Baghdad. In response to questions about how
Saddam could have made so many mistakes that provoked the invasion, Piro
explained that Saddam didn't believe he could be so wrong about US–UK intentions, but he also told Piro that "he initially miscalculated President Bush."[27]
Saddam refused to accept the possibility that the United States and UK would be
able to generate sufficient support for a full invasion, especially in the absence
of UN support for a second resolution. This was perhaps Saddam's most serious
mistake – according to Piro, "he thought the United States would retaliate with
the same type of attack as we did in 1998 under Operation Desert Fox ... He
survived that once, (so) he was willing to accept that type of attack. That type of

[26] Duelfer 2004.   [27] Pelley 2008.

damage."[28] Duelfer (2004: 67) provides additional insights into Aziz's interpretation of Saddam's behavior:

> DEBRIEFER: You appeared confident. Your public statements were exactly what you said – that Iraq was prepared to defeat any American invasion.
>
> AZIZ: Of course I said these things: How could I say "I think we are making a mistake; we are not prepared for an attack?" That would be impossible. I had to say these things because this was my government's position, but it was true. *A few weeks before the attacks Saddam thought that the US would not use ground forces; he thought that you would only use your air force.* (Emphasis added)
>
> DEBRIEFER: Wasn't he aware of the buildup of forces in the region?
>
> AZIZ: Of course he was aware, it was all over the television screen. *He thought they would not fight a ground war because it would be too costly to the Americans. He was overconfident. He was clever, but his calculations were poor. It wasn't that he wasn't receiving the information. It was right there on television, but he didn't understand international relations perfectly.* (Emphasis added)

With respect to whether Saddam believed he could effectively respond to a US–UK attack once it became clear to him that an invasion was imminent, Piro explains that Saddam "asked of his military leaders and senior government officials to give him two weeks. And at that point it would go into what he called the secret war."[29] He believed he could withstand the initial attacks and perhaps even an invasion, prevent the US–UK from moving toward Baghdad, and then win an insurgency. As Gordon and Trainor (2006: 121) point out with references to the ISG and IPP interview transcripts, Iraq's Director of Military Intelligence and other high-level detainees from Saddam's inner circle (and the majority of military staff) believed the war would last only a few days and look very much like 1998, with air strikes, military operations and ground troops, if any, focused primarily in the south of Iraq.

Hundreds of pages of interview transcripts confirm that Saddam seriously underestimated Washington's resolve to fight and win a ground war, including a push to occupy Baghdad if the demands stipulated in UNSCR 1441 were not satisfied. The Iraqi leader failed to consider the importance the United States and UK placed on demonstrating resolve and credibility in this case. "The miscalculation phase," Duelfer (2004: 61–2) explains in his final ISG report, "was marked by a series of poor strategic decisions that left Saddam isolated."

> Iraq's cooperation with UN inspectors was typically uneven, and ultimately the Coalition considered the Regime's efforts to be too little, too late. By January 2003, Saddam believed military action was inevitable. He also felt that Iraqi forces were prepared to hold off the invaders for at least a month,

---

[28] Pelley 2008.   [29] Pelley 2008.

even without WMD, and that they would not penetrate as far as Baghdad. He failed to consult advisors who believed otherwise, and his inner circle reinforced his misperceptions. Consequently, when Operation Iraqi Freedom began, the Iraqi armed forces had no effective military response. Saddam was surprised by the swiftness of Iraq's defeat. The quick end to Saddam's Regime brought a similarly rapid end to its pursuit of sanctions relief, a goal it had been palpably close to achieving.

Saddam's miscalculations were compounded by the fact that he overestimated the support he received (and would receive) from Russia and France and "took comfort in the fact that the Security Council was split and the regional powers and most of America's allies opposed the war" (Gordon and Trainor 2006: 135).[30] Saddam no doubt accepted the French interpretation of 'successful' UN negotiations and believed France managed, through their diplomatic efforts, to prevent an automatic resort to force. In reality, one side was rejoicing over what they perceived to be a requirement for a second resolution, while the other was convinced that the inclusion of "material breach" and "serious consequences" was sufficient for an attack if Iraq failed to comply. The only important item US and UK officials agreed to in the context of UNSCR 1441 was to "consider" a second resolution, not to pass one, and both Colin Powell and Jack Straw believed their subsequent efforts to negotiate another, final resolution clearly satisfied that commitment. Transcripts of IPP interviews with Tariq Aziz reveal the extent of Saddam's overconfidence as it relates to expectations of Russian and French assistance (Woods *et al.* 2006a):[31]

> Deputy Prime Minister Tariq Aziz described the dictator as having been "very confident" that the United States would not dare to attack Iraq, and that if it did, it would be defeated. What was the source of Saddam's confidence? Judging from his private statements, the single most important element in Saddam's strategic calculus was his faith that France and Russia would prevent an invasion by the United States. According to Aziz, Saddam's confidence was firmly rooted in his belief in the nexus between the economic interests of France and Russia and his own strategic goals:
>
> > *Aziz*: France and Russia each secured millions of dollars worth of trade and service contracts in Iraq, with the implied understanding that their political posture with regard to sanctions on Iraq would be pro-Iraqi. In addition, the French wanted sanctions lifted to safeguard their trade and service contracts in Iraq. Moreover, they wanted to prove their importance in the world as members of the Security Council – that they could use their veto to show they still had power.

The authors go on to point out in the final IPP report:

---

[30] Gordon and Trainor 2006.   [31] See Woods *et al.* 2006a. See also Woods *et al.* 2006b.

Ibrahim Ahmad Abd al-Sattar, the Iraqi army and armed forces chief of staff, claimed that Saddam believed that even if his international supporters failed him and the United States did launch a ground invasion, Washington would rapidly bow to international pressure to halt the war. According to his personal interpreter, Saddam also thought his "superior" forces would put up "a heroic resistance and ... inflict such enormous losses on the Americans that they would stop their advance."

In Saddam's own words, "Iraq will not, in any way, be like Afghanistan. We will not let the war become a picnic for the American or the British soldiers. No way!"[32] When the war did start, the IPP report points out:

Saddam stubbornly clung to the belief that the Americans would be satisfied with an outcome short of regime change. According to Ibrahim Ahmad Abd al-Sattar, the Iraqi army and armed forces chief of staff, "*No Iraqi leaders had believed coalition forces would ever reach Baghdad.*" Saddam's conviction that his regime would survive the war was the primary reason he did not have his forces torch Iraq's oil fields or open the dams to flood the south, moves many analysts predicted would be among Iraq's first in the event of an invasion. In the words of Aziz, "*[Saddam] thought that this war would not lead to this ending*". Saddam realized that if his strategic calculus was correct, he would need the oil to prop up the regime. Even with US tanks crossing the Iraqi border, an internal revolt remained Saddam's biggest fear. In order to quell any postwar revolt, he would need the bridges to remain intact and the land in the south to remain unflooded. On this basis, Saddam planned his moves. (Emphasis added)

... As late as the end of March 2003, Saddam apparently still believed that the war was going the way he had expected. If Iraq was not actually winning it, neither was it losing – or at least so it seemed to the dictator. Americans may have listened with amusement to the seemingly obvious fabrications of Muhammad Said al-Sahaf, Iraq's information minister (nicknamed "Baghdad Bob" by the media). But the evidence now clearly shows that Saddam and those around him believed virtually every word issued by their own propaganda machine.

The evidence paints a crystal clear image of a dangerously delusional leader surrounded by close family members, most of whom were selected not because they possessed any skill set that would allow them to manage the crisis but purely on the basis of such family bonds. None of these advisers, including his closest and most senior (Tariq Aziz), challenged Saddam's perceptions and tactics. Even as the war started, the misperceptions remained fully entrenched:

During the first ten days of the war, Iraq asked Russia, France, and China not to support cease-fire initiatives because Saddam believed such moves would legitimize the coalition's presence in Iraq. As late as March 30,

---

[32] See Woods *et al.* 2006a.

Saddam thought that his strategy was working and that the coalition offensive was grinding to a halt. On that day, Lieutenant General Abed Hamid Mahmoud, Saddam's principal secretary, directed the Iraqi foreign minister to tell the French and Russian governments that Baghdad would accept only an "unconditional withdrawal" of US forces because "Iraq is now winning and ... the United States has sunk in the mud of defeat." At that moment, US tanks were a hundred miles south of Baghdad, refueling and rearming for the final push.[33]

These unfolding events speak directly to the failure of US coercive diplomacy. US–UK officials implemented a coercive diplomatic and military strategy they believed was sufficiently credible, resolute and costly to the regime if implemented. The more convinced they became of the credibility of their own threats, the more worrisome and suspicious was Saddam's failure to comply with their demands, and the more certain they were that Saddam must be hiding proscribed weapons. Both errors – the US decision to deploy 200,000 troops to the region based on their mistaken assumptions about WMD, and Hussein's decision to practice strategic ambiguity and deterrence by deception – combined to produce mutually reinforcing fears and actions that led to the war. And neither side saw the holes in their respective strategies: US officials refused to believe Saddam could possibly question US–UK commitment and resolve given their actions, and Saddam refused to believe they would actually invade without a second resolution, despite US–UK actions and statements to the contrary. Saddam completely underestimated the impact of 9/11, and the UNSC failed to appreciate the domestic and regional motivations behind Saddam's use of strategic ambiguity.

Neoconism completely overlooks the causal influence of these mutually reinforcing political-strategic-psychological factors.

Saddam's relatives, advisers and sycophants

Saddam was not the only one responsible for mistakes that pushed the country closer to war – his errors were reinforced by the absence of balanced judgements from key advisers, which most leaders rely on for guidance. As Woods *et al.* (2006b) explain in their summary of the IPP's findings:

> Saddam truly trusted only one person: himself. As a result, he concentrated more and more power in his own hands. No single man could do everything, however; forced to enlist the help of others to handle operational details, Saddam used a remarkable set of hiring criteria. As one senior Iraqi leader noted, Saddam selected the "uneducated, untalented, and those who posed no threat to his leadership for key roles." Always wary of a potential

[33] See Woods *et al.* 2006a.

coup, Saddam remained reluctant to entrust military authority to anyone too far removed from his family or tribe.[34]

This accounts for the regime's failure to reconsider the wisdom of strategic ambiguity and deterrence by deception after 9/11, as well as the credibility and resolve of the US–UK to enforce UNSCR 1441. According to the larger IPP report:

> Another factor reduced Iraq's military effectiveness: sanctions. For more than a dozen years, UN sanctions had frayed the fiber of the Iraqi military by making it difficult for Baghdad to purchase new equipment, procure spare parts, or fund adequate training. Attempts to overcome the effects of the sanctions *led Saddam to create the Military Industrial Commission as a means to sustain the military. The commission and a series of subordinate organizations steadily promised new capabilities to offset the effects of poor training, poor morale, and neglected equipment. Saddam apparently waited for the delivery of wonder weapons that would reverse the erosion of his military strength.* (Emphasis added)[35]
>
> A captured Military Industrial Commission annual report of investments made in 2002–3 showed more than 170 research projects with an estimated budget of about 1.5 percent of Iraq's GDP. The commission divided projects among areas such as equipment, engineering, missiles, electronics, strategic weapons, artillery, and air forces. One senior Iraqi official alleged that the commission's leaders were so fearful of Saddam that when he ordered them to initiate weapons programs that they knew Iraq could not develop, they told him they could accomplish the projects with ease. Later, when Saddam asked for updates on the nonexistent projects, they simply faked plans and designs to show progress.[36]

The key advisers and senior scientists Saddam relied on for information about his WMD programs were clearly providing misleading information (Duelfer 2004).[37] Scientists were in fact deceiving Saddam into believing they were following orders to produce more advanced WMD programs when in fact they could not (because of the effects of sanctions), but were afraid to convey their failure to Saddam.

> This constant stream of false reporting undoubtedly accounts for why many of Saddam's calculations on operational, strategic, and political issues made perfect sense to him. According to Aziz, "*The people in the Military Industrial Commission were liars. They lied to you, and they lied to Saddam. They were always saying that they were producing or procuring special weapons so that they could get favors out of Saddam – money, cars, everything – but they were*

---

[34] Woods *et al.* 2006b.   [35] See Woods *et al.* 2006a: 40.   [36] See Woods *et al.* 2006a: 42–3.
[37] Duelfer 2004, from Volume 3 on Biological Warfare.

liars. If they did all of this business and brought in all of these secret weapons, why didn't [the weapons] work?" (Emphasis added)[38]

The documents they fabricated to prove they were developing new weapons systems were the same files periodically uncovered by inspectors to form part of the WMD case against the regime.

There are many other illustrations of false reporting by regime officials that compounded misperceptions on both sides. In the lead up to the Iraq war, for example, Rihab Rashid Taha (a senior Iraqi scientist) was asked about the unaccounted for anthrax listed in Blix's reports – she failed to provide inspectors with any useful answers. After the war, the same microbiologist confessed to dumping the lethal bacteria close to Saddam's palaces.

> The members of the program were too scared to tell the Regime that they had dumped deactivated anthrax within sight of one of the principal presidential palaces. ISG's investigation found no evidence that Iraq continued to hide BW (biological) weapons after the unilateral destruction of 1991 was complete.[39]

The scientist was obviously worried about her own health if the truth about her actions was revealed to Saddam, but the fact that information about the poor method of anthrax destruction was withheld from inspectors simply reinforced suspicions that WMD were being hidden. The deception, in other words, was understandably misread, but it was unfortunately the most plausible (risk averse) interpretation in light of a decade of deception. The more benign interpretation (i.e., that WMD were destroyed without records) was not as prudent in a post-9/11 world. As Powell cautioned everyone about the quantity of potent anthrax in his UN speech, "tens of thousands of teaspoons ... This is evidence, not conjecture. This is true."[40] The facts regarding the effects of anthrax, when coupled with the most plausible interpretation of the evidence of ongoing deception, made for a strong case. The almost insurmountable challenge was trying to correctly interpret what the deception actually meant.

According to the ISG's David Kay, "some stuff was still around because the sons-in-law, before defecting, had not carried out earlier instructions to destroy everything."[41] Hussein was very concerned about the impact these defections would have on prolonging sanctions, so he instructed Iraq's senior military staff to get rid of any signs of WMD. When the order was communicated to troops on the ground, it was intercepted and misinterpreted by US officials as instructions to hide rather than get rid of WMD evidence, a mistake informed by a decade of similar games by the regime.

---

[38] See Woods *et al.* 2006a: 42.   [39] Woods *et al.* 2006a.
[40] www.guardian.co.uk/world/2003/feb/05/iraq.usa.
[41] Quoted in Pincus 2006: A15.

The most obvious case of American–Iraqi misperceptions (discussed in more detail in Chapter 5) was in 2002 when US intelligence intercepted a communication between two Iraqi Republican Guard commanders discussing the removal of the words "nerve agents" from "the wireless instructions" and ordering troops to "search the area surrounding the headquarters camp and [the unit] for any chemical agents, make sure the area is free of chemical containers, and write a report on it." It is obvious today that this communication should have been interpreted as an effort to *comply* with UN resolutions, but at the time it was not unreasonable to assume proscribed weapons did exist and, once again, the regime was attempting to conceal them.

Summary: strategic ambiguity and the inevitability of war

Members of the national security teams in both the Clinton and Bush administrations believed Saddam retained WMD, as Tenet explains, because "Saddam had an entire organization dedicated to concealing them."[42] Martin Indyk, who worked with Tenet and served on the NSC staff under Clinton, agrees with Tenet's analysis: "We observed how they operated. Saddam refused to account for the material that was missing from the previous war, and logically it did not make sense, since if he would just come clean he could get out of sanctions and we would be screwed."[43] Both administrations failed to imagine the possibility that he was bluffing for reasons we now understand. But neoconists should understand that it is virtually impossible for inspections to succeed when they are searching for weapons everyone expects to find but don't exist. The international community was dealing with a leader who refused to admit he was not a threat, and did not believe the United States was.

But when the same mistakes and miscalculations are repeated over time, their negative effects multiply – the same moves at later points in the crisis raised even higher levels of concern in the minds of Saddam's opponents. For example, Iraq's failures to comply with UN disarmament resolutions before 1998 were considerably less significant than the regime's failure in 2003 to comply with UNSCR 1441 once a threat of "serious consequences" was issued, because infractions at this late stage were much more likely to reinforce suspicions that he must be hiding something – why else would he take these risks? Saddam's biggest error, therefore, was his failure to fully appreciate the diminishing returns of the same strategy after 9/11: "he was a fool," Tenet (2007: 333) argues, "for not understanding, especially after 9/11, that the United States was not going to risk underestimating his WMD capabilities as we had done once before."[44] As the crisis escalated, and as more potent threats were issued, smaller and smaller infractions were perceived as increasingly threatening.

---

[42] Tenet 2007: 331.   [43] Tenet 2007: 331.   [44] Tenet 2007.

Conclusions: *Gore-war* versus *Gore-peace* revisited

Typical neoconist assertions that things would have been different under a Gore administration are never sufficient to produce compelling counterfactual conclusions – these statements say nothing about what those differences would have been, why they were more or less likely to unfold, and what effects they would have had on behavior and outcomes. Of course Saddam could conceivably have behaved differently if faced with a Gore presidency, but how and in what direction?

The key counterfactual question emerging from the discussion in this chapter is whether the Iraqi regime would have been more or less likely to correct its mistakes if Gore's team was in power. More specifically, would Gore have been any more successful than Bush and Blair at correcting Saddam's misperceptions or convincing him that strategic ambiguity was not in his best interests? What would that strategy look like, and how would Gore have managed the political consequences of the required strategy if it was implemented? Conversely, how would Saddam have interpreted the intentions of a Gore administration, and how would these impressions have changed his preference for strategic ambiguity or deterrence by deception? Why would Saddam's reliance on the WMD façade have been any less likely if he was facing a Democratic administration?

Leaving aside important questions about why Saddam's errors are so often ignored in the neoconist literature, it is pretty clear from the evidence that the regime's miscalculations were directly relevant to producing enabling conditions that led to this war. Saddam's working assumptions, threat perceptions and preferences would not have changed if he was facing a Gore administration, for several reasons.

First, it is one thing to speculate about how US intelligence assessments could have improved with a new team (see Chapter 5 for a discussion of why this was unlikely), but it is a far more daunting challenge to change an opponent's entrenched beliefs. From the Iraqi leader's point of view, he was getting everything he wanted: support from France, Germany and Russia (anxious to retain lucrative oil contracts), billions each year from a corrupt oil-for-food program, and rapidly declining global support for the UN sanctions regime.

Second, Saddam would have been even less inclined to believe threats issued by a Democratic president who, throughout his time as vice president in the 1990s, was responsible for shaping many of Saddam's misperceptions in the first place. Why would Saddam have been more inclined to question the credibility of a president who, when vice president, endorsed air strikes but avoided the deployment of ground troops in Baghdad (1991), Somalia (1993), Rwanda (1994), Bosnia (1995), Iraq (1998) and Kosovo (1998)? If these policies were responsible for Saddam's assumptions about Western resolve in 2002–2003, why would Hussein alter his calculations if he was facing a Gore team? Congressional authorization and the subsequent deployment of military troops to the region would still have been misinterpreted by Saddam as an empty threat consistent with those issued repeatedly over the previous decade.

Third, without any human intelligence on the ground to decipher Saddam's serious miscalculations about US intentions, the essential ingredient for crafting an alternative path away from war would still have been missing. Indeed, as noted elsewhere, the likelihood would have been higher that Gore would have relied on WMD intelligence gathered during the two Clinton–Gore administrations.

Fourth, for reasons noted in Chapters 2 and 7, Gore was not the type of political leader prone to suffering the political consequences, after 9/11, of conceding to the French request to take all military options off the table when debates began on the second resolution. Nor is there any evidence on record indicating his advisers would have counseled Gore to accept the French offer. Logically, if Gore, Holbrooke and Lieberman were willing in 1998 to attack Iraq without congressional authorization or a new UN resolution threatening "serious consequences," why would we not expect the same team to be even *more* inclined to accept the need for military action in 2002 *with* congressional authorization, UNSCR 1441 and strong support from its most important ally?

Fifth, there is nothing in the ISG or IPP reports that indicates Saddam's perceptions, values, concerns and interpretation of comparative risks were susceptible to major changes. If cognitive rigidity explains US errors, despite the presence of a much more sophisticated intelligence community, there was very little that was available within Iraq that would have changed Saddam's perceptions of US plans and intentions.

Mutually reinforcing misperceptions on both sides represented a collection of enabling factors and causal mechanisms that would not have been significantly altered under a Gore administration. There is nothing much Gore (or Bush) could have done to change Saddam's assumptions. Gore certainly could have selected different tactics, but it is not clear that these alternatives would have had a significant enough effect on the overall strategy to change the course of history. Any specific counterfactual arguments to the contrary would need to be defended on logical and empirical grounds.

For example, Gore could have put a larger invading force into Kuwait to prepare for a more significant post-conflict occupation and reconstruction effort, but there is no reason to believe Saddam would have been any more likely to find the threat from a larger force credible enough to change his strategy. In fact, a larger force could have been dismissed more easily given Saddam's belief that the United States was not prepared to suffer casualties and was probably compensating for that weakness by deploying more troops. Moreover, once a military threat was issued, and later with a larger coalition supporting serious consequences, the political and financial costs of sustaining the deployment with an indefinite extension to inspections would have been much higher. Gore could also have obtained European support for a second resolution, but that would simply have produced a larger invading coalition once inspections failed to find weapons everyone believed Hussein had – thanks, once again, to Saddam's practice of strategic ambiguity.

Appendix 8.1

Excerpts from final ISG report

Scope Note[45]

This report relays Iraq Survey Group's findings from its creation in June 2003 until September 2004 and provides context and analysis to ISG's physical findings. It also attempts to place the events in their Political-Military context.

The United States' investigation of Iraqi WMD activities began during Operation Iraqi Freedom itself. In prewar planning, it was assumed chemical and possibly biological stocks were likely to be encountered and perhaps employed. Forces were equipped with protective equipment. A military unit designated Expeditionary Task Force-75 (XTF-75) was deployed during the war to investigate suspected locations for WMD stocks. Many sites were inspected but with an aim of discovering WMD, not inspecting and developing an analytical assessment of the Iraqi programs. Wartime conditions prevailed with concern about force protection primary. The work of XTF-75 was therefore aimed at discovery of possible WMD locations (to eliminate a threat), not the compilation of evidence to build a picture of what happened to the weapons and programs.

This early approach, perhaps logical if the goal was simply to find hidden weapons, undermined the subsequent approach of piecing together the evidence of the Iraqi WMD programs such as they existed. In fact, combined with the chaos of the war and the widespread looting in the immediate aftermath of the conflict, it resulted in the loss of a great amount of potentially very valuable information and material for constructing a full picture of Iraqi WMD capabilities. Sites were looted. Documents were either ignored or collected haphazardly or burned by either the Regime or Coalition forces.

To begin a more systematic collection of evidence to build an understanding of Iraqi WMD programs, DOD stood up ISG under the military command of Major General Keith Dayton. He brought together a unique blend of collection, analytic, and force maneuver assets to conduct both the ongoing WMD investigation and secondary tasks that included counterterrorism and the search for Captain Scott Speicher, a US Navy pilot shot down in 1991 during Desert Storm. Elements of ISG included:

Analytic Staff – Experts in the functional areas of Iraqi WMD from the CIA, DIA, DOE, State, DOD, as well as United Kingdom and Australia gathered and

---

[45] Duelfer 2004.

analyzed data to develop a picture of Iraq's WMD program and plan further collection. Several participants were former United Nations inspectors with long experience in Iraq.

Documentation Exploitation – A forward linguistic element in Baghdad (approximately 190) identifies documents of immediate importance from the millions recovered in the course of the war and occupation. A large facility housing more than 900 staff members in Qatar recorded, summarized, and translated documents. At the time of this writing, this facility houses about 36 million pages that have been scanned into a database. Roughly a third of these – all that appeared of direct relevance to ISG's mission – have been examined by a linguist and a gist prepared.

Recently, ISG obtained about 20,000 boxes of additional documents, which had been stored in Coalition-occupied buildings. Many of these documents are from the Iraqi Intelligence Service and the Baath party. This is a volume roughly equivalent to the total received to date – a huge infusion. Triage of these documents will probably take several months. New information will inevitably derive from this process, but may not materially affect the overall elements of this report.

Interrogation and Debriefing – ISG had dedicated linguists and debriefers for the so-called High Value Detainees. Statements by former key players in the Regime formed an important information source, but must be evaluated very cautiously since the prospect of prosecution inevitably affected what they said. It is also important to understand that the population of senior detainees held at the Camp Cropper facility interacted freely among themselves. They could consult on what they were asked, and the pressures and tensions among detainees over cooperation with ISG certainly affected their candor. In addition, debriefers were not experts in the field of Iraq or WMD as a general rule. ISG compensated by having subject matter experts present as often as possible.

9

Summary and implications

Consider the following expanded sample of idiosyncratic, domestic and international factors, derived from the preceding analysis, that would very likely have influenced President Gore during the same crucial period from 2002 to 2003 (see Table 9.1).

Admittedly, Al Gore's preferences in each instance are not likely to be black or white, and there will probably be disputes about what the historical facts actually tell us about Gore's personality, WMD assumptions, or foreign policy legacy. Nevertheless, it is possible to provide at least some estimation of where Gore and his team would fall on a continuum between two extremes across all twenty of these enabling conditions (see Table 9.2). Both extremes represent category 'A' and category 'C' evidence embedded in the mutually exclusive counterfactuals from Figure 1.1.

The main contribution of comparative counterfactual evidence is the logical clarity it demands when specifying the necessary conditions for competing counterfactual claims. The central question is whether Gore's foreign policy legacy, speeches, statements and actions (when combined with the domestic political circumstances, congressional support, rally effects, widely shared intelligence errors, Saddam's miscalculations, inspections impasse, UN politics and other factors outlined in the book) would be more in line with supporting the *Gore-war* (category C) or *Gore-peace* (category A) counterfactual.

With respect to what actually constitutes *Gore-peace* (category A) evidence, consider the following – if the President was someone who was on record strongly opposing the 2003 Iraq war (for example, Congressman Dennis Kucinich or Senator Ted Kennedy), or rejected the use of military force except in cases when the country is directly attacked, or dismissed the WMD evidence against Iraq as exaggerated and accepted Saddam's WMD disarmament declarations as full, complete, accurate and sufficient, or interpreted Saddam's puzzling behavior as a response to misperceived regional security threats from Iran, or refused to believe Iraq was worth the trouble of returning to the UN or restarting UN inspections, or strongly opposed the 1991 Gulf War, 1998 Kosovo bombing campaign or 1998 bombing campaign against Iraq, or never accepted Iraq as part of the 'axis of evil' or claimed the United States should work with allies if possible but "alone, if we must" (see Gore's CFR speech), then

Table 9.1 *Enabling conditions influencing Al Gore presidency – 2002–2003*

Leadership

1. Willingness to use military force (Iraq 1991, 1998; Bosnia 1995; Kosovo 1998)
2. Gore hawkish on foreign policy, Iraq and Saddam Hussein
3. Gore's VP, Secretary of State and senior advisers hawkish on Iraq, Saddam and WMD threats
4. Foreign policy legacy – unilateral application of force (Kosovo 1998)[a]
5. Convinced of Iraq's WMD threat (Desert Fox 1998; 2000–2002 speeches)
6. Accepts 'Axis of Evil' reference to Iraq, Iran and North Korea[b]
7. Supports policy of 'regime change' – Iraq Liberation Act 1998[c]
8. Belief in legal grounds for war based on previous UN Resolutions
9. Expressed strong support for returning inspectors to Iraq (absent since 1998)
10. Expressed strong preference for robust inspections (consistent with UNSCR 1441)[d]
11. Accepts relationship between democratization and US security
12. Supported active internationalism, 'assertive multilateralism', 'forward engagement'
13. Strong belief in utility and moral purpose of US military force in the face of sufficient threat

Domestic Political

14. Majority of Democrats in Congress hawkish on Iraq, Saddam and WMD threats
15. Public opinion strongly favorable to robust inspections
16. Public opinion/Congress favorable to military action (authorization) to enforce UNSCR 1441

Structural

17. Intelligence failures, bureaucratic deficiencies present during Clinton/Gore
18. Would have obtained coalition support for war from same key allies (perhaps others)
19. US vs. France and Russia – similar support (UNSCR 1441) and divisions (rejection of second res.)
20. Serious miscalculations by Saddam; failure to fully comply with UN resolutions

a With respect to the choice between unilateralism and multilateralism, Gore (2002) acknowledges, "The Administration in which I served looked at the challenges we faced in the world and said we wished to tackle these with others, if possible; alone, if we must." http://www.cfr.org/publication/4343/commentary_on_the_war_against_terror.html. Proponents of the Kosovo air campaign are likely to claim that their application of military force was not unilateral, but the arguments they offer to defend the multilateral components of the Kosovo war look very similar to those offered by those who endorsed the 2003 Iraq war. In fact, the collection of multilaterally endorsed UN resolutions compelling Iraq to comply with disarmament obligations or face serious consequences is considerably more apparent than was the case prior to Kosovo. Moreover, military operations in Iraq did benefit directly from NATO assets (see Harvey 2004).

the *Gore-peace* (category A) counterfactual would be much stronger. If these circumstances prevailed, it would be easier to defend the view that Gore would have taken the country down a completely different path, because the likelihood would be much higher that none of the key decisions in the path-dependent sequence I outline in the book would have been taken.

There is nothing in Gore's past, for example, that would indicate he shared the same views on the 2003 war as, for example, Dennis Kucinich. As one of the war's strongest critics, Kucinich was very clear during congressional debates about his much higher standards for using US forces:

> The United Nations has yet to establish that Iraq has *usable* weapons of mass destruction. There is no intelligence that Iraq has the *ability to strike at the United States*. According to the CIA, Iraq has no intention to attack America, but will defend itself if attacked. (Emphasis added)[1]

The former vice president never defended anything approaching these standards when justifying the application of military force, and it was highly unlikely in a post-9/11 world that any sitting president would argue in favor of responding only after Saddam had acquired "usable" WMD capable of "striking at the United States." Obviously it would be too late by then to 'deter' the regime from acquiring WMD – Iraq would already have them.

Of course, critics are likely to dismiss the *Gore-peace* (category A) counterfactual, corresponding to all Xs on the left side of the continuum, as a straw man that

Notes to Table 9.1 (*cont.*)

b Al Gore clearly states in his 2002 Council on Foreign Relations speech, "Since the State of the Union, there has been much discussion of whether Iraq, Iran and North Korea truly constitute an 'Axis of Evil.' As far as I'm concerned, there really is something to be said for occasionally putting diplomacy aside and laying one's cards on the table. There is value in calling evil by its name. One should never underestimate the power of bold words coming from a President of the United States."

See www.cfr.org/publication/4343/commentary_on_the_war_against_terror. html.

c The Iraq Liberation Act was passed on October 31, 1998. Operation Desert Fox took place in December 1998. Both Clinton and Gore relied on the Act when defending (and legitimizing for their domestic audiences) the bombing campaign in the absence of a UN resolution or any other form of UN endorsement.

d With respect to the choice between a strong and weak inspections mandate, it would obviously be far more difficult for the US and UK to establish the case for non-compliance if the requirements were not as strict as those included in UNSCR 1441, or if the requirements were less demanding with respect to full, complete and unfettered compliance.

[1] See Kucinich 2003.

Table 9.2 *Comparative counterfactual profiles of possible Al Gore administrations*

	(Based on 20 Enabling Conditions)						
Category 'A'			*(continuum)*				**Category 'C'**
Gore-peace	←	←	←	→	→	→	Gore-war
1. Diplomacy only						X	Willingness to use force
2. Gore dovish						X	Gore hawkish
3. Gore advisers doves on Iraq					X		Gore advisers hawks on Iraq
4. Need multilateral consensus						X	'Alone, if we must'
5. Rejected WMD threat						X	Accepted WMD threat
6. Rejected 'Axis of Evil'						X	Accepted 'Axis of Evil'
7. Rejected regime change						X	Accepted regime change
8. Unjust/unlawful war						X	War was justified by int'l law
9. Preferred 1998 status quo						X	Return inspectors to Iraq
10. Weak inspections regime not backed by coercive threat						X	Strong, robust coercive inspections
11. Democracy ≠ security						X	Democracy = security
12. Rejects 'forward engagement,' assertive multilateralism'						X	Endorses 'forward engagement,' 'assertive multilateralism'
13. War requires imminent threat						X	War requires sufficient threat
14. Congress dovish on Iraq					X		Congress hawkish on Iraq
15. Public opposition inspect						X	Public support inspect
16. Pub/Congress opposes force						X	Pub/Congress authorizes force
17. Intelligence failures absent						X	Intelligence failures present
18. No UK/ally/coalition support						X	Same UK/ally/coalition support
19. UNSC rejects 1441						X	UNSC accepts 1441
20. Hussein avoids serious miscalculations						X	Hussein seriously miscalculates

does not exist. But that is precisely the central point – no such person existed at the time (except perhaps for Kennedy and Kucinich). Gore and his advisers were certainly not category A leaders and, despite assumptions firmly rooted in conventional wisdom, there is very little evidence to support that position. Once again, this is powerful disconfirmation of the conventional neoconist view that the war was driven exclusively by a bunch of neoconservative, unilateralist ideologues.[2] The entire collection of arguments and historical evidence presented in the preceding chapters is completely absent in Klaus Dodds' (2008) widely cited counterfactual analysis of a Gore presidency.[3] In fact, Dodds relies heavily on speeches that Gore delivered long *after* the war ended, which criticized the Bush and Blair administrations for the very policies (and assumptions) Gore himself endorsed at the time – a serious logical error when applying counterfactual reasoning.

In sum, a comprehensive review of enabling conditions related to Gore's personality, foreign policy preferences, and the domestic, political and bureaucratic pressures he would have faced as president all strongly support the *Gore-war* end of the continuum in almost every instance. The evidence disconfirms expectations derived from the dominant *Gore-peace* (neoconism) interpretation of history. The very same structural conditions that were present during the Bush administration would have been equally relevant to Gore's strategic and political calculations at the time, including societal pressures and security fears after 9/11, public opinion on Iraq and the UN, domestic political support in Congress based on the same WMD consensus, mistaken national intelligence estimates from the previous administrations, divisions within NATO and the UN Security Council, and, of course, strategic ambiguity practiced by Saddam Hussein.

Some neoconists will favor a considerably watered down (weaker) version of *Gore-peace* that concedes many of the points noted throughout the book (and in Table 9.2) but, nevertheless, rejects the view that Gore would have gone to war at the final stage. This qualified version of neoconism is weaker because it does not assign all blame to neoconservative ideologies and acknowledges the role Democrats played in supporting the policies that led to war. Accordingly, Gore's team would likely have made many of the same coercive diplomatic decisions to obtain authorization from Congress, deploy troops, negotiate a new UN resolution and return inspectors – everything except invasion. But even this weak version of neoconism constitutes a major challenge to conventional wisdom, particularly the *failure of the marketplace of ideas* thesis defended by Kellett Cramer (2007), Kaufmann (2004), Krebs and Lobasz (2007) and many

[2] These points are completely overlooked in Dodds (2008). None of my evidence is addressed in his analysis, while all of the evidence in Dodds' paper is directly challenged in mine. In fact, Dodds relies heavily on speeches Gore delivered long after the war criticizing the Bush and Blair administrations – this is one of the most serious errors one could make when applying counterfactual reasoning.

[3] See Dodds 2008.

others. Weak neoconism clearly implies that the marketplace of ideas character-
istic of a healthy democracy was working perfectly well up to the very last stage.
Of course, this version of history begs the obvious question: why would Gore's
team act so logically with respect to all previous decisions, but behave so differently at the very end? Gore would certainly not have come to power with a plan
to invade Iraq, but no such premeditated plan is required for Gore and his team
to see the absence of inspectors in Iraq as an important enough problem after
9/11 to warrant attention. Completely ignoring Iraq was not an option, and a
multilateral approach to inspections would have emerged as the best alternative.
Unfortunately, the actions required to ensure effective and successful inspections also led the country closer to war. Why would Gore have been any more
capable of withstanding the pressure to cross the line?

Finally, there were other important enabling conditions that set the stage
for the Iraq war – the 9/11 attacks are perhaps the most obvious. Strip away
9/11 and you lose the consensus that Saddam is an important enough threat to
invest the time, effort or political resources to return inspectors. In fact, prior to
9/11, France, Russia and China were happy to continue working with Saddam
to exploit a corrupt oil-for-food program and, at the time, were pushing to *lift*
economic sanctions. In addition to transforming US and UK security priorities,
the 9/11 attacks set the stage for a significant measure of European goodwill (or
sympathy) that would have been exploited by any US administration to reinvigorate containment through multilateral inspections.

Momentum, path dependence and the inevitability of war

The debate over the relative strengths of competing counterfactuals must
include a discussion of the sequence of specific decisions leading from one
stage to the next. Each decision represents its own counterfactual point in time.
Deciding to address Iraq through inspections is not as simple as saying, 'OK,
let's get inspectors back into Iraq.' That choice has consequences, and subsequent decisions that form part of the strategy to make inspections work have
consequences as well.

Counterfactual analysis facilitates the construction of 'sequential narratives'
that explain why specific decisions were taken, and how these choices made the
outcome very probable (Pelz 2001: 101).[4] The approach is designed to uncover:

> a continuous series of (necessary) conditions ... causal mechanisms, and
> proximate causes (that) reduce the decision-makers' options and finally
> leaves them little choice but to accept the outcome in question. Such a
> chain of standing conditions and proximate causes constitutes the sequen-
> tial mode of explanation. Such an approach goes beyond simple decision-
> making analysis and is explored under the rubric of "process tracing."

[4] See Pelz 2001.

As explained in the introductory chapter, theory-guided process tracing was used to uncover important details often excluded from standard narratives.[5] As expected, the approach has led to "theoretically explicit narratives that ... capture the unfolding of social action over time in a manner sensitive to the order in which events occur" (Aminzade 1993: 108).[6] Getting this order correct is essential to the quality of an historical account because it clearly exposes relevant information and the stimuli decision-makers relied on to form perceptions, priorities, expectations, preferences and choices. By embracing complexity, nuance and detail, the approach helps to reveal the full context and chronology of choices as they unfolded at crucial points in time. The sequence of these decisions, when viewed in the context of the domestic and international politics at the time, provides a richer and more detailed account of the eighteen-month period from the end of combat operations in Afghanistan through March 2003.

Viewing the case not as a single decision to invade but as a series of rational choices along the path to war provides a considerably more informed account of what happened. Consider the following examples of the many distinct decision points in this case, starting with the invasion and moving backwards in time (see Table 9.3).

Working backwards from T+15, it would be very difficult for neoconists or other proponents of *Gore-peace* to challenge the wisdom or rationality of the choices made at each of the previous stages. Consequently, if ignoring Iraq was not an option at T+1 (see Chapter 2) and other options (containment, sanctions, etc.) were not working because of the absence of inspectors since 1998, then returning inspectors made perfect sense. The logic of all subsequent decisions is interrelated and mutually reinforcing, and the final US–UK decision to invade emerges as a direct product of earlier decisions designed to enhance the success of UN inspectors and, ultimately, end the impasse peacefully. In essence, each decision represents its own counterfactual case study, and each explains the next and subsequent choices.

Both path dependence and momentum are excellent theoretical constructs that can be used to develop a thorough and sophisticated explanation of the 2003 Iraq war – an explanation that is much stronger than neoconism and supported by the evidence in Chapters 1–8. The best way to distinguish the two constricts is to view them in terms of the sequence of events. Path dependence explains the inter-linkages and mutually reinforcing relationship between and among specific decisions in a rational sequence of choices moving forward. Momentum provides a useful account of the combined effects of previous decisions on the final choice for war.

[5] See Falleti 2009; George and Bennett 2005; George and McKeown 1985.
[6] See Aminzade 1993.

Table 9.3 *Sequence of choices leading to war – 2002–2003*

T+15	– invasion and occupation of Iraq with allies;
T+14	– begin air strikes;
T+13	– issue final ultimatum to Saddam and his sons (demand leadership change);
T+12	– calculate as unacceptable the political/military/financial costs of status quo;
T+11	– reject French veto on the threat of military force (retain coercive value of deployment);
T+10	– begin to negotiate a second resolution;
T+9	– interpret Blix report(s) as confirming material breach and non-compliance;
T+8	– interpret Iraq WMD dossier as unacceptable/further deception;
T+7.3	– negotiate reference in UNSCR 1441 to "serious consequences";
T+7.2	– negotiate reference in UNSCR 1441 to "material breach";
T+7.1	– negotiate reference in UNSCR 1441 to "nuclear facilities";
T+6	– deploy 200,000 troops – credibility, resolve, bargaining leverage;
T+5	– begin seven weeks of UN negotiations for strong resolution;
T+4	– obtain congressional authorization to use force (before going to UN);
T+3	– prioritize multilateral approach to Iraq impasse/improve containment;
T+2	– return UN inspectors (essential for effective containment and sanctions);
T+1	– fix failing containment policy to address post-9/11 WMD threat.

There are helpful treatments of path dependence in political science and the social sciences more generally that inform the analysis to follow.[7] As Bennett and Elman (2006: 251) point out:[8]

> There are several different phenomena that exhibit causal complexity, including tipping points, high-order interaction effects, strategic inter-action, two-directional causality or feedback loops, equifinality (many different paths to the same outcome), and multifinality (many different outcomes from the same value of an independent variable depending on context).

"The crucial feature of a historical process that generates path dependence," Pierson (2004: 20) argues, "is positive feedback or self-reinforcement." A path-

---

[7] Greener 2005; Kay 2005; Mahoney 2000, 2001 and 2006; Mahoney and Schensul 2006; Pierson 2000 and 2004; Thelen 1999.
[8] Bennett and Elman 2006.

dependent sequence includes decisions that constitute reactions to previous events, which are then causally connected to subsequent decisions (Mahoney 2006). "Each successive step down the path," Bennett and Elman (2006: 256) note, "increases the likelihood that a particular event or choice will be repeated and/or the magnitude of its subsequent manifestations. Positive feedback is often associated with a tipping point, where the causal pathway becomes fixed after the causal variable increases past a given point." As Bennett and Elman (2006: 258) go on to explain:

> Although the links between the events in this kind of path dependence must have some special characteristics (otherwise any causal story would qualify), it is not yet clear what those features must be. One possibility is that the causal links are characterized by a high degree of sufficiency, that is, once the first step on the path is taken the final outcome is very likely to happen. This would capture the "why actors stay on the path" part of the story.

These insights nicely capture the theoretical construct underlying the counter-factual claims I am developing in this book. The decisions throughout 2002–2003 are essentially links that constitute necessary conditions, "without which the next step in the chain would not have been possible" (Bennett and Elman 2006: 258). Process tracing helps to clarify the relevant sequence of events and facilitates "the search for omitted variables that might lie behind contingent events" (Bennett and Elman 2006: 259).

Major foreign policy decisions involving multiple actors almost never emerge from a simple cost-benefit assessment of available options at a single point in time, by a single person (even a head of state) – big decisions (especially decisions by powerful democracies to launch a major war) usually unfold incrementally over time and through stages. In any given crisis, leaders make a series of calculated political, diplomatic and military moves that constitute their preferred crisis management strategy – a product of the variables and pressures described in the preceding eight chapters. In order to bolster their decisions at each stage, however, officials often underscore the many problems (risks and costs) of rejected alternatives. This common approach to selling policies makes it very difficult later on in a crisis to adopt previously discarded options. For example, a strong case for why Saddam's WMD programs posed a threat to the United States was essential to obtaining (1) public support; (2) bipartisan congressional authorization to use force; (3) deployment of troops to the region; (4) a unanimous UN Security Council Resolution; and (5) a strong inspection regime. Having achieved these goals, in part by persuading *everyone* (except neocons) that returning UN inspectors was the best (multi-lateral) approach to disarmament, it becomes much harder later on to revert to the status quo without suffering political consequences. The stronger the general case against Saddam, the harder it is to back off from the 'serious consequences' stipulated in UNSCR 1441 when "full and complete" compliance was not forthcoming or when so many WMD questions remained unresolved or un-resolvable. The political damage from that kind of flip-flop after 9/11 would have been viewed by many as significant in light of the recommendations outlined in the 9/11 Commission report. Research on crisis tipping points, non-compensatory decision-making and mission creep are all useful in this regard (Goertz andLevy 2007; Hoagland 1993; Mintz 1993; Siegel 2000; Sylvan and Majeski 1998).[9]

There is a natural (almost inevitable) 'momentum' tied to selecting one strategy (e.g., returning inspectors) over another (e.g., ignoring the Iraq problem or downplaying the significance of the WMD threat). When one combines the 9/11 attacks, the heightened fear of WMD proliferation, the complete absence of inspectors in Iraq since 1998 and a weak containment policy that was failing to prevent Saddam (and others) from exploiting the oil-for-food sanctions program, ignoring Iraq was no longer an option. Of all the available diplomatic strategies at the time, the only reasonable, multilateral approach was the one Bush, Powell and Blair were praised for taking at the time – going to the UN for a strong mandate. In fact, Richard Holbrooke was glowing in his endorsement of Bush's strategy:

> [The Bush Administration] finally got their act together and … eliminated the united opposition of both parties on the hill and then they went to the UN and played their hand skilfully and as we talk here tonight we're waiting for the next shoe to drop. The most important thing that happened here is that the President speaks finally, the world rallies to the United States, Saddam finally backs up. Some of the nations of the world then say to the United States, "ok, don't go any further," Bush correctly says "no," we're still going to keep pushing and now the ball is back in Washington's court and it's been well played for the last few days.[10]

The Bush team was universally praised for the diplomacy leading to a unanimous UN resolution declaring Saddam in "material breach" – it was considered by *everyone* to be Colin Powell's shining diplomatic achievement as secretary of state, and it would have been equally impressive for a Democratic secretary of state. Once UNSCR 1441 was passed, however, it would have become very difficult – I would argue inconceivable – for Bush (or Gore) to back down after Chirac removed the military option from the table, because the post-9/11 credibility and resolve of both the United States and UK were at stake. The financial

---

[9] Goertz and Levy (2007: 31–2) refer to the concept of "windows of opportunity" and the importance of three streams conjoining to make specific options more appealing and others less likely: the 'political' stream (confluence of political pressures and benefits), the 'problem' stream and the 'solution' stream. The confluence of these three streams is another way to conceptualize the political challenges of confronting a post-9/11 security crisis and the imperative to address Iraq's WMD threat. See Goertz and Levy 2007.

[10] See Holbrooke 2002b.

costs of sustaining 200,000 American troops in the region would have continued to rise as Gore's approval ratings rapidly dropped; the public, encouraged by a strong and vocal Republican opposition, would have questioned the president's commitment to their post-9/11 security. Gore would have faced the additional problem of maintaining the coalition – at the time, support from 'new' European states was already on shaky grounds after Chirac raised doubts about the status of their EU membership (following the publication of the Vilnius letter), and many of the United States' Arab allies – who, at the time, were providing clandestine support for the coalition (e.g., Saudi Arabia, Egypt and Jordan) – would have backed off if Washington lost its resolve to deal with the Saddam problem once and for all.[11] All of these costs and pressures increased over time as a direct result of the efforts put into defending a widely supported policy. Ending these multilaterally endorsed efforts would have reinstated the status quo, with no option of threatening military force, no proof that Iraq had disarmed in accordance with UNSCR 1441, no proof that the regime had destroyed its weapons, and ongoing revelations of material breach. This would have amounted to a major failure of American foreign policy – both Democrats and Republicans would have criticized Gore for allowing US security to be controlled by a veto from France and Russia, and not authorization from Congress.

Momentum and comparative risks over time

Neoconist critics might concede the previous point on the risks of returning to the status quo in March 2003, but they would also point out that the decision to invade carried enormous risks that were apparently overlooked by the Bush administration. However, the risks and costs of alternative strategies are not static – they are typically calculated over time and through stages, before and after each decision. At T+1, leaders were comparing the political and security *risks* and *costs* of the status quo in 2002 versus a return of inspectors; at the next stage, leaders compared the *risks* of trying to get a new UN resolution with or without first obtaining congressional authorization to deploy troops (generally viewed as essential for enhancing the credibility of the US–UK coercive threat); they then evaluated the *risks*, after authorization, of actually deploying (or not deploying) forces, and how many troops (Gore would have deployed more troops in line with his post-invasion plans); then the *risks* of demanding a strong, coercive resolution with rigid requirements (along with a commitment to consider a second resolution) versus negotiating a weaker resolution with standards that would be easier for Saddam to meet (see item 11 in Table 9.2); then they compared the *risks* of accepting the Iraqi regime's lengthy disarmament

---

[11] For an overview of the support offered by many Arab states in the region (and other 'critics' of the war), see Harvey (2004).

report as sufficient, or rejecting it as more of the same; then the *risks* of accepting Blix's mixed reports as sufficient or demanding clearer evidence of compliance and/or solid proof of WMD disarmament (which Saddam no longer had); then the *risks* of trying (and failing) to get a second resolution; and then, after all of these stages and a decision by France to reject the timeline and threat of military force (stripping away the coercive value of the troops), the *risks* of this status quo (ongoing and costly deployment of hundreds of thousands of troops, ongoing discovery of material breach) versus intervention – all in the context of a post-9/11 environment and an upcoming presidential election campaign. In sum, the costs associated with the status quo in 2002 (T+1, before all of these actions) were not the same as the costs of the status quo at the final stage in 2003 (T+15) – it is the status quo at the final stage that is the one measured against the costs and benefits of intervention, real disarmament and regime change. There were no easy answers, as Krauthammer (2004) explains in his review of the mounting costs of the status quo:

> Of course the lack of Franco-German support made things more difficult. Of course the lack of international consensus constituted a prudential reason not to invade. But … [t]he tense post-Gulf War settlement was unstable and created huge and growing liabilities for all concerned, most especially for the United States. First, it caused enormous suffering for the Iraqi people under a cruel and corrupt sanctions regime – suffering and starvation that throughout the Middle East and in much of Europe w[as] blamed squarely on the United States. Second, the standoff with Iraq made it necessary to maintain a large American garrison in Saudi Arabia, land of the Islamic holy places – for many Muslims, a provocative and deeply offensive presence. Indeed, in his 1998 fatwa against the United States, Bin Laden listed these two offenses as crimes numbers one and two justifying jihad against America. Moreover, the sanctions regime was collapsing. That collapse was temporarily halted by the huge pre-war infusion of American troops into Kuwait that forced the Security Council to reaffirm the sanctions – but only as a way to avert an American invasion.[12]

The idea that the choice in 2003 was between a neocon sanctioned invasion and pre-invasion stability misses too much of what made this dilemma so difficult to resolve.

These are the facts that must be processed to draw historically informed conclusions about how risks and costs were evaluated. In other words there was no prospect, at T+15, of returning to the status quo that existed at T+1.

The logic of coercive diplomacy, momentum and war

In addition to missing the role of path dependence and momentum, neoconism completely overlooks the logic of coercive diplomacy and the effects that the

---

[12] Krauthammer 2004.

application of this strategy has on subsequent calculations and options. Coercive diplomacy adds to the momentum for war because it instantly changes the calculation of risks and costs once threats are issued and resolve is demonstrated.

Many critics of the 2003 war point to the decision to deploy hundreds of thousands of American and British troops to the region in 2002 as the single biggest error because it created the momentum for war that was difficult to reverse. Having that many troops in the region was very costly, especially over an extended period of time, and bringing them home in 2003 would have been viewed as a serious military and diplomatic failure; it would also have been interpreted as another major success for Saddam. The real motivation to use the troops was a product of these political factors, critics argue, not the military security imperatives to address a major WMD threat. Mann (2004: 349) makes the same argument:

> By early January French Officials had recognized that the American armada in the Gulf was becoming far bigger than was needed for coercive diplomacy. The United States was openly preparing for war. Indeed, the huge build up seemed to close off other possibilities; if Bush were [to] reverse course and bring the forces home without a war, he would look silly to the American public, and the United States would lose face overseas.[13]

But these points raise several interesting questions about the requirements for effective deterrence and compellence: how many troops *should* be deployed to mount a 'credible' (successful) coercive threat capable of compelling a leader to comply with UN disarmament demands? There is no set standard of, say, 50,000, 100,000 or 250,000 troops. The truest measure of credibility in any case is derived from the opponent's behavior once the threat is issued – we now know, for example, that Saddam did not believe invasion was imminent despite the deployment of hundreds of thousands of American and British troops and a clear threat to impose serious consequences. This fact is missed by neoconists, who erroneously believe, as Mann does, that the US deployment exceeded the requirements for effective coercion. In this case, coercive diplomacy failed for reasons covered in Chapter 8.

The success of coercive diplomacy is directly related to the costs of backing down. If US officials sent only 100 soldiers to the region, for example, that deployment would certainly be much easier to reverse, but it would also be a very weak coercive threat, because the potential costs to Saddam would have been insignificant to him. With 200,000 troops, on the other hand, the threat is more credible precisely because it is far more difficult to reverse or back down without suffering enormous political costs – costly signals are central to effective coercion. But these moves also mean that escalation is more likely if the threat is still viewed by Saddam as not credible, which is precisely what happened. Perceptions – not troop numbers – are the relevant considerations.

---

[13] Mann 2004.

The paradox of coercive diplomacy in this case is that the decision to deploy this many troops in the first place made perfect sense to the significant majority of US Congress members and British parliamentarians that authorized force, because the move satisfied essential prerequisites for a credible compellent threat – a clear demonstration of resolve, capability and commitment.[14] As UK Foreign Secretary Jack Straw explains (on October 12, 2002):[15]

> What we face here is a paradox: the firmer and tougher we are up-front about the fact that we will use force in Iraq … the more likely there is to be a peaceful solution.

Blair's chief of staff, Alastair Campbell, agreed with Straw's take on the logic of coercive diplomacy: "The clearer we are that we would use force, the likelier it may be that we don't have to."[16] But Straw's interpretation of the prevailing paradox did not go far enough – he is right that strong, credible threats are more likely to work. But credible, resolute threats are also more likely to lead to hostilities if demands are not fully and completely met. In this case, Saddam was *not* convinced the threat was credible, did not believe the invasion was imminent and remained committed to the practice of strategic ambiguity throughout the crisis.

It is important to recall that everyone at the time, including the war's strongest critics, agreed with the need to mount a strong, coercive military threat by deploying American and British troops to the region – everyone shares part of the blame for endorsing a strategy that was responsible for the war. Hans Blix conveyed his strong support for the approach in a conversation with National Security Advisor Condoleezza Rice – "*I have never complained about your military pressure. I think it's a good thing*" (emphasis added).[17] France's President Chirac was asked the following question by CNN's Christiane Amanpour: "You have said that inspections were working in great part because of the massive US and British force that is arrayed outside Saddam Hussein's doorstep. Wouldn't it be even more effective if France had sent troops also to double and triple the threat?" Chirac responded, "*I have said that it is indeed thanks to the pressure of British and American troops that the Iraqi authorities and Saddam Hussein have changed their position and have agreed to cooperate with the inspectors*" (emphasis added).[18] Of course, Chirac's minimalist interpretation of the regime's cooperation was never likely to be accepted by any US administration.

Based on extensive interviews with the Bush's national security team, Bob Woodward confirms the prevalence of the same sentiments regarding the logic of coercive diplomacy.[19] According to Woodward (2004: 254), administration

---

[14] Harvey 1998, 1999, 2006, 2008 and 2010; Huth and Russett 1984, 1988 and 1989; Lebow and Stein 1987, 1989 and 1990.

[15] Quoted in Acronym Institute 2002.   [16] Campbell and Stott 2007: 639–40.

[17] Woodward 2004: 254.   [18] See Kopp 2003.   [19] Woodward 2004.

officials became convinced that "you have to follow through on your threat. If you're going to carry out coercive diplomacy, you have to live with that decision." Woodward (2004: 261) goes on to quote Rumsfeld: "The penalty for our country and for our relationship and potentially the lives of some people are at risk if you have to make a decision not to go forward." The president, Rumsfeld argued, would need "some very highly visible reason not to go forward, like the capitulation or the departure of Saddam Hussein or something like that." This was unlikely, given Saddam's pathological failure to fully appreciate his own predicament or understand who his real enemy was. Even Woodward (2004: 261) acknowledges the logic underpinning the dilemma described by Rice and Rumsfeld – "The president was rapidly losing his options of not going to war." He goes on to quote President Bush in a conversation with Rumsfeld – "Look, we're going to have to do this, I'm afraid. I don't see how we're going to get him to a position where he will do something in a manner that's consistent with the UN requirements, and we've got to make an assumption that he will not." All of these sentiments clearly draw out the paradox of coercive diplomacy. The compulsion to protect US security by strengthening Washington's reputation for issuing credible, resolute threats was identical to the coercive diplomatic strategy used by Clinton and Gore against Iraq (1998) and Kosovo (1998).

The challenges with coercive diplomacy run deeper than simply having to convince Saddam that the threat he was facing was credible. Woodward's (2004: 73) exchange with NSA Condoleezza Rice reveals her understanding of the complexities of coercion and the imperative to send credible signals to both opponents and allies in the region:[20]

> Coercive diplomacy meant living with dissonance and inconsistencies, (Condi) realized. The CIA made it clear that in order to recruit sources inside Iraq they would have to say the US was serious and was coming with its military.

Credibility, commitment and resolve – the essential ingredients for effective coercion and signalling – were not only aimed at Saddam but were also directed at internal groups and allies who required clear proof that Washington was serious about dealing with this problem. In fact, coercive diplomacy in this case – particularly the deployment of troops to the region – was designed to persuade the following audiences of the seriousness of US–UK commitment: (1) supporters in the United States who authorized the use of force; (2) the American and British public and media; (3) European powers, including those on the UNSC; (4) potential allies in the region; (5) opposition groups and allies inside Iraq; (6) the Iraqi military; and (7) Saddam and his chief advisers. Convincing the latter groups was obviously the most important task, but the immense scope of military capabilities deployed to the region was so badly underestimated by Saddam

[20] Woodward 2004: 73

that he actually believed he was winning the war – Saddam was so oblivious to the reality on the ground at the time that he demanded nothing short of unconditional surrender as troops were moving toward Baghdad. This was the most dangerous set of circumstances that could possibly have unfolded; the military threat was perceived by Saddam to be a bluff at the very time US–UK leaders were convinced the threat was so obvious. As stronger threats were issued over time, Saddam's misperceptions meant that war became increasingly more likely.

Conclusions: *Gore-war* versus *Gore-peace* revisited

Based on generally accepted criteria for conducting rigorous counterfactual analyses (Fearon 1991; Ferguson 2000; Goertz and Levy 2007; Lebow 2000; Levy 2008b; Tetlock and Belkin 1996), the combined evidence presented in the preceding eight chapters strongly supports the view that Al Gore would have been compelled to follow the same path. *Gore-war* is firmly rooted in a more precise historical account of the case evidence, satisfies all generally accepted standards for identifying strong counterfactual analysis (minimum re-write, logical consistency, theoretical relevance, cotenability, etc.), and is supported by well established theories in international relations. These theories, derived from multiple levels of analysis, combine to provide a more plausible explanation for the 2003 Iraq war.

Consider the very large number of theories that run through the analysis presented here: misperception theory; political psychology (cognitive and motivational biases on both sides); organizational theory; bureaucratic politics (intelligence failures); cycles of intelligence failures; alliance politics and post-Cold War balancing in the UN; groupthink; public opinion (rally around the flag, externalization theory); rational choice theory; mission creep, escalation and momentum; continuity in American foreign policy, etc. The *Gore-war* counterfactual combines some of the best theoretical work in the field of international relations, compiled from decades of research on these important questions. This entire intellectual legacy is virtually ignored by neoconists, who privilege the power and incredible influence of a few advisers in the Bush administration.

In contrast, *Gore-peace* remains a much more difficult counterfactual to defend on logical, empirical and theoretical grounds. Proponents would have to defend several auxiliary assumptions about Gore and his team in light of the sheer weight of the disconfirming empirical evidence presented throughout this book. What would these circumstances look like – what set of alternative decisions would Gore have selected, based on what facts, supported by what advisers, for what reasons and with what political consequences? How would the Republican and Democratic leadership, public and media respond to these initiatives? One would need to change too much, assume too much and discard too much to make this counterfactual as compelling as *Gore-war*. Perhaps most importantly, one would have to somehow transform Gore's legacy and personality, or at least offer more compelling interpretations of the many speeches described in Chapter 2.

Standard accounts repeatedly ignore the entire body of evidence covered in this book. Neoconism misrepresents the influence of neoconservatives, overlooks the broader international and bipartisan consensus that emerged on how to deal with Iraq, misinterprets post-9/11 public opinion as a *product* rather than a *cause* of Iraq policy, overestimates the impact of exaggerated intelligence on the authorization vote, ignores Saddam's miscalculations and fails to appreciate the path tied to coercive diplomacy. Among the only ways to increase probability of a *Gore-peace* path would have been to avoid *all* of the very reasonable and generally lauded interim decisions that created the impasse in March 2003. And, given his legacy, there is no reason to expect such avoidance would have been Gore's preference.

Many neoconist critics will reject the *Gore-war* counterfactual as revisionist history. On the contrary; the standard neoconist interpretation of the 2003 Iraq war is guilty of revisionist history, for two reasons. First, neoconism ignores almost all of the historical facts outlined in each of the nine chapters of this book, including important facts surrounding Saddam's misperceptions. Second, far too much explanatory weight is assigned to factors (e.g., individuals, ideologies) that were demonstrably less significant to the invasion. As Kagan concludes, "it's interesting to watch people rewrite history, even their own."[21] Far from revising history, the purpose of this book is to embrace the past by exposing a very weak (but popular) theory of the war to more probing and thoughtful analysis. Democratic leaders who no longer acknowledge their initial support for the war, or who remove from their websites the floor speeches they delivered in October 2002 strongly endorsing authorization, are the ones who are practicing revisionist history.

The point here is not to create or ignore history, or to cherry-pick historical facts that bias the case in favor of one or another theory. The objective is to open up the entire historical record as a way of evaluating the comparative strengths of two mirror-image counterfactuals. The purpose of comparative counterfactual history is not to change or revise history – it is to keep history intact, with only one minor change (a Gore victory), and then to process this antecedent condition through the case history, making sure the ripple effects of the alteration are carefully considered. Neoconism, in contrast, is responsible for revising or ignoring a great deal of history by dismissing the relevance of so many other factors that were central to decisions made and supported at the time. It is revisionist (or weak) history to ignore the fact that almost every Democrat, including Gore, shared the same views about Saddam, WMD and the wisdom of the multilateral approach to the disarmament impasse. Revisionist history

---

[21] Kagan 2005b.

ignores the fact that different leaders, with different decision-making styles and personalities, all arrived at the same conclusions and policy recommendations. It is revisionist (or weak) history to ignore the bipartisan support Bush received from Congress and the American public. Ignoring major speeches by Democratic senators, who accepted the bulk of WMD intelligence that required the return of inspectors, is a major oversight. The conventional neoconist account is not good history or good theory – it essentially rejects history and theory.

My arguments are also likely to be interpreted by many critics as a tad deterministic, but major foreign policy decisions (especially decisions to go to war) made by leaders of powerful democracies *are* deterministic, for reasons outlined in the book. Given the choice between two competing interpretations (or counterfactual theories) of American foreign policy, free will versus determinism, the latter argument is consistently much stronger across most historical cases. More importantly, neoconism (*Gore-peace*) can just as easily be dismissed as deterministic – the popular story is firmly rooted in the belief that a neoconservative victory in the 2000 US presidential election virtually guaranteed war, whereas a few more hanging chads would almost certainly have led the country down a different path. If critics reject *Gore-war* as excessively deterministic, they would then have to reject *Gore-peace* (neoconism) on the same grounds, which they never do.

Most of those who subscribe to counterfactual analysis do so in order to demonstrate the transformational effects from small accidents (or different leaders). "Counterfactual history," Lebow (2000) observes, "is a good corrective to the tendency to see developments as 'overdetermined.'"[22] If small changes produce significant alterations in the course of history, then these outcomes are obviously contingent and malleable. But both *Gore-war* and *Gore-peace* are deterministic accounts of history – one supporting the inevitability of change (peace) contingent on a different leader in power, the other view (defended here) supporting the inevitability of continuity (war) based on a combination of leadership, psychological, societal, political organizational and international (structural) conditions. There is no way to get around the assumption of determinism when explaining any event, just as it is impossible to render a factual claim without simultaneously making a counterfactual argument. If one believes neoconservatives caused the war, then neoconservatism must be viewed as highly deterministic, by definition – in the absence of pressure from neocons, Gore's team would not have gone to war. Regardless of which counterfactual argument one prefers, however, both deterministic accounts must be persuasively defended, and the best way to reveal biases in either case is to simultaneously subject both counterfactuals – continuity (*Gore-war*) and change (*Gore-peace*) – to the full body of historical evidence through comparative counterfactual analysis. When

---

[22] www.people.cohums.ohio-state.edu/grimsley1/dialogue/postcolonialism/resistance_22.htm.

this is done well, *Gore-war* emerges as a more powerful account of history than neoconism.

The book's conclusion – that major decisions from 2002–2003 were path dependent, regardless of leadership – is not meant to condone the war, for reasons nicely summarized by the following excerpt:

> To believe that there's a deterministic causal explanation for wrongful behavior is not in any sense to condone or approve it – we still have our standards of right and wrong. Those who believe that to explain is to condone are motivated to suppress natural (biological, psychological and social) explanations for evil, barring us from understanding it and responding to it effectively. So the idea that determinism is a universal excuse disempowers us, making evil more likely. This is yet another reason why it's critical to see that a scientific, naturalistic view of human depravity does not undermine moral standards or moral responsibility. To accept that people don't have free will isn't to condone evil, only to understand it thoroughly instead of chalking it up to a mysterious, ultimately self-originated choice.[23]

The primary objective of the book is to demonstrate why neoconism is wrong, not so we can excuse Bush for his decisions but rather to better understand the case history and the pressures that played such an important role in making these decisions so rational, despite the outcome. These findings will not be appealing to those comforted by simplistic interpretations of history, but their aversion to complexity should not be allowed to prevent other scholars from producing much better historical accounts of one of the most important wars in decades.

When engaged in politically volatile debates, there is a tendency to attribute some measure of motivation to those who subscribe to one or another position. Worse, some critics are convinced the *Gore-war* counterfactual is designed to shift blame or minimize the responsibility Bush and his administration share for a policy that most agree today was a serious mistake. Specifying a more deterministic rather than contingent interpretation of the war does not imply a readiness to forgive officials who led their respective countries to war, just as explaining anti-Semitism, the onset of genocide in Rwanda, ethnic cleansing in Bosnia or Islamic fundamentalism does not condone any of these actions.

Finally, there are likely to be many historians who will be inclined to dismiss my counterfactual conclusions on methodological grounds. Tristram Hunt (2004) summarizes this common critique very well:

> E.H. Carr dismissed such whimsical exercises as a red herring worthy not of scholarly pursuit but an idle "parlour game." Characteristically[,] E.P. Thompson went one stage further, dismissing "counter-factual fiction"

---

[23] Clark 2008.

as "unhistorical shit." Both pointed to the futility of pondering multiple variables in the past and the logical problem of assuming all other conditions
remained constant.[24]

But would any of these renowned historians deny the fact that conventional
('factual') historical analysis, if done poorly, can be "Geschichtswissenschlopff"
(or "unhistorical shit", in Carr's words) as well? Neoconism, for example, is
firmly rooted in a weak, superficial and largely inaccurate historical account of
the participants, key decisions, events and many other facts from 2002 to 2003.
Proponents of this 'factual' account of history subscribe to an excessively simplistic model of behavior that assigns overwhelming causal weight to the ideological predispositions and personal fickleness of a few members of the Bush
administration. Structures and processes are ignored in an attempt to lay the
blame for the war on these committed ideologues. But, if done well, counterfactual analysis can challenge weak 'factual' accounts by being *more* attuned to
all of the facts from the case, as the chapters in this book have demonstrated. A
systematic application of comparative counterfactual analysis reveals the serious problems with simplistic accounts of history and challenges neoconists to
consider the influence of so many other domestic, political, organizational and
psychological variables that, when combined, provide a more comprehensive
account of behavior throughout the relevant time period. The methodology
associated with factual or counterfactual analysis is not the problem – it is the
application and careful attention to historical facts that determines the quality
of any analysis.

Perhaps the most serious error critics make when launching insults at counterfactual analysis is their failure to appreciate the underlying counterfactual
claims embedded in their own explanations. The historical account of the war
put forward by neoconists, for example, is logically associated with a *Gore-peace*
counterfactual. By implication, if critics are prepared to dismiss *Gore-war* as
purely speculative or excessively deterministic, there is no logical reason the
very same criticism could not be leveled against *Gore-peace* and neoconism.
Fortunately, comparative counterfactual analysis forces researchers to explore
the possibility that causality is considerably more complex than neoconists are
prepared to admit. It pushes us to reveal as much of the history as possible in
order to carefully weigh the relative strengths of two mutually exclusive paths.

[24] Hunt 2004.

10

Conclusion

The value of any contribution to knowledge should be measured in terms of the prevailing consensus being challenged – the more sweeping the consensus regarding the crucial role of neoconservatism and other first-image theories of the war, the more pressing the obligation to challenge it, and the more valuable the conclusions if these theories are persuasively challenged, largely disconfirmed or significantly refuted. The objective of this book was not simply to defend an interesting counterfactual thesis on a Gore presidency, or provide a new, innovative way to apply counterfactual methodology to historical cases. The primary goal, as I explain in the Introduction, is to use comparative counterfactual analysis as a tool to construct a more compelling, complete, historically accurate, logically informed, theoretically grounded account of the Bush presidency and the strong support Bush and Blair received for the many key decisions they made from 2002 to 2003.

In light of the alternative explanation for the 2003 Iraq war outlined in the preceding chapters, any suggestion that neoconism or its underlying *Gore-peace* counterfactual deserve to retain their status as the only prevailing 'truths' about this war is, in a word, indefensible. Yet neoconism continues to be assigned a high degree of respect despite the clear *absence* of supporting evidence. If alternative accounts, like the one offered in this book, are summarily rejected despite the *presence* of an overwhelming body of supporting empirical (and theoretical) evidence, we will be destined to retain incomplete or, worse, fundamentally erroneous lessons from one of the most important wars in decades. What is perhaps most ironic about standard neoconist accounts of the war is that they are plagued by the same errors that proponents of neoconism typically attach to the Bush administration's process in dealing with Al-Qaeda and the Iraq war: premature closure of inquiry; failure to challenge consensus; an unwillingness to change assumptions embedded in the prevailing wisdom; a systematic refusal to consider alternative theories that are inconsistent with popular accounts and opinions, etc. There are several reasons, therefore, why the arguments developed here using comparative counterfactual analysis are so important.

First, the book forcefully challenges conventional wisdom on a critically important case, and raises doubts about the validity of a nearly universally held and almost taken-for-granted assumption about the key foreign policy decisions that led to war. It addition to being admittedly provocative, the objective was to generate both vigorous debate and theoretical advances in our understanding of the interaction among (and relative importance of) individual psychology, bureaucratic politics, public opinion, domestic politics, international negotiations and coercive diplomacy.

Second, the book is an essential corrective to what amounts to academic groupthink – like other conspiracy theories, neoconism develops an entire narrative around a simplistic first-image theory about the Machiavellian brilliance and absolute power of a few ideologues who transformed US foreign policy to serve their self-interests. But widely accepted neoconist assumptions about the causes of the 2003 war can be just as dangerous as the intelligence failures that were responsible for the crisis in the first place. These weak narratives are particularly dangerous when proponents refuse to acknowledge anomalies that challenge their entrenched beliefs, or when they continue to rely exclusively on a small portion of the historical record to reconfirm a weak theory.

Third, the findings challenge the tendency in the literature to assign extraordinary causal weight to a few cherry-picked intelligence exaggerations. Neoconists remain convinced that Cheney's distortions were considerably more relevant than many other intelligence errors that encompass the true measure of failure in this case. In fact, the common assertion that Cheney's 'lies' caused the war continues to be issued as if it is an indisputable, irrefutable, incontrovertible fact requiring absolutely no need for proof or historical evidence. It is the gospel, according to almost everyone writing on the causes of this war. But the academic community shares an important obligation to discredit simplistic accounts of the war that overlook the structural and organizational causes of intelligence failure (Chapter 5). If conventional accounts continue to be accepted, very little effort will be devoted to fixing the real problems plaguing US intelligence – the cyclical nature of intelligence failures. The findings from this project, therefore, are considerably more policy relevant.

Fourth, the conclusions reveal several serious deficiencies with first-image (leadership) theories of US foreign policy. Consider the following example from Charles-Philippe David's (2008: 30) research. He lists, among other factors, George W. Bush's presidential style. According to the author, almost all of the *mistakes* Bush made:[1]

> could have been mitigated or entirely eliminated if Bush had surrounded himself with better advisors, had carefully chosen a suitable decision-making system, and had been more alert to the risks of the process going off the tracks. This did not happen because of certain aspects of Bush's presidential style, which help explain, in retrospect, the US debacle in Iraq and the American refusal to take the necessary remedial action. Among the elements of Bush's personal style that contributed to the mistake, *the most*

----

[1] David 2008.

obvious and best documented are probably the following: George W. Bush is an obstinate, combative, stubborn president, prone to overconfidence and certainty in his own rightness … He confuses obstinacy with perseverance … His eagerness to act decisively leads him to neglect the deliberation stage of the decision-making process. Bush is inclined to "trust his gut," as he likes to put it. His stubbornness and his impatience to invade Iraq eliminated all doubt in his mind and led him to ignore the risk of disastrous consequences. His self-confidence is matched by his arrogance and fatalism. Since 9/11, Bush has been disinclined to ask questions. He acts from instinct and resolve, convinced that he is reading events correctly and making the right decisions … Bush is an uncurious president who is disconnected from what is happening on the ground … Bush is a lazy president when it comes to seeking out, absorbing and weighing options … He does not test the merits of his decisions … His demand for unquestioning loyalty prevents him from taking advantage of disagreements between advisors within a competitive decision-making system. (Emphasis added)

Juxtaposed against the analysis presented throughout this book, Charles-Philippe David's observations raise several simple questions that reveal serious weaknesses with his thesis. For example, how exactly does one explain identical assessments by Clinton, Gore and Holbrooke in 1998 and 2002 based on the same flawed intelligence of Iraq's WMD? What is it about *their* decision-making style(s) that could possibly explain the emergence of policy preferences that were entirely consistent with those of Bush and Blair in 2002? They all rejected unilateral pre-emption in favor of UN-based multilateral inspections. Obviously, if their approach to making decisions was as variable as their personalities, then decision-making styles cannot logically be relevant to explaining the consensus on both the threat and appropriate solutions. Similarly, why did so many Democrats accept the WMD intelligence and offer their strongest support for the Bush–Blair strategy responsible for setting their countries on a path to war? Why would so many other Democrats endorse decisions to return inspectors, obtain congressional authorization, deploy troops to the region, and go back to the UN for a strong resolution threatening serious consequences? Tony Blair, Al Gore, Richard Holbrooke, James Baker and Brent Scowcroft must have been plagued by the very same decision-making pathologies Bush suffered, or they were just too stupid to see through Bush's mistakes. But how exactly do we determine which decisions in the above list are rational, based (presumably) on sound decision-making styles, and which are less rational and deserving of scorn and ridicule? If the same basic pathologies listed in the above quote are present during both good and bad decisions, then these pathologies are irrelevant to explaining those choices – something else must be included in the explanatory model. David's analysis ignores almost all of the key variables (and levels of analysis) included in the explanation of the war outlined in this book.

Every one of us has a distinctive psychological profile encompassing different fears, life experiences, egos, talents, intellects, moral compasses and, of course, decision-making styles – all of which have an effect on the choices we make. But they have less influence when decisions involve input from more people, and become increasingly less relevant when a very large group is involved in providing information relevant to the decisions we make. For American presidents, their idiosyncrasies lose more significance when the policies in question involve competing government departments and Congress. And, finally, personality traits become almost insignificant when the issue involves a large democracy and its allies involved in negotiating one of the most important foreign policy decisions a country and its government can make – the decision to invade and occupy another country suspected of developing and possibly using WMD. So many other factors must be included in our models to avoid simplistic (often politically motivated) assumptions about the superhuman capacity of a few individuals to shape the entire direction of a country's foreign policy.[2] In sum, there are strong and weak leadership theories – neoconism is a very weak theory of the Iraq war.

Fifth, the evidence in the book also facilitates the application of larger theoretical frameworks. Take neoclassical realism (NCR) as an example. Strictly speaking, neoclassical realism is not a theory – it is a theoretical framework whose proponents believe foreign policies are products of the interaction among structural (power) and actor-based (domestic) factors. But aside from NCR's recommendation to explore both structure and agency when explaining state actions, the approach says little about how and in what context specific domestic factors might have influenced decisions and outcomes in any given case. Therefore, the specific domestic factors that are hypothesized to have influenced state priorities must be carefully unpacked from the case evidence – simply saying that domestic factors matter is not the same as identifying which factors had what impact on what decisions. Failure to address these important research questions in any given case often leads neoclassical realists to arrive at faulty conclusions about the role of some domestic factors at the

---

[2] See Byman and Pollack 2001. Notwithstanding their effort to highlight the relevance of leadership theories, even these authors are careful to acknowledge the importance of other factors. Also see Rosenau 1966. Rosenau's work on pre-theories is perhaps the definitive account of when and under what conditions idiosyncratic variables are likely to carry more/ less weight. They matter more when power and decision authority rests in the hands of a few people, when power is not shared across branches of government, or when there is little or no accountability to a general, voting public. The relative importance of these factors depends on the extent to which institutions within the state are in conflict, or if the international system is in a state of flux or crisis. In other words, domestic political and structural conditions must be considered prior to assigning all causal weight to first-image explanatory factors, and large, open democracies like the United States are the least likely of all states to be governed by idiosyncratic factors.

expense of exploring the larger role of other domestic, political and societal pressures.

Unfortunately, proponents of neoclassical realism are not immune from being influenced by very popular stories about powerful neoconservatives running the US government in 2002–2003 – they simply apply NCR to reinforce rather than prove (or disprove) neoconist theory. Consider the conclusions by Lobell *et al.* (2009: 3):

> Relative power and shifts in the level of external threat alone cannot explain the nuances of the George W. Bush administration's grand strategy after the September 11, 2001 terrorist attacks. Certainly, any presidential administration (Republican or Democratic) would have responded to the Al Qaeda attacks on New York City and Washington, DC by using American military might to topple the Taliban regime in Afghanistan and destroy Al Qaeda safe havens in that country. However, other aspects of the Bush administration's behavior defy simply systemic or domestic-level explanations. Instead, the so-called Bush doctrine, the March 2003 invasion of Iraq, and the administration's subsequent campaign to eliminate Islamist terrorism by fostering liberal democracy in the Middle East resulted from a veritable witches' brew of systemic and domestic-level factors. In other words, while external threats and preponderant American power set the parameters for a US military response, *unit-level factors such as executive branch dominance in national security, policy entrepreneurship by neoconservatives within the administration and the think tank community, and the dominance of Wilsonian (or liberal) ideals in US foreign policy discourse determined both the character and the venue of that response.* (Emphasis added)[3]

For reasons covered in the preceding nine chapters, the authors have constructed a decidedly weak neoclassical realist interpretation of the war that simply repeats (rather than confirms) the common neoconist view that neoconservatism was relevant to the key strategic decisions that led to the 2003 Iraq war. The authors stay fully grounded in the standard narrative, which remains plagued by mistaken assumptions about neocons – who, contrary to popular accounts, actually lost many key debates along the way. And these domestic political battles were resolved in favor of a strategy that was strongly endorsed by most Democrats and non-neocon Republicans. Lobell *et al.* then cite as their key references several other authors (e.g., Dueck 2004; Jervis 2003; Kaufmann 2004; Monten 2005a) who offer their own versions of the same Bush-neocon-war thesis. The domestic political, organizational and societal variables included in Chapters 4, 5 and 6 of this book are never fully engaged.[4]

---

[3] Lobell *et al.* 2009.   [4] Dueck 2004; Jervis 2003; Kaufmann 2004; Monten 2005b.

The $64,000 question – why the popularity of neoconism?

If the evidence against neoconism is so overwhelming, then why does the consensus prevail? There are several reasons why standard accounts remain popular.

To begin, many of those who espouse the neoconist position in Washington do so for reasons that have nothing whatsoever to do with a commitment to rigorous academic research and analysis. These officials are politically motivated to cover themselves (or their record) and, whenever possible, shift blame to the other party for any foreign policy blunder. Not surprisingly, the conventional wisdom regarding the powerful role of neocons in the Bush administration is endorsed by many Democrats who are desperately trying to distance themselves from that legacy. Unlike his speeches in 2002 (see Chapter 2), more recent speeches by Al Gore have attacked both the Bush and Blair administrations for following a strategy he endorsed at the time. As Robert Kagan explains:[5]

> Prominent intellectuals, both liberal and conservative, have turned on their friends and allies in an effort to avoid opprobrium for a war they publicly supported. Journalists have turned on their fellow journalists in an effort to make them scapegoats for the whole profession. Politicians have twisted themselves into pretzels to explain away their support for the war or, better still, to blame someone else for persuading them to support it.
>
> Al Gore, the one-time Clinton administration hawk, airbrushed that history from his record. He turned on all those with whom he once agreed about Iraq and about many other foreign policy questions. And for this astonishing reversal he has been applauded by his fellow Democrats and may even get the party's nomination.
>
> Apparently, amazingly, dispiritingly, it all works. At least in the short run, dishonesty pays. Dissembling pays. Forgetting your past writings and statements pays. Condemning those with whom you once agreed pays. Phony self-flagellation followed by self-righteous self-congratulation pays. The only thing that doesn't pay is honesty. If Joe Lieberman loses, it will not be because he supported the war or even because he still supports it. It will be because he refused to choose one of the many dishonorable paths open to him to salvage his political career.

The transformation is often facilitated by the conspicuous deletion of key speeches from the websites of congressional leaders, on both sides, who strongly endorsed the authorization to use force (in October 2002). Of course, it is easy to understand in hindsight why a politician would want to avoid any mention of a speech they delivered defending the authorization to use force to compel Saddam's compliance with UNSCR 1441 and UNMOVIC inspectors. Why would anyone want to take credit for a policy that ultimately led to a war most

---

[5] Kagan 2006.

agree today was not necessary? In fact, both sides of the political aisle are equally committed to selling the neoconist narrative, because everyone has an interest in blaming the war on the fewest people possible – neocon ideologues have become the obvious target. But academics have an obligation to work through the political noise to arrive at better explanations; counterfactual historical analysis forces the researcher to revisit this period and shed light on these speeches while assigning less weight to statements delivered long after the war, and long after the leaders relinquished their responsibility to protect the American public.

Second, critics of the Bush administration often conflate strong, detailed explanations for the war (like the one developed in this book) with support for these policies. Consequently, critics are inclined to completely reject the notion that a war they despised, launched by an administration they hated, could possibly have made their decisions on the basis of a rational cost-benefit assessment of reasonable options at the time. Structural or deterministic explanations for unpopular wars are typically rejected, while leadership theories that assign specific blame to a political party, group or individual are consistently more appealing. Leadership theories are embedded in 'war of choice' explanations that elevate the relevance of individuals in order to apportion direct blame or praise, usually in order to gain political leverage. After all, if individuals matter, then changing the leader or political party in power should solve the problem. There is nothing particularly surprising about Democrats perpetuating the myth that things would have been very different if Gore had been in charge, even if it is very clear from their own behavior at the time that very little would have changed. This is a politically astute and pragmatic tactic, especially given what ultimately transpired in Iraq after the invasion. However, for those scholars who are seriously interested in truly understanding significant events, post-hoc political posturing should have no bearing on the careful, balanced analysis of relevant facts.

Third, simple neoconist models are more appealing precisely because they are easier to comprehend and/or more comforting – theories are often defended to make us feel better, not to make us smarter or more knowledgeable. It is so much easier for multilateralists, for example, to blame neoconservative unilateralists than it is to admit that a multilateral approach to dealing with Iraq's disarmament could conceivably have set the country on a path to war. Again, academics have an obligation to enhance the intellectual legacy of the field of foreign policy analysis and international relations – their job is to evaluate the relative strengths of competing explanations and historical accounts. Unfortunately, they are not immune from selecting theories they find more appealing, not because they are right but because they are consistent with their own ideological predispositions. Comparative counterfactual analysis forces everyone to explore the entire historical record through the prism of competing theories and historical accounts.

Fourth, neoconism is a very popular choice for journalists because it fits the 700–800-word sound bite op-eds and editorials 'covering' the administration and its foreign policies. Understandably, there is no real appetite to explore the many facets of the history, domestic politics, Saddam's miscalculations or the international diplomacy that pushed the United States and UK closer to war. The easier approach requires focusing on the actions and statements of a few administration officials. But their complicity in perpetuating the same WMD story, or their explicit endorsement of the Bush–Blair strategy to get UN inspectors back into the country, is never fully acknowledged in the media's black-and-white coverage of the war (see Chapter 6).

Fifth, when assumptions become so entrenched, it is very difficult for people to learn from history or engage in truly objective analysis of facts surrounding important events. As Tetlock (1999: 335) explains, scholars remain wedded to their positions even when confronted with disconfirming evidence, and often go through empirical and theoretical contortions to defend their views.[6] Based on "exploring experts' reactions to the confirmation and disconfirmation of conditional forecasts, the results reveal that experts neutralize dissonant data and preserve confidence in their prior assessments by resorting to a complex battery of belief-system defenses that, epistemologically defensible or not, make learning from history a slow process and defections from theoretical camps a rarity." The intellectual capital invested in defending their positions for so long explains the impediments to adjusting – it is a humbling experience to acknowledge key weaknesses with one's preferred explanation. This pathology afflicts those on the left or right of the political spectrum, and those who are critical or supportive of specific policies. Everyone is susceptible to these compulsions. However, there is some evidence indicating that those who prefer structural theories are more inclined to defend their positions than those who are less deterministic, because the latter tend to reject claims about inevitability and are more likely to accept contingence when accounting for behavior. But the problem remains: those who reject deterministic accounts of history are just as likely to remain overly committed to their contingent explanations (e.g., *Gore-peace*) despite the abundance of disconfirming evidence. The final answer with respect to the relative strengths of any explanation must rest on facts from the case and the quality of the explanation derived from these facts. Comparative counterfactual analysis facilitates this search for evidence.

Sixth, the typical approach to explaining the Iraq war tends to extract specific facts from the case for the purposes of supporting a preferred theory (neoconism, realism, liberalism, neoclassical realism, social psychology, etc.) rather than using all relevant facts from the case (derived from multiple levels of analysis) to explore the comparative advantages and relevance of multiple

---

[6] Tetlock 1999.

theories – the latter being the approach used in this book.[7] Unfocused reviews of partial pieces of evidence strategically selected to fit a theory is not the best approach to understanding the case, because there will always be some evidence to fit a poorly constructed, rudimentary version of a popular theoretical framework. The more important question is whether these theories and supporting evidence, in some combination, can provide a more well-rounded account of events leading to the war.

Seventh, there are sociological, psychological and academic reasons why scholars prefer to bandwagon by endorsing the consensus view on what happened from 2002 to 2003, when the alternative explanation, like the one offered in this book, is so much more complex. Academics, especially those not immersed in international relations, American foreign policy or the details of the case history, will find it much easier to teach neoconism. They will certainly avoid having to suffer criticism from students who already subscribe to simplistic neoconist accounts of this part of American history. This is so much easier than actually engaging in the kind of analysis included in the preceding chapters. Methodologically speaking, comparative counterfactual analysis is difficult and time consuming.

In sum, the conventional wisdom underpinning standard accounts of the war is more popular because it is easier to digest as an explanation and, therefore, more likely than more complex alternatives to be preferred by politicians, journalists, many academics, and former diplomats involved in the crisis.

Projectability as counterfactual confirmation

There are two ways one can assess the quality of a counterfactual argument. One way is through comparative counterfactual analysis and process tracing – the approach used in this book. Another, less formal method is through projectability. More specifically, in addition to disproving *Gore-peace* (neoconism) by processing historical evidence through the prism of a different administration, one can also disprove the Bush-neocon-war thesis by comparing Bush's policies to those defended by a completely different, Democratic administration that followed Bush's (and the neocons') departure from office. To the extent that a completely different president, Barack Obama, proceeds, when in office, to defend many of the same policies on key foreign affairs issues, the notion that Al Gore (or any other Democratic leader) would have followed Bush's path is much easier to contemplate.

---

[7] For example, Lieberfeld (2005) studied the US decision to invade Iraq from the perspectives of "realism, liberalism, elite interests, ideological influences, and personal and social psychology." His objective was to "better understand the causes of the invasion decision and implications of the particular case study for general theories of war causes." www.gmu.edu/programs/icar/ijps/vol10_2/wLieberfeld10n2IJPS.pdf.

CONCLUSION

For example, on January 22, 2009 President Barack Obama issued his first executive order to close the Guantánamo Bay detention facility:[8]

> The detention facilities at Guantánamo for individuals covered by this order shall be closed as soon as practicable, and no later than 1 year from the date of this order. If any individuals covered by this order remain in detention at Guantánamo at the time of closure of those detention facilities, they shall be returned to their home country, released, transferred to a third country, or transferred to another United States detention facility in a manner consistent with law and the national security and foreign policy interests of the United States.

The order went on to state, without any apparent ambiguity or equivocation:

> Individuals currently detained at Guantánamo have the constitutional privilege of the writ of habeas corpus.

The writ is a mandate to bring accused prisoners to trial quickly, both to establish a justification for their imprisonment and to give them an opportunity to hear and challenge the charges against them. These protections were suspended for Guantánamo detainees in 2001 (by President Bush's executive order establishing the military commissions) and then officially in 2006 when Congress passed the Military Commissions Act. The suspension of habeas corpus was overturned by the Supreme Court in 2008, and Obama's executive order clearly commits the administration to the court's ruling. As Obama declared at the time, these changes will go a long way toward re-establishing the moral standing of the United States in the world.

This was the official story, but how credible is the spin from Obama's White House?

The committee tasked to review the full range of issues surrounding Guantánamo detentions was scheduled to submit its recommendations in July 2009, long before the January 2010 deadline for closure, but, instead, requested a six-month extension. As many observers expected, the very brief interim report provided no details on how the administration planned to resolve the outstanding legal hurdles that confounded the Bush administration.

As late as September 2010 there were about 230 detainees at the facility and most were scheduled for release, but only a handful of prisoners had been returned to Saudi Arabia and Iraq. A few European allies (France, Spain and Italy) agreed to accept some of the detainees, and the release of almost 100 Yemenis was delayed due to lingering concerns about torture if they were returned. About sixty-five prisoners were scheduled for prosecution by military commission or federal courts.

---

[8] See www.whitehouse.gov/the_press_office/ClosureOfGuantanamoDetentionFacilities.

In May 2009, congressional Democrats and Republicans joined forces in a rare bipartisan rejection of the president's budget request to cover the costs of closure. The 90–6 vote in the Senate meant that all but six Democrats opposed the president, demanded a clearer plan for the disposition of remaining detainees after the facility is shut down, and barred the transfer of Guantánamo detainees to US soil unless they were sent there to be prosecuted. In other words, none of the detainees scheduled for release would be relocated to the United States, which likely hampered the president's efforts to convince European allies to help out by accepting detainees to their countries.

Of course, the most difficult challenge for the president was the disposition of the fourteen high-value detainees, including Khalid Sheikh Mohammed, Abu Zubaydah, Ramzi Binalshibh, Abu Faraj al Libi and about ten others. At the time of writing (July 2011), they continue to be imprisoned at Guantánamo indefinitely without the benefit of a federal or military commission trial. Obama's new and 'improved' policy was outlined in a major speech in May 2009:[9]

> There remains the question of detainees at Guantanamo *who cannot be prosecuted yet who pose a clear danger to the American people.* And I have to be honest here – *this is the toughest single issue that we will face.* We're going to exhaust every avenue that we have to prosecute those at Guantanamo who pose a danger to our country. But even when this process is complete, *there may be a number of people who cannot be prosecuted for past crimes, in some cases because evidence may be tainted, but who nonetheless pose a threat to the security of the United States.* Examples of that threat include people who've received extensive explosives training at al Qaeda training camps, or commanded Taliban troops in battle, or expressed their allegiance to Osama bin Laden, or otherwise made it clear that they want to kill Americans. These are people who, in effect, remain at war with the United States ... Let me repeat: *I am not going to release individuals who endanger the American people. Al Qaeda terrorists and their affiliates are at war with the United States, and those that we capture – like other prisoners of war – must be prevented from attacking us again.* (Emphasis added)

The revised policy directly challenges both the 2008 Supreme Court ruling and the president's own executive order. Apparently, only *some* "individuals currently detained at Guantánamo have the constitutional privilege of the writ of habeas corpus," and only *if* the evidence is not "tainted." In essence, Obama has endorsed the Bush–Cheney policy of preventive detention. This clear reversal was supported by senior Democrats, including the Secretary of State, Hillary Clinton:[10]

---

[9] Obama 2009, Remarks by the President on National Security. The White House, Office of the Press Secretary, Washington, DC, May 21, www.whitehouse.gov/the_press_office/Remarks-by-the-President-On-National-Security-5-21-09.

[10] Hillary Clinton 2009, www.weeklystandard.com/weblogs/TWSFP/2009/07/clinton_100_percent_committed.asp.

> The president, and certainly I and our entire administration, are 100 percent committed to the closure of Guantanamo and to proceeding with the transfer of those who can be transferred, the trial of those who can be tried, and the continuing detention of those who pose a grave threat.

Obama's policy shift is even more perplexing, if not paradoxical, in light of the reasons the president was compelled to adjust his views. Every one of the high-value detainees was waterboarded dozens of (some reportedly over 100) times. Because the evidence obtained from these confessions was "tainted" it would not be admissible in a federal court or military commission trial. However, the Obama team obviously accepted as credible the confessions obtained from these sessions, and continued to rely on this "tainted" evidence to justify indefinite detention and denial of habeas corpus. Now, if the information obtained from torture is accepted as reliable enough to detain prisoners without trial, isn't this a crystal clear admission by Obama that torture and waterboarding work?

The Supreme Court's ruling made no exceptions for high-value detainees – in fact, moral standards are typically revealed when legal rulings are applied to the hardest of cases. Aside from a few superficial adjustments to the military commission process, however, the legal standards the Obama administration applied to the hardest cases were identical to those Bush adopted.

In an effort to pressure the administration to try all remaining cases in federal courts, Human Rights First published a major report highlighting the 90 percent successful conviction rate of federal courts when processing terrorist cases. But government officials in the Obama administration remained concerned that the high-value detainees might fall into the 10 percent failure rate if prosecuted, given the tainted evidence collected from torture – Obama was not prepared to take that risk, despite the legal consequences. Obama went on to use his exceptionally refined communication skills to finesse the politics surrounding this issue, but the fact that these policies were now being defended by a popular president does not make the policies any more or less ethical. Obama's reversal was aptly described by the *Wall Street Journal* as "Bush's Gitmo Vindication," and, as predicted, human rights groups raised the same concerns: "Any effort to revamp the failed Guantanamo military commissions or enact a law to give any president the power to hold individuals indefinitely and without charge or trial," warned Anthony Romero (the ACLU's executive director), "is sure to be challenged in court and it will take years before justice is served."[11] Obama's campaign slogan, "change you can believe in," came back to bite him in numerous editorials.

---

[11] Anthony Romero 2009, quoted in www.articles.cnn.com/2009–07–21/politics/obama.gitmo_1_military-commissions-guantanamo-bay-controversial-prison/2?_s=PM:POLITICS.

But the Guantánamo case is only one of several important foreign policy initiatives, which include Iran and North Korea,[12] extraordinary rendition,[13] intelligence sharing and transparency,[14] nuclear proliferation, Iraq, Afghanistan, counterterrorism legislation, and the Middle East. In most cases, Obama's policies appear strikingly similar to the ones neocons were defending during the previous administration: those retaining military commissions for Guantánamo, deciding against the release of additional photos of Iraqi prison abuse (released May 13–14, 2009), spending more on missile defense, Obama's slow progress on his campaign promises to revisit federal policies on gay marriage and "don't ask, don't tell," strengthening North Korean sanctions, and continuing the Bush administration's Iraq surge strategy.[15] As the *Guardian* noted in a June 1, 2009 editorial:[16]

> The most interesting question ... is how (Obama) will describe his vision of what America can do to promote democracy and liberty. Yes, these were neocon goals. But it's not the goals that were wrong, just the means (military force). During the Bush years, some American liberals came to reject even these goals just because Bush endorsed them. So one of Obama's tasks on Thursday is to reclaim these goals, yank them out of their neoconservative context and place them in a liberal-internationalist one.

If Obama's foreign and security policies look very similar to Bush's, then we are compelled as academics to look at factors other than ideology, personality and leadership style for explanations. If the approach helps us understand why Obama's policies look similar to Bush's, then we should also at least consider the reasons (outlined in this book) for why Gore's foreign policies would have looked similar to Clinton's and Bush's. The mistake many Democratic legislators made when the Bush administration was replaced by Obama's was that they began to believe their own rhetoric about the 'Democratic Party' having

---

12 Sanger 2009.
13 See Johnson 2009: "The Obama administration will continue the Bush administration's practice of sending terrorism suspects to third countries for detention interrogation, but pledges to closely monitor their treatment to ensure that they are not tortured, administration officials said on Monday. 'It is extremely disappointing that the Obama administration is continuing the Bush administration practice of relying on diplomatic assurances, which have been proven completely ineffective in preventing torture,' said Amrit Singh, a lawyer with the American Civil Liberties Union."
14 "The White House opposes the provision to expand the number of briefing participants from the current eight to 40 members of Congress." Obama threatened to veto any such provision to expand the number privy to briefings. So much for transparency push. See www.articles.cnn.com/2009–07–09/politics/cia.congress_1_cia-officials-house-intelligence-committee-house-democrats/4?_s=PM:POLITICs.
15 www.network.nationalpost.com/np/blogs/fullcomment/archive/2009/04/21/don-martin-napolitano-s-makes-bush-administration-look-well-informed.aspx; www.salon.com/opinion/greenwald/2009/02/18/savage/index.html.
16 Tomasky 2009.

a different set of beliefs and foreign policy values. Speaker of the House Nancy Pelosi believed the differences were so stark that she conveniently forgot her own legislative legacy in which she condoned the decision to use enhanced CIA interrogation techniques for Guantánamo detainees. Until she was reminded of her own record, Pelosi continued to spin the official Democratic line that this was a conservative Republican mistake forced down the throats of Democrats who were desperately trying to battle the evil neoconservative empire. The truth, of course, is that Democrats were not only intimately involved in (and endorsed) the decisions that led to the Iraq war, but they were also briefed on the administration's decisions regarding detainee interrogation. Leon Panetta (CIA director under Obama) defended the CIA's 2002 briefings to the Senate Intelligence Committee and directly contradicted Pelosi's claims that she had been out of the loop.

With respect to additional evidence supporting projectability, McGough (2007) provides an excellent overview of the significant bipartisan support for anti-terrorism legislation and other elements of the Patriot Act, implying that domestic and international pressures would have resulted in the same limitation to civil liberties and allowances for the government's wiretapping programs and surveillance of domestic communication under a Democratic administration.[17] Like the October 2002 authorization to use force (see Chapter 4), Democrats were as enthusiastic as Republicans when passing legislation that prioritized security over civil liberties, because they faced the same pressures to demonstrate a commitment to public safety (Harvey 2008).

Without question, President Obama's response to the crisis in Libya in March, 2011, is perhaps the most vivid and compelling illustration of how projectability serves to confirm the counterfactual arguments defended in this book. Consider the following – no one in 2008 would have come close to predicting that, within three years of being elected president, and exactly eight years after the start of the Iraq war, Obama (among the strongest critics of Bush's Iraq policies) would make the following series of decisions on the path to war with Libya: (1) construct an international coalition to impose sweeping economic sanctions against Libya; (2) approach the UN for a strong UN Security Council Resolution 1973 with a clear Chapter Seven mandate to use "all necessary means" to enforce a no-fly zone over Libya (to prevent Muammar Gaddafi's air force from attacking civilian populations); (3) bypass congressional authorization and unanimous UN Security Council endorsement of the use of force (Germany, Russia and China abstained); (4) apply a broad interpretation of the no-fly zone resolution to include the targeting of Libyan ground forces and equipment used in attacks on Benghazi and Misrata; (5) endorse, along with France, an explicit policy of regime change not included in UNSCR 1973; and (6) invest hundreds of millions of dollars to conduct yet another war against a Muslim state.

---

[17] McGough 2007.

Democrats will no doubt craft detailed arguments identifying what they believe to be obvious differences across the 2003 and 2011 cases, but a careful reading of the relevant historical evidence reveals obvious similarities – a patterned and consistent commitment to facilitating liberal internationalist principles through the application of coercive military power (and preventive war) in support of regime change and democratization. The policy objectives are virtually indistinguishable from those ascribed to George W. Bush by neoconists. And, as was true with Bush's Iraq policy and strategy, neither the Project for a New American Century nor neoconservatism more generally were relevant to Obama's preferences.

The one significant difference Democrats will highlight to distinguish Obama's approach to multilateralism from Bush's is the size of the coalition and, by extension, the higher measure of international 'legitimacy' it received. Staunch supporters of Obama's intervention in Libya will praise the operation as a textbook illustration of how to construct a truly multilateral coalition with combined endorsements from the Arab League, United Nations Security Council and NATO. Obama's coalition, Democrats will argue, established a much higher measure of legitimacy essential to maintaining public and international support, both of which were required to sustain the military operation against Muammar Gaddafi. Of course, the key piece of Obama's coalition was endorsement from the Arab League – an historical precedent highlighted by the president and consistently repeated by every member of his national security team.

Far from representing the mother of all multilateral endorsements, however, there are clear costs to Obama's rigid commitment to this kind of multilateral consensus that threatened to undermine the capacity of Western leaders to facilitate change and transformation in the region.

Few observers have given serious thought to why the Arab League enthusiastically endorsed the UN's no-fly zone resolution, or whether their specific interests and values mesh with those expressed by Obama and other European allies. Arab League members were obviously not motivated by a sudden epiphany regarding the wisdom of democratization, or driven by a new imperative to protect the rights and freedoms of Libyan rebels, or their own citizens. Like any leader on the planet, these officials are motivated by self-interest and the preservation of their regimes.

Paradoxically, Obama's precondition of obtaining Arab League endorsement prior to negotiating the UN resolution sets an important precedent – it essentially established an Arab League veto over future humanitarian, no-fly zone or military interventions in, for example, Syria, Saudi Arabia, Jordan, Bahrain or any of the other 22 members of the Arab League. The same folks responsible for suppressing their own citizens now hold the "legitimacy" prerequisite at the heart of the West's willingness to stop them. Is this the standard of legitimacy the international community should be relying on to address the new and emerging challenges in North Africa and the Middle East?

Obama's multilateralism certainly has its benefits, but a rigid commitment to multilateral consensus is not cost free. And while the multilateral legitimacy that comes from Arab League support carries a great deal of surface appeal, the subtext to this legitimacy should be clearly understood. Those who believe Obama's approach to multilateralism is the best or only way forward should consider this – it was the international community's rigid commitment to multilateral consensus that prevented any state from intervening in Rwanda in 1994, and Darfur today. The same narrow interpretation of multilateral legitimacy threatens to create identical barriers at a time when those in the Middle East need the international community's help and support. The question is whether Obama remains committed to a weak interpretation of legitimacy grounded in Arab League support or will revise the Obama Doctrine accordingly.

Non-existent grand strategies and the myth of a Bush Doctrine

A number of scholars remain convinced that the best explanations for the 2003 Iraq war can be found by exploring the main principles underlying American 'grand strategy' or the 'Bush Doctrine.' The problem with these assumptions is that US foreign policies in practice are never really guided by grand strategies or doctrines – this is a myth.

Grand strategies and presidential doctrines are nothing more than convenient templates that are occasionally useful in some instances to *describe* an administration's policies, but they do not *explain* or *predict* anything. Although grand strategies and related documents (e.g., Quadrennial Defense Reviews; United States National Security Strategies) purport to convey the big game plans, they are actually nothing more than summaries of very general themes officials deem relevant at the time – they rarely vary from one administration to another and whatever differences do exist have more to do with the imperative to distinguish the text from one administration to another rather than the policies themselves. These documents say nothing about what Washington will or will not do in any specific situation or crisis. Therefore, the notion that the Bush administration was driven by a neoconservative ideology and a single-minded agenda (to push an invasion of Iraq to satisfy some higher moral calling to democratize the Middle East) is a myth promoted primarily by critics of the administration (and there are many).

American leaders have always followed a standard set of priorities and approaches when designing foreign policy initiatives, and these major policy decisions are typically reactionary and incremental, not planned or very structured. Consider the 2002 USNSS (pp. 6, 15):

> We will disrupt and destroy terrorist organizations by: defending the United States, the American people, and our interests at home and abroad by identifying and destroying the threat before it reaches our borders. While the

United States will constantly strive to enlist the support of the international community, *we will not hesitate to act alone*, if necessary, to *exercise our right of self-defense by acting preemptively* against such terrorists, to prevent them from doing harm against our people and our country. (Emphasis added)

The United States has long maintained the option of preemptive actions to counter a sufficient threat to our national security. The greater the threat, the greater is the risk of inaction – and the more compelling the case for taking anticipatory action to defend ourselves, *even if uncertainty remains* as to the time and place of the enemy's attack. To forestall or prevent such hostile acts by our adversaries, the United States will, if necessary, act preemptively. The United States will not use force in all cases to preempt emerging threats, nor should nations use preemption as a pretext for aggression. *Yet in an age where the enemies of civilization openly and actively seek the world's most destructive technologies, the United States cannot remain idle while dangers gather.* (Emphasis added)

This policy statement was the basis for speculating about a major shift in American foreign policy and related predictions about the United States' new pre-emption doctrine. These excerpts are consistently linked today to the Bush administration's 'neoconservative' agenda and represent the core thesis (and evidence) presented in almost every book on the subject of Bush's US foreign policy and the Iraq war. Now, with respect to policy guidance and priorities for addressing new and emerging threats from terrorism and WMD proliferation, there is no question that unilateralism, pre-emption and preventive war were viewed as essential to post-9/11 US security. But the basic principles underlying this 'new' grand strategy were not the product of a right-wing, neoconservative administration determined to rid the world of the scourge of multilateralism. The very same underlying themes run through the previous US National Security Strategies produced by the Clinton administration in 1996 and 1999 (pp. 1, 14, 19, 20). Consider the following excerpts:

There are three basic categories of national interests that can merit the use of our armed forces. The first involves America's vital interests, that is, interests that are of broad, overriding importance to the survival, security and vitality of our national entity – the defense of US territory, citizens, allies and our economic well-being. We will do whatever it takes to defend these interests, including – when necessary – the *unilateral* and decisive use of military power. (Emphasis added)

The United States will do what we must to defend our vital interests including, when necessary and appropriate, using our military *unilaterally* and decisively … We act in alliance or partnership when others share our interests, but *unilaterally* when compelling national interests so demand … The decision whether to use force is dictated first and foremost by our national interests. In those specific areas where our vital interests are at stake, our use of force will be decisive and, if necessary, *unilateral* … We act in concert with the international community whenever possible, but do not hesitate to act *unilaterally* when necessary. (Emphasis added)

These documents are basically rhetorical representations of Washington's stated preferences. They are not legally or politically binding strategic documents that need to be parsed for specific words – like pre-emption or unilateralism. They do not automatically establish the plans or operational deployment schedules for the US military. They are simply general statements that rarely change from administration to administration, don't mean very much beyond their publication (and related press conference) and determine nothing that is predictable.

The claim that the inclusion of the word "pre-emption" somehow fundamentally transformed US grand strategy is a myth. The Bush administration did nothing more or less than a Democratic administration under Clinton did in 1998 against Iraq, and nothing different from what Al Gore recommended in his 2000 campaign speeches on US foreign policy, in his 2002 speeches on Iraq, or when he was vice president (see Chapter 2 and Appendix 2.1). The US president can be expected to do essentially the same things when faced with the same circumstances, threats, enemies and allies, for the same reasons.

Preventive diplomacy and military strategy did not begin with the Bush administration. As Levy (2007: 190–1) concludes from his research on the historical roots of the policy, the American public "appears to be quite open to preventive logic as a justification for military action."[18] Similarly, As Daalder and Lindsay (2003: 36) point out, Bush's foreign policy was consistent with every other major presidential candidate since World War II – "he accepted Woodrow Wilson's view that the United States' foreign policy should seek to promote its values as well as its interests."[19] There was nothing particularly unique about the Bush administration's priorities. A balanced comparison of the content of Bush's speeches would confirm the presence of core, standard messages. Daalder and Lindsay go on to argue (2003: 39) that "Bush's stances on the two foreign policy issues that would come to define his presidency – terrorism and Iraq – were equally conventional." None of the three pillars of the so-called Bush Doctrine are new. Indeed, the classification of a struggle between 'good' and 'evil' and the belief that the spread of liberal democracy is a fundamental solution to the root cause of conflict is common to many American administrations throughout history (Kaufman 2007: 127).

These same morally grounded justifications were exploited by President Clinton, Al Gore, Richard Holbrooke and Madeleine Albright in the lead up to the Bosnia and Kosovo wars in the 1990s. The title of 'neoconservatives' may serve the opposition's political agenda, because it provides a compact derogatory title to encapsulate an unpopular foreign policy, but the 'neoconservatism-equals-war' thesis is not a very useful analytical tool to help understand or

---

[18] Levy 2007.   [19] Daalder and Lindsay 2003.

explain the policies themselves. The principles, values and policies running through the 2001 United States National Security Strategy (USNSS) – e.g., American exceptionalism, the indispensible value of American military power, the need for coalitions of the willing (to replace exclusive reliance on European style 'principled' multilateralism or unanimity), preventive war (dealing with threats 'before' they escalate), spreading democracy to enhance American security, the threat from rogue states, the risks associated with uncontrolled biological, chemical and nuclear proliferation, links between rogue states and terrorism, etc. – are all common to the USNSS outlined by Bill Clinton and George H.W. Bush. If neoconists are right about the role of these strategic principles in pushing Bush to war in 2003, then there is no logical reason why the same principles defended by Clinton and Gore in their USNSS would be any less likely to compel a Gore administration down the same path under the same circumstances. To illustrate the point, Robert G. Kaufman (2007) provides a thorough review of key speeches from past American presidents that reveal dozens of identical references to many of the same concepts, values and principles ascribed to neoconservatives – freedom, democracy, American exceptionalism, and the obligation to share and spread these values.[20] As Kaufman (2007: 127) points out:

> Like Ronald Reagan and Harry Truman with regard to the Soviet Union, and like Franklin Roosevelt with regard to Nazi Germany and imperial Japan, President Bush sought to inject moral clarity in the struggle with our enemies. Like his great predecessors, he defines regime change and the spread of stable, liberal democracy to address the real root cause of aggression as the ultimate goal in the war on terror.

Of course, whether or not Clinton or Bush succeeded in accomplishing these objectives in Bosnia, Kosovo, Iraq or Afghanistan can be vigorously debated by reasonable people, but to claim that these core values are distinguishable or, in the case of the Bush administration, represent a significant neoconservative departure from US policy is simply false. Marvin Zonis (2007: 230) reinforces this view in his assessment of the Bush Doctrine's commitment to "Democracy," which, he argues,

> deepened and became the primary focus of his foreign policy when the initial rationales for American invasion of Iraq proved to be baseless … As the rationales disappeared and as the war turned from a campaign against the army of Hussein to a war against an Iraqi insurgency honed by foreign terrorists eager to damage the United States, the President turned to his Democracy Doctrine to justify the entire enterprise.[21]

President Bush would no doubt have exploited the same sentiments had stockpiles of WMD been found in Iraq, but these policies, 'doctrines' and strategies

[20] Daalder and Lindsay 2003.   [21] Zonis 2007.

were incremental and reactive, not directive as is commonly assumed in the Bush Doctrine literature.

Dispelling the myth of a Bush Doctrine

Ironically, the 2003 Iraq war is perhaps the worst case study to use when defending claims regarding a doctrine of pre-emption, primarily because the lead up to war required dozens of enabling conditions. If anything, the Iraq war is a great example of the impediments to pre-emption. Consider the prerequisites or enabling conditions for US pre-emption in this case:

(1) seventeen UN resolutions directly charging Iraq with 'material breach' of clear UN disarmament mandates based on intelligence estimates compiled over a decade by US and UN inspectors;

(2) failure on the part of the international community (indeed, its complicity) in perpetuating a corrupt oil-for-food program (i.e., a failure of containment/sanctions);

(3) congressional endorsement and official authorization to use military force;

(4) the deployment of 100,000 US and UK troops to Kuwait to establish a credible, coercive threat;

(5) support from key allies, particularly Britain's Tony Blair;

(6) a unanimous UNSC resolution, 1441, repeating the 'material breach' indictment and threatening "serious consequences";

(7) overwhelming consensus in the US and international community based on the same flawed (but non-distorted) intelligence on Iraq's WMD; and

(8) serious misperceptions by Saddam regarding US intentions and UN power to prevent an attack.

With these prerequisites in mind, the Iraq crisis is a much better case study for confirming how incredibly difficult it is to mount a multilaterally endorsed attack – it is not a compelling case to support claims regarding a move toward unilateral pre-emption.

Moreover, the other two corners of the axis of evil – Iran and North Korea – have never provoked a neoconservative attack, despite the fact that threats from these two cases are considerably clearer and more obvious – e.g., initiative shown on uranium enrichment, ballistic missile deployment and nuclear testing, explicit threats to wipe Israel off the map, statements regarding the impending death of Israel and the United States, refusal to abide by UN resolutions and IAEA commitments, etc. In other words, two of the three cases actually refute the very premise of the unilateralism-pre-emption doctrine. Iraq is the exception to the rule, and, for reasons outlined above, it is not a particularly good illustration of unilateralism or pre-emption, nor of the power and influence of neoconservatives that were recommending this strategy.

Closing thoughts

The material presented in the book constitutes only a fraction of the evidence that could be compiled to support the conclusion that President Gore would have been compelled to make many of the same rational moves to get inspectors back into Iraq. These sensible interim decisions would have been made despite the absence of neocons on Gore's national security team. Perhaps the only significant difference would have been the size of the invading force – Gore would probably have recommended a much larger troop deployment, in line with General Anthony Zinni's plan under the Clinton administration (OP PLAN 1003–98, originally approved in 1996 and updated in 1998, called for 400,000 troops).[22] Boosted by the confidence of deploying this many troops, and concerned about the cost of sustaining such a large force through prolonged (and unsuccessful) inspections, Gore would have been more, not less, inclined to accept the risks of war. It is highly unlikely that a sitting Democratic president would have survived the 2004 election if he decided against enforcing "all necessary means" or "serious consequences" in favor of the French–Russian position. As military historian Victor Davis Hanson (2003) pointed out, the combat part of operations turned out to be a huge success:

> In a span of about three weeks, the United States military overran a country the size of California. It utterly obliterated Saddam Hussein's military hardware ... and tore apart his armies. Of the approximately 110 American deaths in the course of the hostilities, fully a fourth occurred as a result of accidents, friendly fire, or peacekeeping mishaps rather than at the hands of enemy soldiers. The extraordinarily low ratio of total American casualties per number of US soldiers deployed ... is almost unmatched in modern military history.[23]

Nor would a larger initial invading force have altered the misperceptions of Saddam Hussein regarding American willingness to invade. Even with more troops deployed to the region, there is nothing much President Gore (or Bush) could have done to prevent the significant strategic miscalculations by the Iraqi regime. For whatever reason, Saddam believed his survival depended on convincing Iranian officials he had WMD – he succeeded. Ironically, his main concern was not that UNMOVIC inspectors would uncover stockpiles, but that they would ultimately conclude he had nothing left. Similarly, even at the eleventh hour, Saddam remained convinced that coalition forces would stop short of invasion and regime change – the result of mistaken assumptions regarding American casualty-aversion and faulty interpretations of past conflicts.

[22] Woodward 2004.   [23] Hanson 2003.

Strong theories are supported by facts, but their real strength is sustained by the absence of powerful evidence that disproves them. The strongest theories are those that are susceptible to falsification yet survive the test. Neoconism has failed the test. The arguments outlined throughout this book may not convince neoconists to discard their theory, but if it convinces those with an open mind to reconsider the value of such a simple theory of the Iraq war, or to re-evaluate the relative importance of other factors, it will have accomplished something important.

BIBLIOGRAPHY

Aaronovitch, D., 2007. Does a Terrorist Care who's in the White House? Democrat Fantasies about Foreign Policy. *Times Online*, March 6 [online]. Available at: www.timesonline.co.uk/tol/comment/columnists/david_aaronovitch/article1475277.ece [accessed October 2010].

Acronym Institute, 2002. Iraq Agrees to Readmit Inspectors as US, Britain Insist on War Option. *Disarmament Diplomacy* 67 (October–November) [online]. Available at: www.acronym.org.uk/dd/dd67/67nr01.htm#01 [accessed October 2010].

Aita, J., 2001. *Holbrooke: Iraq Will Be a Major UN Issue for Bush Administration – UN Ambassador Reviews Issues for 2001*. Italy: US Embassy, January 1 [online]. Available at: www.usembassy.it/file2001_01/alia/a1011102.htm [accessed October 2010].

Albright, M., 1997. Weapons of Mass Destruction: Sec. State Albright Policy Speech on Iraq, March 26, Global Security.org [online]. Available at: www.globalsecurity.org/wmd/library/news/iraq/1997/bmd970327b.htm [accessed October 2010].

1998. Albright to Begin Iraq Talks with US Allies. Washington, DC. CNN.com, January 28 [online]. Available at: www.cnn.com/WORLD/9801/29/iraq.albright [accessed October 2010].

1999. Democratic Quotes about Iraq. Freerepublic.com, November 10 [online]. Available at: www.freerepublic.com/focus/f-news/1003520/posts [accessed October 2010].

2003. Bridges, Bombs, or Bluster? *Foreign Affairs* 82(5): September/October [online]. Available at: www.foreignaffairs.com/articles/59179/madeleine-k-albright/bridges-bombs-or-bluster [accessed October 2010].

2009. Public Statements, November 10 [online]. Available at: www.freerepublic.com/focus/f-news/1003520/posts [accessed October 2010].

Ali, T., 2004. Available at: www.socialistworker.org/2004-2/509/509_06_ABB.shtm.

Allison, Graham, 2004. How to Stop Nuclear Terror. *Foreign Affairs*. January/February.

Alternatehistory.com, *Another America*. March [online]. Available at: Alternatehistory.com.

American Enterprise Institute for Public Policy Research, 2008. Public Opinion on the War with Iraq. *AEI Public Opinion Studies*, July 24 [online]. Available at: www.aei.org/docLib/200701121_roody2.pdf [accessed October 2010].

Aminzade, R., 1993. Class Analysis, Politics, and French Labor History. In L.R. Berlanstein, ed. *Rethinking Labor History: Essays on Discourse and Class Analysis*. Urbana and Chicago: University of Illinois Press, 90–113.

Attwood, T., 2004. *Hegemony and the Bush Administration's Foreign Policy: A Reconfiguration of American Grand Strategy*, in Annual Meetings of the International Studies Association. Montreal.

Baker III, J.A., 2002. The Right Way to Change a Regime. *New York Times*, August 25 [online]. Available at: www.nytimes.com/2002/08/25/opinion/the-right-way-to-change-a-regime.html [accessed October 2010].

Banchoff, T. 2004. Value Conflict and US-EU Relations: The Case of Unilateralism, *American Consortium on European Union Studies Working Paper* [online]. Available at: www1.american.edu/aces/Working%20Papers/2004[1].3.pdf [accessed October 2010].

Barger, Deborah, 2004. It is Time to Transform, Not Reform, US Intelligence. *SAIS Review of International Affairs* 24(1) (Winter–Spring).

BBCNews.com, 1998. Madeleine Albright, "Kosovo Diplomacy Reaching its Limits." October 8 [online]. Available at: www.news.bbc.co.uk/2/hi/europe/189504. stm [accessed October 2010].

    2002. www.news.bbc.co.uk/2/hi/uk_news/politics/2239887.stm [accessed October 2010].

Bell, M., 2005. "With Us or With the Terrorists: A Canadian Academic Argues that the Days of Multilateral Action are Over" – Book Review of *Smoke and Mirrors: Globalized Terrorism and the Illusion of Multilateral Security*, by Frank P. Harvey (University of Toronto Press). *Literary Review of Canada* 13(2) (March) [online]. Available at: www.cronus.uwindsor.ca/users/m/mbell/ research.nsf/54ef3e94e5fe816e85256d6e0063d208/90c652c5f792d5468525 72fa0054b61e/$FILE/Literary%20Review%20of%20Canada%20March%20 2005.pdf [accessed October 2010].

Belsham Moki, S., 2006. *Bush and Gulf War II: A Study in Presidential Leadership*. Frederick: Publish America.

Bennett, A. and Elman, C., 2006. Complex Causal Relations and Case Study Methods: The Example of Path Dependence. *Political Analysis* 14(3): 250–67.

Bennett, A. and George, A.L., 2001. Case Studies and Process Tracing in History and Political Science: Similar Strokes for Different Foci. In C. Elman and M. Fendius Elman, eds. *Bridges and Boundaries: Historians, Political Scientists and the Study of International Relations*. Cambridge, MA: MIT Press.

Berger, S., 1998. Press Briefing by National Security Adviser Sandy Berger. FAS News, December 16 [online]. Available at: www.fas.org/news/iraq/1998/12/16/ index.html [accessed October 2010].

2004. Foreign Policy for a Democratic President. *Foreign Affairs* 83(3) (May/ June) [online]. Available at: www.foreignaffairs.com/articles/59892/samuel-r-berger/foreign-policy-for-a-democratic-president [accessed October 2010].

Betts, Richard K., 1978. Analysis, War, and Decision: Why Intelligence Failures Are Inevitable. *World Politics* 31(2): 61–89.

2002. Fixing Intelligence: The Limits of Prevention. *Foreign Affairs* 81(1): 43–59.

2004. The New Politics of Intelligence: Will Reform Work this Time? *Foreign Affairs* 83(3): 2–9.

2007. Two Faces of Intelligence Failure: September 11 and Iraq's Missing WMD. *Political Science Quarterly* 122(4): 585–606.

Biden, J., 2003. *Congressional Record – Senate*. January 23 [online]. Available at: www.frwebgate.access.gpo.gov/cgi-bin/getpage.cgi?dbname=2003_record&page=S1481&position=all [accessed October 2010].

Blair, T., 2003. Full Text: Tony Blair's Speech. *Guardian*, March 18 [online]. Available at: www.guardian.co.uk/politics/2003/mar/18/foreignpolicy.iraq1 [accessed October 2010].

2010. *A Journey: My Political Life*. Toronto: Knopf Canada.

Blix, H., 2003a. Briefing of the Security Council, February 14 [online]. Available at: www.un.org/Depts/unmovic/blix14Febasdel.htm [accessed October 2010].

2003b. Update on Inspections. Delivered to the UN Security Council, January 27, by Executive Chairman of UNMOVIC [online]. Available at: www.un.org/Depts/unmovic/Bx27.htm [accessed October 2010].

2003c. Briefing of the Security Council, January 27: An Update on Inspections [online]. Available at: www.un.org/Depts/unmovic/new/pages/security_council_briefings.asp#5 [accessed October 2010].

2004. *Disarming Iraq*. New York: Pantheon Books.

Bonn, S., 2010. *Mass Deception: Moral Panic and the U.S. War on Iraq*. New Jersey: Rutgers University Press.

Bowman, K.H., 2008. America and the War on Terror. American Enterprise Institute [online]. Available at: www.aei.org/docLib/20050805_terror0805.pdf [accessed October 2010].

Boyle, M., 2007. *The War on Terror in American Grand Strategy*, in Annual Meetings of the International Studies Association. Chicago.

Bozdaglioglu, Y., 2004. *Hegemonic (In)stability and the Limits of US Hegemony in the Middle East*, in Annual Meetings of the International Studies Association. Montreal.

Broder, J.M., 2000. The 2000 Campaign: Gore's National Security Advisers Assemble as Part of a Government-in-Waiting. *New York Times*, May 17.

Bronson, R., 2002. U.S. has "Strategically Sound and Morally Just" Reasons to Invade Iraq. Interview with Bernard Gwertzman, Consulting Editor, CFR.org, December 12.

Buckley, M. and Singh, R., eds., 2006. *The Bush Doctrine and the War on Terrorism: Global Reactions, Global Consequences*. New York: Routledge.

Burbach, R. and Tarbell, J., 2004. *Imperial Overstretch: George W. Bush and the Hubris of Empire*. London: Zed Books.

Busby, J.W., 2003. Last Stop Baghdad: Origins of the Transatlantic Trainwreck. *Global Dialogue* 5(3–4): 49–62.

Bush, G.W., 2003. *State of the Union Address*, January 28 [online]. Available at: www.usgovinfo.about.com/library/weekly/aasou2003_text.htm.

Buzan, B., 2004. *US Hegemony, American Exceptionalism and Unipolarity*, in Annual Meetings of the International Studies Association. Montreal.

Byman, D. and Pollack, K., 2001. Let us Now Praise Great Men: Bringing the Statesman Back in. *International Security* 25(4): 107–46.

Bzostek, R. and McCall, K.W., 2004. *The Bush Doctrine: An Application of Crabb's Doctrinal Criteria and Illustration of Resulting Changes in American Foreign Policy*, in Annual Meetings of the International Studies Association. Montreal.

Calabresi, M., 2002. Exclusive: Scott Ritter in his Own Words. Time.com, September 14 [online]. Available at: www.time.com/time/nation/article/0,8599,351165,00.html [accessed October 2010].

Campbell, A. and Stott, R., 2007. *The Blair Years: Extracts from The Alastair Campbell Diaries*. London: Hutchinson.

Carr, Edward Hallett, 1961. *What is History?* London: Penguin.

Carter, A.B. and Perry, W.J., 1999. *Preventive Defense: A New Security Strategy for America*. Washington, DC: Brookings Institute Press.

Central Intelligence Agency, 2002a. *Unclassified Report to Congress on the Acquisition of Technology Relating to Weapons of Mass Destruction and Advanced Conventional Munitions*. January 1 through June 30, 2001 [online]. Available at: www.cia.gov/library/reports/archived-reports-1/jan_jun2001.htm.

2002b. Iraq's Weapons of Mass Destruction Programs. National Intelligence Estimate, October [online]. Available at: www.gwu.edu/~nsarchiv/NSAEBB/NSAEBB129/nie_first%20release.pdf [accessed October 2010].

Chaudet, D., 2008. *The Neoconservative Movement at the End of the Bush Administration: Its Legacy, its Vision, its Political Future*, in Annual Meetings of the International Studies Association. San Francisco.

Chirac, J., 2002. Interview. *L'Orient-Le Jour*, October 16 [online]. Available at: www.globalpolicy.org/security/issues/iraq/attack/2002/1016chirac.htm [accessed October 2010].

Christie, T.B., 2006. Framing Rationale for the Iraq War: The Interaction of Public Support with Mass Media and Public Policy Agendas. *International Communication Gazette* 68(5–6): 519–32.

Clark, General Wesley, 2002. Testimony – House Armed Services Committee Hearing on US Policy toward Iraq, September 26. Available at: www.drudgereportarchives.com/data/2004/01/15/20040115_165004_mattwc.htm.

Clark, T., 2008. Misrepresenting Naturalism: An Open Letter to R. Albert Mohler, Jr [online]. Available at: www.naturalism.org/misrepresenting.htm [accessed October 2010].

Clarke, Richard A., 2004. *Against All Enemies: Inside America's War on Terror*. New York: Free Press.

Clinton, B., 1998a. Text of Clinton Statement on Iraq. CNN.com/AllPolitics, February 17 [online]. Available at: www.cnn.com/ALLPOLITICS/1998/02/17/transcripts/clinton.iraq [accessed October 2010].

1998b. Speech to Joint Chiefs and Pentagon Staff. February 17 [online]. Available at: www.articles.cnn.com/1998-02-17/politics/transcripts_clinton.iraq_1_national-security-american-people-freedom?_s=PM:ALLPOLITICS [accessed October 2010].

1998c. Transcript: President Clinton Explains Iraq Strike. CNN.com/ALL POLITICS, December 16 [online]. Available at: www.cnn.com/ALLPOLITICS/stories/1998/12/16/transcripts/clinton.html [accessed October 2010].

1999a. Text of a Letter from the President to the Speaker of the House of Representatives and the President Pro Tempore of the Senate. The White House, Office of the Press Secretary, March 3 [online]. Available at: www.casi.org.uk/discuss/1999/msg00185.html [accessed October 2010].

1999b. Clinton Justifies U.S. Involvement in Kosovo. CNN.com/All Politics, May 13 [online]. Available at: www.cnn.com/ALLPOLITICS/stories/1999/05/13/clinton.kosovo/transcript.html [accessed October 2010].

Clinton, H., 2001. Speech. WavSource.com, September 11 [online]. www.wavsource.com/news/20010911a.htm [accessed October 2010].

2002. Speech. WavSource.com, October 10 [online]. Available at: www.clinton.senate.gov/speeches/iraq_101002.html [accessed October 2010].

2009. Quoted in William Kristol, Clinton: 100 Percent Committed. Weeklystandard.com, July 17 [online]. Available at: www.weeklystandard.com/weblogs/TWSFP/2009/07/clinton_100_percent_committed.asp.

Cockburn, A. and St. Clair, J., 2000. *Al Gore: A User's Manual*. New York: Verso.

Collier, D. and Mahoney, J., 1996. Insights and Pitfalls: Selection Bias in Qualitative Research. *World Politics* 49: 56–91.

Congressional Record (Senate), 2002a. Congressional Record via GPO Access, October 9: S10191-S10195 [online]. Available at: www.clarkiw.wordpress.com/2002/10/ [see DOCID:cr09oc02-79; accessed October 2010].

Congressional Record, 2002b. Proceedings and Debates of the 107th Congress, second session Volume 148 – Part 15. October 10–November 8: 20215–21285 (quote from p. 20454) [online]. Available at: www.sweetness-light.com/archive/obama-gets-rockefeller-iraq-vote-wrong [accessed October 2010].

Congressional Record, 2002c. Joint Resolution to Authorize the Use of United States Armed Forces against Iraq. H.J. Resolution 114, 107th Congress, October 16 [online]. Available at: www.c-span.org/Content/PDF/hjres114.pdf [accessed October 2010].

Cooper, Jeffrey R. and Brown, John Seely, 2005. Intelligence: We've Lost Our Edge. *Washington Post*, 10 May.

Cordyack, B., 2004. Bush Approval Ratings. *Washington Post* [online]. Available at: www.washingtonpost.com/wp-srv/politics/daily/graphics/bushApproval_ 031305.gif [accessed October 2010].

Cosgrove-Maher, B., 2002. What Should the US do about Saddam Hussein and Iraq? *Face the Nation*, CBSNews.com, August 4 [online]. Available at: www.cbsnews. com/stories/2002/08/05/ftn/main517523.shtml [accessed October 2010].

Coughlin, C., 2006. *American Ally: Tony Blair and the War on Terror*. New York: HarperCollins.

Daalder, I.H. and Destler, I.M. (moderators), 2000. *The National Security Council Project: Oral History Roundtables – The Clinton Administration National Security Council*. The Brookings Institution, Washington, DC, September 27 [online]. Available at: www.brookings.edu/fp/research/projects/nsc/ transcripts/20000927.pdf [accessed October 2010].

Daalder, I.H. and Lindsay, J.M., 2003. *America Un-bound: The Bush Revolution in Foreign Policy*. New York: John Wiley and Sons.

Daschle, T., 2002. House gives Bush Authority for War with Iraq. CNN.com, October 10 [online]. Available at: www.archives.cnn.com/2002/ALLPOLITICS/10/10/ iraq.us [accessed October 2010].

David, C.P., 2008. Five Years after the Invasion of Iraq: Lessons Learned from U.S. Decision-Making. Paper presented at the International Studies Association (ISA) meeting in San Francisco, Hilton Hotel, March 28.

2010. How not to do Post-invasion: Lessons Learned from US Decision-making in Iraq (2002–2008). *Defense & Security Analysis* 26(1): 31–63.

Davidstuff.com, n.d. Democrat Quotes on Iraq Weapons of Mass Destruction [online]. Available at: www.davidstuff.com/political/wmdquotes.htm [accessed October 2010].

Deyoung, K., 2007. *Soldier: The Life of Colin Powell*. New York: Vintage Books.

Diamond, John M., 2008. *The CIA and the Culture of Failure: U.S. Intelligence from the End of the Cold War*. Palo Alto: Stanford University Press.

Dietrich, J., 2004. *Candidate Bush to Incumbent Bush: The Development of an Internationalist, Unilateralist and Interventionist*, in Annual Meetings of the International Studies Association. Montreal.

Dodds, K., 2008. Counter-Factual Geopolitics: President Al Gore, September 11th and the Global War on Terror. *Geopolitics* 13(1) (December): 73–99.

Doggett, T., 1999. Cohen Fears 100,000 Kosovo Men Killed by Serbs. *Face the Nation*, CBS, May 16 [online]. Available at: www.washingtonpost.com/wp-srv/inatl/ longterm/balkans/stories/cohen051699.htm [accessed October 2010].

Draper, R., 2007. *Dead Certain: The Presidency of George W. Bush*. New York: Free Press.

Dueck, C., 2004. Ideas and Alternatives in US Grand Strategy, 2000–2004. *Review of International Studies* 30(3): 511–35.

Duelfer, C., 2004. *Comprehensive Report of the Special Advisor to the Director of Central Intelligence On Iraq's WMD*, US Central Intelligence Agency, September 30 [online]. Available at: www.cia.gov/library/reports/general-reports-1/iraq_wmd_2004/index.html [accessed October 2010].

2009. *Hide and Seek: The Search for Truth in Iraq*. New York: Public Affairs.

Duncan, H., 2006. *Bush and Cheney's War: A War Without Justification*. London: Trafford Publishing.

Duncan, G., 2008. *Democracy Held Hostage: How Neocon Arrogance, George Bush's Incompetence and Dick Cheney's Criminality Subverted the Constitution, Destroyed Iraq and Weakened America. Letters to the Editor 2004–2008.* Bloomington: Trafford Publishing.

Dunn, D., 2004. *911, the Bush Doctrine and the Implications of the War on Iraq*, in Annual Meetings of the International Studies Association. Montreal.

2005. *The Transformation of American Foreign Policy and the Conflicting Strategies of the War on Terrorism*, in Annual Meetings of the International Studies Association. Honolulu.

Economist, The, 2001a. If Al Gore had Won. November 15 [online]. Available at: www.economist.com/world/united-states/displaystory.cfm?story_id=E1_RGPGGN [accessed October 2010].

2001b. Al Gore Discovers Himself. November 15.

Edwards, J., 2002a. Late Edition with Wolf Blitzer. CNN.com/Transcripts, February 24 [online]. Available at: www.cnn.com/TRANSCRIPTS/0202/24/le.00.html [accessed October 2010].

2002b. US Senate Floor Statement, *Authorization of the Use of United States Armed Forces Against Iraq*. October 10 [online]. Available at: www.frwebgate.access.gpo.gov/cgi-bin/getpage.cgi?dbname=2002_record&page=S10233&position=all.

Eisendrath, C. and Goodman, M.A., 2004. *Bush League Diplomacy: How the Neoconservatives are Putting the World at Risk*. New York: Prometheus Books.

Enée, A.C., 2008. Wag the Dog: A Memory List for those Afflicted with Political Alzheimer's. June 19 [online]. Available at: www.thepanelist.net/general-finance-10103/1060-wag-the-dog-a-memory-list-for-those-afflicted-with-political-alzheimers [accessed October 2010].

Entessar, N., 2004. *Permanent War, Elusive Peace: The Next US War in the Middle East*, in Annual Meetings of the International Studies Association. Montreal.

Fahrenheit 9/11, 2004. [Film] Directed by Michael Moore. USA: Dog Eat Dog Films.

Falleti, T.G., 2009. *Theory-Guided Process-Tracing in Comparative Politics: Something Old, Something New*. Unpublished manuscript. Philadelphia: University of Pennsylvania.

Fearon, J., 1991. Counterfactuals and Hypothesis Testing in Political Science. *World Politics* 43(2): 169–95.

Fehl, C. and Thimm, J., 2008. American Unilateralism Reconsidered: A Research Program on US Participation in Multilateral Treaties. *Annual Convention of the International Studies Association (ISA)*, March 26–29, 2008, San Francisco.

Feltus, W. and Ingraham, L., 2000. What if Al Gore had Won in Florida? *The Washington Times*, November 30 [online]. Available at: www.uchronia.net/bib.cgi/author.html?id=F [accessed October 2010].

Ferguson, N., 2000. *Virtual History: Alternatives and Counterfactuals*. New York: Basic Books.

Fleischer, A., 2003. Speaks on Iraq's Need to Comply with UN Resolution. Interview on *CNN Breaking News*, January 7 [online]. Available at: www.transcripts.cnn.com/TRANSCRIPTS/0301/07/bn.02.html [accessed October 2010].

Flibbert, A., 2007. *Who Lost Iraq? Policy Entrepreneurs and the War Decision*, in Annual Meetings of the International Studies Association. Chicago.

Ford, H., Graham, B., Lantos, T., Lieberman, J. and McCain, J., 2001. *Letter to President George W. Bush*. December 5 [online]. Available at: www.house.gov/ford/12_06_01a.htm.

Franke, V., 2005. *W's Manifest Destiny: Faith-Based US Foreign Policy for the 21st Century?* in Annual Meetings of the International Studies Association. Honolulu.

Frum, D., 2004. The Chads Fall off in Florida. In A. Roberts, ed. *What Might Have Been: Imaginary History from Twelve Leading Historians*. London: Weidenfeld & Nicholson, 179–88.

   2005. *The Right Man: An Inside Account of the Bush White House*. New York: Random House.

Fuerth, L., 2002a. One Terrorist at a Time. *New York Times*, January 4.

   2002b. America's New War: Should Iraq be Next? A Point-Counterpoint with R. James Woolsey. *DLC/Blueprint Magazine*, May 21 [online]. Available at: www.ndol.org/ndol_ci.cfm?contentid=250508&kaid=124&subid=161 [accessed October 2010].

   2003. An Air of Empire. *Washington Post*, March 24. Available at: www.forwardengagement.org/index.php?option=com_content&task=view&id=17&Itemid=46.

   2005. www.globetrotter.berkeley.edu/people5/Fuerth/fuerth-con5.html [accessed October 2010].

Fuerth, L. and Perle, R., 2002. Getting Saddam: A Debate. *Council on Foreign Relations*, January 22 [online]. Available at: www.cfr.org/publication/4324/getting_saddam.html?breadcrumb=%2Fbios%2F3325%2F%3Fgroupby%3D3%26hide%3D1%26id%3D3325%26filter%3D2002 [accessed October 2010].

Fuerth, L. and Zoellick, R., 2000. *The Middle East in US Global Strategy*. Washington Institute for Near East Policy Annual Soref Symposium Special Forum Report #462, May 23 [online]. Available at: www.washingtoninstitute.org/print.php?template=C07&CID=177 [accessed October 2010].

Fukuyama, F., 2003. The Real Intelligence Failure: What if it Turns Out Saddam didn't have Weapons of Mass Destruction? *Wall Street Journal*, August 5 [online]. www.fukuyama.lindosblog.com.

2006. *America at the Crossroads: Democracy, Power, and the Neoconservative Legacy*. New Haven: Yale University Press.

Furmanski, L., 2008. *Eyes too Blind to See: Foreign Policy Making in the Bush Administration*, in Annual Meetings of the International Studies Association. San Francisco.

Gaddis, J., 2004. *Surprise, Security, and the American Experience*. Cambridge, MA: Harvard University Press.

Gadinger, F., 2007. *Practices of Security in the Light of 9–11: From a US-identity Crisis to a Crusade of Freedom*, in Annual Meetings of the International Studies Association. Chicago.

George, A. and McKeown, T., 1985. Case studies and theories of organizational decision making. In R.F. Coulam and R.A. Smith, eds. *Advances in Information Processing in Organizations, Volume II, Research on Public Organizations*. Greenwich, CT: JAI Press.

George, A.L. and Bennett, A., 2005. *Case Studies and Theory Development in the Social Sciences*. Cambridge, MA: MIT Press.

George, J., 2005. *The Neo-Conservative Ascendancy and US Hegemony: History, Legacies and Implications*, in Annual Meetings of the International Studies Association. Honolulu.

Gill, S., 2005. *The New Imperialism and the War in Iraq*, in Annual Meetings of the International Studies Association. Honolulu.

Goertz, G. and Levy, J.S., 2007. Causal Explanation, Necessary Conditions, and Case Studies. In Gary Goertz and Jack S. Levy, eds. *Explaining War and Peace: Case Studies and Necessary Condition Counterfactuals*. New York: Routledge.

Goertz, G. and Starr, H., 2003. *Necessary Conditions: Theory, Methodology and Applications*. Lanham: Rowan and Littlefield.

Goldberg, J., 2006. Analogy vs. Analogy. *Los Angeles Times*, September 7.

Goldberg, M., 2002. Wellstone was Right. Salon.com, November 2 [online]. Available at: www.dir.salon.com/story/politics/feature/2002/11/02/war/print.html [accessed October 2010].

Gordon, M.R. and Trainor, B.E., 2006. *Cobra II: The Inside Story of the Invasion and Occupation of Iraq*. New York: Pantheon Books.

Gordon, P.H., 2006. The End of the Bush Revolution. *Foreign Affairs* 85(4) (July/August) [online]. Available at: www.foreignaffairs.com/articles/61734/philip-h-gordon/the-end-of-the-bush-revolution [accessed October 2010].

Gore, A., n.d. On the Issues. Available at: www.ontheissues.org/al_gore.htm.

1991a. *Congressional Record*. April 18. Available at: www.gpoaccess.gov/index.html.

1991b. *Nightline*. ABC, April 18.

1997. Final Report to President Clinton: White House Commission on Aviation Safety and Security. February 12. Available at: www.fas.org/irp/threat/212fin~1.html

1998a. *Special Report.* ABC News, December 16.

1998b. Excerpts: Gore Comments on Iraq Strike. Vice President interviewed by CNN's Larry King, December 16. GlobalSecurity.org [online]. Available at: www.globalsecurity.org/wmd/library/news/iraq/1998/98121664_tlt.html [accessed October 2010].

1999. Speech on 50th Anniversary of NATO. Ellis Island, New York, April 21, quoted in: www.query.nytimes.com/gst/fullpage.html?res=950DE6DB153AF931A15757C0A96F958260.

2000a. Al Gore on Defense. University Of New Hampshire, Durham, New Hampshire. *On the Issues*, January 5 [online]. Available at: www.issues2000.org/Celeb/Al_Gore_Defense.htm [accessed October 2010].

2000b. Press Release on Vice Presidential Speech. Boston, April 30. Available at: www.issues2000.org/celeb/Al_Gore_Foreign_Policy.htm.

2000c. Late Edition with Wolf Blitzer. CNN, April 30.

2000d. *Soldiers for the Truth*, May 23 [online]. Available at: www.americandaily.com/article/84.

2000e. Candidate Al Gore on Israel. *American Israel Public Affairs Committee Conference.* Washington Hilton Hotel, Washington, DC, May 23 [online]. Available at: www.jewishvirtuallibrary.org/jsource/US-Israel/Gore.html [accessed October 2010].

2000f. The Hyde Park Declaration. *On the Issues*, August 1 [online]. Available at: www.ontheissues.org/Notebook/Note_00-DLC12.htm [accessed October 2010].

2000g. Presidential Debate, Wake Forest University. *On the Issues*, October 11 [online]. Available at: www.ontheissues.org/Wake_Forest_debate.htm [accessed October 2010].

2000h. Excerpts from an Interview with Gore about Foreign Policy. *New York Times*, October 5 [online]. Available at: www.nytimes.com/2000/10/05/politics/o5GTEX.html [accessed October 2010].

2000i. Bush/Gore Second Presidential Debate October 11 [online]. Available at: www.fas.org/news/usa/2000/usa-001011.htm [accessed October 2010].

2002a. *A Commentary on the War Against Terror: Our Larger Tasks.* Remarks to the US Council on Foreign Relations. Washington, DC. February 12 [online]. Available at: www.cfr.org/publication.html?id=4343 [accessed October 2010].

2002b. *Iraq and the War on Terror.* Remarks to the Commonwealth Club of California. San Francisco, CA. September 23 [online]. Available at: www.commonwealthclub.org/archive/02/02-09gore-speech.html [accessed October 2010].

2002c. Transcript of the Former US Vice-President's Speech on Iraq and the War on Terrorism. *Guardian*, September 23 [online]. Available at: www.guardian.co.uk/usa/story/0,12271,797999,00.html [accessed October 2010].

2002d. Text of Gore Speech. *USA Today*, September 23. Available at: www.usato-day.com/news/nation/2002-09-23-gore-text_x.htm.

2002e. A Conversation with Al and Tipper Gore. *The Charlie Rose Show*, November 19 [online]. Available at: www.charlierose.com/view/interview/2276 [accessed October 2010].

2003. Former Vice President Al Gore: Remarks to MoveOn.org. New York University, August 7 [online]. Available at: www.moveon.org/gore-speech. html [accessed October 2010].

Goss, P.J., 2009. Security Before Politics. *Washington Post*, April 25.

Gourevitch, A., 2006. *National Insecurities: Narcissism, Neoconservatism, and the American National Interest*, in Annual Meetings of the International Studies Association. San Diego.

Gourevitch, P., 2003. US-European Relations Post-Iraq. *Council for European Studies*, Columbia University [online]. Available at: www.councilforeuropean-studies.org/pub/Gourevitch_sep03.html [accessed October 2010].

Government of the United Kingdom, 1998. The Iraq Crisis: UK Government Research Paper 98/28, 16 February [online]. Available at: www.parliament. uk/documents/commons/lib/research/rp98/rp98-028.pdf.

2002. *Iraq's Weapons of Mass Destruction: The Assessment of The British Government*; Foreword by Prime Minister Tony Blair, September [online]. Available at: www.fco.gov.uk/resources/en/pdf/pdf3/fco_iraqdossier [accessed October 2010].

GovTrack, 2002a. *H.J. Res. 114 [107th]: Authorization for Use of Military Force Against Iraq Resolution of 2002*. Govtrack.us, October 11 [online]. Available at: www.govtrack.us/congress/vote.xpd?vote=s2002-237 [accessed October 2010].

2002b. *H.R. 3162 [107th]: Uniting and Strengthening America by Providing Appropriate Tools Required to Intercept and to Deter and Punish Terrorist Acts in the United States and Around the World, to Enhance Law Enforcement Investigatory Tools, and for Other Purposes*. Govtrack.us, October 11 [online]. Available at: www.govtrack.us/congress/vote.xpd?vote=h2001-398 [accessed October 2010].

Graham, B., Lieberman, J., Ford, H. and Lantos, T. 2001. *Letter to President George W. Bush*, December 6.

Greener, I., 2005. The Potential of Path Dependence in Political Studies. *Politics* 25: 62–72.

Greenwald, G., 2008. *Tragic Legacy: How a Good vs. Evil Mentality Destroyed the Bush Presidency*. New York: Three Rivers Press.

Gwertzman, B., 2002. Iraqi Resolution is "Enormously Important." CFR.org, November 8.

Haass, R.N., 2009. *War of Necessity, War of Choice: A Memoir of Two Iraq Wars*. New York: Simon & Schuster.

Hagel, C., 2004. A Republican Foreign Policy. *Foreign Affairs* 83(4) (July/August) [online]. Available at: www.foreignaffairs.com/articles/59921/chuck-hagel/a-republican-foreign-policy [accessed October 2010].

Halper, S. and Clarke, J., 2005. *America Alone: The Neo-Conservatives and the Global Order*. Cambridge: Cambridge University Press.

Hamza, K., 2001. Khidhir Hamza: Saddam Hussein and the Iraqi Weapons Program. CNN.com, October 22 [online]. Available at: www.cnn.com/2001/COMMUNITY/10/22/hamza.cnna [accessed October 2010].

Hanes, M., 2007. *Where You Stand, Where You Sit and How You Think; Bureaucratic Roles and Individual Personalities*, in Annual Meetings of the International Studies Association. Chicago.

Hanes, M. and Schafer, M., 2007. *The Private-Psychological Sources of a Public War: Why George W. Bush went to War with Saddam*, in Annual Meetings of the International Studies Association. Chicago.

Hanson, V.D., 2003. Lessons of the War. *Commentary Magazine* [online]. Available at: www.commentarymagazine.com/index.html [accessed October 2010].

Harkin, T. and Specter, A., 2002. Joint Resolution. July 18. Available at: www.gpoaccess.gov/crecord/02crpgs.html.

Hartung, W.D., 2000. Quick on the Trigger: Are you Prepared for Gore's Foreign Policy? *The Progressive*, November [online]. Available at: www.thirdworldtraveler.com/Foreign_Policy/QuickOnTrigger.html [accessed October 2010].

Harvey, F.P., 1998. Rigor Mortis or Rigor, More Tests: Necessity, Sufficiency and Deterrence Logic. *International Studies Quarterly* 42(4): 675–707.

1999. Practicing Coercion: Revisiting Success and Failures Using Boolean Logic and Comparative Method. *Journal of Conflict Resolution* 43(6): 840–71.

2004. *Globalized Terrorism and the Illusion of Multilateral Security*. Toronto: University of Toronto Press.

2006. Getting Nato's Success in Kosovo Right: The Theory and Logic of Counter-Coercion. *Conflict Management and Peace Science* July: 139–58.

2008. Deterrence and Compellence in Iraq, 1991–2003: Lessons for a Complex Paradigm. In T.V. Paul and J. Wirtz, eds. *Complex Deterrence*. Chicago: University of Chicago Press.

2010. Counter-Coercion, the Power of Failure and the Practical Limits of Deterring Terrorism (with Alex S. Wilner). In *Deterring Terrorism: Theory and Practice*. Stanford: Stanford University Press.

Hayes, S., 2005. Rolling Rockefeller. *The Weekly Standard*, June 6.

Heilbrunn, J., 2008. *They Knew They Were Right: The Rise of the Neocons*. New York: Doubleday.

Heilemann, J., 2006. What if 9/11 Never Happened? *New York Magazine*, August 14 [online]. Available at: www.nymag.com/news/features/19147

Heinbecker, P., 2004. Canada Got it Right on Iraq. *The Globe and Mail*, March 19.

Hitchens, C., 2005a. Moral and Political Collapse, *Free Republic*, June 16 [online]. Available at: www.freerepublic.com/focus/f-news/1457374/posts [accessed October 2010].

2005b. Losing the Iraq War: Can the Left Really Want Us To? Slate.com, August 8 [online]. Available at: www.slate.com [accessed October 2010].

Hoagland, J., 1993. Beware "Mission Creep" in Somalia. *Washington Post*, July 20.

Holbrooke, R., 1999. *A New Realism for a New Era: The US and the UN in the 21st Century*. United States Representative to the United Nations Address to the National Press Club, November 2.

2002a. High Road to Baghdad: Bush Must Return to the UN if He Wants International Backing. *Guardian*, August 29 [online]. Available at: www.guardian.co.uk/world/2002/aug/29/iraq.comment1 [accessed October 2010].

2002b. Interview, *The Charlie Rose Show*, September 17.

Holmes, S., 2000. The 2000 Campaign: Gore Assails Bush on Plan to Recall US Balkan Force. *New York Times*, October 22.

Hunt, A.R., 2001. The Gore Nightmare: We're Lucky Bush is President – and it's the Republicans' Fault. *Wall Street Journal*, December 1.

Hunt, T., 2004. Pasting Over the Past: Far from being a Harmless Intellectual Pursuit, "What if" History is Pushing a Dangerous Rightwing Agenda. *Guardian*, April 7 [online]. Available at: www.guardian.co.uk/education/2004/apr/07/highereducation.news [accessed October 2010].

Hunter, Robert E., 2002a. Iraq Needn't Be a Vietnam. Rand Corporation. Available at: www.rand.org/commentary/2002/08/12/LAT.html.

2002b. Peering into Postwar Future. Rand Corporation. Available at: www.rand.org/commentary/2002/10/15/BS.html.

2002c. What Must Follow Next War in Iraq? Rand Corporation. Available at: www.rand.org/commentary/2002/12/16/ATU.html.

2003. Learn the Lessons: Know the Price of Iraq War Before Fighting Erupts. Rand Corporation. Available at: www.rand.org/commentary/2003/03/17/DN.html.

Hurst, S., 2005. Myths of Neoconservatism: George W. Bush's "Neo-conservative" Foreign Policy Revisited. *International Politics* 42: 75–96.

Huth, P. and Russett, B., 1984. What Makes Deterrence Work? Cases from 1900–1980. *World Politics* 35: 496–526.

1988. Deterrence Failure and Crisis Escalation. *International Studies Quarterly* 32: 29–45.

1989. Testing Deterrence: Rigor Makes a Difference. *World Politics* 42: 466–501.

Ikenberry, J., 2000. *After Victory: Institutions, Strategic Restraint, and the Rebuilding of Order after Major Wars*. Princeton: Princeton University Press.

Iraq Liberation Act, 1998. HR 4655. Iraqwatch.org, n.d. [online]. Available at: www.iraqwatch.org/government/US/Legislation/ILA.htm [accessed October 2010].

Ish-Shalom, P., 2006. *The Civilization of Clashes: Neoconservative Reading of the Theory of the Democratic Peace*, in Annual Meetings of the International Studies Association. San Diego.

Isikoff, M. and Corn, D., 2006. *Hubris: The Inside Story of Spin, Scandal, and the Selling of the Iraq War*. New York: Random House.

Janis, I., 1972. *Victims of Groupthink*. Boston: Houghton Mifflin Company.

Janis, I. and Mann, L., 1977. *Decision Making: A Psychological Analysis of Conflict, Choice, and Commitment*. New York: Free Press.

Jentelson, B.W., 2003. Tough Love Multilateralism. *The Washington Quarterly* 27(1): 7–24 [online]. Available at: www.twq.com/04winter/docs/04winter_jentelson.pdf [accessed October 2010].

Jervis, R., 1976. *Perception and Misperception in International Politics*. Princeton: Princeton University Press.

1986. What's Wrong with the Intelligence Process? *International Journal of Intelligence and Counterintelligence* 1(1): 28–41.

1987. Intelligence and Foreign Policy: A Review Essay. *International Security* 11(3): 141–61.

2001. International History and International Politics: Why Are They Studied Differently? In C. Elman and M. Fendius Elman, eds. *Bridges and Boundaries: Historians, Political Scientists and the Study of International Relations*. Cambridge, MA: MIT Press.

2003. Understanding the Bush Doctrine. *Political Science Quarterly* 118(3): 365–88.

2006. Reports, Politics, and Intelligence Failure: The Case of Iraq. *The Journal of Strategic Studies* 29(1): 3–52.

Johnson, D., 2009. U.S. Says Rendition to Continue, But With More Oversight. *New York Times*, August 24 [online]. Available at: www.nytimes.com/2009/08/25/us/politics/25rendition.html [accessed October 2010].

Kagan, R., 2002. Multilateralism American Style. *Washington Post*, September 13, A39.

2003. A Plot to Deceive? Carnegie Endowment for International Peace – *Washington Post*. June 6 [online]. Available at: www.carnegieendowment.org/publications/index.cfm?fa=view&id=1295 [accessed October 2010].

2005a. It wasn't just Miller's Story. *Washington Post*, October 25 [online]. Available at: www.carnegieendowment.org/publications/index.cfm?fa=view&id=17644&prog=zgp&proj=zusr [accessed October 2010].

2005b. On Iraq, Short Memories. *Washington Post*, September 12.

2006. The Last Honest Man. *Washington Post*, August 6.

2008a. Neocon Nation: Neoconservatism, c. 1776. *World Affairs Journal*, Spring [online]. Available at: www.worldaffairsjournal.org/articles/2008-Spring/full-neocon.html [accessed October 2010].

2008b. Interview with Robert Kagan, Author, Dangerous Nation. C-span [online]. Available at: www.c-span.org/special/kegan.asp [accessed October 2010].

Kagan, R. and Ferguson, N., 2004. American Power, Past and Present. *Slate Magazine*, May 6 [online]. Available at: www.slate.msn.com/id/2099751 [accessed October 2010].

Kagan, R. and Kristol, W., 2003. Why We Went to War. *The Weekly Standard*, October 20.

Kahneman, D. and Tversky, A., 1979. Prospect Theory: An Analysis of Decision under Risk. *Econometrica* 47: 313–27.

    1992. Decision under Risk. *Journal of Risk and Uncertainty* 5: 297–323.

Kahneman, D., Slovic, P. and Tversky, A., eds., 1982. *Judgment Under Uncertainty: Heuristics and Biases*. New York: Cambridge University Press.

Kane, P., 2009. CIA Says Pelosi Was Briefed on Use of "Enhanced Interrogations". Washington Post.com, May 7 [online]. Available at: www.voices.washington-post.com/capitol-briefing/2009/05/cia_says_pelosi_was_briefed_on.html [accessed October 2010].

Kaplan, F., 2008. *Daydream Believers: How a Few Grand Ideas Wrecked American Power*. New York: John Wiley and Sons.

Katzenstein, L., 2004. *Assessing US Intent in the Onset of the Iraq War*, in Annual Meetings of the International Studies Association. Montreal.

Kaufman, R.G., 2007. *In Defence of the Bush Doctrine*. Lexington: University of Kentucky Press.

Kaufmann, C., 2004. Threat Inflation and the Failure of the Marketplace of Ideas: The Selling of the Iraq War. *International Security* 29(1) (Summer): 5–48.

Kay, A., 2005. A Critique of the Use of Path Dependency in Policy Studies. *Public Administration* 83: 553–71.

Kay, D., 2003. ISG Interim Report to Congress, October 2 [online]. Available at: www.merln.ndu.edu/merln/pfiraq/archive/cia/david_kay_10022003.pdf [accessed October 2010].

    2004. Transcript: David Kay at Senate Hearing. CNN.com, January 28 [online]. Available at: www.cnn.com/2004/US/01/28/kay.transcript [accessed October 2010].

Keller, J., 2004. *The Making of a Crusader: George W. Bush, September 11th, and the War Against Iraq*, in Annual Meetings of the International Studies Association. Montreal.

Kellett Cramer, J., 2007. Militarized Patriotism: Why the US Marketplace of Ideas Failed Before the Iraq War. *Security Studies* 16(3) (July–September): 489–524.

Kengor, P., 1997. The Foreign Policy Role of Vice President Al Gore. *Presidential Studies Quarterly* 27(1): 14–38.

Kerry, J., 2002a. *Face The Nation*, September 15.

    2002b. US Senate Floor Statement, *Authorization of the Use of United States Armed Forces Against Iraq*. October 9 [online]. Available at: www.gpoaccess. gov/crecord/02crpgs.html.

    2003a. Bush Lied? Truthorfiction.com, January 23 [online]. Available at: www. truthorfiction.com/rumors/b/bushlied.htm [accessed October 2010].

    2003b. John Kerry on War and Peace. OntheIssues.org, September 9 [online]. Available at: www.ontheissues.org/2004/John_Kerry_War_+_Peace.htm [accessed October 2010].

2004. Statement from Kerry's 2004 Democratic Party Platform [online]. Quoted in: www.isreview.org/issues/37/one_agenda.shtml.

King, G. and Zeng, L., 2002. Improving Forecasts of State Failure. *World Politics* 53(4): 623–58 [online]. Available at: www.gking.harvard.edu/files/abs/civil-abs.shtml [accessed October 2010].

2005. When Can History Be Our Guide? The Pitfalls of Counterfactual Inference [online]. Available at: www.GKing.Harvard.Edu.

2006. The Dangers of Extreme Counterfactuals. *Political Analysis* 14(2): 131–59 [online]. Available at: www.gking.harvard.edu/files/abs/counterft-abs.shtml [accessed October 2010].

Kissinger, Henry, 2004. Better Intelligence Reform. *Washington Post*, 16 August.

Klein, J., 2010. Karl Rove's Memoir: Act of Vengeance. *Time*, March 11 [online]. Available at: www.time.com/time/politics/article/0,8599,1971211,00.html [accessed October 2010].

Klein, R. 2009. Intelligence Report: Pelosi Briefed on Use of Interrogation Tactics in Sept. '02. *The Note/ABCNews.com*, May 7 [online]. Available at: www. blogs.abcnews.com/thenote/2009/05/intelligence-re.html [accessed October 2010].

Knorr, K., 1983. *Power, Strategy, and Security*. Princeton: Princeton University Press.

Knox, P., 2003. Showdown at the UN as US sets March 17 Deadline. *The Globe and Mail*, March 8.

Kopp, C., 2003. Chirac Makes His Case on Iraq: French President Argues Hiw View on "60 Minutes" [online]. Available at: www.cbsnews.com/ stories/2003/03/16/60minutes/main544161.shtml [accessed October 2010].

Krauthammer, C., 2004. Commentary on Francis Fukuyama. *The National Interest* 77: 15–26.

2005. The Realist Who Got it Wrong. *Washington Post*, October 30: B07.

Krebs, R. and Lobasz, J.K., 2007. Fixing the Meaning of 9/11: Hegemony, Coercion, and the Road to War in Iraq. *Security Studies* 16(3) (July–September): 409–51.

Kucinich, D., 2003. www.kucinich.us/index.php?option=com_content&task=view &id=237.

Kurlantzick, J., 2004. Another America. *Prospect Magazine* 96 (March 20) [online]. Available at: www.prospect-magazine.co.uk/article_details.php?id=5860 [accessed October 2010].

Lebow, R.N., 1984. *Between Peace and War: The Nature of International Crisis*. Washington, DC: The Johns Hopkins University Press.

2000. What's so Different about a Counterfactual? *World Politics* 52: 550–85.

2001. Social Science and History: Ranchers versus Farmers? In C. Elman and M. Fendius Elman, eds. *Bridges and Boundaries: Historians, Political Scientists and the Study of International Relations*. Cambridge, MA: MIT Press.

2006. Franz Ferdinand Found Alive: World War I Unnecessary. In P. Tetlock, R.N. Lebow and N. Parker, eds. *Unmaking The West: Counterfactual Thought Experiments In History*. Ann Arbor: University of Michigan Press.

Lebow, R.N. and Stein, J.G., 1987. Beyond Deterrence. *Journal of Social Issues* 43: 5–71.

1989. Rational Deterrence Theory: I Think Therefore I Deter. *World Politics* 41: 208–24.

1990. Deterrence: The Elusive Dependent Variable. *World Politics* 42: 336–369.

Leffler, M., 2005. 9/11 and American Foreign Policy. *Diplomatic History* 29: 395–413.

Leigh, David and Wilson, James, 2001. Counting Iraq's Victims. *Guardian*, October 10.

Levin, E., 2004. Did Reagan End the Cold War? *Weekly Standard* 10(9), November 15.

Levy, J., 2001. Explaining Events and Developing Theories: History, Political Science, and the Analysis of International Relations. In C. Elman and M. Fendius Elman, eds. *Bridges and Boundaries: Historians, Political Scientists and the Study of International Relations*. Cambridge, MA: MIT Press

2007. Preventative War and the Bush Doctrine: Theoretical Logic and Historical Roots. In *Understanding the Bush Doctrine: Psychology and Strategy in an Age of Terrorism*. New York: Routledge.

2008a. Preventive War and Democratic Politics. *International Studies Quarterly* 52: 1–24.

2008b. Counterfactuals and Case Studies. In J.M. Box-Steffensmeier, H.E. Brady and D. Collier, eds. *Oxford Handbook of Political Methodology*. New York: Oxford University Press.

Lewis, D., 1973a. *Counterfactuals*. Cambridge, MA: Harvard University Press.

1973b. Causation. *Journal of Philosophy* 70: 556–67.

Library of Congress. Available at: www.gpoaccess.gov/crecord/index.html.

Lieberfeld, Daniel, 2005. Theories of Conflict and the Iraq War. *International Journal of Peace Studies* 10(2) (Autumn/Winter). Available at: www.gmu.edu/programs/icar/ijps/vol10_2/wLieberfeld10n2IJPS.pdf.

Lieberman, Joseph, 2002. *Congressional Record*, V. 148, Pt. 14, October 2, 2002 to October 9, 2002, p. 19213.

Lind, M., 2003. The Weird Men behind George W. Bush's War. *The New Statesman*, April 7 [online]. Available at: www.newstatesman.com/200304070003 [accessed October 2010].

Lobasz, J. and Krebs, R., 2006. *Fixing the Meaning of 9/11: Rhetorical Coercion and the Iraq War*, in Annual Meetings of the International Studies Association. San Diego.

Lobell, S.E., Ripsman, N.M. and Taliaferro, J.W., 2009. *Neoclassical Realism, the State, and Foreign Policy*. Cambridge: Cambridge University Press.

Lynch, T. and Singh, R.S., 2008. *After Bush: The Case for Continuity in American Foreign Policy*. New York: Cambridge University Press.

Macleod, A., 2008. *The Consequences of the "Day Nothing Much Changed" for Realist Theory*, in Annual Meetings of the International Studies Association. San Francisco.

McDermott, R., 1992. Prospect Theory in International Relations: The Iranian Hostage Rescue Mission. *Political Psychology* 13: 237–63.

McDonald, M. and Jackson, R., 2008. *Selling War: The Coalition of the Willing and the "War on Terror,"* in Annual Meetings of the International Studies Association. San Francisco.

McGough, M., 2007. If Gore had Won…Would Civil Liberties be Much Better? *Los Angeles Times*, August 23 [online]. Available at: www.latimes.com/news/opinion/la-oew-mcgough23aug23,0,4734827.story [accessed October 2010].

Mahoney, J., 2000. Path Dependence in Historical Sociology. *Theory and Society* 29: 507–48.

    2001. *The Legacies of Liberalism: Path Dependence and Political Regimes in Central America*. Baltimore: Johns Hopkins University Press.

    2006. Analyzing Path Dependence: Lessons from the Social Sciences. In A. Wimmer and R. Kössler, eds. *Understanding Change: Models, Methodologies, and Metaphors*. Basingstoke: Palgrave Macmillan.

Mahoney, J. and Schensul, D., 2006. Historical Context and Path Dependence. In R. Goodin and C. Tilly, eds. *Oxford Handbook of Contextual Political Analysis*. Oxford: Oxford University Press.

Mann, J., 2004. *Rise of the Vulcans: The History of Bush's War Cabinet*. New York: Penguin.

Maoz, Z., 2009. Intelligence Failures: An Analytic Framework. Prepared for presentation at the annual meeting of the American Political Science Association, August 31 to September 3, Philadelphia.

Martinez, A., 2008. Assessing the Gore Presidency. *Washington Post*, July 8 [online]. Available at: www.voices.washingtonpost.com/stumped/2008/07/assessing_the_gore_presidency.html [accessed October 2010].

Martorana, G., 2008. *Evangelical Protestants: The Soteriological Impetus Behind Recent Foreign Policy Initiatives*, in Annual Meetings of the International Studies Association. San Francisco.

Mazarr, M.J., 2007. The Iraq War and Agenda Setting. *Foreign Policy Analysis* 3(1) (January): 1–23.

Mearsheimer, J. and Walt, S., 2007. *The Israel Lobby and US Foreign Policy*. New York: Farrar, Straus and Giroux.

Mercurio, J., 2002. Gore Challenges Bush Iraqi Policy. CNN.com/Inside Politics, September 23 [online]. Available at: www.archives.cnn.com/2002/ALL POLITICS/09/23/gore.iraq [accessed October 2010].

Meyerson, H., Waldman, P., Franke-Ruta, G. and Yglesias, M., 2004. He's Back. *The American Prospect*, February 23 [online]. Available at: www.prospect.org/cs/articles?article=hes_back [accessed October 2010].

Middle East Media Research Institute, 2002. "Why We Fight America" – Al-Qa'ida Spokesman Explains September 11 and Intentions to Kill 4 Million

Americans with Weapons of Mass Destruction. June 12 [online]. Available at: www.memri.org/bin/articles.cgi?Page=archives&Area=sd&ID=SP38802 [accessed October 2010].

Mintz, A., 1993. The Decision to Attack Iraq: A Noncompensatory Theory of Decision Making. *Journal of Conflict Resolution* 37(4): 595–618.

Monten, J., 2005a. *Neoconservatism and the Promotion of Democracy Abroad*, in Annual Meetings of the International Studies Association. Honolulu.

2005b. The Roots of the Bush Doctrine: Power, Nationalism, and Democracy Promotion in Grand Strategy. *International Security* 29(4): 112–56.

Monten, J. and Busby, J., 2008. *Winner Takes All: How did Unilateralism Triumph in the Republican Party?* in Annual Meetings of the International Studies Association. San Francisco.

Morkevicius, V., 2006. *Faith-Based War? Religious Rhetoric and Foreign Policy in the Bush Administration*, in Annual Meetings of the International Studies Association. San Diego.

Most, Benjamin A., Starr, H. and Puchala, D.J., 1989. *Inquiry, Logic, and International Politics*. Columbia: University of Southern Carolina Press.

Moyers, Bill. 2008. Buying the War: How Did the Mainstream Press Get it So Wrong? Available at: www.pbs.org/moyers/journal/btw/watch.html

Murphy, G., 1969. On Counterfactual Propositions. *History and Theory* 9: 14–38.

Mylroie, L., 1998. Clinton Signs Iraq Liberation Act: Statement by the President. Iraq News/FAS News, October 31 [online]. Available at: www.fas.org/news/iraq/1998/11/01/981101-in.htm [accessed October 2010].

Nabers, D. and Patman, R., 2007. *9/11 and the Rise of Political Fundamentalism in the US: Domestic Legitimatisation versus International Estrangement?* in Annual Meetings of the International Studies Association. Chicago.

Nader, R., 2004. Meet the Press. NBC News: interview transcript, February 22 [online]. Available at: www.msnbc.msn.com/id/4304155 [accessed October 2010].

Nagourney, A., 2002. A Nation Challenged: The Democrat; Gore, Championing Bush, Calls for a "Final Reckoning" with Iraq. *New York Times*, February 13 [online]. Available at: www.nytimes.com/2002/02/13/world/nation-challenged-democrat-gore-championing-bush-calls-for-final-reckoning-with.html [accessed October 2010].

New Republic, The, 1998. Fuerth In Line. December 7, 16.

New York Times Magazine, 2006. What If 9/11 Never Happened? A Counter-history. August 14 [online]. Available at: www.nymag.com/news/features/19147 [accessed October 2010].

Noonan, P., 2002. The Great Iraq Debate: Richard Offers Perles of Wisdom, and Leon Says Fuerth Things First. *The Wall Street Journal*, February 15.

Nunn, S., 2002. www.pbs.org/newshour/bb/congress/jan-june02/agenda_1-31.html; www.nti.org/c_press/speech_samnunn_102202.pdf [accessed October 2010].

Nye, Joseph, 2002. Owls are Wiser About Iraq Than Hawks. *Financial Times*, October 21. Available at: www.belfercenter.ksg.harvard.edu/publication/

1224/owls_are_wiser_about_iraq_than_hawks.html?breadcrumb=%2Ftopic
%2F7%2Fdirty_bombs%3Fpage%3D14.

Obama, Barack, 2009. Remarks by the President on National Security. The
White House, Office of the Press Secretary, Washington, DC, May 21. Avail-
able at: www.whitehouse.gov/the_press_office/Remarks-by-the-President-On-
National-Security-5-21-09.

O'Driscoll, C., 2006. *Anticipatory War and the Just War Tradition: Sufficient Threats,
Just Fears, Unknown Unknowns, and the Invasion of Iraq*, in Annual Meetings
of the International Studies Association. San Diego.

O'Hanlon, M., 2002. How the Hardliners Lost. *Washington Post*, November 10, B7.

Oliphant, T., 2007. *Utter Incompetents: Ego and Ideology in the Age of Bush*. New
York: Thomas Dunne Books.

Onea, T.A., 2008. *Jacksonian Idealism: Prestige, Iraq, and American Empire*, in
Annual Meetings of the International Studies Association. San Francisco.

O'Reilly, M. and Renfro, W. 2006. *Like Father, Like Son? A Comparison of the Foreign
Policies of George H.W. Bush and George W. Bush*, in Annual Meetings of the
International Studies Association. San Diego.

Payne, R. and Dombrowski, P., 2005. *Preemptive War: Crafting a New International
Norm*, in Annual Meetings of the International Studies Association.
Honolulu.

Pelley, S., 2008. Interrogator Shares Saddam's Confessions. *60 Minutes Online*,
January 27 [online]. Available at: www.cbsnews.com/stories/2008/01/24/
60minutes/main3749494.shtml [accessed October 2010].

Pelz, S., 2001. Toward a New Diplomatic History: Two and a Half Cheers for
International Relations Methods. In C. Elman and M. Fendius Elman,
eds. *Bridges and Boundaries: Historians, Political Scientists and the Study of
International Relations*. Cambridge, MA: MIT Press.

Phythian, M., 2006. The Perfect Intelligence Failure? US Pre-War Intelligence on
Iraqi Weapons of Mass Destruction. *Politics and Policy* 34(2) (May): 400–24.

Pierson, P., 2000. Increasing Returns, Path Dependence, and the Study of Politics.
American Political Science Review 94: 251–67.

2004. *Politics in Time: History, Institutions, and Social Analysis*. Princeton:
Princeton University Press.

Pillar, P., 2006. Intelligence, Policy, and the War in Iraq. *Foreign Affairs* 85(2):
15–27.

Pincus, W., 2006. U.S. Said to Misread Hussein on Arms: Report Cites Suspicions of
Ruse. *Washington Post*, March 14.

Piro, G., 2008. Interrogator Shares Saddam's Confessions: Tells 60 Minutes Former
Iraqi Dictator didn't Expect U.S. Invasion. *60 Minutes*, January 27.

Podhoretz, Norman, 2007. *World War IV: The Long Struggle against Islamofascism*.
New York: Random House, 154.

Pollack, K.M., 2002. Next Stop Baghdad? *Foreign Affairs*, 81(2) (March/April).
Available at: www.cfr.org/publication/4484/next_stop_baghdad.html.

Pollack, K., 2004. Spies, Lies, and Weapons: What Went Wrong. *The Atlantic* (January/February) [online]. Available at: www.theatlantic.com/doc/200401/pollack [accessed October 2010].

Porpora, D., 2004. *Structure, Ideology, and the New American Hegemony*, in Annual Meetings of the International Studies Association. Montreal.

Powers, T., 2007. What George Tenet Really Knew about Iraq: Unraveling the Former CIA Chief's Cover Story about Bogus Intelligence – and the Grand Scheme that Launched the War. Salon.com, July 2/*The New York Review of Books*, July 19 [online]. Available at: www.salon.com/opinion/feature/2007/07/02/tenet_iraq/index1.html [accessed October 2010].

Prados, J., 2004. *Hoodwinked: The Documents that Reveal How Bush Sold Us a War*. New York: New Press.

Press, E., 2001. Smart Bomb? *Prospect Magazine*, December 17 [online]. Available at: www.prospect.org/cs/articles?article=smart_bomb [accessed October 2010].

Preston, J., 2002. Threats and Responses: Shift Toward the US Stand On Iraq is Noted in Council. *New York Times*, November 1.

Proulx. J., 1999. Tapping an Empty Well: What's Happening in Iraq Today. *Columbia Chronicle Online*, 33(9), November 22 [online]. Available at: www.columbia-chronicle.com/back/1999_fall/99nov22/vp2.html [accessed October 2010].

Purdum, T.S. and Tyler, P.E., 2002. Top Republicans Break With Bush On Iraq Strategy. *New York Times*, August 16.

Ragin, C. and Becker, H., eds. 1992. *What is a Case?* Cambridge: Cambridge University Press.

Record, J., 2010. *Wanting War: Why the Bush Administration Invaded Iraq*. Dulles: Potomac Books Inc.

Redd, S.B., 2002. The Influence of Advisers on Foreign Policy Decision Making: An Experimental Study. *Journal of Conflict Resolution* 46(3): 335–64.

Rice, C., 2000. Promoting the National Interest. *Foreign Affairs*, 79 (January/February): 45–62.

Ricks, T.E., 2007. *Fiasco: The American Military Adventure in Iraq*. New York: Penguin.

Risen, J., 2006. *State of War: The Secret History of the CIA and the Bush Administration*. New York: Free Press.

Ritter, S., 1999. *Endgame: Solving the Iraq Problem Once and for All*. New York: Simon & Schuster.

2002. Ritter: Facts Needed Before Iraq Attack. CNN.com/WORLD, July 17 [online]. Available at: www.archives.cnn.com/2002/WORLD/meast/07/17/saddam.ritter.cnna [accessed October 2010].

Rivkin, David B. and Casey, Lee A., 2003. Saddam, Nikita and Virtual Weapons of Mass Destruction: A Question of Threat Perception and Intelligence Assessment. *The National Interest*, June 11 [online]. Available at: www.nationalinterest.org/article/saddam-nikita-and-virtual-weapons-of-mass-destructiona-question-of-threat-percep-2362.

Robb, C.S. and Silberman, L.H., 2005. *The Commission on the Intelligence Capabilities of the United States Regarding Weapons of Mass Destruction: Report to the President of the United States*, March 31 [online]. Available at: www.globalsecurity.org/intell/library/reports/2005/wmd_report_31mar 2005.pdf.

Rodriguez, E., 2004. *George W. Bush and the End of the New World Order*, in Annual Meetings of the International Studies Association. Montreal.

Romero, A., 2009. Quoted in Ed Henry, Deadline Missed for policy on detaining terror suspects. CNN.com, July 21 [online]. Available at: www.articles. cnn.com/2009-07-21/politics/obama.gitmo_1_military-commissions-guantanamo-bay-controversial-prison/2?_s=PM:POLITICS

Rosenau, J.N., 1966. Pretheories and Theories of Foreign Policy. In R.B. Farrell, ed. *Approaches to Comparative and International Politics*. Evanston: Northwestern University Press.

Rove, K., 2010. *Courage and Consequence: My Life as a Conservative in the Fight*. New York: Threshold Editions (Simon & Schuster).

Rowley, J., 2009. Panetta Says CIA Agents "Truthfully" Briefed Pelosi (Update2). Bloomberg.com, May 15 [online]. Available at: www.bloomberg.com/apps/ news?pid=20601087&sid=ax..5s0JJ5rI&refer=home [accessed October 2010].

Rubin, J., 2002. Quoted in PBS documentary "Saddam's Ultimate Solution." July 11 [online]. Available at: www.pbs.org/wnet/wideangle/shows/saddam [accessed October 2010].

Russell, K., 2004. The Subjectivity of Intelligence Analysis and Implications for the US National Security Strategy. The US National Security Strategy, *SAIS Review* XXIV(1) (Winter–Spring): 147–63.

Ryan, D., 2004. *Framing the Response: US Hegemony after September 11*, in Annual Meetings of the International Studies Association. Montreal.

Saletan, W., 2004. Iraq War? No. Slate.com, August 12 [online]. Available at: www. slate.com [accessed October 2010].

San Francisco Chronicle, 2002. Missing: A Case for War. Chronicle Editorial, August 29: A-20 [online]. Available at: www.sfgate.com/cgi-bin/article.cgi?file=/ chronicle/archive/2002/08/29/ED186178.DTL [accessed October 2010].

Sanger, D., 2000. The 2000 Campaign: Rivals Differ on US Role in the World. *New York Times*, October 30 [online]. Available at: www.nytimes.com/2000/10/30/ world/2000-campaign-world-views-special-report-rivals-differ-us-role-world.html [accessed October 2010].

2009. U.S. Weighs Intercepting North Korean Shipments. *New York Times*, June 7.

Santora, M., 2007. A Democratic Drive to War? *New York Times*, May 21 [online]. Available at: www.thecaucus.blogs.nytimes.com/2007/05/21/a-democratic-drive-to-war [accessed October 2010].

Saunders, E.N., 2008. *Wars of Choice: Leadership, Threat Perception, and Military Interventions*, in Annual Meetings of the International Studies Association. San Francisco.

Schiff, J., 2003. Holbrooke: After War, US must Mend Bonds with Other Countries, UN. *University Record Online*. University of Michigan, March 31 [online]. Available at: www.ur.umich.edu/0203/Mar31_03/08.shtml [accessed October 2010].

Schmidt, B.C. and Williams, M.C., 2008. The Bush Doctrine and the Iraq War: Neoconservatives Versus Realists. *Security Studies* 17(2) (April): 191–220.

Schonberg, K., 2006. *Wilsonian Unilateralism: Rhetoric and Power in American Foreign Policy since 9/11*, in Annual Meetings of the International Studies Association. San Diego.

Schroeder, G., 2003. www.news.bbc.co.uk/1/hi/not_in_website/syndication/monitoring/media_reports/2756893.stm [accessed October 2010].

Schuler, D., 2007. What if? The Al Gore Presidency (Updated). *The Glittering Eye* [online]. Available at: www.theglitteringeye.com/?p=3343 [accessed October 2010].

Sciolinoi, E., 2000. The Insider: A Gore Adviser Who Basks in the Shadows. *New York Times*, April 25 [online]. Available at: www.partners.nytimes.com/library/politics/camp/042500wh-gore-fuerth.html [accessed October 2010].

Scowcroft, B., 2002. Don't Attack Saddam: It would Undermine Our Anti-terror Efforts. *Wall Street Journal*, August 15.

Selfa, L., 2004. The Democratic Party and the Politics of Lesser Evilism. International Socialist Organization [online]. Available at: www.internationalsocialist.org/pdfs/democrats_lesserevilism.pdf [accessed October 2010].

Senate Select Committee on Intelligence on the US, 2004. Report on the US Intelligence Community's Prewar Intelligence Assessments on Iraq, July 7 [online]. Available at: www.gpoaccess.gov/serialset/creports/iraq.html [accessed October 2010].

Sevan, B.V., 2005. Oil for Food: Far from a Failure. *International Herald Tribune*, September 12 [online]. Available at: www.nytimes.com/2005/09/12/opinion/12iht-edsevan.html [accessed October 2010].

Sickles, M., 2005. *A Neoconservative Just War: Implications of the Iraq Campaign*, in Annual Meetings of the International Studies Association. Honolulu.

Siegel, A., 2000. Mission Creep or Mission Misunderstood? *Joint Force Quarterly*. National Defence University [online]. Available at: www.ndu.edu/inss/Press/jfq_pages/1825.pdf [accessed October 2010].

Smith, G.F., 2006. *Deadly Dogma: How Neoconservatives Broke the Law to Deceive America*. New York: Institute for Research.

Sniegoski, S.J., 2008. *The Transparent Cabal: The Neoconservative Agenda, War in the Middle East, and the National Interest of Israel*. Norfolk: Ihs Press.

Sobieraj, S., 2000. Associated Press in *L.A. Times*, May 23.

Specter, A., 2002. Bill Summary & Status – 107th Congress (2001–2002) – S.J. RES.41 – All Information [online]. Available at: www.thomas.loc.gov/cgi-bin/bdquery/D?d107:41:./list/bss/d107SJ.lst:@@@L&summ2=m& [accessed October 2010].

Stempel, J., 2005. *The Ideology and Reality of American Primacy: Hope, Error, and Incompetence*, in Annual Meetings of the International Studies Association. Honolulu.

Straw, J., 2002. www.downingstreetmemo.com/strawtext.html [accessed October 2010].

2010. www.iraqinquiry.org.uk/media/44940/100208pm-straw.pdf [accessed October 2010].

Sylvan, D. and Majeski, S., 1998. A Methodology for the Study of Historical Counterfactuals. *International Studies Quarterly* 42(1): 79–108.

Tenet, G., 2007. *At the Center of the Storm: My Years at the CIA*. New York: HarperCollins.

Tetlock, P., 1999. Theory-Driven Reasoning About Plausible Pasts and Probable Futures in World Politics: Are We Prisoners of Our Preconceptions? *American Journal of Political Science* 43(2): 335–66.

Tetlock, P. and Belkin, A., 1996. *Counterfactual Thought Experiments in World Politics: Logical, Methodological and Psychological Perspectives*. Princeton: Princeton University Press.

Tetlock, P. and Lebow, R.N., 2001. Poking Counterfactual Holes in Covering Laws: Cognitive Styles and Historical Reasoning. *American Political Science Review* 95(4): 829–43.

Tetlock, P. and Mellers, B., 2002. The Great Rationality Debate: The Impact of the Kahneman and Tversky Research Program. *Psychological Science* 13: 94–9.

Tetlock, P., Lebow, R.N. and Parker, N., 2000. *Unmaking the West: "What if" Scenarios that Re-write History*. Ann Arbor: University of Michigan Press.

Thelen, K., 1999. Historical Institutionalism in Comparative Politics. *Annual Review of Political Science* 2: 369–404.

Theurkauf, R.S., 2008. *Theological Identities in International Relations Theory*, in Annual Meetings of the International Studies Association. San Francisco.

Thorson, S. and Sylvan, D.A., 1982. Counterfactuals and the Cuban Missile Crisis. *International Studies Quarterly* 26(4): 539–71.

Thrall, A. and Cramer, J., 2007. *Why Did the US Invade Iraq? Survey and Evidence*, in Annual Meetings of the International Studies Association. Chicago.

Tomasky, Michael, 2009. The Obama Doctrine? Let's See What He Says to Mubarak. *Guardian*, May 31.

Tully, A.F., 2002. Are Influential Senator's Comments about War with Iraq Tacit Approval? Washington, DC: Radio Free Europe/Radio Liberty [online]. Available at: www.globalsecurity.org/wmd/library/news/iraq/2002/020807_08200215535.htm [accessed October 2010].

Tunç, H., 2005. What Was it All About After All? The Causes of the Iraq War. *Contemporary Security Policy* 26(2) (August): 335–55.

Turque, B., 2000. *Inventing Al Gore*. New York: Houghton Mifflin Company.

Unger, C., 2007. *The Fall of the House of Bush: The Untold Story of How a Band of True Believers Seized the Executive Branch, Started the Iraq War, and Still Imperils America's Future*. New York: Scribner.

2008. *American Armageddon: How the Delusions of the Neoconservatives and the Christian Right Triggered the Descent of America.* New York: Scribner.

United Nations Monitoring, Verification and Inspection Commission, 2003a. *Twelfth quarterly report of the Executive Chairman of the United Nations Monitoring, Verification and Inspection Commission in accordance with paragraph 12 of Security Council resolution 1284 (1999),* February 28 [online]. Available at: hwww.un.org/News/dh/iraq/unmovic-feb03-en.pdf [accessed October 2010].

2003b. *Unresolved Disarmament Issues: Iraq's Proscribed Weapons Programmes.* United Nations, March 6 [online]. Available at: www.un.org/Depts/unmovic/new/documents/cluster_document.pdf [accessed October 2010].

United Nations Security Council, 2002. *Security Council Holds Iraq in "Material Breach" of Disarmament Obligations, Offers Final Chance to Comply, Unanimously Adopting Resolution 1441.* Security Council 464th Meeting, November 8 [online]. Available at: www.un.org/News/Press/docs/2002/SC7564.doc.htm [accessed October 2010].

United Nations Special Commission, 1998. *Letter Dated 15 December 1998 from the Secretary-General Addressed to the President of the Security Council.* United Nations, December 15 [online]. Available at: www.un.org/Depts/unscom/s98-1172.htm [accessed October 2010].

Urbina, I., 2000. Rogues' Gallery: Who Advises Bush and Gore on the Middle East? *Middle East Report* 216 (Fall).

US Department of Defense, 2002. Rumsfeld on Iraq: "Goal is Disarmament." CNN. com, September 21, Interview with CNN's Jamie McIntyre [online]. Available at: www.defenselink.mil/transcripts/transcript.aspx?transcriptid=3659 [accessed October 2010].

US Department of Justice, Federal Bureau of Investigation, 2009. Saddam Hussein Talks to the FBI: Twenty Interviews and Five Conversations with "High Value Detainee # 1" in 2004. National Security Archive Electronic Briefing Book No. 279. Edited by Joyce Battle, Assisted by Brendan McQuade. Declassified on May 21, 2009.

US Department of State (Office of the Spokesman), 2003. FACT SHEET: Historic Review of UNMOVIC's Report on Unresolved Disarmament Issues. GlobalSecurity.org, March 10 [online]. Available at: www.globalsecurity.org/wmd/library/news/iraq/2003/iraq-030310-state-unmovic_2003-269.htm [accessed October 2010].

Van Apeldoorn, B. and De Graaff, N., 2008. *The Making of the "Long War": Neoconservative Networks and Continuity and Change in US "Grand Strategy,"* in Annual Meetings of the International Studies Association. San Francisco.

Vasquez, Betsy R., 2003. Thank God Bush was our President on 9/11, not Al Gore. *The Moderate Independent,* September 16–30, 1(11).

Vertzberger, Y., 1990. *The World in their Minds: Information Processing, Cognition and Foreign Policy Decision-Making.* Palo Alto: Stanford University Press.

Voice of America News, 2003. US Rejects Canadian Proposal to Give Iraq More Time. *State Department: Voice of America News*, February 26 [online]. Available at: www.voanews.com/english/archive/2003–02/a-2003–02–26–38-US.cfm?moddate=2003–02–26 [accessed October 2010].

Voice of America News *W.*, 2008. [Film]. Directed by Oliver Stone. USA: Lions Gate Productions.

Wahlrab, A., 2004. *Realism, Security, and Democracy: A "Sophisticated" Realist Critique of the War on Terrorism*, in Annual Meetings of the International Studies Association. Montreal.

Warrick, J. and Eggen, D., 2007. Hill Briefed on Waterboarding in 2002. *Washington Post*, December 9, A01.

Washington Post, 2005. UNcorruptible? WashingtonPost.com, August 10, A16.

Washington Times, 2005. Oil-for-Bribes Program. *Washington Times*, August 10.

Weintraub, J., 2003. Al Gore on Iraq. *Jeff Weintraub: Comments and Controversies* [online]. Available at: www.jeffweintraub.blogspot.com/2003/11/al-gore-on-iraq-february-12-2002.html [accessed October 2010].

Weisberg, J., 2002. Iraq Now? *Slate.com*, February 7 [online]. Available at: www.slate.com/id/2061799 [accessed October 2010].

2008. *The Bush Tragedy*. New York: Random House.

Western, J., 2005. The War over Iraq: Selling War to the American Public. *Security Studies* 14(1) (October): 106–39.

2007. *Discounting the Costs of War in Iraq: Resurrecting the Ideology of the Offensive*, in Annual Meetings of the International Studies Association. Chicago.

Wilson, J., 2004. Interview. *Meet the Press*, NBC, May 2.

Wisconsin Project on Nuclear Arms Control, 2006. *H.R.4655 Iraq Liberation Act of 1998* (Enrolled Bill [Sent to President]). Iraq Watch, August [online]. Available at: www.iraqwatch.org/government/US/Legislation/ILA.htm [accessed October 2010].

Woodward, B., 2004. *Plan of Attack: The Definitive Account of the Decision to Invade Iraq*. New York: Simon & Schuster.

Woods, K.M., Lacey, J.R. and Murray, W., 2006b. Saddam's Delusions: The View from the Inside. *Foreign Affairs* (May–June) [online]. Available at: www.foreignaffairs.com/articles/61701/kevin-woods-james-lacey-and-williamson-murray/saddams-delusions-the-view-from-the-inside [accessed October 2010].

Woods, K.M., Pease, M.R., Stout, M.E., Lacey, J.R. and Murray, W., 2006a. *Iraqi Perspectives Project: A View of Operation Iraqi Freedom from Saddam's Senior Leadership*. Joint Center for Operations Analysis, Washington, DC [online]. Available at: www.jfcom.mil/newslink/storyarchive/2006/ipp.pdf [accessed June 2008].

Woollacott, M., 2004. Americans and the Rest of the World: Who Needs Whom? *Arab News*. London, 24 January.

Youtube user, 2006. *Democrats on Iraq's WMD*. August 12 [online]. Available at: www.youtube.com/watch?v=i87cZ3Og6ts [accessed October 2010].

2008. *Democrats, WMD's & The Iraq War*. April 8 [online]. Available at: www. youtube.com/watch?v=iSwSDvgw5Uc [accessed October 2010].

Zonis, M., 2007. The Democracy Doctrine of President George W. Bush. In *Understanding the Bush Doctrine: Psychology and Strategy in an Age of Terrorism*. New York: Routledge.

INDEX